THE LEGAL TENDER OF GENDER

Extensive welfare, law and policy reforms characterized the making and unmaking of Keynesian states in the twentieth century. This collection highlights the gendered nature of these regulatory shifts and, specifically, the roles played by women as reformers, welfare workers and welfare recipients, in the development of welfare states historically. The contributors are leading feminist socio-legal scholars from a range of disciplines in Canada, the United States and Israel. Collectively, their analyses of women, law and poverty speak to long-standing and ongoing feminist concerns: the importance of historically informed research, the relevance of women's agency and resistance to the experience of inequality and injustice, the specificity of the experience of poor women and poor mothers, the implications of changes to social policy, and the possibilities for social change. Such analyses are particularly timely as the devastation of neo-liberalism becomes increasingly obvious. The current world crisis of capitalism is a defining moment for liberal states—a global catastrophe that concomitantly creates a window of opportunity for critical scholars and activists to reframe debates about social welfare, work, and equality, and to reinsert the discourse of social justice into the public consciousness and political agendae of liberal democracies.

Oñati International Series in Law and Society

A SERIES PUBLISHED FOR THE OÑATI INSTITUTE FOR THE SOCIOLOGY OF LAW

Titles in this Series

Social Dynamics of Crime and Control: New Theories for a World in Transition *edited by Susanne Karstedt and Kai Bussmann*

Criminal Policy in Transition *edited by Andrew Rutherford and Penny Green*

Making Law for Families *edited by Mavis Maclean*

Poverty and the Law *edited by Peter Robson and Asbjørn Kjønstad*

Adapting Legal Cultures *edited by Johannes Feest and David Nelken*

Rethinking Law, Society and Governance: Foucault's Bequest *edited by Gary Wickham and George Pavlich*

Rules and Networks *edited by Richard Appelbaum, Bill Felstiner and Volkmar Gessner*

Women in the World's Legal Professions *edited by Ulrike Schultz and Gisela Shaw*

Healing the Wounds *edited by Marie-Claire Foblets and Trutz von Trotha*

Imaginary Boundaries of Justice *edited by Ronnie Lippens*

Family Law and Family Values *edited by Mavis Maclean*

Contemporary Issues in the Semiotics of Law *edited by Anne Wagner, Tracey Summerfield and Farid Benavides Vanegas*

The Geography of Law: Landscapes, Identity and Regulation *edited by Bill Taylor*

Theory and Method in Socio-Legal Research *edited by Reza Banakar and Max Travers*

Luhmann on Law and Politics *edited by Michael King and Chris Thornhill*

Precarious Work, Women and the New Economy: The Challenge to Legal Norms *edited by Judy Fudge and Rosemary Owens*

Juvenile Law Violators, Human Rights, and the Development of New Juvenile Justice Systems *edited by Eric L Jensen and Jørgen Jepsen*

The Language Question in Europe and Diverse Societies: Political, Legal and Social Perspectives *edited by Dario Castiglione and Chris Longman*

European Ways of Law: Towards a European Sociology of Law *edited by Volkmar Gessner and David Nelken*

Crafting Transnational Policing: Police Capacity-Building and Global Policing Reform *edited by Andrew Goldsmith and James Sheptycki*

Constitutional Politics in the Middle East: With special reference to Turkey, Iraq, Iran and Afghanistan *edited by Saïd Amir Arjomand*

Parenting after Partnering: Containing Conflict after Separation *edited by Mavis Maclean*

Responsible Business: Self-Governance and Law in Transnational Economic Transactions *edited by Olaf Dilling, Martin Herberg and Gerd Winter*

Rethinking Equality Projects in Law *edited by Rosemary Hunter*

Regulating Deviance: The Redirection of Criminalisation and the Futures of Criminal Law *edited by Bernadette McSherry, Alan Norrie and Simon Bronitt*

Living Law: Reconsidering Eugen Ehrlich *edited by Marc Hertogh*

Multicultural Jurisprudence: Comparative Perspectives on the Cultural Defense *edited Marie-Claire Foblets and Alison Dundes Renteln*

Legal Institutions and Collective Memories *edited by Susanne Karstedt*

The Legal Tender of Gender: Welfare, Law and the Regulation of Women's Poverty *edited by Shelley AM Gavigan and Dorothy E Chunn*

The Legal Tender of Gender

Welfare, Law and the Regulation of Women's Poverty

Edited by
Shelley AM Gavigan
and
Dorothy E Chunn

Oñati International Series in Law and Society

A SERIES PUBLISHED FOR THE OÑATI INSTITUTE
FOR THE SOCIOLOGY OF LAW

• HART •
PUBLISHING
OXFORD AND PORTLAND, OREGON
2010

Hart Publishing, 16c Worcester Place, Oxford, OX1 2JW
Telephone: +44 (0)1865 517530 Fax: +44 (0)1865 510710
E-mail: mail@hartpub.co.uk
Website: http://www.hartpub.co.uk

Published in North America (US and Canada)
by Hart Publishing
c/o International Specialized Book Services
920 NE 58th Avenue, Suite 300
Portland, OR 97213-3786
USA
Tel: +1 503 287 3093 or toll-free: (1) 800 944 6190
Fax: +1 503 280 8832
E-mail: orders@isbs.com
Website: www.isbs.com

British Library Cataloguing in Publication Data
Data Available

ISBN: 978-1-84113-314-0 (hardback)
ISBN: 978-1-84113-315-7 (paperback)

Typeset by Compuscript, Shannon
Printed and bound in Great Britain by
Lightning Source UK Ltd

Acknowledgements

We are indebted to many people for their assistance in bringing this book to fruition. Professor Dr Joxerramon Bengoetxea Caballero, Scientific Director of the International Institute for the Sociology of Law, provided generous intellectual and material support for our Workshop. We acknowledge with great thanks the superb work of Ms Malen Gordua Mendizabal and the IISL staff more generally for their assistance with the Workshop. The gracious, generous and professional manner in which they took care of local arrangements helped to make the Workshop a memorable experience. We also thank Dr José Antonio Azpiazu, IISL publications, for his encouragement to publish a book in the Oñati International Series in Law and Society.

We want to acknowledge as well the invaluable contributions of our two co-organizers, Mimi Abramovitz and Mimi Ajzenstadt, and all the Workshop participants who, in addition to the authors in this collection, included Wendy Chan, Margaret Little, Dorothy Roberts, and Anna Marie Smith. With respect to the publication of this book, we thank Johannes Feest and Judy Fudge, Co-Editors of the Oñati International Series in Law and Society. In particular, we want to express our appreciation to Professor Fudge for her patience and professionalism at every stage of the process from submission to review to production. The two anonymous reviewers provided excellent, wonderfully detailed and constructive comments on the collection and strengthened the final work. Laurie Cormack of Osgoode Hall Law School, York University, provided invaluable support in the early stages of planning the Workshop and Hazel Pollack, Gautam Janardhanan, Jonathan Cevallos, Anita Leung, and Sheetal Rawal (Osgoode 2011), also at Osgoode Hall Law School provided invaluable assistance in the preparation of the revised manuscript. It was a great pleasure to work with Richard Hart and his colleagues at Hart Publishing, and we thank them for their exceptional work. Karen E Andrews and Robert Menzies, as always, buoyed us through the entire process.

Shelley AM Gavigan and Dorothy E Chunn
June 2009

Contents

List of Contributors

Mimi Abramovitz, MSW, DSW (Columbia) is The Bertha Capen Reynolds Professor of Social Policy at Hunter School of Social Work and The CUNY Graduate Center. She is author of *Regulating the Lives of Women: Social Welfare Policy From Colonial Times to the Present,* the award-winning *Under Attack, Fighting Back: Women and Welfare in the US* and co-author of *Taxes Are A Women's Issue: Reframing the Debate*. A scholar/activist and recipient of numerous awards from major professional associations, Dr Abramovitz is frequently interviewed by the print and broadcast media and regularly invited to keynote national and international meetings.

Mimi Ajzenstadt is Lionel Cohen Senior Lecturer in Law, a Professor at the Baerwald School of Social Work and Social Welfare and at the Institute of Criminology, Faculty of Law, and the Chair of the Lafer Center for Gender Studies at the Hebrew University of Jerusalem. Her research interests lie in the areas of sociology of law and in the areas of gender, social policy and the welfare state. She has examined the development of social policy towards women in the Israeli welfare state. Currently, she is researching the societal reaction to crime committed by legal and illegal migrants in Israel.

Felice Batlan is a professor at Chicago-Kent College of Law. She holds a JD from Harvard Law School, a doctorate in US history from New York University, and specializes in feminist jurisprudence and women's legal history. She has written extensively on the gendered origins of public interest law and the role that women played as legal activists and lay lawyers in the late nineteenth century. Before entering the academy, she practised law for nine years.

Dorothy E Chunn, MA, PhD (Toronto), is Professor of Sociology and Co-Director of the Feminist Institute for Studies on Law and Society at Simon Fraser University. Her recent research and publications focus on poor women's perceptions and experiences of welfare reform; feminism, law and social change since the 1960s; and the politics of Canadian custody law reform. She is co-editor (with Susan B Boyd and Hester Lessard) of *Reaction and Resistance: Feminism, Law, and Social Change* (University of British Columbia Press, 2007).

Shelley AM Gavigan, BA, LLB (Sask), MA (Toronto), LLM (Osgoode/York), SJD (Toronto) is a Professor of Law at Osgoode Hall Law School in Toronto, Canada, and a member of the Bars of Saskatchewan and Ontario. Her research interests focus on socio-legal theory and history in the areas of Canadian criminal law; law and poverty; legal regulation and definition of family; access to justice and social justice.

Joan M Gilmour, BA, LLB (Toronto), JSM, JSD (Stanford), is an Associate Professor at Osgoode Hall Law School in Toronto, Canada, and a member of the Bar of Ontario and British Columbia. She is Director of Osgoode's Master's programme specializing in Health Law, and has served as a consultant to Health Canada and the Ontario Law Reform Commission. Her research spans a range of issues, including the interrelation of disability, gender, inequality and law, the effects of the tort system on patient safety, and health system restructuring.

Hester Lessard is a Professor at the University of Victoria Faculty of Law in Victoria, BC Canada. The following general areas are the focus of her teaching and research: feminist legal theory, human rights law, social movements and law, and Canadian constitutional rights jurisprudence. She is co-editor (with Susan B Boyd and Dorothy E Chunn) of *Reaction and Resistance: Feminism, Law, and Social Change* (University of British Columbia Press, 2007).

Janet Mosher is an Associate Professor of Law and Associate Dean at Osgoode Hall Law School, York University, in Toronto, Canada. Her research has focused on legal interventions that impact upon women abused in their intimate relationships, and she is currently engaged in a research project exploring the multiple ways in which state policies and practices are implicated in sustaining woman abuse. She has also published on poverty law, access to justice for disadvantaged groups, legal aid and legal ethics. She is currently the English language editor of the *Canadian Journal of Women and the Law.*

Premilla Nadasen is an Associate Professor of History at Queens College, CUNY. She writes and speaks about social policy and activism. She is author of *Welfare Warriors: The Welfare Rights Movement in the United States* (winner of the John Hope Franklin Prize) and is currently working on a book about domestic worker organizing.

Karen Swift holds a doctorate in Social Work and is a Professor in the School of Social Work, York University. She is the author of numerous publications on issues of gender and social policy, including *Manufacturing 'Bad Mothers': A Critical Perspective on Child Neglect* (1995). She is also the co-author of a social policy text, called *Canadian Social Policy: An Introduction*, which is in its third edition (2008). Her latest book is *At Risk: Social Justice in Child Welfare and Other Human Services*, co-authored with Marilyn Callahan, and will be published by University of Toronto Press in autumn 2009.

Margot Young is Associate Professor of Law at the Faculty of Law, University of British Columbia. She researches and teaches in the areas of constitutional law and social justice. She is co-editor of *Poverty: Rights, Social Citizenship and Legal Activism* (University of British Columbia Press, 2008). She has worked for some years with women's equality-seeking groups on NGO submissions to United Nations committees documenting Canada's failures to observe international human rights obligations. She is a Research Associate with the Canadian Centre for Policy Alternatives, BC Office.

Introduction

THE CHAPTERS IN this collection were originally presented as papers at a workshop that took place at the International Institute of the Sociology of Law in June 2007.[1] The workshop brought together leading feminist scholars from Canada, the United States and Israel, all of whom were engaged in socio-historical and socio-legal research that analyzes the construction and experience of poverty of working and poor women and their children. Participants were asked to historicize and theorize the changing nature of states (ie liberal state, post-war Keynesian state, and neo-liberal state), the gendered nature of their socio-legal policies, and the analytic frames that feminist scholars deploy to document and explain these historical forms and social relations. The workshop papers principally addressed the role of welfare policy and law in nation states that developed historically as settler societies, primarily through colonialization, massive European immigration, and displacement of indigenous peoples.[2]

A focus on the extensive welfare law and policy reforms that marked the emergence and development of Keynesian states during the twentieth century, and their neo-liberal (re)formation, lent a thematic unity to the workshop that also is reflected in this book. Changes in the form and content of social welfare legislation and policy over time are examined through feminist lenses. Despite the reluctance of most liberal states to provide forms of income security and social supports to the working poor and the destitute, some from within their ranks managed to be seen as more deserving of modest forms of support. Historically, sole-support mothers, for instance, were among those considered, however precariously and unevenly, to merit the status of most 'deserving' as recipients of public funding in liberal states; but they are no longer so 'privileged'. Therefore, analyses of how increasingly punitive treatment has rendered them 'undeserving' or 'never deserving' can help illuminate the profound changes that have occurred across many jurisdictions under neo-liberalism.

[1] 'The Legal Tender of Gender: International Perspectives on Welfare Law, State Policies and the Regulation of Women's Poverty' A Workshop held at the IISL, University of Oñati, Euskadi, Spain, 7–8 June 2007.

[2] Many similarities and differences between the nation states reflected in this collection are of interest: for instance, Canada and the United States are among the least developed welfare states, whereas Israel the only liberal democratic state in the Middle East and, like Canada, having close ties to the United States, has until recently been one of the most developed Keynesian states.

The analyses offered in this collection are particularly timely now as the devastation of neo-liberalism becomes increasingly obvious. The current crisis of capitalism is the worst since the Great Depression of the 1930s and the always precarious situation of both working poor women and mother-headed families that rely on social assistance has been greatly exacerbated. The current crisis, arguably, is a defining moment for liberal states—an undeniable global catastrophe that also creates a window of opportunity for critical scholars and activists to attempt to reframe debates about social welfare, work and equality, and to reinsert the discourse of social justice into the public consciousness and political agendae of liberal democracies.

The considerable extant critical scholarship and research can contribute to such a reframing. Critical socio-legal scholars who analyze the state and forms of law and social welfare have used a range of useful theoretical concepts to explain the form and content of state and socio-legal policies of early-twentieth-century and post-World War II socialist and Keynesian welfare states.[3] Key concepts include social control, regulation, race, class and patriarchal relations, among others. Feminist analyses of liberal welfare states have made original and important contributions to knowledge on the constructions and experiences of women in these social formations and on the role of law and state policy.[4] Most notably, feminists in different

[3] See, eg, John Clarke, *Changing Welfare, Changing States: New Directions in Social Policy* (London, SAGE, 2004); John Clarke and J Newman, *The Managerial State: Power, Politics and Ideology in the Remaking of Social Welfare* (London, SAGE, 1997); David Garland, *Punishment and Welfare* (Brookfield VT, Gower, 1985); Stuart Hall, 'Reformism and the Legislation of Consent' in National Deviancy Conference (ed), *Permissiveness and Control: The Fate of the Sixties Legislation* (London, Macmillan, 1980); Stuart Hall, et al, *Policing the Crisis: Mugging, the State, and Law and Order* (London, Macmillan, 1978).

[4] See, eg, Mimi Abramovitz, *Regulating the Lives of Women: Social Welfare Policy From Colonial Times to the Present* (Boston MA, South End Press, 1996), *Under Attack, Fighting Back: Women and Welfare in the United States* (New York, Monthly Review Press, 2000); Mimi Ajzenstadt and J Gal, 'Appearance Can Be Deceptive: Gender in the Israeli Welfare State' (2001) 8 *Social Politics* 292; Sylvia B Bashevkin, *Welfare Hot Buttons: Women, Work and Social Policy Reform* (Toronto, University of Toronto Press, 2002); Susan B Boyd (ed), *Challenging the Public/Private Divide: Feminism, Law, and Public Policy* (Toronto, University of Toronto Press, 1997); Janine Brodie, *Politics on the Margins: Restructuring and the Canadian Women's Movement* (Halifax NS, Fernwood Publishing, 1995); Nancy Christie, *Engendering the State: Family, Work, and Welfare in Canada* (Toronto ON, University of Toronto Press, 2000); Dorothy E Chunn and Shelley AM Gavigan, 'Welfare Law, Welfare Fraud and the Moral Regulation of the "Never Deserving" Poor' (2004) 13 *Social and Legal Studies* 219; Brenda Cossman and Judy Fudge (eds), *Privatization, Law, and the Challenge to Feminism* (Toronto ON, University of Toronto Press, 2002); Nancy Fraser, *Justice Interruptus: Critical Reflections on the 'Postsocialist' Condition* (New York, Routledge, 1997); Linda Gordon (ed), *Women, the State and Welfare* (Madison WN, University of Wisconsin Press, 1990), *Pitied But Not Entitled: Single Mothers and the History of Welfare 1890–1935* (Cambridge MA, Harvard University Press, 1994); Janet Mosher, 'Managing the Disentitlement of Women: Glorified Markets, the Idealized Family, and the Undeserving Other' in Sheila Neysmith (ed), *Restructuring Caring Labour: Discourse, State Practice and Everyday Life* (Don Mills ON, Oxford University Press, 2000); Janet Mosher and Joe Hermer, *Welfare Fraud: The*

jurisdictions have demonstrated that, in many ways, the history of all welfare states is inextricably bound up with the history of women and women's struggles within and against the state. In particular, feminist socio-legal scholars problematize women as agents of change and emphasize the complex and contradictory contributions of law, state and welfare policy to the social and legal position of women.

The contributors to this collection draw liberally on this body of critical work. Consequently, while they represent a range of disciplines—social work, sociology, law, women's studies, and history—their respective chapters are connected in several ways. First, they reflect a feminist-informed, interdisciplinary approach to scholarly research that engages with the premises of the liberal welfare state, the ascendance of neo-conservative and neo-liberal discourses, and changing forms of welfare state and social policy. Secondly, they highlight and interrogate the structural contexts—local, national, and, for some, international—in which income security laws and policies have been developed and (re)formed. Thirdly, the chapters all address to a greater or lesser degree a number of overarching questions: Given that most women have always straddled the public/private divide, how have discursive and material changes (re)formed their relationships to state, family, labour, and market and shaped the constructions of women, particularly sole-support mothers, in welfare law and social policy historically? What has been the impact of welfare legislation and social policy on poor working women and mothers at different points during the twentieth century? To what extent have feminists and other activist women influenced the content and form of state welfare law and policy in ways that challenge the status quo?

The authors in this collection offer analyses of women, law and poverty through a combination of historical and theoretical perspectives and wide-ranging case studies. Their essays reflect and contribute to long-standing feminist concerns: the importance of historically-informed research and analyses, the relevance of women's agency and resistance to the experience of inequality and injustice, the specificity of the experience of poor women and poor mothers, the implications of changes to social policy, and always the possibility of social change. Taken together, the authors in this collection, look back, look here, and look forward—understanding the past and current context, never doubting the necessity and possibility of a better, more socially just future.

Constitution of Social Assistance as Crime (Ottawa, Law Reform Commission of Canada, 2005); Premilla Nadasen, *Welfare Warriors: The Welfare Rights Movement in the United States* (New York, Routledge, 2005); Frances E Olsen, 'The Family and the Market: A Study of Ideology and Legal Reform' (1983) 96 *Harvard Law Review* 1497; Margot Young et al (eds), *Poverty: Rights, Social Citizenship and Legal Activism* (Vancouver BC, University of British Columbia Press, 2007).

Within these broad overarching themes, the contributors focus on different issues. Their differing foci are reflected in the thematic organization of the book. Part I presents longitudinal analyses of the making and unmaking of welfare states in liberal democracies during the twentieth century. While feminist researchers have tended to investigate one or the other development for a number of good reasons, including constraints on time and resources, taking the long view reveals important continuities as well as differences across time as the authors of the chapters in this Part illustrate. Their essays historicize the two defining moments that (re)formed social reproduction and welfare law and policy during the last century in the United States and Canada respectively.

In chapter one, 'Women, Social Reproduction, and the Neo-Liberal Assault on the US Welfare State', Mimi Abramovitz uses the feminist concept of social reproduction, or 'care work', to assess the impact on women's lives of the response of the American state to two major economic crises of the twentieth century—the collapse of the economy in the 1930s and the crisis of corporate profitability in the 1970s. The solution to the former rested on public policy that distributed income downwards and expanded the role of the state, including the welfare state. The solution to the latter was the reverse: the redistribution of income upwards and the downsizing of the state.

Abramovitz draws on government trend data to compare the expansion of the US welfare state from 1945 to 1975 with the retrenchment of revenues and spending since the mid-1970s using the changes in the three core welfare state programmes—Temporary Assistance for Needy Families (TANF), Social Security, and Unemployment Insurance—as a case study. She argues that the responses to both economic crises had mixed impact on women. The welfare state underwrote the costs of social reproduction conducted by women in the home (a policy that paradoxically lessened women's economic dependence on both men and markets and created the conditions for their mobilization), while concomitantly reproducing the patriarchal and racialized social relations of the wider society. The neo-liberal state has undercut social reproduction and strengthened patriarchal and racialized controls by shifting responsibility for care work from the state back to individual women, but has also done little to create economic growth, thereby generating contradictions that create possibilities for progressive change.

In chapter two, 'Women, the State, and Welfare Law: The Canadian Experience', Shelley AM Gavigan and Dorothy E Chunn analyze two waves of welfare law reform through an historically-informed feminist lens, using the exemplar of poor mother-headed families to examine changes in the form and content of Canadian welfare law. Their analysis of how the state dealt with sole-support mothers in several Canadian provinces throughout the twentieth century reveals important continuities, as well as discontinuities, between past and present that have shaped, regulated and reshaped the lives and experiences of poor women and their children.

Gavigan and Chunn demonstrate that the form and content of the first wave of Canadian welfare legislation, intended to provide for certain low-income lone mothers, supported and never dislocated or supplanted, the premises of patriarchal familial ideology. The onerous requirements of much of the legislation also meant that these mothers were also working mothers, either by working whilst waiting out waiting periods for eligibility or by supplementing their modest allowances. This legislation nonetheless did represent a form of recognition by the pre-Keynesian state in Canada that worthy lone mothers with young dependent children merited modest financial support in order to raise their children. When Gavigan and Chunn turn to recent reforms in Canadian welfare law, in which mothers have been rendered invisible, and in which families are no longer regarded as worthy of state support, the nature of neo-liberal (re)formation of the Keynesian state in Canada is illuminated, in particular the recasting of poor mothers as 'undeserving' or 'never deserving' of any assistance that is not tied to workfare.

Part II of the book shifts the analytic focus to women's agency and women's activism as reformers, workers and 'clients' of the welfare state. Considerable feminist scholarship has demonstrated the ways in which women engaged in advocacy, organizing and resistance, helped to shape welfare law and policy, and even found employment in welfare state structures; this research has countered the image of women as passive, always powerless and 'done to', never in control or recipients of positive outcomes.[5] The two comparative, historical papers in this section address these often neglected aspects of welfare state history and exemplify the feminist challenge to conventional wisdoms about women, welfare, and the state.

In chapter three, 'Gender and the Rise of the Welfare State in Fin-de-Siècle New York City: The Case of Tenement Regulation', Felice Batlan illuminates 'the interactions between welfare, regulation, law, gender, and the state' through a focus on urban housing and, in particular, municipal regulation of tenements. Contrary to scholars who locate the origins of the American welfare state at the state and federal levels, she argues that the proto-welfare state first emerged on the local level and that it was a 'deeply gendered' development in which women, though denied the franchise, were able to exert enormous influence over municipal government to shape both a regulatory state and urban space, often using the courts to assert new rights. Their efforts contributed to a reformulation of the division between public and private spheres that created a basis for state intervention in the 'private' domestic realm.

[5] See above n 4.

Batlan illustrates this general phenomenon using a case study of the interactions between law and tenement houses in New York City in the early twentieth century. She examines differing conceptions of 'the tenement problem' among a range of historical actors, including tenement residents and settlement house workers, many of whom were women, and details how proponents of regulation attempted to construct tenements as both private domestic spaces and public spaces that were legitimate sites for state supervision. Women's advocacy around tenement housing helped to generate a new conception of law and a jurisprudence that was deeply grounded in the daily life of home, neighbourhood and women's domestic work. Through their complaints to city officials about sub-standard living conditions, many immigrant women living in tenements came to understand that they had a right to decent housing. However, they often came under intense scrutiny from middle-class and elite women settlement workers who, through their role in enforcing tenement laws, not only contributed to the development of a 'benevolent' regulatory welfare state but also imposed their own sense of morals and 'appropriate' home life and public order upon them.

In chapter four, '"Mothers at Work": The Welfare Rights Movement and Welfare Reform in the 1960s', Premilla Nadasen examines women's grassroots struggles for welfare rights at a later, and defining, moment in the history of the American welfare state. Specifically, she documents the contributions of African-American women to the development of a mass movement of poor black women who came together in local groups to challenge the discriminatory, punitive policies of the Aid to Families with Dependent Children programme. Ideologically, and inaccurately, identified as a programme helping black families only,[6] the AFDC came to be associated politically and culturally with laziness and immorality and viewed as a source of many social problems, from 'broken' black families to teenage pregnancies to rising taxes. This new discourse of welfare led to new work rules and punitive measures on the national level that transformed the programme from one that supported and encouraged women in their motherhood roles to one that devalued their care work and required poor women to enter the paid labour force.

Nadasen argues that women in the 1960s welfare rights movement challenged with some success the dominant discourse that constructed welfare recipients as unworthy and not deserving of assistance. They fought for protection of their basic civil rights, worked to increase benefits, demanded better treatment from case workers and sought to bring dignity and respect to their work as mothers. They engaged politicians, the press, the public and welfare administrators, articulating their own notions of

[6] White women were the majority of AFDC recipients during the late 1950s and early 1960s.

rights, responsibility, and welfare reform. In doing so, they inserted their voices into political and policy-making circles and made themselves agents in the process of welfare reform.

Part III of this collection turns to the contemporary era of neo-liberal welfare reform. The chapters illuminate the legal construction of poor women and the increased precariousness of their always tenuous citizenship in the shift from the liberal welfare state to one informed by and committed to neo-liberalism. Feminist work in this area has demonstrated how women's historically-assigned responsibility for social reproduction (which is rendered invisible in a regime that conceptualizes everyone as an entrepreneurial citizen engaged in paid employment) and the historical conceptualization of (married) women as part-time or secondary earners at best, have exacerbated their exclusion from full social and political citizenship.[7] Feminists have also demonstrated how the neo-liberal emphasis on sameness obscures the differential impact of (welfare) law and policy on the citizenship of women who are differently situated by virtue of race, sexual orientation, disability, entanglement in abusive relationships and so on.[8] The authors in this Part offer innovative analyses of the gendered implications of neo-liberalism, and in particular neo-liberal law reform to labour, child protection, and welfare laws, as they affect labouring and poor women in different national contexts.

A central argument of the collection is that the examination of the relation between women, work, and the state must be contextualized within particular economic, social and historical circumstances. Such an examination must focus on the particularities of gender relationships in a specific society, paying attention to issues of power and ideology. The relationship between women, the labour market and the state, and the ways in which neo-liberalism has contributed to the erosion of women's income and women's rights lie at the heart of Mimi Ajzenstadt's chapter, 'Women in the Workforce in the Context of Neo-Liberalism: The Case of Israel' (chapter five). This chapter shows that historical conditions and

[7] See, eg, Eileen Boris and E Prugl (eds), *Homeworkers in Global Perspective: Invisible No More* (New York, Routledge, 1996); Marjorie Griffin Cohen and Jane Pulkingham (eds), *Public Policy for Women: The State, Income Security, and Labour Market Issues* (Toronto, University of Toronto Press, 2009); Judy Fudge and Rosemary Owens (eds), *Precarious Work, Women and the New Economy: The Challenge to Legal Norms* (Oxford, Hart Publishing, 2006).

[8] See Kiran Mirchandani and Wendy Chan, *Criminalizing Race, Criminalizing Poverty: Welfare Fraud Enforcement in Canada* (Halifax NS, Fernwood Publishing, 2007); Janet Mosher et al, *Walking on Eggshells: Abused Women's Experience of Ontario's Welfare System*, Final Report of Research Findings from the Woman and Abuse Welfare Research Project (5 April 2004); Dorothy Roberts, *Killing the Black Body: Race, Reproduction and the Meaning of Liberty* (New York, Vintage Books, 1997) and *Shattered Bonds: The Color of Child Welfare* (New York, Basic Books, 2002); Anna-Marie Smith, *Welfare Reform and Sexual Regulation* (New York, Cambridge University Press, 2007); Karen Swift, *Manufacturing 'Bad' Mothers* (Toronto ON, University of Toronto Press, 1995).

socio-economic-political events shaped material and discursive conditions for women in North America and in other places, such as Israel. Ajzenstadt analyzes the impact of neo-liberal governance on women in Israel, through an examination of changes in the labour market during the late twentieth century. She argues that since the mid-1980s processes of privatization and globalization, in tandem with declining unionization, erosion of state responsibility for the welfare and rights of individuals, and attacks on the public sector, have governed labour market policies as well as policies related to health, education and welfare.

Ajzenstadt illustrates her argument using data from her case study on the impact of a set of labour laws enacted by the neo-liberal state in Israel which were expressly intended to secure and promote gender equality, including a guarantee of paid maternity leave and of post-leave job security and a prohibition on the firing of pregnant women. After tracking the outcomes of cases brought before the labour court and files opened at Israeli agencies that provide legal aid, Ajzenstadt concludes that enforcement of the legislation aimed at establishing gender equality in the labour force is weak and, as a result, working mothers' rights are not being upheld. Following an analysis of the process through which the new set of labour legislation was introduced, she undertakes a close examination of the various claims and justifications used by employers and law enforcement agents dealing with the abuse of working mothers' rights in the labour market.

In chapter six, '"Risky Women": The Role of "Risk" in the Construction of the Single Mother', Karen Swift moves the analytic focus from the ineffectiveness of labour laws premised on gender equality to the re-conceptualization of women's unpaid (mother)work under neo-liberalism. She argues that low-income single mothers were viewed more positively for brief periods in the Canadian welfare state, but public attitudes became more punitive with the emergence of neo-liberal social policy and law, which are based on the idea of individual rather than social responsibility for risks. As a result, low-income, single mothers, and indeed women in general, increasingly bear the responsibility and are held accountable for managing the risks associated with social reproduction.

Using the example of child protection law, Swift draws on data from interviews with low-income mothers and social workers in two Canadian provinces to explore some effects of including the notion of 'risk' in child protection law. Her analysis suggests that the concept of 'risk' operates as an ideology which obscures and marginalizes the unequal relations of class, race and gender that are structured into child welfare. She concludes that in the field of child protection, the definition of 'risk' as a real, identifiable and value-neutral thing, supported in law, allows the construction of a 'risk class', composed mostly of low-income women, who can legitimately be subjected to ongoing state surveillance and regulation on the basis of possible future harm as opposed to any actual harm to their children. As a result, more families become involved with child protection authorities for more reasons and often with more substantial consequences under neoliberalism than was the case historically.

In chapter seven, 'Intimate Intrusions: Welfare Regulation and Women's Personal Lives', Janet Mosher provides a similar analysis of how late-twentieth-century welfare reforms have profoundly reshaped the citizen-state relationship and in particular the state's role in disciplining welfare recipients. Like Swift, Mosher reminds us that the fleetingly liberal moment in Canadian welfare policy and its modest, imperfect contributions to the wellbeing of women and children, should not be forgotten, especially in the wake of its crushing demise. Considerable research has documented the discursive transformation of single mothers from full-time mothers whose work of social reproduction was at least partially acknowledged into full-time workers who have been removed from the ranks of the 'deserving' poor. Mosher agrees this shift is important, but her work addresses the less studied topic of how welfare reforms have simultaneously reordered the welfare system to discipline and regulate women's intimate lives.

Using interview data on the effects of welfare reforms in the province of Ontario, she focuses specifically on the role of the welfare fraud regime in the regulation and disciplining of women's bodies. Close attention to the intersections of the fraud regime and the concept of 'spouse' at play in Ontario's welfare system reveals that women's intimate relational lives are viewed as criminally suspect, and consequently are subject to intense surveillance. Although the state's interest in fraud detection is not new, Mosher maintains that the scope of surveillance, the ready acceptance of demeaning stereotypes and the widespread characterization of non-criminal conduct as 'fraud' have created 'a dense, intractable web of control over women's relational lives'. Forming an intimate relationship is thus profoundly 'risky' for single mothers on welfare. Moreover, this is a deeply gendered and patriarchal form of discipline, exercised upon the bodies of women but not men, often mirroring the exercise of power and control by abusive men.

In chapter eight, 'Retrenchment Not Reform: Using Law and Policy to Restrict the Entitlement of Women with Disabilities to Social Assistance', Joan M Gilmour examines how women with disabilities are regulated and their citizenship rights subverted in the context of establishing eligibility for social assistance. She documents how Canadian governments' discursive commitments to framing and evaluating policies affecting people with disabilities in terms of advancing citizenship contrast starkly with welfare law reform that has led to tighter eligibility criteria, substantially reduced social assistance payments, rigid reliance on a medical model of disability in determining entitlement to benefits, and increasingly intrusive surveillance of welfare recipients.

Gilmour argues that women are even more severely affected by the harsh economic realities frequently associated with disability than men and depend more on income support. Consequently, they are particularly vulnerable to cut-backs in governments transfer programmes, uninformed judgements about eligibility, and restrictive interpretations of the legislation and regulations. With few challenges to bureaucratic/administrative power, the final arbiters of claims are usually administrative decision-makers. Further, the medicalized conception of disability that women must embrace to successfully navigate the disability determination process 'becomes what disability, and they themselves are (ie *un*able to function) thereby reinforcing and validating both the judgement of incapacity and their exclusion'. Many women with disabilities thus are ensnared in a system of discretionary administrative allocations of minimal assistance, deeply shaped by historical distinctions between deserving and undeserving poor, in which claims based on citizenship (with rights and entitlements) are not heeded.

Part IV of this book addresses the question that emerges from all of the chapters discussed above: Where do we go from here? Feminists have generated an extensive literature which documents the mixed consequences of socio-legal reform[9] and of welfare reform in particular,[10] and the need to develop strategies that will be more resistant to appropriation by anti-feminists. The papers in this final section point to ways in which feminists may be able to influence the reformation of state legislation and policy related to welfare that will have more positive outcomes for women than the strategies that clearly have had their day and are now counter-productive in the current context.

In chapter nine, 'Substantive Universality: Reconceptualising Feminist Approaches to Social Provision and Child Care', Hester Lessard interrogates the language of universality and its relation to feminist theorizing with respect to questions of social provision. To reframe social welfare, she argues, feminists require more 'nuanced' conceptions of universality. While accepting the centrality of the redistributive element in universal programmes, she insists that the 'everyone' implied by the universal sometimes reinforces social inequalities and must be challenged. But when the 'everyone' fails to deliver on its promise not because of a formal gap in coverage or a hidden 'claw-back' under another regime, but because of a failure to reflect significant historical, social and cultural differences and practices, it must be complicated rather than rejected.

[9] See, eg, Janine Brodie, Shelley AM Gavigan and Jane Jenson, *The Politics of Abortion* (Toronto, Oxford University Press, 1992); SB Boyd, *Challenging the Public/Private Divide* (above n 4); Dorothy E Chunn, Susan B Boyd and Hester Lessard (eds), *Reaction and Resistance: Feminism, Law and Social Change* (Vancouver BC, University of British Columbia Press, 2007); B Cossman and J Fudge, *Privatization, Law, and the Challenge to Feminism* (above n 4); Carol Smart, *Feminism and the Power of Law* (London, Routledge & Kegan Paul, 1989).

[10] Jennifer Mittelstadt, *From Welfare to Workfare: The Unintended Consequences of Liberal Reform 1945–1965* (Chapel Hill NC, University of North Carolina Press, 2005); M Young et al, (above n 4).

Lessard revisits the historical universality/selectivity division in social programmes, and examines key Canadian government initiatives in the child care field to illustrate how the recent turn to tax-based delivery of social benefits disrupts this dichotomy. She concludes that from a feminist perspective, the strategic relevance of the universality/selectivity binary is much reduced. She suggests, therefore, that in reformulating universality, feminists should examine the parallel between the conceptual and practical problems generated by the terminology of universality in social provision and the conceptual and practical problems generated by the language of equality in constitutional rights discourses. Feminist analyses of the tension between formal and substantive equality provide a useful guide for developing a feminist conception of universality that addresses substantive differences in material conditions, social locations, needs and relationships.

In chapter ten, 'Women's Work and a Guaranteed Income', Margot Young addresses the issue of universality in relation to adequate income and how to ensure that everyone in society has one. Canadian women have experienced increasing, disproportionately high rates of poverty, and lone-mother-led families are especially reliant on social assistance regimes. Thus, the idea of a guaranteed income with the promise of 'adequacy' and the severing of economic security from paid employment could potentially transform the lives of sole-support mothers. Feminists are divided, however, about whether basic income policies might simply entrench the gendered division of labour that assigns the work of social reproduction to women within the 'private' family.

Young argues that the public-private divide and its gendered character must be central in any appraisal of such proposals. Feminist analyses of marriage, employment and citizenship can contribute much to discussions about income security reform and the development of policies that will meet the needs of diverse groups of women. While mindful that many basic income schemes would be highly disadvantageous for women, she concludes that a guaranteed income proposal that is grounded in the idea of ensuring all Canadians a fair share of economic resources and attentive to related issues such as the need for child care and social housing, is extremely compelling and must be part of any income security reforms.

In sum, the chapters in this collection demonstrate the importance and relevance of history and feminist theorizing in the area of women, the state and welfare law to an analysis and understanding of the gendered impact of neo-liberal welfare policy in the current context. The collection also demonstrates the significance of feminist analysis that renders visible the agency and struggles of poor women—from the tenements of late-nineteenth-century New York City to the streets of Tel Aviv to African-American communities in contemporary USA, and small towns and slightly larger Canadian cities—to resist oppressive shifts in law and policy and to attempt to forge a better life for their children and themselves. It is their legacy that we honour and to their future that our ongoing work is dedicated.

Part I

Historicizing Social Reproduction, Welfare and Neo-liberalism

1

Women, Social Reproduction and the Neo-Liberal Assault on the US Welfare State

MIMI ABRAMOVITZ

'The test of our progress is not whether we add more to the abundance of those who have much; It is whether we provide enough for those who have too little'.

President Franklin Roosevelt, 32nd President of the United States (1882–1945)

I. INTRODUCTION

THE INTELLECTUAL REVOLUTION sparked by feminism revealed that the study of gender, like that of race and class, uncovered previously ignored information and introduced new analyses of social, economic and political relations—including the welfare state. Traditional welfare state analyses in the United States and other countries focused on male workers and class conflict, paying little attention to the relationship of women to the welfare state. When feminists applied a gender lens to the discourse they discovered that women reformers played a central role in the origins of the welfare state and that women comprised the majority of welfare state clients and workers.

They also discovered that the welfare state underwrote women's unpaid care work in the home—often called social reproduction.[1] Social reproduction refers to those activities established by societies to further procreation, socialization, sexuality, nurturance and family maintenance. Carried out by the family as well as schools, religious organizations and other societal institutions, social reproduction includes (a) reproducing the next generation of workers; (b) ensuring the health, productivity and socialization of

[1] K Bezanson and M Luxton, 'Social Reproduction and Feminist Political Economy' in K Bezanson and M Luxton (eds), *Social Reproduction: Feminist Political Economy Challenges Neo-Liberalism* (MontrealMcGill-Queen's Press, 2006).

the current work force; (c) managing consumption; and (d) caring for those too old, young, sick, disabled or jobless to support themselves. Care work or social reproduction is typically carried out by women in the home, and is critical for family well-being but also for business profits and for the smooth functioning of the entire social order. Crises in social reproduction can arise when the market fails to yield the level of jobs and income needed for family maintenance and when social change challenges the norms that hold the gender division of labour in place.

This chapter compares the different ways in which those in charge of US national policy responded to the breakdowns in social reproduction associated with the two major economic crises of the twentieth century: the collapse of the economy in the 1930s and the crisis of profitability the 1970s. Each crisis reflected the unravelling of the social, economic, and political structures that had been put into place during the previous 40–50 years to stabilize the social order. They no longer worked for the elite and had to be reformed.[2] In response to the first emergency—the Great Depression—the nation's leaders blamed the workings of the laissez-faire market. For the first time, however unwillingly, they called upon the federal government to restore economic growth, to support families in need (social reproduction) and to mute the social unrest sparked by the economic disaster. In sharp contrast, in the 1970s the nation's decision-makers made a dramatic U-turn in public policy. They blamed their falling profits on the government programmes that been created in the 1930s in response to the first crisis. Driven by conservative ideology, the resulting retrenchment undercut government support for women's care work in the home—once regarded as critical for the wellbeing of families, business profits, and the smooth functioning of the entire social order.

II. THE FIRST CRISIS: THE RISE OF THE US WELFARE STATE

The first crisis, the collapse of the United States (US) economy, revealed that the laissez-faire structures that had ensured profits, political stability and family well-being since the 1890s no longer worked. Hidden beneath the rapid economic growth, booming profits and the giddy consumerism of the 'roaring '20s' the poor and working class suffered a falling standard of living and mounting social problems. Rising rates of poverty, hunger, unemployment, evictions, overcrowding and depleted savings were accompanied by alcoholism, desertion, marital breakup, sickness, child neglect, malnutrition and other family problems. The distress went unnoticed until

[2] DM Kotz, 'Interpreting The Social Structures of Accumulation Theory' in DM Kotz, T McDonough and M Reich (eds), *Social Structures of Accumulation: The Political Economy of Growth and Crises* (New York, Cambridge University Press, 1994); VC Lippit, 'Social Structure of Accumulation Theory' (Unpublished manuscript, Paper Presented at the conference on 'Growth and Crisis: Social Structure of Accumulation Theory and Analysis', National University of Ireland, Galway, Ireland, 2–4 November 2006).

the Great Depression caused both material hardship and social problems to spread from the working to the middle class.[3]

A crisis of social reproduction that simmered during the 1920s was fuelled as well by the victories of the first wave of feminism that challenged prevailing gender norms.[4] More women in paid work, lower birth rates, fewer marriages, and a sexual revolution reduced access to women's unpaid domestic labour on which social reproduction relied and otherwise undermined the patriarchal underpinnings of the 'traditional' family.[5] During the same period the combination of 'Jim Crow laws', a series of calamities that devastated the cotton crop, and labour shortages in the North and the West caused more than half a million blacks to leave the rural South in search of urban industrial jobs. The turmoil of the 'Great Migration' disrupted social reproduction in the black community. The employment of large numbers of black women and black men in domestic service or dirty and dangerous industrial jobs also deprived the black family of women's unpaid labour at home.[6] With few government programmes in place in the late 1920s, troubled or needy white and black families swamped their respective (ie segregated and unequal) private social agencies that tried to maintain families.[7] Extreme hardship also led the dispossessed of all races to take to the streets. Groups representing the elderly, the jobless, struggling housewives and racialized communities demanded that the federal government step in to help families survive; that is to underwrite social reproduction.[8]

A. The Modern Welfare State in the United States: Mediating Contradictions

The Great Depression exposed a contradiction built into market economies: the tension between profitable economic production and effective social reproduction. On the one hand, profits depended on the ability of

[3] S Coontz, *The Social Origins of Private Life, A History of American Families 1600–1900* (London, Verso, 1988); S Mintz and S Kellog, *Domestic Revolutions: A Social History of American Family Life* (New York, The Free Press, 1988); DM Scott and W Wishy, *America's Families: A Documentary History* (New York, Harper & Row, 1982); S Ware, *Holding Their Own: American Women in the 1930s* (Boston MA, Twayne, 1982).

[4] D Brown, *Setting the Course: American Women in the 1920s* (Boston MA, Twayne Publishers, 1987), 81.

[5] Coontz et al, *Social Origins* (above n 3), Mintz and Kellog, *Domestic Revolutions* (above n 3); Scott and Wishy, *America's Families* (above n 3); Ware, *Holding Their Own* (above n 3).

[6] DL Franklin, *Ensuring Inequality: The Structural Transformation of the American Family* (New York, Oxford, 1997); J Jones, *Labor of Love, Labor of Sorrow; Black Women, Work and the Family from Slavery to Present* (New York, Basic Books, 1985).

[7] M Abramovitz, *Regulating the Lives of Women: Social Welfare Policy From Colonial Times to the Present* (Boston MA, South End Press, 1996).

[8] FF Piven and RM Cloward, *Poor People's Movements: Why They Succeed, How They Fail* (New York, Vintage, 1977); M Triece, *On The Picket Line: Strategies of Working Class Women During the Depression* (Urbana IL, University of Chicago Press, 2007).

families to sustain themselves; that is to buy goods and services, to ensure the productivity of the current and future work force, and to care for those who could not support themselves. However profits also depended on low wages and high unemployment both of which undercut the capacity of families to carry out these critical tasks. In the 1930s, the failure of the market, the breakdown in social reproduction, and the demands from social movements made it clear that the smooth running of the entire society required that the federal government play a major new role in ensuring general welfare, including support for social reproduction. However reluctantly, the leaders in business and government offered the public a 'New Deal' based on redistributing income downwards and expanding the role of the state, including the welfare state.

The 1935 Social Security Act[9] is widely viewed as the birth of the US welfare state because it transferred social welfare responsibility from the states to the federal government and created an entitlement to income support. The historic shift in social policy was legitimized in the late 1930s by two major events. The Supreme Court finally upheld the constitutionality of federal responsibility for the general welfare and officialdom accepted the economic theory of the British economist, John Maynard Keynes that called for greater government spending to increase aggregate demand and otherwise stimulate economic growth.

From the New Deal (1930s) to the Great Society (1970s) the welfare state expanded in response to prosperity, population growth, the emergence of new needs, and the demands made by the increasingly militant trade union, civil rights, women's liberation, and other movements.[10] The resulting income support and social service programmes provided families with a minimum standard of living and contributed to family maintenance. The subsidization of social reproduction eased the contradiction between business profits and family needs by benefiting both.

(i) Business Profits

The post-war welfare state helped to create the conditions for profitable economic activity. Its programmes (1) ensured the daily consumption of goods and services that companies produced, (2) cushioned employers against loss during economic downturns, and (3) supplied business with a healthy, educated and socialized workforce. The welfare state also (4) supplemented wages, which enabled employers to pay less; and (5) helped to quiet the social unrest produced by market inequality.

[9] 42 USC A § 301 et seq.

[10] M Abramovitz, 'The Reagan Legacy: Undoing Class, Race, and Gender Accords' (1992) XIX *Journal of Sociology and Social Welfare* 91.

(ii) Meeting Family Needs

The post-war expansion of the welfare state also compensated millions of people for income lost due to old age, illness, disability, joblessness, and absence of parental support. Its comprehensive array of health, education, housing, employment, and social services helped families from all income groups to address a wide range of physical, emotional, and social needs. This basic support enabled families to more effectively carry out the tasks of social reproduction: to reproduce the next generation; to ensure the health, productivity and socialization of the current work force; to manage consumption; and to care for those too old, young, sick or disabled to provide for themselves.

(iii) The Gender Division of Labour

Social reproduction depends on women's unpaid labour in the home that the welfare state has helped to enforce.[11] Most welfare state programmes incorporated the male breadwinner-female homemaker model, based on the idea that women's place is in the home and economically dependent on a male earner. Programme rules and regulations favoured married or previously married women—such as widows and wives of sick, disabled or temporarily unemployed men—who were viewed as lacking a male breadwinner through no fault of their own and thus 'deserving' of aid. These 'deserving' women received higher benefits and better treatment than the so-called 'undeserving', deserted, abandoned or never-married women who were viewed as wilfully departing from prescribed wife and mother roles.[12]

(iv) Welfare Racism

From the start, however, the welfare state favoured social reproduction by white households, especially married heterosexual couples. Its early programmes excluded African American and Latino families and over the years provided them with lower benefits, reinforced discriminatory labour market policies, disadvantaged single mothers, and implemented other forms of 'welfare racism' that deprived families of colour of the resources needed to adequately care for their families.[13] In the final analysis a distinction

[11] Abramovitz, *Regulating The Lives* (above n 7); JE Lewis, 'Gender and Welfare in Modern Europe', *Past & Present* (2006 Supplement) 39–54; D Sainsbury, *Gender, Equality and Welfare States* (Cambridge, Cambridge University Press, 1996).

[12] Abramovitz, *Regulating the Lives of Women* (above n 7).

[13] KJ Neubeck and NA Casenav, *Welfare Racism: Playing the Race Card Against America's Poor* (New York, Routledge, 2001); M Brown, *Race, Money and the American Welfare State* (Ithaca NY, Cornell University Press, 1999).

between the 'deserving' and 'undeserving' poor was built into most welfare state programmes. Based largely on class, race and marital status, it upheld the economic dependence of women on men; rewarded women who complied with prevailing gender norms; and penalized single mothers, employed wives and childless women who could not or chose not to play by these patriarchal rules. These rewards and penalties regulated the lives of women. They encouraged white women to engage in the unpaid domestic labour required for successful social reproduction in the home while channelling black women into low-paid jobs, making it harder to provide care for their families and communities.

The post-war welfare state helped to save capitalism from itself by mediating the contradiction between profitable economic production and effective social reproduction, although it enforced the contradiction between the democratic promise of equal opportunity and the unequal treatment of people by gender, class and race. The arrangements held steady until the mid-1970s when the nation faced its second major economic crisis of the twentieth century.

III. THE SECOND ECONOMIC CRISIS: THE FALL OF THE US WELFARE STATE

In the mid-1970s, structural shifts in the domestic and global economies fuelled the second major crisis of profitability in the twentieth century. The changes—third world revolutions, the loss of US world hegemony, reduced access to cheap raw materials from third world nations, mounting international economic competition, and the victories of US social movements—eventually weakened the institutional arrangements set up in the 1930s to promote profits, political stability, and family well-being, and to otherwise address the first major crisis of the century.[14] Beginning in the mid-1970s, business and government became less willing to support the welfare state that once benefited them in various ways.

For one de-industrialization at home, the exportation of production abroad, and technological advances reduced corporate America's reliance on US workers and weakened the power of labour unions. With these developments, employers became less interested in social welfare programmes that previously helped business to maintain the current and future workforce, sustain social reproduction and appease social movements. Once less-developed and formerly communist countries began to purchase goods produced in the United States, American businesses had

[14] T Weisskopf, 'The Current Economic Crisis in Historical Perspective' (1981) 57 *Socialist Review* 9.

less need to raise wages or social welfare benefits to ensure consumption of their products.[15]

Leaders in business and government additionally blamed the rising cost of investment dollars on the welfare state. They attributed high interest rates, the mounting deficit, and the massive debt to social welfare spending rather than to other factors that had more significantly increased the cost of borrowing and otherwise interfered with investment and economic growth.[16]

Finally, business and government faulted the welfare state for raising the cost of maintaining the political peace, especially by increasing social benefits. Although they had hoped that welfare state programmes would ensure political stability by mediating inequality and otherwise appeasing social movements, the welfare state paradoxically had raised these costs by emboldening individuals and social movements. Similar to a strike fund, access to income outside of the market reduced workers' fears of unemployment, increased labour's bargaining power, and yielded higher wages and improved working conditions. The expanded welfare state fostered the democratic promise of equal opportunity by undercutting patriarchal controls and white hegemony. Its programmes contained the potential to help women choose welfare over low-paid, dangerous jobs, to leave unhappy or unsafe marriages, to decide to raise children on their own, and to otherwise gain autonomy. Likewise, pressed by the civil rights movement, the state gradually began to protect racialized persons and/or compensate them for the impact of discrimination. This made it possible for them to avoid the worst jobs and otherwise undercut white hegemony and business profits.

In the early 1980s, the New Right also gained a strong grip on US public policy. Troubled by changes in the class, racial and gendered status quo, its leaders blamed the welfare state for creating a 'crisis' in the family (ie the employment of women, high rates of divorce, single motherhood, greater female autonomy and gay rights). In addition to increasing women's bargaining power at home and on the job, the Right argued that the expanded welfare state had undermined the patriarchal family by undercutting gender norms, weakening personal responsibility, parental authority and traditional 'family values'.[17] The Right also argued that the civil rights movement had solved the problem of racism leaving no other anti-racism work to be done.[18]

[15] T Amott, *Caught in the Crisis: Women and the U.S. Economy* (New York, Monthly Review Press, 1993).

[16] *Ibid.*

[17] AS Orloff, 'Gender and the Social Rights of Citizenship: The Comparative Analysis of Gender Relations and Welfare States' (1993) *American Sociological Review* 303; RE Klatch, *Women of the New Right Philadelphia* (Philadelphia PA, Temple University Press, 1987).

[18] D D'Souza, *The End of Racism: Principles for a Multiracial Society* (New York, The Free Press, 1995).

A. Neo-Liberalism: The U-Turn in Public Policy

In contrast to the crisis of the '30s, in the 1970s the national elite concluded that the welfare state was part of the problem, rather than part of the solution and called for its demise. The resulting attack on the welfare state was part of a broader economic recovery strategy designed to restore profitability by redistributing income and wealth upwards from the have-nots to the haves, downsizing the state, and advancing family values. This historic U-turn in public policy known as neo-liberalism but also Reaganomics and Supply-Side Economics, first surfaced in the mid-1970s when President Carter campaigned for the Democratic Party's nomination on an anti-Washington platform.[19] Launched in full by the Reagan Administration in 1981, the policies have been pursued in varying degrees by every US administration since then.

Hoping to promote economic growth by returning to the old laissez-faire or market-driven economic model, the neo-liberal strategy sought to undo the New Deal by (1) limiting the role of the federal government, (2) shrinking the welfare state, (3) lowering labour costs, and (4) weakening the influence of social movements best positioned to resist this austerity plan. The now familiar tactics include (1) tax cuts, (2) retrenchment of social programmes, (3) devolution or the shift of social welfare responsibility from the federal government back to the States, and (4) privatization or the transfer of public responsibility of the private sector. At the same time, the New Right called for (5) restoring patriarchal 'family values' and a colour-blind social order.

Now that three decades have passed, we can ask: How has neo-liberalism worked? The rest of the chapter contextualizes well-known policies and events in relation to long-term trends. Using federal budget data from the late 1940s to the present it both (1) documents the U-turn in public policy that occurred in the mid- to late 1970s and the early 1980s and (2) assesses the impact of this historic paradigm shift on the capacity of families to maintain themselves, that is to carry out the complex tasks of social reproduction. The data show that, in the short run, neo-liberalism helped to: (1) downsize the state (domestic side), (2) redistribute income upwards, (3) restore 'family values' and a colour-blind social order, (4) shift costs of social reproduction from the state to women and families, and (5) weaken social movements. However, in the long run, the data suggest that neo-liberalism may be undermined by its own internal contradictions.[20]

[19] RJ Bresler, 'Liberalism's Third Act?' *USA Today* (Society for the Advancement of Education, January 2008); H Sklar, *Reagan, Trilateralism and the Neoliberals: Containment and intervention in the 1980s* (Cambridge MA, South End Press, 1980).

[20] D Kotz, 'The Financial and Economic Crisis of 2008: A Systemic Crisis of Neoliberal Capitalism', paper prepared for a panel on 'The Global Financial Crisis: Heterodox Perspective', at the Annual convention of the Allied Social Science Association, 4 January 2009.

(i) Downsizing The State: The Era of Big Government is Over

The first goal of neo-liberalism aimed at downsizing the domestic role of the state on the grounds that large tax cuts and less social spending would stimulate economic growth by favouring private over public spending and putting money in the hands of those most likely to save and invest. The following federal budget data document the reversal of the New Deal policies marked by the decline of federal tax revenues and federal spending, and the retrenchment of three core welfare state programmes: Aid To Dependent Children/Temporary Aid to Needy Families, Unemployment Insurance, and Social Security. As President Bill Clinton explained in 1996, 'the era of big government is over'.[21]

(a) Reduced Tax Revenues

During the post-war years revenues based on a progressive income tax system covered the cost of running the country reasonably well.

With some fluctuation (see Table 1) federal tax revenues rose as a percentage of the Gross Domestic Product (GDP) from 1949 (14.5 per cent) to

Table 1—Federal Revenues as a % of the GDP, 1948–2007

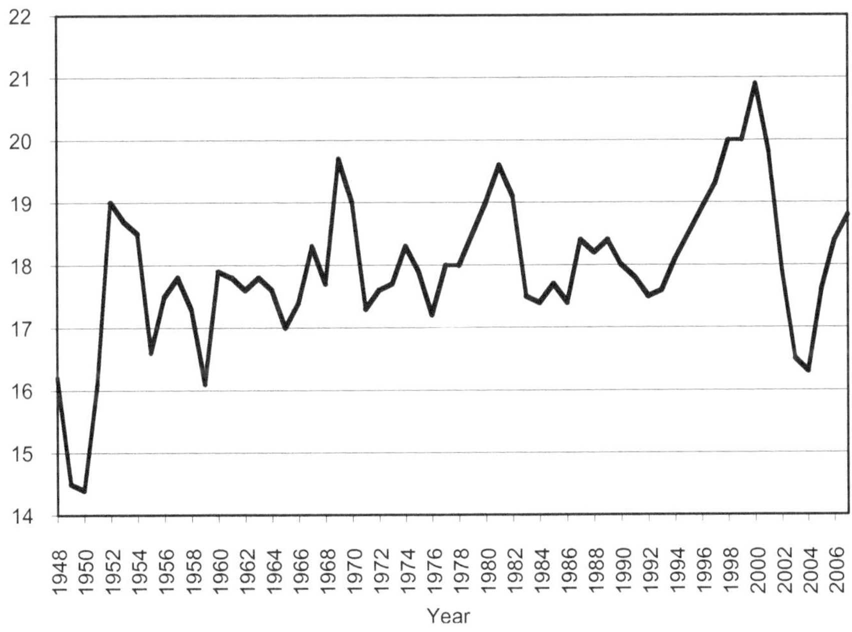

[21] W Clinton, 'The Era of Big Government is Over', CNN Transcript of President Clinton's Radio Address (16 January 1996), at: www.cnn.com/US/9601/budget/01-27/clinton_radio/.

a post-war high in 1969 (19.7 per cent). However, as neo-liberalism eroded the progressivity of tax collections federal revenues gradually declined as a share of the economy. Except for two economic booms, revenues remained below the 1969 peak and by 2004 had dropped back to their lowest level since 1950.[22] Although record high profits and wealth increased federal revenues to 18.8 per cent of the GDP in 2007, they still fell below the pre-neo-liberal high of 19.5 per cent in 1969.[23]

(b) Reduced Federal Spending

Federal spending followed the same pattern of post-war expansion and neo-liberal contraction. Total federal spending (see Table 2) rose from 1948 (11.6 per cent of GDP) to a post-war peak in 1983 (23.5 per cent of GDP). During the neo-liberal '80s and '90s federal spending dropped steadily reaching 18.4 per cent of the GDP in 2000.[24]

Table 2—Total Federal Spending as a % of the GDP, 1948–2006

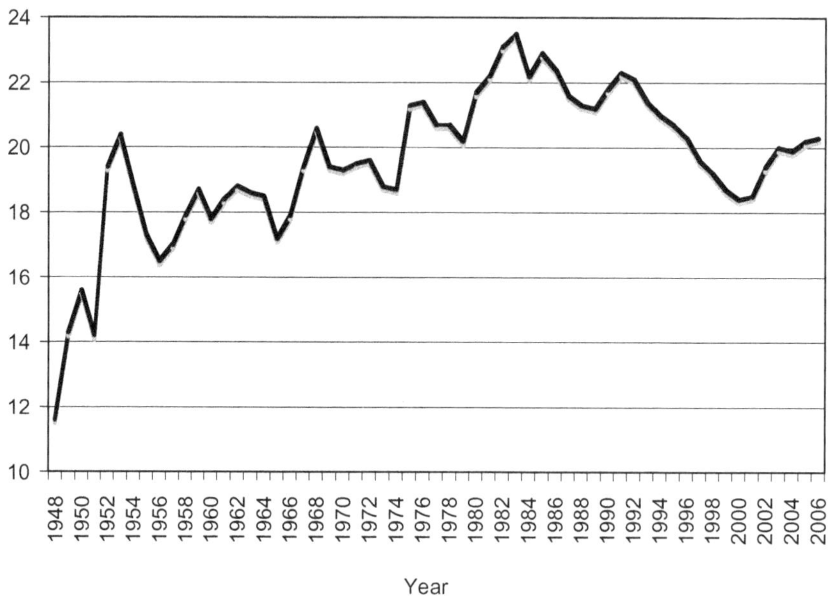

[22] J Irons, 'Federal Budget Continues Fiscal Decline?', *OMB Watch*, 4 February 2004, at: www.ombwatch.org/article/articleview/2028/1/18/.

[23] Tax Policy Center, Historical Data. Table 1.2: 'Summary of Receipts, Outlays and Surplus or Deficits in Current and Constant Dollars FY 2000, and as Percentages of GDP, 1940–2013', at: www.taxpolicycenter.org/taxfacts/displayafact.cfm?Docid=200.

[24] *Ibid.*

Due largely to rising military and health care costs, overall outlays jumped to 20 per cent of the GDP in 2007, the same as 1954—before Medicare, Medicaid, and the Interstate Highway system existed—and below the 1983 high! Domestic discretionary (non-military, non-international) spending (see Table 3 below) rose from 2.5 per cent of the GDP in 1962 (first reliable data) to a peak of 4.8 per cent in 1978.

In the following period, neo-liberal retrenchment led these outlays to fall steadily to 3.1 per cent of the GDP in 1989. They rose to 3.4 per cent in the early 1990s and to 3.6 per cent in 2001 due largely to increasing health care costs but then fell back to 3.4 per cent in 2007.[25] Total mandatory or entitlement spending (see Table 4 below) also grew as a share of the economy from 4.9 per cent of the GDP in 1962 to 10.6 per cent in 1983.

With the advent of neo-liberalism the mandatory spending stream fell as a percentage of the GDP and did not exceed its 1982 high (10.6 per cent) until 2001 when the growth of Medicare, Medicaid and Social Security (the

Table 3—Federal Discretionary Spending (Domestic) as a % of the GDP, 1962–2008

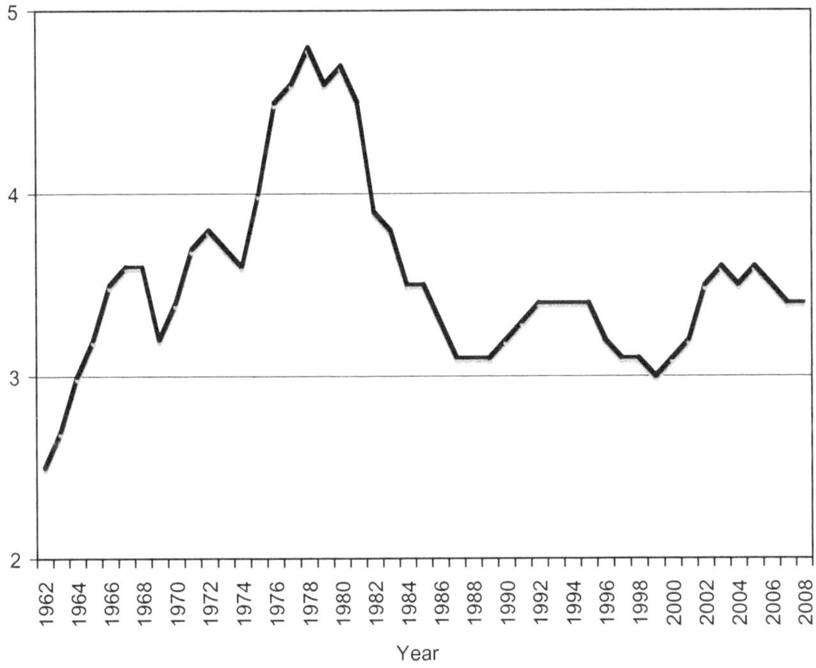

[25] US Congress, *The Budget and Economic Outlook: Fiscal Years 2009–18* (Washington DC, Government Printing Office, 2008) Table F-8 p 155.

Table 4—Federal Mandatory Spending as a % of the GDP, 1962–2007

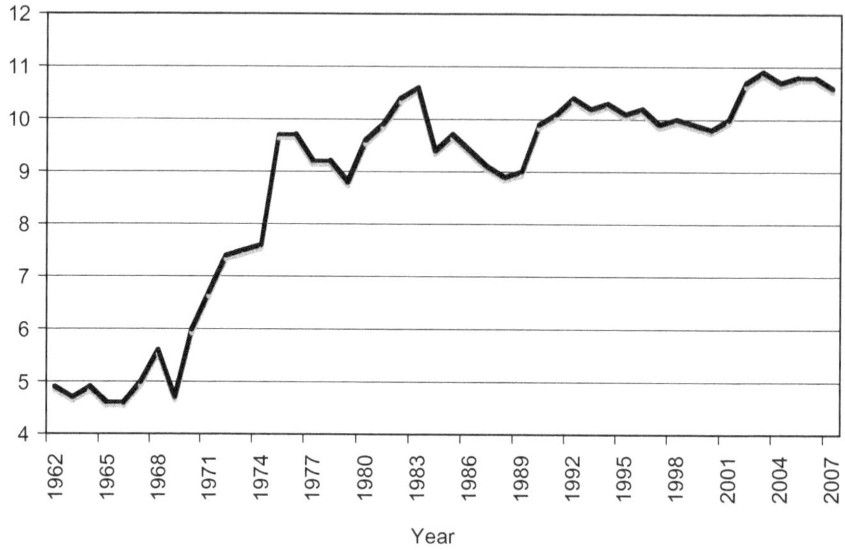

'big three') increased spending to 10.9 per cent of the GDP. By 2007 mandatory spending had fallen back to 10.6 per cent of the GDP.[26] All other entitlements grew more slowly than the 'big three'. If current policy does not change, the other entitlements will consume a much smaller share of the nation's resources in 2050 than they do today.[27]

(c) Retrenchment of Core Welfare State Programmes

The neo-liberal 'reformers' viewed the welfare state as a barrier to cheap labour and cheap money and sought to retrench the nation's three core social welfare programmes: Aid to Families for Dependent Children/ Temporary Aid to Needy Families (AFDC/TANF), Unemployment Insurance (UI), and Social Security (SS). They argued that cutting back these programmes would promote profits and growth by making it harder for people to avoid the lowest-paid jobs and easier for corporations to borrow investment dollars due to lower interest rates. The retrenchment fell especially hard on women, the majority of welfare state clients and workers. In particular, it undercut women's capacity for care work by reducing benefits and/or shifting the costs of social reproduction from

[26] *Ibid*, Table F-10, p 157.

[27] R Kogan and A Aron-Dine, 'There Is No General 'Entitlement Crisis' (Center on Budget and Policy Priorities, 29 January 2007), at: www.cbpp.org/1-29-07bud2.htm.

the state back to women. Given their overrepresentation among the poor (due to racism) women of colour were hit especially hard by the loss of welfare state support.

(d) AFDC/TANF

Neo-liberal reformers pointed to the post-war rise in the cost of AFDC/TANF to build public support for retrenching both this programme for single mothers and the wider welfare state. They regularly reported that total AFDC/TANF spending grew steadily from US$4.9 billion in 1970 to a high of US$26 billon in 1994, just prior to the 1996 welfare reform. However, they won their argument by misleading the public on two fronts. First they played the race and gender cards to demonize single mothers as lazy and unfit. Then they presented dollar figures that failed to account for the impact of inflation on programme costs. When controlled for inflation (2005 dollars) it is clear that spending peaked in 1976, much earlier and long before welfare reform. Thereafter actual spending fell steadily from 1976 (US$33.8 billion) to 1996 (US$29.2 billion). Since the 1996 federal welfare overhaul spending plummeted to a low of US$12.9 million in 2002 and US$13.billion in 2005.[28] The deep cuts left many eligible women and children out in the cold (see below).

The reformers also pointed to the growing number of women and children on AFDC to discredit the programme. But once again they did not publicize the most accurate numbers. The total number of individuals on welfare rose steadily from the end of World War II to 1994 when it peaked at nearly 14 million[29] (see Table 5 below). Following welfare reform the numbers dropped steadily reaching 3.7 million in 2008.[30]

However, the public was not informed that when measured as a proportion of the total population (see Table 6 below) the proportion actually fell much earlier—from a peak of 5.2 per cent in 1973 to a low of 4.4 per cent in 1988. The essentially flat percentage inched up to 5.4 per cent in 1993 and then dropped back to 4.5 per cent in 1996—also prior to welfare reform.

[28] US Department of Health and Human Services, *Indicators of Welfare Dependence, Annual Report to Congress 2007, Program Data*, Table TANF 4: 'Total AFDC/TANF Expenditures on Cash Benefits and Administration 1970–2005', at: aspe.hhs.gov/hsp/Indicators07/apa.pdf.

[29] *Ibid*, Table TANF 1: 'Trends in AFDC/TANF Caseloads: 1962–2007', at: aspe.hhs.gov/hsp/Indicators07/apa.pdf.

[30] US Department of Health and Human Services, Administration For Children and Families, Office of Family Assistance, TANF: 'Total Number of Recipients, Fiscal and Calendar Year 2008', at: www.acf.hhs.gov/programs/ofa/datareports/caseload/2008/2008_recipient_tan.htm.

Table 5—Total Number of AFDC/TANF Recipients, 1970–2005

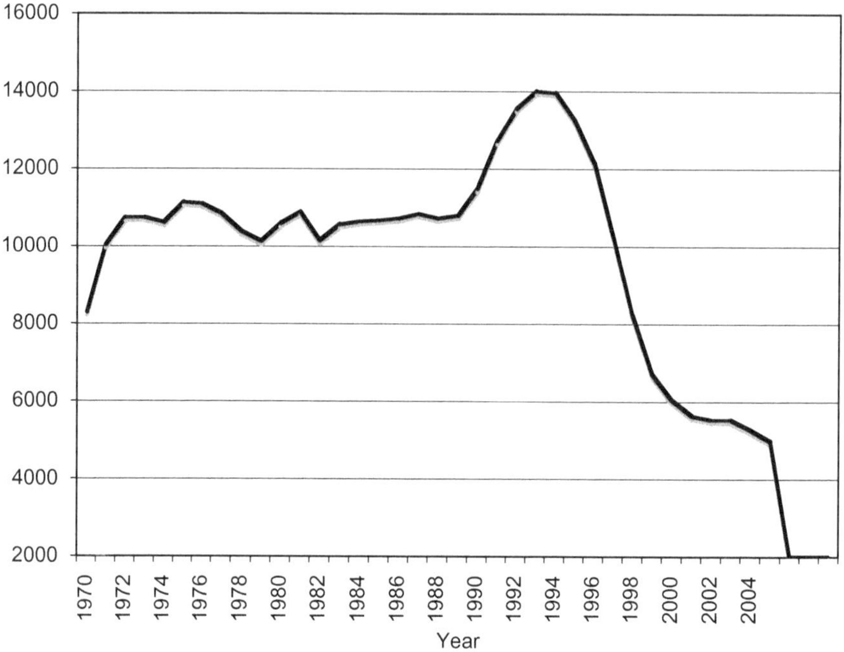

Table 6—Recipients as a % of the total population and the poverty population, 1970–2005

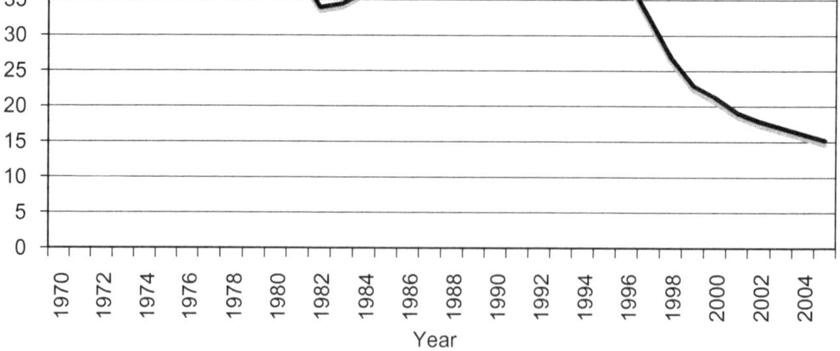

During the post-war years, the AFDC caseload also grew as a share of the poverty population (the pool from which eligible recipients are actually drawn) (see Table 6 above). But like its share of the total population the caseload peaked as a share of the poverty population in 1973 at 46.7 per cent—much earlier than touted by the welfare reformers. Then it fell steadily to 33.3 per cent in 1996—the year Congress passed the federal welfare overhaul but before it was implemented.[31] By 2005 only 1.7 per cent of the total population and 13.5 per cent of the poverty population received benefits.[32] Since welfare reform the per cent of the eligible families helped by the programme dropped by half from 80 per cent in 1980s and 85.7 per cent in 1993 to only 42 per cent in 2005![33] How are the others making ends meet?

(e) Unemployment Insurance (UI)

The UI programme followed the same up and down pattern. Pressed during the post-war years by the trade union and civil rights movements, Congress added more occupations to the UI programme so that today it extends to more than 90 per cent of US civilian employment.[34] Funded by a tax on employers, the average tax amounted to 0.96 per cent of payroll from 1947 to 2005[35] However, tax cuts for employers led tax collections to fall by 33 per cent during the 1990s. The rate reached a record low of just half of one per cent (0.51 per cent) in 2001 and averaged only 0.64 per cent from 2000–2005.[36] In addition, Congress deprived the States of the federal resources necessary to cover the basic costs of administering their UI programmes. Of the 21 high-income Organization for Economic Development and Cooperation (OECD) countries with populations of at least one million persons, only Greece and Japan spend less than the US on UI benefits as a percentage of payroll.[37]

Despite widespread occupational coverage, not all workers in covered occupations qualify for benefits. With periodic ups and down, the percentage of jobless workers receiving UI benefits (the recipiency rate) has declined

[31] US Department of Health and Human Services, *Indicators of Welfare Dependence* (above n 28).

[32] *Ibid.*

[33] *Ibid*, Table IND 4A, at: aspe.hhs.gov/hsp/indicators07/ch2.pdf.

[34] DP McMurrer and AB Chasanov, 'Trends in Unemployment Insurance Benefits' (1995) September, *Monthly Labor Review* 30–39.

[35] W Vroman, 'Strengthening Unemployment Insurance: A Critique of Individual Accounts and Wage-Loss Insurance' EPI Briefing Paper #202 (23 October 2007), at: www.epi.org/content.cfm/bp202.

[36] M Emsellem, National Employment Law Project Testimony. Hearing Before the US House of Representatives, Ways & Means Committee, Sub-committee on Income Security and Family Support (15 March 2007), at: www.nelp.org/docUploads/UIHearingTestimony2007%2Epdf.

[37] Vroman, 'Strengthening Unemployment Insurance' (above n 35).

steadily from nearly 50 per cent in the 1950s to just over 40 per cent in the 1960s and 1970s. The neo-liberal changes in the UI programme marked the end of a strong and stable relationship between the number of UI claimants and the number of job losers.[38] The recipiency rate fell to 28.5 per cent in the 1980s—the lowest recorded percentage since 1947. In the 1990s for the first time, the ratio of claimants to the total number of unemployed workers did not increase significantly even as the unemployment rate peaked.[39] The recipiency rate rose to 31 per cent in 2004 and 36 per cent in 2006—but remained below the 1960s and 1970s level.[40] In 2007 in nine states less than 25 per cent of unemployed workers collected jobless benefits. The UI programme has always served only a minority of unemployed workers, but not the worst off.[41] Although low-waged workers (where women and racialized people predominate) are almost two and a half times as likely to be out of work as higher-wage workers, they are half as likely to receive UI benefits.[42]

(f) Social Security (SS)

The push to shrink SS took longer given the programme's historic widespread public support. Spending on SS rose from 2.5 per cent of the GDP (1962) to a high of 4.9 per cent in 1983. As the Reagan Administration raised the retirement age from 65 to 67, reduced the age at which benefits for the children of a widow or widower ceased from 18 to 16 years, cut benefits for post-secondary school students, and otherwise tightened the rules,[43] SS spending dropped steadily, reaching 4.2 per cent of the GDP, the same as in the late 1970s. The effort to cut the programme by diverting a portion of the payroll tax into the stock market rose to the top of President Bush's agenda but failed to gain ground even before the financial meltdown in 2008.

(ii) Redistributing Income Upwards

The second the major goal of the neo-liberal strategy sought to redistribute income and profits upwards by simultaneously lowering market wages, shrinking the welfare state, and reversing the post-war trend toward greater equality.

[38] McMurrer and Chasanov, Trends in Unemployment Insurance Benefits (above n 34).
[39] McMurrer and Chasanov (above n 34).
[40] Emsellem, Testimony (n 36 above); Vroman (above n 35).
[41] Emsellem (n 36 above).
[42] Government Accounting Office. 'Unemployment Insurance: Role as a Safety Net for Low Wage Workers in Question'. GAO-01-181 (December 2000), at: www.gao.gov/new.items/d01181.pdf.
[43] US House. Committee on Ways and Means, Overview of Entitlement Programs, 2004 Green Book (Washington DC, Government Printing Office, Social Security, Legislative History, 2004) 1-35–1-39 and Tables: 1-17, 1-18, at: frwebgate.access.gpo.gov/cgibin/getdoc.cgi?dbname=108_green_book&docid=f:wm006_01.pdf.

(a) Lower Market Wages

A central feature of the relatively peaceful and productive post-war period was mass upward mobility: the income of individuals rose sharply through much of their careers and each generation lived better than the last. From 1947 to 1973 productivity and real median income grew hand-in-hand, increasing by 103.7 per cent and 103.9 per cent respectively.[44] The real minimum wage (in 2006 dollars) increased from US$2.82 an hour in 1948 to a high of US$7.17 in 1968[45] and real private sector wages grew from US$7.86 per hour (in 1982 dollars) in 1964 to a high of US$8.99 in 1976.[46] Median family income also improved during these years more than doubling from US$20,102 in 1947 to US$40,656 in 1977[47] as the rising tide of productivity lifted most, if not all, boats.

However, during the second crisis of the twentieth century this close relationship broke down. Since the mid-1970s, productivity gains have not translated into raised income for most US workers. Faced with rising global competition and falling profits firms searched for ways to lower labour costs. They moved manufacturing jobs and production from the high-paid states in the US North (the 'frost belt') to the low-unionized states in the US South (the 'sunbelt') and from US cities to foreign nations. Employers also slashed manufacturing pay-cheques, sacked thousands of industrial workers, and wrung major concessions from organized labour.

And wages fell. America's median hourly wage is barely higher than it was 35 years ago when adjusted for inflation. The real average hourly wage declined from a 1972 high of US$8.99 an hour to US$8.24 an hour in 2006 (1982 dollars).[48] From 2006 to 2007 real hourly (and weekly) earnings fell about one per cent.[49] The real minimum wage (in 2006 dollars) dropped from the 1968 high of US$7.71 an hour to US$5.15 an hour in 2005—the lowest in over 50 years.[50] From 1973 to 2004 productivity grew by only 75.7 per cent and family median income rose by only 21.8 per cent—less than one-third the rate of productivity and less than during the post-war

[44] L Mishel, J Bernstein and S Allegretto (Economic Policy Institute), *The State of Working America 2006–2007* (Ithaca NY, Cornell University Press, 2007) 45–6, at: www.stateofworkingamerica.org/swa06-01-family_income.pdf.

[45] Economic Policy Institute, *Issue Guide, Minimum Wage* (April 2007), Table 4: The Real Value of the Minimum Wage, 1947–2006, at: www.epi.org/issueguides/minwage/table4.pdf.

[46] US Department of Labor, Bureau of Labor Statistics, *Employment, Hours, and Earnings from the Current Employment Statistics Survey (National)* (nd)[?] 'Total Private Average Hourly Earnings, 1982 Dollars', at: data.bls.gov/cgi-bin/surveymost?ce.

[47] US Bureau of the Census, *Measuring 50 Years of Economic Change* (1998) 60–203. Table 2.1, at: www.census.gov/prod/3/98pubs/p60–203.pdf.

[48] US Department of Labor, Bureau of Labor Statistics, *Employment Hours and Earnings (nd).*

[49] J Bernstein, Economic Policy Institute, Issue Brief #240 'Real Wages Decline in 2007', 18 January 2008, at: www.epi.org/content.cfm/ib240.

[50] *Ibid.*

years.[51] The income of a man in his 30s is now 12 per cent below that of a man his age three decades ago.[52] The fall in the standard of living since the mid-1970s led family members, especially women, to greatly increase their time in the workforce just to help households make ends meet. While boosting family income and women's independence, women's employment lessened the time available for the work of social reproduction—given the prevailing gender division of labour and the lack of needed supports for working mothers.

(b) Lower Social Welfare Benefits

Following the neo-liberal paradigm, leaders in business and government took aim at cash benefits as well as market wages to increase profits but also to contain the role of the government. Cash benefits increased government spending, and as noted earlier, strengthened the bargaining power of workers on the job, women in the home, racialized persons in white-dominated society. Although the monthly AFDC/TANF benefit per family grew steadily from US$121 in 1962 to US$370 in 2005,[53] when inflation is taken into account the real value of the welfare cheque reached its post war high of US$805 (in 2005 dollars) much earlier—in the 1970s. With the advent of neo-liberalism the purchasing power fell steadily to US$370 in 2005.[54] Benefits failed to match the rising cost of living due to both the anti-government agenda and State budget cuts. Today the combination of welfare and food stamps does not lift a family of three above the poverty line in any State.

The value of weekly UI benefit also dropped from its post war levels under neo-liberalism. Reduced revenues lowered the ratio of the average UI weekly benefit to the average weekly wage in covered employment. Known as the replacement rate, the ratio rose during the post-war years from 33.6 per cent in 1943 to 37.7 per cent in 1976 and in 1982. During the 1990s the ratio fell to 32.9 per cent as Washington taxed workers' UI benefits and cut payments to the states forcing them to restrict eligibility. The share of lost income replaced by UI benefits declined by five percentage points across the nation so that in 1999 UI benefits replaced only 33 per cent of an average worker's lost earnings.[55] By 2000, the replacement rate equaled 32.9 per cent. It inched up to 34.1 per cent in 2007[56]—still below the 1968 level and far

[51] M Bernstein and S Allegretto, *The State of Working America* (above n 44).

[52] RD Reich, 'Totally Spent', *The New York Times*, 13 February 2008, p A25.

[53] US Department of Health and Human Services, *Indicators of Welfare Dependence* (2007), Table TANF 6, A-14.

[54] *Ibid.*

[55] H Boushey and J Wenger, 'Coming Up Short: Current Unemployment Insurance Benefits Fail To Meet Basic Family Needs' (October 2001) *Economic Policy Institute Brief #169*.

[56] US Department of Labor, Employment and Training Administration, *ET Financial Data Handbook* (2006) 394, at: ows.doleta.gov/unemploy/hb394.asp.

below what a family of four needs just to get by.[57] Similarly, the number of workers who exhausted their benefits prior to finding a job fell during the post-war years from about from 27.5 per cent in 1948 to about 21.5 per cent in 1965.[58] In contrast, by 2003 the number had soared to a new high of 43.7 per cent, despite relatively low joblessness. This is the highest rate since 1941. It is also higher than the 1985 rate of 31.2 per cent—a year when unemployment exceeded 10 per cent. The rate dropped steadily from 2003 to a low 35 per cent in 2007 but has since crept up to nearly 42 per cent.[59]

Likewise for Social Security benefits. The wage replacement rate for the average worker rose steadily from 15.8 per cent in 1948 to a high of 51.7 per cent in 1981. Once the Reagan Administration programme changes set in the wage replacement of the average earner's SS benefit fell steadily to 41.7 per cent in 2007.[60] It is expected to drop to 36 per cent over the next two decades as Social Security's 'normal retirement age' rises to 67 years.[61] Since the introduction of the automatic cost of living adjustment (COLA) from 1975 to 1981 the annual benefit increase fluctuated between five per cent and 14 per cent. In contrast, except for 1990, the much lower increase varied from only 1.3 per cent to 4.7 per cent between 1982 and 2007.[62]

In sum, lowering spending and benefits helped to downsize the scale, scope and cost of the welfare state. The retrenchment both transferred the cost of care work from the state back to women and helped to drive labour costs down by flooding the labour market with thousands of desperate workers in need of jobs. In 2004, *The New York Times* reported that the influx of women into low-wage jobs since the welfare overhaul had depressed the median wage of all workers.[63] The increased competition for jobs created by declining welfare, UI and SS benefits made it easier for employers to pay less and harder for unions to negotiate good contracts. Given their overrepresentation among programme recipients, the cuts hit

[57] Boushey and Wenger, *Coming Up Short* (above n 55).

[58] US Department of Labor, Employment, and Training Administration, ET Financial Data Book (2007); Economic Policy Institute, 'Annual Unemployment Insurance Exhaustion Rate at Highest Level in 60 Years' (2004) Economic Snapshots, at: www.epi.org/content.cfm?id=1900.

[59] US Department of Labor, Employment, and Training Administration, State UI Employment Data, US Totals as of 4 April 2008, at: ows.doleta.gov/unemploy/5159report.asp.

[60] Social Security Administration, Office of Chief Actuary, VI.F10—'Estimated Annual Scheduled Benefit Amounts[1] for Retired Workers with Scaled Medium Pre-Retirement Earnings Pattern Based on Intermediate Assumptions Calendar Years 1940–2080', at: www.ssa.gov/OACT/TR/TR05/lr6F10-2.html.

[61] R Greenstein, 'So Called "Price Indexing" Proposal Would Result in Deep Reductions Over Time in Social Security Benefits' (Center on Budget and Policy Priorities, 25 January 2005), at: www.cbpp.org/12-17-04socsec.htm.

[62] Social Security Administration, Office of the Chief Actuary, 'Cost of Living Adjustments', at: ssa.gov/OACT/COLA/colaseries.html.

[63] L Utichelle, 'Gaining Ground on the Wage Front', *The New York Times*, 31 December 2004, col c3.

women and racialized individuals especially hard and belied the promise of equal opportunity for all. Championing the neo-liberal victory, Alan Greenspan, the former chair of the US Federal Reserve Board, declared that the economy's 'extraordinary' and 'exceptional' performance during the late 1990s was, in part, due to 'a heightened sense of job insecurity' that helps to subdue wage gains.[64]

(c) Less Economic Equality

Rather than causing resources to trickle down to the average household as promised, the neo-liberal policies reversed the downward distribution of income launched by the New Deal. During the post-war years, everyone prospered, but those at the bottom gained the most. From 1947 to 1979 the real family income of the bottom fifth income group rose by 116 per cent, compared to 111 per cent for the middle fifth and 99 per cent for the top fifth. From 1979 to 2005 neo-liberalism reversed this equalizing trend. During this time real family income for the bottom fifth dropped by one per cent, while the middle fifth gained 25 per cent, and the top fifth gained a stunning 53 per cent.[65] The personal saving rate evidenced the same pattern. It rose from five per cent in 1949 to 11.2 per cent in the 1976 after which it fell steadily to 1.1 per cent in 2006.[66]

The data on real after tax income—one of the best measures of income distribution collected since 1979—documents the widening gap. According to the Congressional Budget Office the after-tax income of the top 20 per cent of households rose 80 per cent (or US$76,500) from 1979 to 2005 compared to 21 per cent (or US$8700) for the middle fifth and just six per cent (or US$900) for the bottom fifth. The after-tax income for the top one per cent rose by 228 per cent (or US$745,100)![67] Given that the neo-liberal tax cuts favoured the highest earners, by 2007 the concentration of after-tax income at the top was greater than at any time since 1929.[68] The experts predict that if tax policy does not change, the top 20 per cent of households will receive 75 per cent of the future tax cuts compared to just eight per cent for the middle group and a dramatic zero per cent for the bottom fifth.[69] Grover Norquist, President of Americans for Tax Reform championed this neo-liberal victory. He told *US News and World Report* that tax cuts for the rich had a strategic value because they 'drain the government of its lifeblood'

[64] FF Piven, 'The Welfare State as Work Enforcer (Sept/Oct 1999) *Dollars and Sense* 34.
[65] 'By the Numbers', at: Inequality.org.www.demos.org/inequality/numbers.cfm.
[66] *Ibid.*
[67] A Sherman, 'Income Inequality Hits Record Levels, New CBO Data Show' (Center on Budget and Policy Priorities, 14 December 2007), at: www.cbpp.org/12-14-07inc.htm.
[68] *Ibid.*
[69] C Huang and G Brunet, 'The Skewed Benefits of the Tax Cuts' (Center on Budget and Policy Priorities, 24 November 2008), at: www.cbpp.org/2-4-08tax.htm.

and 'make the average person's blood boil with rage, leading them to call for even more tax cuts'.[70]

(iii) Restoring Family Values and a Colour-Blind Social Order

The third neo-liberal/Right agenda item focused on restoring family values and a colour-blind social order. The Right argued that the welfare state created a crisis in the family by undermining personal responsibility, appropriating parental authority, and perhaps most important, increasing women's autonomy at home and on the job. To stem these tides the Right endorsed a family values agenda in all three core welfare state programmes. The results exploited women's financial needs by forcing them to comply with prescribed gender roles in exchange for government support and undercut state support and responsibility for care in the home.

(a) AFDC/TANF

Welfare reform supports 'family values' by punishing single motherhood and promoting heterosexual marriage 'as the foundation of society'.[71] Reflecting the historic distrust of social reproduction carried out by single mothers especially by single mothers of colour,[72] the 1996 federal welfare law included distinct efforts to curb their child bearing. The child exclusion rule denied aid to children born to women on welfare, the 'illegitimacy bonus' divided US$100 million a year among the five states reporting the largest decrease in non-marital birth without an increase in abortions, and the 'abstinence-only' policy earmarked US$250 million for school programmes that taught children to postpone sex until marriage but prohibited talk of contraception or safe sex. The Bush Administration has also actively pursued a large-scale marriage-promotion programme. Pro-family-values rules additionally limit access to public housing and other social programmes. Some see welfare's harsh work mandates as a punishment for single motherhood.

(b) Unemployment Insurance

The differential treatment of women and men by the UI programme also upholds family values. Throughout the post-war years the UI programme reflected family values by employing eligibility criteria that reflected

[70] P Krugman, 'The Tax Cut Con', *The New York Times Magazine*, 4 September 2003, 54, at: www.ufenet.org/econ/taxes/KrugmanTaxCutCon.html.
[71] Personal Responsibility and Work Opportunity Reconciliation Act of 1996/Public Law 104–193, 104th Congress, 22 August 1996, 110 Stat 2105.
[72] D Robert, *Killing The Black Body: Race, Reproduction and the Meaning of Liberty* (New York, Pantheon Books, 1997).

white male work patterns. Endorsing the outdated male-breadwinner framework it ignored how women's care-giving responsibilities limited women's work options.[73] The rules penalized employed women and low-wage workers of colour, in particular in several ways. They required recipients to show a 'substantial' labour force attachment, meaning full time work, in order to qualify for benefits and measured 'attachment' in terms of wages earned rather than hours worked. The programme also shut out new entrants to the work force (eg workers with no reported work experience in the last 18 months) and workers who 'voluntarily' left work due to pregnancy, to care for a family member or to relocate with a spouse—two groups in which women predominate due to the gender division of labour.

Pressed by the women's movement, in the mid-1970s some States began to weaken or eliminate some of these sexist rules, but with only partial success. For example by the late 1990s although 25 per cent of women who left their jobs did so because of care-giving responsibilities, only 20 States included domestic circumstances in their 'good-cause quit' regulations. Fewer than 15 States provided benefits to women if they 'voluntarily' quit their job due to sexual harassment at work or male violence at home. Thus women who quit their jobs were 32 per cent less likely than were men who quit to qualify for benefits.[74] In 1976 the Supreme Court finally allowed UI benefits to pregnant women. In 2008, 67.7 million women or 56.6 per cent of all women aged 16 and over worked outside the home.[75] Yet in 2007 the UI programme served 57.2 per cent of jobless men but only 42.7 per cent of jobless women, a pattern that existed in 41 of the 50 States.[76]

(c) Social Security (SS)

The SS programme also encoded an outdated male-breadwinner framework that ignored how the economic dependence of women on men and the gender division of labour kept women economically insecure. Its programmes favour married over husbandless women and full-time homemakers over working wives, and end all benefits once a women's care-giving responsibilities cease (eg, once her husband and/or children are no longer in the

[73] R Smith, R McHugh, A Stettner and N Segal, *Between a Rock and a Hard Place: Confronting the Failure of State UI Systems to Serve Women and Working Families* (New York, National Employment and Law Project, 2003).

[74] A Um'rani and V Lovell, *Research In Brief*, (Place, Institute for Women's Policy Research, November 1999) #A122; Smith, McHugh, Stettner and Segal, *Between a Rock and a Hard Place* (above n 73).

[75] US Department of Labor, Bureau of Labor Statistics, *Women in the Labor Force: A Data Book* (2009) T.1, p 5, at: www.bls.gov/cps/wlf-table1-2008.pdf.

[76] US Department of Labor, Employment & Training Administration, Unemployment Insurance 'Percent Distribution of Characteristics of the Insured Unemployed. Report for Calendar Year 2007', at: workforcesecurity.doleta.gov/unemploy/chariu/dstrpt.asp.

home). The benefit formula continues to privilege high-earning workers and those with long work histories—a practice that mirrors male work patterns and disadvantages women of all races who earn low wages and take time out of the workforce for family responsibilities. Women often do better by taking one-half of their husband's pension rather than the smaller amount available to them on their own work record, marking them as economic dependents of men. The same pattern disadvantages low-earning men of colour.

These rules continue to enforce the prevailing gender division of labour despite the massive entry of women into the workforce. While the number of women entitled to benefits as workers rose from 43 per cent in 1960 to 70 per cent in 2006,[77] the Reagan Administration ignored the gender-equity proposals proposed by mainstream feminist groups in favour of neo-liberal 'reforms' that disadvantaged women. The Reagan 'reforms' included the elimination of the minimum benefit, the later retirement age, the reduced benefit for early retirees, and the lowering of the age at which benefits ended for children of a deceased parent. The proposed privatization of SS—that is, the investment of some social security dollars in the stock market by individuals or the government—would also be problematic for women retirees, leading to lower grants, and ending the spousal benefit, the life and disability insurance for parents caring for children under age 16, and the current guarantee of benefits in later life. The reliance on the stock market would expose women to many unaffordable financial risks[78]—as the 2008 financial meltdown made all too clear.

(iv) Social Movements: Weakened

The fourth neo-liberal goal targeted the influence of the social movements that had contributed to the strength of the welfare state in the post-war years. Beginning in the mid-1970s, business and government placed the social movements—well positioned to resist the new austerity programme—on the defensive. On top of the loss of income and jobs incurred by changes in the domestic and global economy, the neo-liberal assault on workers, women, and racialized communities took its toll. One administration after another along with the courts have taken back many of the hard won gains made by the trade union, civil rights, gay rights, and women's liberation movements, as well as weakened workplace, consumer and environmental protections.

[77] Social Security Administration, *Annual Statistical Supplement* (2007), Table 5.A14: 'Number and Percentage Distribution of Women Aged 62 or Older, By Basis Of Entitlement, Type of Benefit & Dual Entitlement Status, December 1960–2006, Selected Years', at: www.ssa.gov/policy/docs/statcomps/supplement/2007/5a.html#table5.A14.

[78] C Hill, 'Privatizing Social Security is Bad, Particularly for Women (Nov/Dec 2000) *Dollars and Sense* 17–19, 35.

Despite strenuous efforts it has been very difficult for the movements to defend past gains or to secure new ones.

IV. THE IMPACT OF NEO-LIBERALISM: SOCIAL REPRODUCTION UNDERMINED

For almost 30 years US economic policy has been guided by the idea that the market is unfailingly wise, that the government should stay out of its way, and that the benefits of laissez-faire policies would trickle down to all. In the short run corporate America clearly enjoyed the economic fruits of neo-liberalism. The share of national income going to profits soared from nine per cent in 1970 to an all-time high of 13.6 per cent in 2006 while the share going to wages fell from 59.3 per cent to 51.6 per cent—the lowest level since 1929! This contrasts sharply with the post-war period when the share of national income going to profits dropped from 13.6 per cent to nine per cent while the share going to wages grew from 55.7 per cent (1950) to 59.3 per cent (1970).[79] Neo-liberalism reversed the trend toward greater equality, exposed the nation to the perils of slavish reliance on market forces, and increased the cost and burdens of women's care work in the home. Sluggish economic growth, a new pattern of economic recoveries without job growth, a less equal distribution of income, and compromised social reproduction—plus the economic crisis of 2008—suggest that in the long run the neo-liberal strategy is failing and appears to have created the conditions of its own its demise.

A. Less Economic Growth

The promised economic growth has failed to materialize. In fact economic growth during the earlier post-war years outdid that of the neo-liberal period. Between 1948 and 1973—the era of so-called 'big government'—the real per capita GDP (the average share of output per person) grew about 2.47 per cent a year. However, from 1973 to 2006—the era of neo-liberal tax and spending cuts—the per capita GDP increased by only 1.85 per cent a year.[80] Peter Orszag, Director of the Office of Management and Budget under President Barack Obama pointed to a lasting impact: 'deficit-financed tax cuts [the central neo-liberal retrenchment strategy] are unlikely to have

[79] A Aron-Dine and I Shapiro, *Share Of National Income Going To Wages and Salaries at Record Low In 2006: Share of Income Going to Corporate Profits at Record High* (Center on Budget and Policy Priorities, rev 29 March 2007), at: www.cbpp.org/8-31-06inc.htm.

[80] Measuringworth.com (Annualized Growth Rate of Various Historical Economic Series, at: www.measuringworth.com/growth/growth_resultf.php?begin%5B%5D=1973&end%5B%5D=2007&beginP%5B%5D=&endP%5B%5D=&US%5B%5D=GDPCP.

significant positive effects on economic growth in the long term, and may well reduce it'.[81] Even before the economic meltdown of 2008 became a reality, the Congressional Budget Office projected that real gross domestic product would be lower in 2007 and every year for the next 10 years than it had earlier projected.

B. Longer (and Jobless) Economic Recoveries

During the post-war period the economy, especially employment, typically bounced back to pre-recession levels reasonably quickly. It took payrolls 17 months to regain their pre-recession level in 1945 and 24 months in 1963. Since 1981 the number of months for payrolls to reach pre-recession peaks has jumped from 28 (1981) to 46 (2001).[82] Similarly, in the post-war years, job growth five years after the high-point of a business cycle increased steadily from 9.9 per cent (April 1960 to April 1965) to 13.5 per cent (November 1973 to November 1978). In contrast the neo-liberal period is known for its jobless recoveries. Job growth five years after a business cycle peak declined steadily from 8.6 per cent (July 1981 to July 1986), to 6.8 per cent (July 1990 to July 1995) to a low of 1.9 per cent (March 2001 to March 2006).[83] Reporting in January 2008, the Center on Budget and Policies Priorities stated that current economic recovery is either the weakest or among the weakest since World War II.[84]

Long before the economic crisis of 2008, the middle class had no margin for error. The slowed economy and jobless recovery had people worrying that worse was yet to come. In June 2007 34 per cent of Americans said that they worry 'all of the time' (21 per cent) or 'most of the time' (13 per cent) that their total household income will be not be enough to meet their family's expenses and bills, more so among blacks and Hispanics, up from 21 per cent in 1998 and 24 per cent in 2004.[85] In a January 2008 Gallup Poll, 82 per cent of Americans said that they thought that economic conditions were

[81] P Orszag, 'The Budget Deficit: Does It Matter?' Speech Before the City Club of Cleveland (16 July 2004), at: www.brookings.edu/views/speeches/20040716orszag.pdf; P Orszag, 'The Cost of Tax Cuts' (Brookings Institute, 19 September 2004), at: www.brookings.edu/articles/2004/0919useconomics_gale.aspx.

[82] Mishel, Bernstein and Allegretto (above n 44).

[83] Economic Policy Institute, Jobs Picture, 'Steadily Improving Job Market, But Little Sign Of Inflationary Pressure' (April 2006), at: www.epi.org/content.cfm/webfeatures_econindicators_jobspict_20060407.

[84] A Aron-Dine, C Stone and R Kogan, *How Robust Is The Current Economic Expansion?* (Center on Budget and Policy Priorities, rev 29 August 2008), at: www.cbpp.org/8-9-05bud.htm.

[85] Gallup.com. Polls Business and Economy, *Nearly Half Blacks-Hispanics Worry About Paying Bills*, at: www.gallup.com/poll/103489/Nearly-Half-Blacks-Hispanics-Worry-About-Paying-Bills.aspx.

getting worse—a Gallup poll high up to that point.[86] They were not wrong. Nearly half of America's top 1,000 companies were actively experimenting with sending service as well as manufacturing jobs off-shore. Between 2001 and 2004 business has exported from 400,000 to one million white-collar jobs abroad, mostly to India and other Asian nations. Experts expect 3.3 million more to follow over the next decade, saving US corporations 30 to 80 per cent on labour costs and eliminating roughly 25,000 American jobs per month. In 2004 a University of California study concluded that international wage disparities have rendered 14 million domestic service jobs vulnerable to possible displacement.[87] In autumn 2008, the US economy collapsed. By early December private and government payrolls combined had shrunk for 11 months in row for a total loss of 1.9 million jobs—two-thirds of them between September and November. The percentage of the population with a job fell to 61 per cent, the lowest since 1993. Economists predicted that should this 'recession' continue past April 2009, it would produce a recession longer than any in the post-war record.[88]

C. Less Time for Care Work

Social reproduction depends heavily on women's unpaid care work in the home. However, the time available for care work has declined since the 1970s when the ideas of the women's movement and the rapid expansion of low-paid service jobs converged with declining wages and reduced public benefits to draw more and more women into the paid work force. In 2005, 75 per cent of prime-age women (aged 25 to 45) and 71 per cent of mothers worked for wages outside the home. Their earnings represented more than one-third of the family's income.[89] The typical American now works more each year than he or she did 30 years ago, putting in 350 more hours a year than the average European.[90] From 1979 to 2004 middle-income wives aged 25–54 with children increased their annual hours of work by 56 per cent (from 849 to 1327 hours) the equivalent of more than 13 full-time weeks. Their husbands increased their annual work hours from 2134 hours in 1979 to 2195 hours in 2004, or only 2.9 per cent during the same

[86] Gallup.com. Polls Business and Economy, *About 40% of American Worrying About Money*, at: www.gallup.com/tag/Business%2band%2bEconomy.aspx.
[87] WM O'Leary, 'A Victim of Free Trade, Economic Populism May Yet Enjoy Revival', *Maine Sunday Telegram*, 18 January 2004, at: www.commondreams.org/views04/0418-04.htm.
[88] C Stone, 'On The November Employment Report' (Center on Budget and Policy Priorities, 5 December 2008), at: www.cbpp.org/12-5-08ui-stmt.htm.
[89] H Boushey, Testimony, Equal Employment Opportunity Commission, *Perspectives on Work/Family Balance and the Federal Equal Employment Opportunity Laws*, Washington DC (17 April 2007), at: www.cepr.net/content/view/1134/.
[90] Reisch 'Total Spent' (2008).

period.[91] There are also more single-parent families than a generation ago: one-in-six in 2005, up from one-in-sixteen in 1964.[92]

The gender division of labour continues to assign women near-exclusive responsibility for care work—even when they work outside the home. The employment of women has increased their economic independence but reduced the time available to women for care work in the home.[93] The toll taken on social reproduction is exacerbated by the lack of child care programmes, the absence of paid family leave, flexi time, and minimal help from men—all of which would allow women to better balance work and family responsibilities. During the 1980s, men temporarily increased their hours of housework and the gender gap in housework grew smaller. However, by the end of the 1990s, men's hours of housework had fallen below their 1970 level.[94]

D. More Hardship

The economy's failure to assure the level of income needed for families to buy basic necessities often results in serious hardships that both reflect reduced support for social reproduction and undermine the household's future capacity to successfully carry out its tasks. Rising poverty, falling wages and reduced cash benefits translate into serious deprivation even among the non-poor. The Economic Policy Institute reported that in 1996 almost 30 per cent of US poor but also working-class families with children did not earn enough to buy needed food, housing, health services and child care—even in prosperous times.[95] In 2003, 20 per cent of all families with children surveyed by the Census Bureau, 47 per cent of poor families, and 16 per cent of non-poor families experienced at least one such hardship: either overcrowded housing, hunger or the risk of hunger (ie food insecurity) or lack of needed medical care—with greater hardship rates for families of colour. In 2007, some one million households containing 36.2 million people did not earn enough to buy needed groceries. In one-third of these someone skipped meals or otherwise ate less due to lack of money.[96] Forty-five million Americans, or more than 15 per cent of the population, also lacked health insurance in 2007 far above the 39.8 million or 14.1 per cent

[91] Mishel, Bernstein and Allegretto (above n 44).

[92] Boushey (above n 89).

[93] SM Bianchi, A Melissa, L Milkie, C Sayer, C and JP Robinson, 'Is Anyone Doing the Housework? Trends in the Gender Division of Household Labor' (2000) 79 *Social Forces* 191.

[94] Boushey (above n 89).

[95] H Boushey, G Gunderson, C Brocht and J Bernstein, *Hardships in America: The Real Story of Working Families* (Washington DC, Economic Policy Institute, 2001).

[96] S Dean, 'On The New USDA Report On Hunger' (Center on Budget and Policy Priorities, 17 November 2008), at: www.cbpp.org/11-17-08fa-stmt.htm.

in 2001.[97] In 2007 more than 40 million adults had skipped at least one type of needed health care (medical, dental, mental health, prescription drugs, etc) in the previous year due to lack of money.[98]

In 2005, 16 million poor households paid more of their income in rent than the federally-defined affordability standard or lived in overcrowded or substandard housing. Six million of these paid more than half of their income for rent and utilities or lived in severely substandard housing. Almost two million poor households could not pay their full rent (or mortgage) at least once in the previous year. Nearly three million poor households fell behind on their gas, oil or electric bill. In 2007 some 1.5 million homeowners received foreclosure notices, more than twice as many as in 2006. About half—disproportionately low-income and homeowners of colour—had the now infamous 'sub-prime' mortgage.[99] Exposure to substandard housing also increased health problems. The 2.5 million households occupying substandard housing in 2002 were more likely than those living in better-housing to suffer serious problems such as asthma, stunted growth, lead poisoning and other debilitating conditions that often lead to learning disorders, reading disabilities, school failure, aggression, anti-social behaviour[100] and other problems that are known to complicate the work of social reproduction.

Meanwhile neo-liberal budget cuts compromised the ability of families as well as schools, health care programmes, and other societal institutions to cushion the impact of the conflict between the requirements of profitable economic production (low wages, high unemployment) and successful social reproduction (health, food and housing security). Estimates made prior to the current economic free-fall predicted that the 'big three' programmes (Medicare, Medicaid and Social Security) would grow faster than the economy between 2007 and 2050 but that all other domestic programmes would shrink.[101]

[97] A Sherman, R Greenstein and S Parrott Sharon, 'Poverty and Share Of Americans Without Health Insurance Were Higher In 2007—and Median Income For Working-Age Households Was Lower—Than At Bottom Of Last Recession' (Center on Budget and Policy Priorities, 26 August 2008), at: www.cbpp.org/8-26-08pov.htm.

[98] Center on Budget and Policy Priorities, *Poverty and Hardship Affect Tens of Millions of Americans* (20 December 2007), at: www.cbpp.org/12-20-07pov.htm#_edn5.

[99] *Ibid*; J Leland, 'Baltimore Finds Subprime Crisis Snags Women', *The New York Times*, 15 January 2008, at: www.nytimes.com/2008/01/15/us/15mortgage.html?pagewanted=all.

[100] PL Chase-Lansdale, RK Coley, BJ Lohmanm and LD Pittman, *Welfare Reform: What About the Children?* Welfare Children and Families Study, Policy Brief 02-01, Johns Hopkins University (2002); A Sherman, *Poverty Matters: The Cost of Child Poverty in America* (Washington DC, Children's Defense Fund, 1997).

[101] R Kogan, M Fiedler, A Aron-Dine and J Horney, '*The Long-Term Fiscal Outlook is Bleak Restoring Fiscal Sustainability Will Require Major Changes to Programs, Revenues, and the Nation's Health Care System*' (Center on Budget and Policy Priorities, 29 January 2007), at: www.cbpp.org/1-29-07bud.pdf.

E. Less Well-being and More Stress

Such material hardship often generates stress that can further undermine family wellbeing. A 1997 Urban Institute survey found high stress among many families that experienced overcrowding, poor health, insufficient food, mortgage payment problems, and lack of access to health services. Twenty-two per cent of all the surveyed children under age 18 lived in a stressful family environment; 50 per cent in lower-income households. Family stress was, in turn, linked to less engagement in school, more behavioural and emotional problems, and parental distress that clearly interferes with effective social reproduction.[102]

Lynch et al also reported that sustained economic hardship led to poorer physical, psychological and cognitive functioning.[103] A 2004 study of Mexican American and European American families found that unstable work led to feelings of economic pressure that, in turn, were associated with higher rates of depression for mothers and fathers. Despite income differences between the two national groups, in both, economic deprivation correlated with depression and depressive symptoms and yielded more marital problems and more hostile parenting.[104] Indeed, parents pre-occupied with stressful circumstances often cannot provide an optimal home environment for their children. When overwhelmed some may even become harsh or coercive. During the neo-liberal era the rate per 1000 children under age 18 in foster care jumped from 4.2 in 1982 to 6.2 in 1990, to a high of 8.1 in 1999 before falling to 7.0 in 2005[105] due to pressure to lower the child welfare caseload as well as the TANF caseload.

The mounting stress associated with low wages, reduced benefits and material hardship provide graphic measures of the ways in which the neo-liberal agenda has undermined the capacity of families to meet basic needs, provide essential care, and otherwise carry out the tasks of social reproduction. These adverse outcomes suggest how much neo-liberalism

[102] KA Moore, and S Vandivere, *Stressful Family Lives, Child and Family Well-Being*, New Federalism, Brief B17 (Washington DC, Urban Institute, 2000).

[103] JW Lynch, GA Kaplan and SJ Sheman, 'Cumulative Impact of Sustained Economic Hardship on Physical, Cognitive, Psychological, and Social Functioning' (2007) 337 *New England Journal of Medicine* 1889.

[104] RD Parke, S Coltrane, S Duffy, R Buriel, J Powers, S French and KF Widaman, 'Economic Stress, Parenting and Child Adjustment in Mexican-American and European American Families' (2004) 75 *Child Development* 296, at: www.srcd.org/journals/cdev/11/Parke%20public%20summary.pdf.

[105] US Department of Health & Human Services, Administration for Children and Families, Children's Bureau, *Trends in Foster Care and Adoption* (FY2000–FY2005), at: www.acf.hhs.gov/programs/cb/stats_research/afcars/trends.htm; Child Trends Data Bank, 'The Number and Rate of Foster Children Ages 17 and Under, 1990–2005', at: www.childtrendsdatabank.org/figures/12-Figure-1.gif. Child Trends, Research Brief: 'Children Of All Ages Entering Foster Care, Leaving Foster Care and In Foster Care at End of Year, 1980–2000', at: www.childtrends.org/files/FosterCareRB.pdf.

has also limited the capacity of the welfare state to mediate the structural contradiction between profitable economic production and successful social reproduction—its historic function. The question is: How long can corporate capitalism manage without the programmes that keep the current and future workforce healthy, educated and productive, and that mediate the disruptive impact of too much class, race and gender inequality? Can capitalism thrive if its success means undermining effective social reproduction on which both family wellbeing and profitable production depends? Or will the falling standard of living generate pressure for change?

V. CONCLUSION

Corporate America—whose profits had fallen during the post-war period—clearly benefited from the ensuing neo-liberal policies that produced economic expansion and massive profits. However, as it runs its course, neo-liberalism appears to be undoing the very conditions required for the long-term survival of capitalism (as well as patriarchy and white hegemony). More specifically, the ability of neo-liberalism to promote expansion and profits may have reached its end in the mid-2000s.[106] The record high inequality and the falling standard of living have given pause to some who influence national policy. Writing in *The New York Times*, Peter Goodman noted in 2007 that 'unease with market forces can be heard ... [t]he invisible hand is being asked to account for what it has wrought'.[107] Cited in the April 2000 issue of *Business Week*, William R Cline, a trade expert at the Institute of International Finance Inc. observed: 'What worries many people about globalization [strongly linked to neo-liberalism] is that the US does little to help those who lose out. You want to make sure that the benefits of trade are fairly shared'.[108]

Mainstream economists including Robert E Rubin (Clinton's Treasury Secretary, and Economic Advisor to President Obama) and scholars at The Brookings Institute worry about the impact of mounting inequality on economic growth and political stability. Brookings's Hamilton Project led by Robert Rubin recommends greater government investment in both human capital and greater fairness.[109] Its 2006 report concluded that

[106] D Kotz, 'The Financial and Economic Crisis of 2008: A Systemic Crisis of Neoliberal Capitalism', paper prepared for a panel on 'The Global Financial Crisis: Heterodox Perspective', at the Annual convention of the Allied Social Science Association, 4 January 2009 (Place).

[107] PS Goodman, 'The Free Market: A False Idol After All', *The New York Times*, 30 December 2007, at: www.nytimes.com/2007/12/30/weekinreview/30goodman.html?_r=1&pagewanted=all&oref=slogin.

[108] A Bernstein, 'Backlash: Behind the Anxiety over Globalization', *Business Week Online*, 24 April 2000, at: www.businessweek.com/2000/00_17/b3678001.htm.

[109] RC Altman, JE Brodoff, PR Orszag and RE Rubin, *The Hamilton Project. An Economic Strategy for Advance Opportunity, Propserity and Growth* (The Brookings Institution, April 2006), at: www.brookings.edu/es/hamilton/THP_Strategy.pdf.

simply 'getting government out of the way' is fundamentally misguided, since sound government policy is essential to 'maximizing long-term [economic] growth'. To advance 'America's promise of opportunity, prosperity and growth' the Report calls for government supported access to financial assistance, educational training opportunities, and basic health care to ensure the productivity of workers but also to 'lessen political demands against protectionism and other growth-diminishing policies'.[110] Market forces 'must be supported and supplemented by an effective public role, one in which government ensure[s] that the rules of the game are fair, transparent, and binding for all parties'.

Others worry that mounting inequality will lead to a backlash by those with less. As early as 1998 economic report for Morgan Stanley, Stephen Roach stated:

> With worker rewards (compensation) lagging worker contributions (productivity) since the early 1980s, I have argued that is was only a matter of time before a politically-inspired backlash would occur that would shift the pendulum of economic power from capital (shareholders) back to workers. While it hasn't happened yet, there is no reason to believe that such a reflex action won't occur at some point in the not-so-distant future.[111]

More recently former Federal Reserve Chairman Alan Greenspan stated that

> an increased concentration of income ... is not the type of thing which a democratic society, a capitalist democratic society can really accept without addressing ... because excluding significant parts of the population from the fruits of economic growth risks a backlash that can threaten prosperity.[112]

Writing during the 2008 Presidential primaries, David Brooks, the conservative *New York Times* columnist, declared that 'Supply Side Economics had a good run, but continual tax cuts can no longer be the centerpiece of Republican economic policy [because] workers are walking away from the GOP'. The only way to 'win back them back is by listening to their economic concerns'. He added that today's 'Republicans [must] envision a different role for government than the 1980's Republicans ... They [workers] want a government that is on their side'.[113] Brooks goes on to call for child tax credits to reduce stress on young families, a tuition tax credit to help with education, universal health care, and wage subsidies for laid-off workers forced to take low-paying jobs.[114]

[110] *Ibid.*

[111] Editors, 'The Stagnation of Employment' (April 2004) *Monthly Review* 3–17.

[112] Altman, Brodoff, Orszag and Rubin (above n 109).

[113] D Brooks, 'Middle Class Capitalists', *The New York Times* (11 January 2008), at: www.nytimes.com/2008/01/11/opinion/11brooks.html?scp=7&sq=brooks+david&st=nyt.

[114] *Ibid.*

Despite their political differences, Brooks and the Hamilton Project openly now regard neo-liberal tax cuts and hostility to government as counterproductive. While the policies they recommend rely more on tax credits than direct spending, they implicitly acknowledge that the government needs to restore its support for social reproduction in order to foster family well-being, profitable economic growth, and political stability. That is, the state must mediate rather than continue to exacerbate the inherent conflict between economic production and social reproduction as well as the conflict between the democratic promise of equal opportunity and the persistence of class, race and gender inequality. According to Kotz, rather than just another financial downturn, the United States and the world may be facing a systemic crisis of capitalism that will only be resolved through major restructuring of the political economy That is the state will inevitably step in to mediate the neo-liberal crises.[115]

However, whoever benefits from the eventual restructuring of the economy will depend on the outcome of political struggle among various groups and classes. If social movements remain weak, state intervention is more likely to promote profits over people. In contrast, the revitalization of mass movements has the potential to force business to compromise with these movements in ways that will redistribute income, power and other resources downward and otherwise mediate the tension between profitable production and sustained social reproduction, The next step is for the public to rise up angry and to demand policies that truly value care-giving, put people before profits, and promote equality and justice for all.

[115] D Kotz, 'The Financial and Economic Crisis of 2008: A Systemic Crisis of Neoliberal Capitalism', paper prepared for a panel on 'The Global Financial Crisis: Heterodox Perspective, at the Annual convention of the Allied Social Science Association, January 4, 2009.

2

Women, the State and Welfare Law

The Canadian Experience*

SHELLEY AM GAVIGAN AND DOROTHY E CHUNN

'The origins of income security in Ontario begin with motherhood'.[1]

'[T]he beauty of the system [Chicago's Court of Domestic Relations in 1920], from the perspective of its officials, was that all of that money came from delinquent husbands—not the public coffers'.[2]

'The parenting needs of the children of sole mothers appear singularly unaddressed in the welfare reform debate'.[3]

I. INTRODUCTION

IN CANADA, AS elsewhere, extensive welfare law and policy reforms that effectively erased the category of 'deserving poor' marked the neoliberal (re)formation of the Keynesian state during the late twentieth century. In this chapter, we examine the contemporary changes in the form and content of Canadian welfare law through a historical, feminist lens,

* This chapter combines two individual papers that were presented by each of the authors at the workshop held at IISL in June 2007. A longer version of this chapter appears in (2007) 44 *Osgoode Hall Law Journal* 733. We acknowledge with thanks research assistance of Kaeleigh Kuzma, Piper Henderson and Yui Funayama; discussions with Cynthia Wilkey and Karen Andrews; comments of Mary Jane Mossman, Jamie Cameron, and the two anonymous reviewers for the Hart-Oñati series on earlier versions; and Robin Senzilet (Osgoode, 2008) and Judy Fudge for their editorial assistance.

[1] James Struthers, *The Limits of Affluence: Welfare in Ontario, 1920–1970* (Toronto, University of Toronto Press, 1994) 19.

[2] Michael Willrich, 'Home Slackers: Men, the State, and Welfare in Modern America' (2000) 87 *Journal of American History* 460, 486. See also Michael Willrich, *City of Courts: Socializing Justice in Progressive Era Chicago* (Cambridge, Cambridge University Press, 2003).

[3] Maggie Walter, 'Working Their Way Out of Poverty? Sole Motherhood, Poverty, Welfare and Material Well-Being' (2002) 38 *Journal of Sociology* 361, 377.

using the exemplar of mother-headed families. Although public spending on the poor has always been grudging, sole-support mothers historically were considered, within the dominant discourses of welfare, to be among the most deserving recipients of public assistance. Therefore, an analysis of how they have been rendered 'undeserving' or 'never deserving' can illuminate the profound changes that have occurred since the 1970s in Canada and elsewhere with the ascendancy of neo-liberalism.

Our point of departure is the burgeoning, extant literatures that are centred on discrete substantive and theoretical concerns related to women and welfare. We draw liberally on a large body of feminist historical work that traces the socio-legal roots and administration of mothers' allowances or pensions in five Canadian provinces during the first half of the twentieth century. This research tells us much about the development of pre-Keynesian state formation in Canada. In the contemporary context, we begin with the use of history and historiography in feminist analytical work on women, welfare law and policy, and neo-liberalism. Our primary focus is social policy and welfare reform in Ontario in the mid-1990s, which was arguably the most dramatic in the recent Canadian context. This was achieved through a restructuring of welfare law, a reduction of rates, a rejection of long-term need based on parental responsibility for children, and a virtual redefinition of welfare as fraud.[4] In these ways, the provincial Conservative government's legislation heralded a major break from some of the historic premises of and rationales for social assistance. Of particular relevance to our analysis is the theoretical work that is premised upon assertions of a shift from the past to the present, expressed, for instance, as 'a shift from public responsibility to private self-reliance, from social welfare rights to individualized support obligations' through what are said to be 'dual strategies' of reprivatization and familialization of 'once-public' goods.[5]

Feminists who write about women or mothers and welfare have tended to conceptualize the issues in an either/or manner. They look at women in the family or women in the market; they focus on past history or history of the here and now; they examine discursive or structural change. These bifurcated forms of framing arguably distort important issues in two ways that we attempt to avoid in our analysis.

First, they implicitly accept the dominant construction of welfare as policy that relates only to poor people. This acceptance has the unintended consequence of rendering invisible the fact that those once characterized as 'corporate welfare bums'[6] have always fared well by Canadian social and

[4] Ontario Works Act, 1997 (SO 1997, c 25) Sch A [Ontario Works Act].

[5] See eg Brenda Cossman, 'Family Feuds: Neo-Liberal and Neo-Conservative Visions of the Reprivatization Project' in Brenda Cossman and Judy Fudge (eds), *Privatization, Law, and the Challenge to Feminism* (Toronto, University of Toronto Press, 2002) 169, 170–71.

[6] David Lewis, *Louder Voices: The Corporate Welfare Bums* (Toronto, James Lewis & Samuel, 1972).

economic policies, enjoying all manner of incentives, land grants, favourable tariff policies, tax incentives, tax breaks, and so on.[7] So, while our article is devoted primarily to the emergence, development and transformation of the ways in which welfare and state support have been structured in relation to poor mothers in Canada, we resist the construction of the poor as the only recipients or beneficiaries of 'state welfare.'

Secondly, we attempt to avoid the other pitfall of an either/or (or 'that was then, this is now') approach to women and welfare that neglects the important historical continuities in the way(s) in which welfare for the poor has been defined and administered. We therefore identify and attend to continuities as well as discontinuities in Canadian social policy, both historically and in the present.

There are some striking continuities between the first wave of mothers' allowance legislation and the neo-liberal reforms of the 1990s. Both occurred during periods of structural change and reformation of the relationships between the state, the market and the family, including a particular concern about the 'crisis' of the (nuclear) family. However, we also identify important discontinuities including, among others, the different forms of liberal state (pre-Keynesian and post-Keynesian), and different forms of welfare law and policy in the two periods.

In particular, we analyze the larger structural contexts in which welfare law and policy have been developed and reformed. Drawing on feminist critiques that have demonstrated the ideological nature of the public/private divide,[8] we argue that the relationships between public and private in liberal states have been reformed rather than transformed. Specifically, we investigate two questions through an analysis of official documents, law reform and policy initiatives, and case law. First, given that most women have always straddled the so-called public/private divide, how have their relationships to state, market and family influenced the constructions of single mothers in Canadian welfare law and policy historically? And secondly, to what extent do changes in legal and other forms of discourse, as well as changes in social and economic relations, reflect and shape those constructions?

[7] See, eg Elizabeth Wallace, 'The Origin of the Welfare State in Canada 1867–1900' (1950) 16 *Canadian Journal of Economics & Political Science* 383; Claire FL Young, *Women, Tax, and Social Programs: The Gendered Impact of Funding Social Programs Through the Tax System* (Ottawa, Status of Women Canada, 2000); Harry Glasbeek, *Wealth by Stealth: Corporate Crime, Corporate Law, and the Perversion of Democracy* (Toronto, Between the Lines, 2002). In the United States context, see Mimi Abramovitz, 'Everyone is Still on Welfare: The Role of Redistribution in Social Policy' (2001) 46 *Social Work* 297.

[8] See eg Susan B Boyd (ed), *Challenging the Public/Private Divide: Feminism, Law and Public Policy* (Toronto, University of Toronto Press, 1997); Frances E Olsen, 'The Family and the Market: A Study of Ideology and Legal Reform' (1983) 96 *Harvard Law Review* 1497; Judy Fudge, 'The Public/Private Distinction: The Possibilities of and the Limits to the Use of Charter Litigation' (1987) 25 *Osgoode Hall Law Journal* 485; and Margaret Thornton, 'The Public/Private Dichotomy: Gendered and Discriminatory' (1991) 18 *Journal of Law & Society* 448.

Our argument proceeds through the following three sections of the chapter. In the next section, we examine the pre-Keynesian development of welfare for lone mothers and their children and demonstrate the long-standing relationship between women's labour (both paid and unpaid) and mothers' allowances (welfare). Next, we analyze the recent era of neo-liberal welfare reform, which we argue is shaped by the principle that 'mothers need not apply', in which responsibility for children has been rendered invisible (at best) and been relegated to no one (at worst). In the conclusion, we synthesize welfare law reform 'then and now' and identify the continuities and discontinuities that have shaped and reshaped the lives and experiences of poor women and their children.

II. WOMEN AND WELFARE THEN: PRE-KEYNESIAN FOUNDATIONS

Viewed retrospectively, welfare reforms that were implemented from the late nineteenth to the mid-twentieth century collectively reformed the public/private divide (state/family/market), and constructed the foundations of a pre-Keynesian state in Canada and other jurisdictions. This reshaping of social legislation and policy occurred in the context of massive structural change marked by industrialization, urbanization, and the establishment of 'universal' (but still racialized) suffrage during and after World War I. While it is important to bear in mind the unevenness of change both within and across cultures, all liberal states experienced a growing concentration of people along class lines in specific urban areas that made the poor (especially the racialized and immigrant poor) more visible, and fuelled middle-class and elite fear of potential threats to social order. Apparent increases in the number of 'deviant' families—including sole-support mothers and their children—at different times throughout the period from the 1880s to the 1940s supported perceptions that the (nuclear) family was in crisis and under siege. Conviction among the middle and elite classes that the nuclear family was the means of achieving integration and 'social control' in mass society focused attention on the role of mothers in the social reproduction of 'good' citizens.[9] Deviant families had to be prevented if possible and rehabilitated if necessary. To that end, reformers demanded forms of state intervention (eg, fiscal and legal) to shore up nuclear family life in the community.[10]

[9] Dorothy E Chunn, *From Punishment to Doing Good: Family Courts and Socialized Justice in Ontario, 1880–1940* (Toronto, University of Toronto Press, 1992); Jacques Donzelot, *The Policing of Families* (New York, Pantheon, 1980); David Garland, *Punishment and Welfare* (Brookfield VT, Gower, 1985).

[10] Chunn, *ibid*; Ann Vandepol, 'Dependent Children, Child Custody, and the Mothers' Pensions: The Transformation of State-Family Relations in the Early 20th Century' (1982) 29 *Social Problems* 221.

Two types of gendered welfare legislation and policy resulted from these efforts. The first category included legislation aimed primarily at male providers, which incorporated laissez-faire conceptions of the poor and of poverty as an individual responsibility, but with a new emphasis on the legal obligations of husbands and fathers to support their dependants, and on the role of the state in enforcing these patriarchal obligations. From the late nineteenth century onward, legislation was enacted in Canada that was intended to enforce the obligation of husbands and fathers to support their wives and their children. The new laws included federal Criminal Code provisions criminalizing the failure to provide the necessaries of life, and a spate of provincial legislation pertaining to the maintenance of deserted wives (later deserted wives and children), children of unmarried parents, and indigent parents.[11]

This legislation also placed an onus on individual women to conform to the criteria that historically were associated with the 'deserving poor'. Although male judges showed disdain for men who were 'home slackers',[12] they were no more receptive to 'undeserving' women. As we outline and demonstrate more fully below, in order to be eligible for assistance a wife was required to have been abandoned, not be responsible for the separation, and be morally impeccable as a mother, and to have made every effort to locate her absconding spouse prior to seeking help from the courts. Similarly, an unmarried mother, although morally compromised, was expected to pursue the (putative) father of her child(ren) for support.[13] However, women's notable lack of success in obtaining support from their husbands and the fathers of their children generated both internal and external pressure on the provinces to help local governments to create and finance specialized tribunals to deal with non-support.

The result was the establishment of domestic relations divisions in the traditional criminal courts and new family courts to enforce family welfare legislation.[14] Among other things, these socialized tribunals helped 'deserving' women track down deserting husbands and collected support on their behalf. While many reformers advocated such tribunals as a more humane

[11] Chunn, *ibid*. See also Willrich, 'Home Slackers' (above n 2); Willrich, *City of Courts* (above n 2). Examples from the Canadian legal context include the Criminal Code, (RSC 1927, c 36) ss 238, 239, 242 regarding the duty to provide necessaries (see especially the patriarchal responsibility and liability imposed in s 242(3)(a) on a man 'as a husband or head of a family'); Married Women (Maintenance in Case of Desertion) Act (SO 1888, c23); Deserted Wives' Maintenance Act, 1901 (SBC 1901, c 18); Children of Unmarried Parents Act (RSO 1927, c 88); and Children of Unmarried Parents Act (RSBC 1922, c 9).

[12] Willrich, 'Home Slackers' (above n 2).

[13] Lori Chambers, *Misconceptions: Unmarried Motherhood and the Ontario Children of Unmarried Parents Act, 1921–1969* (Toronto, The Osgoode Society/University of Toronto Press, 2007); Chris Clarkson, *Domestic Reforms: Political Visions and Family Regulation in British Columbia, 1862–1940* (Vancouver, University of British Columbia Press, 2007).

[14] Chunn (above n 9).

and effective way to deal with problem families, government bureaucrats and politicians were concerned primarily with ensuring that individual men, and not the state, bore the primary (fiscal) responsibility for family maintenance. Enforcement and collection always remained a problem, but that phenomenon never displaced the location or relation of the primary responsibility.[15]

The second type of legislation and policy, aimed at shoring up flawed versions of the nuclear family, provided forms of financial assistance to sole-support mothers. In a departure from laissez-faire conceptions of poverty as strictly an individual problem, both the political right and left came to agree that the state should provide some financial support for poor, sole-support mothers.[16] However, differences emerged about the social policy, about the form and content of the legislation, and about who would assume the fiscal responsibility for such assistance. In Canada, the entire period from the late nineteenth century to the mid-twentieth century was marked by ongoing strained relations between different levels of government about who should pay for what. The assumption of local fiscal responsibility for welfare by the provincial and federal governments was grudging, slow and uneven. This trajectory of welfare development is illustrated by the implementation of two types of social legislation that benefited sole-support mothers: one was rights-based, and employment or service-related as exemplified by provincial workers' compensation laws and the Canadian Patriotic Fund;[17] the other, as exemplified by the provincial statutes dealing with mothers' pensions or allowances, was needs-based and means-tested.[18]

During World War I, proponents of state aid to sole-support mothers often characterized such support as analogous to pensions for soldiers' service rather than as 'an extension of private charity',[19] and some sought a federal-level mothers' pension.[20] The most radical advocates of such policies also

[15] Willrich, 'Home Slackers' (above n 2) 486, found the same emphasis on individual (male) responsibility for family maintenance. See also Chunn (above n 9).

[16] Nancy Christie, *Engendering the State: Family, Work, and Welfare in Canada* (Toronto, University of Toronto Press, 2000).

[17] *Ibid*, 50, 51–2. The Canadian Patriotic Fund (CPF) 'originated during the Boer War as a private organization to help the wives and children of volunteer recruits'. However, the CPF became a large-scale national relief organization with semi-official status when a centralized national fund was established in 1914.

[18] A related family welfare initiative was the means-tested old age pension, introduced by the federal government by the Old Age Pensions Act (RSC 1927, c 156), which theoretically worked in tandem with provincial parents' maintenance legislation aimed at enforcing children's obligations to support their parents.

[19] Christie, *Engendering the State* (above n 16) 135.

[20] In British Columbia, eg, Helena Gutteridge, a feminist trade-unionist, persuaded the Vancouver Trades and Labour Council to lobby for a national pension in 1915. See Margaret Little, 'Claiming a Unique Place: The Introduction of Mothers' Pensions in B.C.' (1995) 105–106 *British Columbia Studies* 80, 88.

sought legislation that would entrench a breadwinner-homemaker model based on the concept of a male family wage, albeit for different reasons. Whereas feminists sought to reinforce the woman's role as full-time homemaker and envisaged state funding that would enable sole-support mothers to devote all their energies to mothering, organized labour supported state aid to single mothers rather as a means of protecting men's position in paid labour by keeping such women from competing with men for jobs and undercutting men's wages.

During the inter-war period, however, movements for provincial mothers' allowances gained momentum.[21] Ultimately, social conservatives who embraced old ideas about poverty prevailed. Feminists on the political right,[22] together with state bureaucrats, politicians, and others concerned about undermining self-reliance and encouraging pauperization successfully argued against the idea that the state should provide single mothers with funding equivalent to the missing husband's contribution to the family wage. It was this much more circumscribed vision of state assistance that was incorporated into the mothers' allowance legislation implemented by most provincial governments in Canada during the inter-war period.[23]

A. Poor Single Mothers and Pre-Keynesian Welfare Reform

As feminists from a range of disciplines have demonstrated, the legislation and policies of liberal capitalist states have long contemplated and supported a particular family form—heterosexual, patriarchal and nuclear—with a breadwinner husband, a stay-at-home wife, and legitimate

[21] Christie (above n 16).

[22] For example, Charlotte Whitton, Executive Director of the Canadian Council on Child Welfare (CCCW), later the Canadian Council on Child and Family Welfare (CCCFW), had initially evinced fierce opposition to mothers' pensions and allowances. See Dennis Guest, *The Emergence of Social Security in Canada* (Vancouver, University of British Columbia Press, 1980) 56–7; Christie (above n 16) 162–4.

[23] Legislation was enacted in Manitoba (1916); Saskatchewan (1917); Alberta (1919); British Columbia (1920); Ontario (1920); Nova Scotia (1930); Quebec (1937); and New Brunswick (1944). See eg The Mothers' Allowance Act (SO 1920, c 89); An Act to Provide for the Payment of Allowances towards the Maintenance of the Dependent Children of Certain Mothers (SNS 1930, c 4). Likewise, 39 of 48 American States had similar legislation by 1920. See Megan Davies, '"Services Rendered, Rearing Children for the State": Mothers' Pensions in British Columbia 1919–1931' in BK Latham and RJ Pazdro (eds), *Not Just Pin Money: Selected Essays on the History of Women's Work in British Columbia* (Victoria, Camosun College, 1984) 249; Little, 'Claiming a Unique Place' (above n 20) 81; Margaret Little, *No Car, No Radio, No Liquor Permit: The Moral Regulation of Single Mothers in Ontario, 1920–1997* (Toronto, Oxford University Press, 1998); Veronica Strong-Boag, 'Wages for Housework: Mothers' Allowances and the Beginnings of Social Security in Canada' (1979) 14 *Journal of Canadian Studies* 24; and Veronica Strong-Boag, 'Canada's Early Experience with Income Supplements: The Introduction of Mothers' Allowances' (1979) 4 *Atlantis* 35; Christie (above n 16).

children.[24] In this section, we demonstrate and emphasize that commitment to this model of family and, to a certain extent, its needs, informed the pre-Keynesian welfare state. Our review of Canadian income security legislation illustrates the primacy of the patriarchal family form over this period; the plans were designed to compensate for its losses or failures rather than transform or alter its shape or place. We have reviewed the first mothers' allowance/pension legislation enacted in five Canadian provinces (British Columbia, Alberta, Saskatchewan, Ontario and Nova Scotia) between 1917 and 1930. These provinces represent three western provinces, home to many new immigrants who were not British subjects; one maritime province; and Ontario, Canada's most populous province. Our review demonstrates that while the five provincial regimes contained many congruities, there were also interesting differences, not the least of which was the date of initial enactment. For instance, of these five provincial regimes, Nova Scotia's first legislation was enacted in 1930, more than a full decade later than the others.

It is clear that despite their regional and population differences, the statutes in this first wave of provincial mothers' allowance legislation each imposed detailed and demanding conditions for entitlement upon indigent mothers seeking to avail themselves of the modest allowances provided by the state.[25] The eligibility hurdles were high and numerous, and included long waiting periods, as well as requirements concerning marital status, residency, number and age of children, and specified reasons for the absence or incapacitation of a husband.

All five provincial statutes required women to provide evidence of both Canadian and provincial residency, although the precise length of the residency requirement varied by province. While immigrant women were not formally precluded from accessing mothers' allowance, some provinces required women to be British subjects (ie born in Canada or elsewhere in

[24] See eg Mary McIntosh, 'The State and the Oppression of Women' in Annette Kuhn and Ann Marie Wolpe (eds), *Feminism and Materialism* (London, Routledge & Kegan, 1978) 254; Elizabeth Wilson, *Women and the Welfare State* (London, Tavistock, 1977); Linda Gordon, *Heroes of Their Own Lives: The Politics and History of Family Violence, 1880–1960* (New York, Penguin Books, 1989); Linda Gordon, *Women, the State, and Welfare* (Madison WN, University of Wisconsin Press, 1990); Linda Gordon, *Pitied But Not Entitled: Single Mothers and the History of Welfare, 1890–1935* (Cambridge MA, Harvard University Press, 1995); and Nancy Fraser, *Justice Interruptus: Critical Reflections on the 'Postsocialist' Condition* (New York, Routledge, 1997) 41.

[25] Mothers' Allowances Act (SO 1920, c 89) [MAA (Ontario)] s 3(g); Mothers' Allowances Act (SNS 1930, c 4) [MAA (NS)] s 5(1)(b); Mothers' Pensions Act (SS 1917, c 68) [MPA (Saskatchewan)] s 2; Mothers' Allowances Act, 1922 (SS 1921–22, c 73) [MAA (Saskatchewan)]; and Mothers' Pensions Act (SBC 1920, c 61) [MPA (BC)] s 4(d). Alberta's legislation was couched in slightly different terms. See Mothers Allowance Act (SA 1919, c 6) [MAA (Alberta)] s 4, which provided that if a female widow or a wife of a man committed to a hospital for the insane was unable to 'take proper care' of her sons under the age of 15 and/or her daughters under the age of 16, she was permitted to apply for assistance under this legislation.

the British Empire), or wives or widows of British subjects.[26] The prairie provinces, home to many European immigrants, did not require the mothers to be British subjects.[27] First Nations women were excluded by two provinces—at first expressly,[28] and later implicitly[29]—ostensibly because of the federal government's constitutional responsibility for Indians.

Widows figured significantly in the early legislation, though benefits were gradually extended to women whose husbands were institutionalized in mental hospitals or penitentiaries, or who were incurably ill.[30] Even when the benefits appeared to be available only to widows, these provinces demonstrated legislative ingenuity in expanding the definition of a widow.[31] Although deserted wives were expressly encompassed by some provinces from the earliest days,[32] these women nonetheless faced onerous, indeed

[26] MAA (Ontario) s 3(e); MPA (BC) s 4(a); and MAA (NS) s 5(1)(g).

[27] Their legislation was silent in this respect.

[28] Nova Scotia's legislation expressly excluded mothers who were Indians, as defined by the federal Indian Act. See MAA (NS) s 5(1)(h).

[29] In 1956, Alberta restricted eligibility to persons who, for the purposes of health and welfare services, were the responsibility of the federal government. See Mothers' Allowance Act (SA 1956, c 35) s 4.

[30] Saskatchewan and British Columbia extended eligibility to women whose husbands had been sentenced to a penitentiary, had been committed to an institute for incurables, or were permanently incapacitated by reason of incurable disease or insanity. See MAA (Saskatchewan); MPA (BC). The British Columbia statute also extended to women whose husbands were sick or in an accident while the women were residing in British Columbia. Ontario provided that women who were widows or wives of inmates of mental hospitals or whose husbands were permanently disabled were eligible to apply. Nova Scotia limited eligibility to widows with at least two dependent children. See MAA (NS) s 5(1).

[31] As other provinces amended their legislation to allow mothers with one child to apply for assistance, Nova Scotia steadfastly limited mothers' allowances to widows with two dependent children until 1943 when, by regulation, the definition of 'widow' was expanded to include women whose husbands were unable to support their family due to permanent physical or mental disability. See Mothers' Allowances Act (SNS 1943, c 26) s 3. In 1936, Alberta allowed deserted wives to apply and extended the definition of 'widow' in its mother's allowance legislation to include 'any married woman who by order of a District Court Judge is declared to have been deserted, without reasonable cause, by her husband for a continuous period of five years or upwards'. See Mothers' Allowance Act (SA 1936, c 38) ss 2(b), 3. In 1942, Alberta broadened the definition of 'widow' to include wives who had obtained a judicial order declaring that they had been deserted by their husbands, without reasonable cause, for a continuous period for five years or more. See An Act to Aid Indigent Widows and Wives of Insane Person in the Support of Children (RSA 1942, c 302) s 2(e).

[32] British Columbia expressly encompassed a deserted wife within its earliest mothers' allowances legislation. See Mothers' Allowance Act (SBC 1920, c 61) s 2. Ontario followed suit in 1921, making it possible for 'abandoned' women with children under the age of sixteen to receive an allowance; Mothers' Allowance Act (SO 1921, c 79) ss 2, 6. It should be noted as well that Saskatchewan, and later Ontario, made it possible for 'dependent husbands' to apply for assistance under social assistance legislation. Saskatchewan's legislation provided that allowances were to be made available to indigent persons or to a person in 'necessitous circumstances' for the support or partial support of a dependent child. See Social Aid Act (SS 1944, c 61), as amended by SS 1946, c 92 [Social Aid (Saskatchewan)] s 2. Saskatchewan's 1949 regulations under this statute provided that an allowance could be paid to either a mother or a father; in order to be eligible, a father had to be 'incapacitated' and his wife either deceased, a patient in a mental hospital, serving a prison sentence, or had deserted the home.

punitive, requirements in the form of waiting periods of as long as five[33] and seven years.[34] Then, if a woman remarried, her assistance was terminated;[35] a stipulation which was relevant only for the handful of deserted wives who could manage to obtain a divorce in the period prior to Canada's first federal Divorce Act in 1968.[36] Many feminists have focused on another moral criterion in this early legislation: most provinces included an explicit requirement that the mother be a fit and proper person to have care and/or custody of her children.[37] While this legislative requirement has been an obvious target for feminist critique, it is important to note that it was not, as some have intimated,[38] an expression or an extension of the British subject requirement. The 'fit and proper' requirement was linked directly to the woman's abilities as a mother; the British subject requirement, under those provincial schemes that required it, was a separate limiting condition.

No discussion of this early social assistance legislation is complete without a consideration of family law support measures, which the provinces also began to enact in the post-World War I period in order to impose child support obligations on parents (read: fathers)[39] This is partly because, as discussed above, provinces began to require women to pursue their husbands and the fathers of their children for financial support in order to be eligible for social assistance.[40] At the same time, an important aspect

The Saskatchewan Regulations defined 'incapacitated' as a 'condition of physical or mental illness or disability from which there appears to be no prospect of improvement for a period of nine months from the date of application for an allowance, of such a nature as to render a person incapable of maintaining himself or his family'. See S Reg 127/1949, Sch 'A'. Ontario's legislation also provided for a widowed or dependent father whose wife was a patient in a sanatorium, hospital, or similar institution. See Mothers' and Dependent Children's Allowance Act (RSO 1960, c 247) s 2(b). In Saskatchewan, a woman's marriage or remarriage had the effect of terminating her entitlement to an allowance. S Reg 127/1949 s 22(a).

[33] See eg Alberta's Mothers' Allowance Act s 2(e).

[34] Child Welfare Act (SS 1930, c 70) s 1.

[35] See Saskatchewan's Social Aid Act s 22(a).

[36] Divorce Act (SC 1968, c 24).

[37] In Ontario, the phrase was 'fit and proper person to have the care and custody of her children'. See MAA (Ontario) s 3(f). In Nova Scotia, the mother had to be 'in every respect a fit, proper and suitable person to have the custody and care of her children'. See MAA (NS) s 5(1)(a). Saskatchewan's first statute to deal with this issue made no mention of the 'fit' criterion. See MPA (Saskatchewan) s 2. However, its MAA (Saskatchewan) s 3(2)(d) required a mother to be a 'fit and proper person to have care and custody of such child or children'. In British Columbia the phrase was 'a fit and proper person to have the custody of her child or children'. See MPA (BC) s 5(a). Alberta's legislation was couched in slightly different terms, containing no explicit reference to this criterion, although by s 4, an inspector was mandated to do a thorough investigation to ensure that the case was a 'proper one for assistance'. See MAA (Alberta) s 5.

[38] See eg Little, 'Claiming a Unique Place' (above n 20).

[39] This legislation took the form of deserted wives and children's maintenance legislation] and, later, legislation to impose support obligations upon parents who were not married; see Chunn (above n 9), Willrich (above n 2) and the legislation cited in n 11 above.

[40] A relationship between eligibility for benefits or allowances and the pursuit of remedies or support under other statutes began to appear as early as 1945, when Saskatchewan replaced abandonment as one criterion for eligibility and instead provided that a deserted wife could

of Deserted Wives' initiatives was the legislative restrictions upon those women who could make applications. For instance, Ontario's legislation required that a woman had to be living separately from her husband because of his cruelty or his failure (without sufficient cause) to support her and their children. Also, the woman herself could not be 'guilty' of adultery, nor could she make a claim against an adulterous husband if she had condoned his adultery.[41]

In sum, this overview of the first wave of mothers' allowance and social assistance legislation demonstrates that the over-riding policy of the legislation was to provide for indigent wives or widows and their children when the husband/father was deceased, incapacitated, incarcerated, or had deserted the family. The family unit had to include dependent children in the custody of the mother, who had to be a fit and proper person to care for children. As the criteria for eligibility gradually and unevenly increased, so too did the requirements imposed on women, such as waiting periods and mandatory efforts to pursue absconding husbands for support. Clearly, these allowances contemplated and circumscribed a particular family unit with a missing or defective breadwinner. Support for the family was a (patriarchal) responsibility of a husband or father. The family had to be supported, and when he was not able to provide, for either good or bad reasons, the state responded with modest support that came bundled with conditions.

B. Pre-Keynesian Welfare Reform and the 'Principle of Less Eligibility'

The means-tested nature of the first wave of mothers' allowance and related post-World War I welfare legislation left intact not only the distinction between the deserving and undeserving poor discussed above, but also the 'principle of less eligibility' that characterized the nineteenth-century

claim under the statute if she had made reasonable efforts to execute an order from the court under the provincial Deserted Wives and Children's Maintenance Act or the Criminal Code. See Child Welfare Act (SS 1945, c 100) s 26(6). The reference to the Criminal Code in this section refers to the criminal offence of failing to provide the necessities of life to one's wife and children, for which husbands in the period could be prosecuted. (Today, prosecutions under this section tend to involve parents who have failed to provide proper medical care for their children or who have failed to protect their child from an abusive parent or spouse.) This requirement was continued in the Social Aid Act (Saskatchewan). Under that statute, a mother was only eligible for social assistance if her husband had deserted the family for at least one year and the husband was convicted for non-support; a court order for support had been issued; or the Welfare Board was satisfied that a reasonable effort has been made to obtain support. See S Reg 127/1949 s 4(g). Divorced mothers were also eligible for social assistance, subject to the same requirements. See S Reg 127/1949 s 4(j). Similarly, an unmarried mother with a dependent child was eligible if she could satisfy the Director of Child Welfare that reasonable effort to obtain support from the father had failed. See S Reg 127/1949 s 4(f).

[41] This was the case as early as 1888 in Ontario. See Married Women (Maintenance in Case of Desertion) Act 1888 (SO 1888, c 23) s 5.

residual concept of welfare.[42] In relation to poverty, this principle implicitly requires that those deemed to be worthy of assistance, including mothers who receive state aid, should not be better off materially than the least affluent families among the working poor. While this principle has many implications, two in particular merit discussion. First, 'less eligibility' meant that the rates of assistance for mothers who qualified for allowances remained at subsistence levels. Although more minimal in some provinces than others, all rates for mothers' allowances were dramatically lower than rates for other welfare measures of the era, such as the Canadian Patriotic Fund and Workmen's Compensation. The latter were rights-based pensions, not allowances, which generated benefits for wives and mothers because of past (male) services to the war effort or to the paid labour force.[43] In contrast to mothers' allowances, these welfare measures also provided money to the wife-recipient in her own right as well as money for her children.

Secondly, 'less eligibility' meant that recipients of mothers' allowances were expected to generate supplemental income. Research indicates this was the norm among women in working poor families where both husbands and wives may have embraced the sexual division of labour, but lacked the family wage that would enable them to live in conformity with the breadwinner-homemaker model.[44] Denyse Baillargeon's study on working poor families in Montreal during the Depression of the 1930s suggested, for instance, that 'the image of the homemaker wholly dependent on the male wage and exclusively dedicated to housework and child care represented a virtually unattainable ideal for the majority of these poor working-class households'.[45]

Without a family wage, 'family survival depended by necessity on intensive domestic production and the extremely close management of the household budget, to which were often added the earnings from paid work of the mother of the family'.[46] Notwithstanding the social disapproval of

[42] Guest, *The Emergence* (above n 22) 36.

[43] Christie (above n 16) 51–2.

[44] Denyse Baillargeon, 'Indispensable But Not a Citizen: The Housewife in the Great Depression' in R Adamoski, DE Chunn and R Menzies (eds), *Contesting Canadian Citizenship: Historical Readings* (Peterborough, Broadview Press, 2002) 179; Eileen Boris and S J Kleinberg, 'Mothers and Other Workers: (Re)Conceiving Labor, Maternalism, and the State' (2003) 15 *Journal of Women's History* 90; Christie (above n 16); Gwendolyn Mink, *The Wages of Motherhood: Inequality in the Welfare State, 1917–1942* (Ithaca NY, Cornell University Press, 1995); Joy Parr, *The Gender of Breadwinners: Women, Men, and Change in Two Industrial Towns, 1880–1950* (Toronto, University of Toronto Press, 1990); and Joan Sangster, *Earning Respect: The Lives of working Women in Small-Town Ontario, 1920–1960* (Toronto, University of Toronto Press, 1995).

[45] Baillargeron (above n 44) 182. Baillargeon's qualitative research is based on 30 interviews with francophone women.

[46] *Ibid.*

and the legal restrictions on wage-earning (married) women,[47] many mothers with young children engaged in paid employment and/or a range of other paid work: including sewing; knitting; taking in laundry, boarders or other people's children; selling home-baked goods; performing domestic work in other people's homes; engaging in forms of prostitution; and making 'moonshine'.[48]

The many mother-supported families among the working poor were equally important to the link between 'less eligibility' and mothers' allowances. Suzanne Morton found that between 1921 and 1931, 16 per cent of all Halifax families with children were headed by a single woman (mostly widows), many of whom engaged in the types of paid work outlined above.[49] Joy Parr's research on the gendered labour force in the industries in two Ontario towns from 1880 to 1950 revealed that women wage-earners in a knitting mill in one town included a large number of single mothers with children. In 1936, for example, more than 25 per cent of female employees lived in single-headed households, most of which included children.[50] Moreover, because of low textile wages, the acute financial need in single-mother-headed households made lone mothers reliant on the wages of their children.[51] According to Parr,

> [m]any women lived alone with their children. Some were widowed, deserted, or never-married mothers who moved to Paris [Ontario] with their children because it was a place where they, with help from their teenagers, could assemble a family wage in the absence of a male breadwinner.[52]

Given the precarious economic situation of the working poor, it is hardly surprising that early mothers' allowance legislation implicitly or explicitly contemplated that women would supplement their 'allowance' with money from paid work even when their children were of tender years, since the rates did not differentiate on the basis of children's age. From a policy standpoint, the provision of such state assistance was based on the express policy that it was temporary, it was supplementary to home-based or other earnings, and it was intended to help worthy single mothers until they

[47] See Judy Fudge, 'From Segregation to Privatization: Equality, the Law, and Women Public Servants, 1908–2001' in Brenda Cossman and Judy Fudge (eds), *Privatization, Law, and the Challenge to Feminism* (Toronto, University of Toronto Press, 2002) 86.

[48] See Janice Acton, Penny Goldsmith and Bonnie Shepard (eds), *Women at Work: Ontario, 1850–1930* (Toronto, Canadian Women's Educational Press, 1974) on making 'moonshine'; Sangster (above n 44).

[49] Suzanne Morton, 'Women on Their Own: Single Mothers in Working-Class Halifax in the 1920s' (1992) 21 *Acadiensis* 90. See Morton's discussion (at 91) of Jessie Muir (a widow and her seven children) who 'survived the way most widows did before the welfare state: she used her home to generate income, and perhaps also accepted occasional day work in the critical period before she could depend on her children's labour'.

[50] Parr, *Gender of Breadwinners* (above n 44) 28–9.

[51] *Ibid*, 83.

[52] *Ibid*.

were able to (re)marry or to receive money from wage-earning children, especially sons.[53] Therefore, it is important to be aware of the class-based aspects of legislation. At that time—and still to this day—middle-class women were exhorted to be homemakers and were criticized if they engaged in paid work. In contrast, the working poor and/or single mothers received contradictory messages. They were told that they should engage in paid labour either to stay off the dole or to demonstrate that they were not idle and lazy yet, ironically, those who engaged in paid labour at that time were criticized for doing so.[54]

In Nova Scotia, for example, there was 'a general prejudice against wage-earning mothers'; the Reports of the Commission on Mothers' Allowances adopted a contradictory position: they stated that engaging in wage labour and taking in boarders was 'inappropriate' for mothers, but 'accepted the belief that a mother should be able to support at least one child'.[55] Joan Sangster has also identified the social stigma as well as the economic marginalization suffered by single mothers, and even widows. If women on mothers' allowance took on supplementary wage work, 'they were criticized for "taking jobs away from others"' and 'criticized by other citizens, including women, for taking state money rather than working!'[56]

The strong adherence of many women on mothers' allowance to familial ideology and the breadwinner ideal was equally contradictory. Noting that 89 per cent of mothers' allowance applicants in Ontario 'reported that they had had no employment outside the domestic sphere',[57] Nancy Christie concluded that in the absence of a male breadwinner, married women 'preferred to receive government welfare assistance rather than to seek work for wages and thereby transgress on the breadwinner's role'.[58] She also argued that '[i]t is in the context of *women's* wages, not the wages of the male breadwinner, that the economic contribution of mothers' allowances must be assessed'.[59] For widows in particular, '[b]ecause work was an enforced necessity, it was not seen as an expression of self-worth and economic

[53] Christie (above n 16) 154–5; Morton, 'Women on Their Own' (above n 49) 96–7; and Sangster (above n 44) 129.

[54] These contradictions were also evident in other jurisdictions. Gwendolyn Mink cites a 1919 US study which found 69% of the children of wage-earning mothers were between five and 15 years old. As a result, maternalists made recommendations that both recognized and discouraged the need for wage work by women; it was recommended that while women could seek part-time outside employment, they should be barred from industrial home work, night work, and part-time work when they had two or three children under the age of 16, and from any outside work if they had five or more children under the age of 16. For maternal feminist leaders, 'the real solution to poverty and its consequences was a husband for every woman and a family wage for every father'. See Mink, *Wages of Motherhood* (above n 44) 44, 46.

[55] Morton (above n 49) 96.

[56] Sangster (above n 44) 131.

[57] Christie (above n 16) 146.

[58] *Ibid*, 314.

[59] *Ibid*, 147.

independence when it conflicted with responsibilities in the home'.[60] We accept the argument advanced by Christie that the nuclear family model became hegemonic among working-class as well as middle-class families during the early twentieth century. However, we also think the analysis needs to address the question of the double day—an often implicit, if not ubiquitous, implication of women's participation in the labour market, and the extent to which the challenges of child care or leaving children alone, for example, may have made the male breadwinner model attractive.[61]

Viewed retrospectively, the reformation of the laissez-faire form of state from the late nineteenth to the mid-twentieth century in Canada, was both discursive and material. On the discursive level, the distinction between crime as a state responsibility and poverty as an individual problem shifted as new discourses about poverty emerged and competed with old ones that linked public assistance to pauperization and a pauper class.[62] Thus, in the pre-Keynesian state poverty came to be viewed, to a limited extent, as a collective, public problem (ie not solely a private, moral failing) to which the appropriate response was state intervention and/or assistance. At the level of actual welfare provision, the change over time was clearly more discursive than substantive. Economic welfare has always been conceptualized in terms of the poor. As noted above, although state subsidization of business has been a constant in Canada, it is never defined as such.[63]

Mothers' allowances did represent a qualitative moment in Canadian welfare's legal history, however, inasmuch as the provinces assumed some direct fiscal responsibility for supporting some poor, sole-support mothers. Much of the new legislation incorporated provisions that were designed to ameliorate some forms of stigmatization. Significantly, mother-recipients were constituted discursively not as charity cases, but rather as government employees on contract, who were charged with the responsibility of raising 'good' citizens. Efforts were also made to avoid public exposure and identification of recipients; in many jurisdictions, for example, allowance

[60] *Ibid*, 148.

[61] In contrast, Gwendolyn Mink's research shows that in mid-1920s Pennsylvania, although women who received pensions were supposed to be full-time mothers, many recipients were 'moonlighting'. Less than half of recipients' income came from pensions; 56.5% came from mothers' and children's wage work and rent from boarders/lodgers. Moreover, notwithstanding maternalist policy-makers' expectations that local policies would subsidize domesticity, states permitted recipients to work outside the home under limited circumstances. The state of Illinois even factored women's potential wages into determining eligibility and grant levels; two out of every three recipients between 1913 and 1915 worked for wages. See Mink (above n 44) 42.

[62] Chunn (above n 9); Garland, *Punishment and Welfare* (above n 9); and Willrich (above n 2).

[63] Wallace, 'Origin' (above n 7). See also Abramovitz, 'Everyone is Still on Welfare' (above n 7).

cheques were mailed, thereby sparing a woman the indignity of having to collect her cheque at a public welfare office.

Nonetheless, mothers' allowance legislation did not fundamentally depart from residual conceptions of welfare,[64] despite factors including diversity in rates and qualifying criteria.[65] The legislation was clearly aimed at reinforcing 'private family welfare and self-support in the future' which was a rejection of the maternal feminist argument 'that poverty and gender were linked'.[66] The introduction of mothers' allowances and pensions thus challenged the notion that sustaining families was an individual responsibility, but it actually did so in a way that reasserted that the primary responsibility was an individual one. The state's assumption of a role in providing for women—and later children—was minimal, grudging and always residual. Moreover, as Christie argues, 'the notion that welfare was primarily a private and family responsibility continued to animate the discourse on welfare even during the Second World War when the modern social security state was being created'.[67]

III. RECENT WELFARE LAW REFORM: 'MOTHERS NEED NOT APPLY'

Canadian feminist socio-legal scholars have begun to grapple with the form and implications of the restructuring of the Canadian welfare state for feminist analyses of law.[68] In particular, the ascendance of the neo-liberal discourse of, and preoccupation with, privatization has been the focus of much recent work. This new literature has tended to reflect the disciplinary and research preoccupations of the scholars, and it is marked by neither a deep immersion in nor an appreciation of the history of the relationship between women and welfare, or of the history of the relationship between welfare law and family law.[69]

[64] Guest (above n 22) 1–2 defines a residual concept of social security as a 'minimal, temporary type of service, offered at the discretion of the social welfare agency, meeting need only after evidence had been presented that all other avenues of help had been explored'.

[65] Christie (above n 16) 132–5; Little, *No Car, No Radio* (above n 23) 39.

[66] Christie (above n 16) 149.

[67] Christie (above n 16) 4. In Christie's view, the province of Manitoba was the worst in using mother's allowances 'to bolster a widow's incentive to work' (at 165). In 1917, only 56% of Manitoba beneficiaries earned supplemental wages; by 1926–27, 80% worked outside the home.

[68] See Boyd, *Public/Private*; Marlee Kline, 'Blue Meanies in Alberta: Tory Tactics and the Privatization of Child Welfare' in Susan B Boyd (ed), *Challenging the Public/Private Divide: Feminism, Law and Public Policy* (Toronto, University of Toronto Press, 1997) 330; and Brenda Cossman and Judy Fudge (eds), *Privatization, Law, and the Challenge to Feminism* (Toronto, University of Toronto Press, 2002).

[69] For a notable early contribution, see Mary Jane Mossman and Morag MacLean, 'Family Law and Social Welfare: Toward a New Equality' (1986) 5 *Canadian Journal of Family Law* 79.

Feminist legal scholars, whose primary research interests lie in family rather than welfare law, have been particularly attentive to the 'familial ideological' dimensions of welfare law, as expressed most clearly in the much amended definition of 'spouse'.[70] Not surprisingly, much of their focus, informed by family law concerns, has been on the various 'spouse in the house' reforms and the extension of the definition of spouse in welfare law to an ever-widening net of cohabiting relationships, including same-sex cohabitation. In the current context, Janet Mosher's research especially stands out because of her interrogation of the impact of welfare law and welfare law policy on the lives of women attempting to leave abusive relationships.[71]

Through interviews with 'welfare mothers', Mosher and her colleagues were able to identify a number of implications of the Ontario government's cuts to welfare rates and restructuring of welfare for women attempting to flee abusive relations. Mosher's research made a number of key thematic findings, not the least of which was that 'women's safety has been further compromised' by the welfare reforms, which resulted in 'grossly inadequate benefits, workfare, increased scrutiny, and the changed definition of spouse, [that] have all operated to make it even harder for women to leave their abusers and re-establish their lives'.[72] The threat of exposure for alleged welfare fraud was found to be empowering for the 'louse in the house' men.[73]

[70] See eg Cossman, 'Family Feuds'; Susan B Boyd, '(Re)Placing the State: Family, Law and Oppression' (1994) 9 *Canadian Journal of Law & Society* 39; Shelley AM Gavigan, 'Paradise Lost, Paradox Revisited: The Implications of Familial Ideology for Feminist, Lesbian, and Gay Engagement to Law' (1993) 31 *Osgoode Hall Law Journal* 589; and Shelley AM Gavigan 'Legal Forms, Family Forms, Gender Norms: What is a Spouse?' (1999) 14 *Canadian Journal of Law & Society* 127.

[71] Janet E Mosher et al, *Walking on Eggshells: Abused Women's Experience of Ontario's Welfare system, Final Report of Research Findings from the Woman and Abuse Welfare Research Project*, 5 April 2004. See also Janet E Mosher, 'Managing the Disentitlement of Women: Glorified Markets, the Idealized Family, and the Undeserving Other' in Sheila M Neysmith (ed), *Restructuring Caring Labour: Discourse, State Practice, and Everyday Life* (Toronto, Oxford University Press, 2000) 30; Janet E Mosher, 'Welfare Reform and the Re making of the Model Citizen' in Margot Young et al (eds), *Poverty: Rights, Social Citizenship, and Legal Activism* (Vancouver, University of British Columbia Press, 2007) 119.

[72] Mosher et al (above n 71) 5.

[73] This refers to men who could be found to be a spouse for the purposes of welfare law, but in no other family law context. In the words of one woman interviewed by Mosher et al: 'He's got all kinds of thing he could do with me: report me to welfare for fraud ... He can get away with assaulting me, you know ... He lived off me, sponged off me. I had no way to um, I had absolutely no way to get off the system. And not only that, the pressure of the system. I couldn't even tell what was going on because they would cut my cheque. I couldn't even tell them that this guy was sponging off me ... I mean you can't even get a guy outta' your house because now he has all the power in the world. Welfare fraud, welfare, that's what it's all about. They just gained the biggest stronghold they could ever gain and there'll be so many women that will be um, affected by that' (above n 71, at 57–8). Another woman spoke of her experience as follows: 'he feels like he has the upper hand, because like I said they were harassing me because he kept calling and saying that he was living with me when he wasn't. And you know, when he wasn't, but they were harassing me though' (*ibid*, 58).

Despite the feminist scholarly preoccupation with the 'spouse in the house' issue, it appears that for the abused, poor women who were interviewed, the 'spouse in the house' issue is only one of a litany of concerns. In *Walking on Eggshells*, Mosher and her colleagues found that abused women experienced many forms of abuse; their abuse was not confined to an abusive spouse, and their abuse could occur both inside and outside of their homes. Mosher and her colleagues identified the depth and range of neo-liberal welfare law reform's adverse impacts. These included inadequate benefits and a resulting inability to both feed the kids and pay the rent; the empowerment of abusive men who used welfare, such as using 'fraud snitch' lines as a means to harass their former spouses; a myriad of impenetrable and changing eligibility rules; and the debilitating effects of living under constant surveillance.[74]

Additionally, *Walking on Eggshells* confirms that extremely low welfare rates and the alleged 'culture of fraud' that has been created extend beyond the discourse of 'welfare cheats' to encompass everyone who is on welfare: the never-deserving poor.[75] Even abused women on welfare who are 'walking on eggshells' express the belief that they are also 'stealing from the government' when they are forced to rely on social assistance.[76]

Recent feminist analysis of women and welfare, especially of the 'spouse in the house' amendments in Ontario, has invoked the discourse of privatization to characterize the 1990s welfare reforms.[77] According to this argument, in the restructuring of the welfare state along leaner and meaner neo-liberal lines, the focus of welfare policy has shifted. The state is now said to be 'reinforcing certain private familial responsibilities for women's poverty ... while diminishing public societal commitment to alleviating that poverty'.[78] In this context, Brenda Cossman has observed that '[f]amily law is displacing social welfare as the primary source for persons without market income'.[79] Relying on scholarship on the gendered nature of privatization, Cossman argues that there are in fact two 'stories' in the re-privatization strategy: the dislocation of the 'public' in favour of 'private

[74] *Ibid.*

[75] Dorothy E Chunn and Shelley AM Gavigan, 'Welfare Law, Welfare Fraud, and The Moral Regulation of the Never Deserving Poor' (2004) 13 *Social & Legal Studies* 219. On the ascendancy and implications of a preoccupation with welfare fraud, see also, Janet Mosher and Joe Hermer, *Welfare Fraud: The Constitution of Social Welfare as Crime* (Ottawa, Law Commission of Canada 2005); Kiran Mirchandani and Wendy Chan, *Criminalizing Race, Criminalizing Poverty: Welfare Fraud Enforcement in Canada* (Halifax NS, Fernwood Publishing, 2007).

[76] Mosher et al, *Walking on Eggshells* (above n 71).

[77] See Cossman (above n 5) 170 regarding the discursive nature of '[t]he shift from public responsibility to private self-reliance, from social welfare rights to individualized support obligations ... [I]t is important to emphasize that this shift operates at the level of the discursive and not necessarily at the concrete level of women and children's lives'.

[78] *Ibid*, 173, quoting Susan B Boyd.

[79] *Ibid.*

support' in family; and the fact that social welfare law co-exists with a 'rearticulation of the "traditional family"'.[80]

We do not deny the social, economic and rhetorical force of neo-liberal attacks on welfare law, nor are we suggesting that the 1995 reforms in Ontario, for instance, were anything less than a full out assault on the poor. However, for us two questions remain. First, when did the provision of social welfare ever dislocate or displace the patriarchal family in fact, law or social policy as the primary site of responsibility for the support of family members? Secondly, when was welfare ever more than at best a residual reinforcement of and support for patriarchal responsibilities for the nuclear family?

In the decade following the initial neo-liberal reforms, litigation, research and advocacy campaigns attempted to restrain and redirect welfare law and policy, with mixed results. Litigation based on the Canadian Charter of Rights and Freedoms[81] that challenged the constitutionality of the dramatic reduction in welfare rates was unsuccessful,[82] whereas the challenge to the definition of 'spouse' ultimately enjoyed more success.[83]

In roughly this same time period, while the government of Ontario, in particular, was pursuing an aggressive campaign against people on welfare, the federal and provincial governments increased the Canadian Child Tax Benefit for low-income families in Canada by adding a new National Child Benefit Supplement (NCBS). The NCBS was said to have been created 'to help prevent and reduce the depth of child poverty'.[84] However, the very poorest families never received the NCB because of a provincial claw-back

[80] *Ibid.*

[81] Canadian Charter of Rights and Freedoms, Part I of the Constitution Act, 1982, being Sch B to the Canada Act 1982 (UK) (c 11) [Charter].

[82] See *Masse v Ontario (Ministry of Community & Social Services)* (1996) 89 OAC 81 (Ont Div Ct). This deferential judicial approach to the substantive components of welfare policy was supported by the Supreme Court of Canada in *Gosselin v Québec (Attorney-General)* [2002] 4 SCR 429, where the Court effectively empowered provincial governments to set whatever limitations on welfare programs they saw fit, even if it meant immiseration of welfare recipients. The majority of the Court rejected any claims based on, inter alia, s 15 and s 7 of the *Charter*.

[83] *Falkiner v Ontario (Ministry of Community and Social Services, Income Maintenance Branch)* (2002) 59 OR (3d) 481 (Ont CA). The definition of 'spouse' was challenged declared unconstitutional by the Ontario Court of Appeal. The provincial government received leave to appeal this decision to the Supreme Court of Canada, but following a change of government, the new Attorney-General announced that the Liberal government would not appeal the decision. Instead, they amended the regulations under the *Ontario Works* legislation to meet the Ontario Court of Appeal's requirements. The Family Benefits Act was replaced by the Ontario Works Act; however, the 1995 definition [under the Family Benefits Act regulations] remained in force in substantially the same form in the Ontario Works Act. Opposite sex partners are defined in a separate definition in the regulation, but are also covered by sub-s (2). O Reg 134/98 amended to O Reg 231/04.

[84] 'The National Child Benefit', at: www.nationalchildbenefit.ca/ncb/thenational1.shtml. See also 'Hands Off our Baby Bonuses' at: www.incomesecurity.org/campaigns/HandsOff/.

that resulted in a deduction from the benefits of parents on assistance.[85] Despite the previous promise of the Ontario Liberals, this claw-back did not end with their first electoral victory.

Following the defeat of the provincial Conservative government in the autumn of 2003, the new Liberal government did, however, adopt a different tone in relation to those people who are extremely poor. The Minister of Community and Social Services condemned the previous Conservative government for treating people on welfare as a 'typical punching bag' and she immediately committed the Liberal government to a 'series of [welfare] reforms'.[86] Although the new Liberal government invoked the now axiomatic incantation of all governments—'no tolerance for welfare fraud'—it also repealed the legal expression of the Conservative government's punitive 'zero tolerance' policy that had been introduced in 2000. In January 2003, the permanent ineligibility sections of the regulations under the Ontario Works Act were repealed.[87] In December 2004, the Liberal government also introduced a series of amendments to the regulations, which ameliorated some of the worst excesses of the previous administration. For instance under the amended regulations, the earnings of a dependent child ceased to be considered an asset in the determining of the eligibility of a benefit unit,[88] and Registered Education Savings Plans also became exempt from the determination of assets (and thus no longer needed to be cashed before the benefit unit became eligible for benefits).[89] In June 2004, the Liberal government announced a modest increase in benefits under the statutes.[90]

Two welfare rights campaigns expressed the ongoing struggles against the ideology and impact of neo-liberal welfare reform: 'Feed the Kids and Pay the Rent' and 'Hands Off!' These welfare rights campaigns—led by welfare mothers, their advocates, and their allies—drew attention to the impact of extremely low welfare rates and the targeted claw-back of the NCBS from the very poorest families. At the same time, these campaigns reasserted the need for a form of 'mothers' allowance' in order to meet the needs of children with mothers on welfare.[91] These campaigns reinserted the relationship

[85] See Wanda A Wiegers, 'The National Child Benefit: Social Inequality Under the New "Social Union"' (2001–02) 33 *Ottawa Law Review* 25.

[86] Ontario, Legislative Assembly, *Official Report of Debates (Hansard)*, 17A (17 December 2003) 868 (Hon Sandra Pupatello).

[87] O Reg 456/03.

[88] O Reg 395/04 s 6(3).

[89] O Reg 395/04 ss 12(1), 13(4).

[90] Ontario Ministry of Community and Social Services, 'Ontario Social Assistance Rate Increase and Special Payments' (30 June 2004), at: www.cfcs.gov.on.ca/CFCS/en/newsRoom/factSheets/040630.htm.

[91] These campaigns were commenced and coordinated by an Ontario legal clinic, the Income Security Advocacy Centre (ISAC), in collaboration with a number of community partners. The campaigns involved a multi-pronged, integrated law reform strategy that included a write-in campaign addressed to Premier Dalton McGuinty, urging him to honour an election promise to end the claw-back of the NCBS made prior to his first election intervention

between poor mothers and their children into the public discourse about social assistance and reminded the public of the vulnerability of single-parent families, mostly mother-led, who continued to be relegated to the lowest ranks of the poor.[92]

In many ways, the most telling illustration of the neo-liberal agenda in recent Canadian history continues to be Ontario's dramatic cuts to benefit levels in order to save the public purse from paying people 'to do nothing'. The sharply reduced welfare rates implemented by the Conservative government in 1995 have witnessed only marginal increases, while the reporting requirements, the scrutiny and discretion of welfare workers, and the dearth of community and social supports remain ongoing.

In our view, the implications of 'Feed the Kids', 'Hands Off!' and '*Walking on Eggshells*' for feminist analyses of welfare, family law and neo-liberalism are significant. It is clear that the impact of neo-liberal welfare law reform on the concrete lives of poor women and their children extended further and deeper than the 'spouse in the house' definitions.

The two-year long 'Hands Off!' campaign against the claw-back of the NCB experienced a bitter-sweet victory of sorts in March 2007, when the provincial government announced the creation of a new Ontario Child Benefit for all low-income families in Ontario. The provincial government also promised that poor families would receive the Ontario Child Benefit in addition to the NCB.[93] The introduction of the Ontario Child Benefit was combined with a 'rate restructuring', which lowered social assistance rates, and allocated items that were previously covered by those rates (eg, winter clothing allowance) to the separate NCB. The formal separation of children (as beneficiaries) from their parents is both discursive and material.

in electoral campaigns; all-candidates meetings; community education and organization; a media strategy; and commencing litigation on *Charter* issues in the case of *Chomolkin, Lance & Prine v Her Majesty the Queen in Right of Canada, et al.* For information on this still pending litigation, see Income Security Advocacy Centre at: www.incomesecurity.org/challenges/ChokomolinLancePrincev.Her MajestytheQueeninRightofCanadaetal.html. For information and an assessment of the campaign, see Income Security Advocacy Centre, at: www.incomesecurity.org/campaigns/Handsoff Campaign.html.

[92] Mother-led families in Canada account for 90% of all poor single-parent families and continue to have the highest poverty rate out of all the most common family types. Their incomes are less than half of Canada's 'poverty line'—Statistics Canada's low-income cut-offs. See National Council of Welfare, *Poverty Profile, 2002–2003* (Ottawa, Minister of Public Works and Government Services Canada, 2006) 12, fig 1.6. See also Wanda Wiegers, *The Framing of Poverty as 'Child Poverty' and its Implications for Women* (Ottawa, Status of Women Canada, 2002).

[93] 'The implementation of the Ontario Child Benefit, and the resulting restructuring of social assistance in July, 2008, reduces the claw-back of the National Child Benefit Supplement (NCBS) but doesn't end it. As of July 2008, the NCBS is no longer deducted from the monthly cheques of families on Ontario Works (OW) or the Ontario Disability Support Program (ODSP)'. See Income Security Advocacy Centre, at: www.incomesecurity.org/campaigns/HandsoffCampaign.html.

In our view, analyses of 'privatization' and 're-privatization' in the context of welfare law do not sufficiently attend to the way in which poverty, welfare and family have historically been framed in liberal states. Rendered invisible in these analyses is the precise nature of the Keynesian form of privatization which really involved public support for the private sector and the family, and which left the assumptions of patriarchal familial ideology firmly intact and embedded. For the Keynesian welfare state, bolstering the family via health care, education, welfare and so on, was the goal.[94] Recent feminist literature speaks of the Keynesian state as if the public realm really supplanted the private—when all it ever did at best was to shore it up.

While the definition of spouse has expanded to include same-sex relationships, the nuclear form of the family has retained its hegemony.[95] Through its emphasis on marriage and its asserted importance to the children of same-sex couples, the same-sex marriage campaign has in fact contributed to the further marginalization of single mother families.[96] Thus, what we are seeing is a reformation of the privatization principle, which is always patriarchal. We do not share the view that there is a new gender order.[97] Rather, we believe there is a reformed gender order in which patriarchal norms and values remain unchanged (even if modified, as evidenced by the successful same-sex marriage campaign in Canada).

Legislation that was gender- and sex-specific made the patriarchal basis of the Keynesian form of welfare state transparent. What was less obvious, but still remained, were long-standing ideas about individual responsibility. With respect to women, their role as mothers was explicit. The legislation also entrenched the individual responsibility of mothers to supplement their benefits (see the first Ontario Mothers' Allowance Act); and later, under Keynesianism, the express principle was that mother work was women's work, and that the payment of the allowance itself was for a form of mother work available only to certain mothers. With gender-neutral legislation, the individual responsibility of everyone, including mothers, to become engaged in wage labour is articulated, while the individual responsibility for domestic labour becomes less visible and less articulated. The unpaid labour of women is increasing. This is especially the case since the words 'health care' have been redefined to include only urgent care, early discharge from hospitals, and the increasing use of homecare for the sick and the elderly.

[94] See McIntosh, 'The State' (above n 24).

[95] Gavigan, 'Legal Forms' (above n 70).

[96] See also, Shelley AM Gavigan, 'Equal Families, Equal Parents, Equal Spouses, Equal Marriage: The Case of the Missing Patriarch' (2006) 33 *Supreme Court Law Review* (2d) 219.

[97] See Janine Brodie, *Politics on the Margins: Restructuring and the Canadian Women's Movement* (Halifax NS, Fernwood Publishing, 1995).

As Cossman has argued, there could be more of a discursive shift—and on this we might agree; however, we need to interrogate the discursive shift within the material context. In our view, within the Keynesian welfare state there was a discourse of helping the poor that translated into alleviating (but not supplanting) the historical expectation that people are responsible for their own poverty and that it is up to them to rely upon their own family, friends and community before they go to the state.

The new rhetoric and policies of privatization are linked to the notion of reduced public spending. Yet, clamping down on welfare fraud does not save the state any money since there is an increase in state-initiated intervention and state expenditure. What has shifted is the extent of privatization—but that is different from saying that privatization is completely new. There is a reorganization and retrenchment of the state; a renegotiating of the public/private divide; and a redefinition not simply of where the line is drawn, but also of what 'content' belongs in each sphere.

Despite the important insights of feminist family law scholars who are analyzing forms of privatization in family and social welfare law,[98] it appears that important sites of privatization remain un- or under-theorized.[99] In particular, compelling illustrations of privatization in family law may be seen in the context of the increasingly permissive approach to 'private ordering' in family law, such as mediation and arbitration. This also includes judicial approval at the highest levels of the Canadian judiciary of permitting the 'contracting out' of family law and holding spouses to their 'freely contracted' bargains. In many ways, the emerging dominant discourse in family law (but not welfare law) is 'freedom of contract'—the sine qua non of the private.

IV. WELFARE LAW REFORM, THEN AND NOW: SOME CONCLUSIONS

In this chapter, we have analyzed two important waves of welfare law reform and the implications thereof for poor lone mothers and their children. We do not suggest that we have covered the entire history of the construction and regulation of poor mothers and their relationship to forms of social assistance—from mothers' allowances, to family benefits, to new notions of workfare: that larger project awaits us on another day. However, our analysis here leads us to the conclusion that the continuities, as well as the discontinuities, between 'then' and 'now' need to be acknowledged and understood.

[98] Susan B Boyd, *Child Custody, Law, and Women's Work* (Toronto, Oxford University Press, 2003) 215–19; Cossman (above n 5).

[99] See especially *Miglin v Miglin* [2003] 1 SCR 303; *Hartshorne v Hartshorne* (2004) 236 DLR (4th) 193.

There are some striking continuities or similarities between the first wave of mothers' allowances and the neo-liberal reforms of the 1990s. Both periods were ones of structural change and reformation of the public and the private (state/market/family). Both periods were marked by concern about a 'crisis' of the (nuclear) family. Both periods saw the enactment of welfare legislation that assumed the participation of (female) beneficiaries in paid labour, in conjunction with the implementation of other legislation (child support guidelines, maintenance acts) aimed at enforcing individual male responsibility to provide for dependent women and children. Both periods saw feminists push for welfare reforms that had mixed impact. While these reforms challenged the patriarchal status quo and (re)formed the gender order, feminists were ultimately unable to control the content, form and administration of the legislation.

However, we have also identified important differences and discontinuities in the periods we have examined. The reformation of the public and private produced different forms of liberal state (ie pre- and post-Keynesian) and of welfare law and policy. The earlier 'crisis' of the family revolved around concern about 'white' Canada, specifically a concern about bolstering the nuclear family (especially in the wake of World War I and the influenza epidemic). The late-twentieth-century 'crisis' of the family reflected anxiety about perceived threats to the traditional (white) nuclear family posed by the proliferation of opposite and same-sex common law relationships and more recently by the legalization of same-sex marriage.

In the early twentieth century, welfare reforms (such as mothers' allowances and pensions) prioritized women's unpaid labour over their paid labour. The basis of women's citizenship thus derived from their status as mothers. In the late twentieth century, welfare reforms prioritized paid labour and assumed the performance of unpaid labour. Women and mothers disappeared and were replaced by the gender-neutral worker whose basis of citizenship is participation in paid employment.

In the pre-Keynesian state, welfare legislation and policy were premised on the family wage—a sexual division of labour in which the male is the breadwinner and the female is the homemaker. This model of social and familial relations constructed women as the 'natural' economic dependants of men. Mothers/wives were conceptualized and regulated primarily in terms of their relationships to the (private) family and not their relationship to the (public) market. The reverse was true for fathers/husbands. This commitment to a family wage rarely translated into a living wage for members of low-income households, and consigned women in particular to poverty, unemployment, or socially invisible forms of (under)employment.[100]

[100] Baillargeon (above n 44); Boris and Kleinberg, 'Mothers and Other Workers' (above n 44); Mink (above n 44); Parr (above n 44); and Sangster (above n 44).

For single mothers, the implications of this emphasis on the (dependent) homemaker role were expressed and experienced through (1) legislation and welfare policies that required them to pursue the (putative) fathers of their children for support; and (2) after World War I, the limited government provision of allowances to destitute, widowed, and (later) abandoned mothers in recognition solely of their role in the social reproduction of future citizens, and not as women per se. This form of state financial assistance was means-tested, based on the 'principle of less eligibility', contingent on closely-scrutinized 'fit and proper' behaviour, and enforced, if need be, through disqualification and/or criminalization. Moreover, the provision of such assistance was based on the express policy that it was temporary, as well as supplementary to home-based earnings, to help worthy single mothers until they were able to (re)marry.

The welfare legislation and policy of the neo-liberal state are premised on the formal equality and gender-neutrality of the freely choosing, self-reliant actor (and more substantively worthy and equal taxpayer). Women are now expected to be employed. The 'feminization' of paid labour, together with the restructuring of the welfare state, has 'equalized' the experience of (under)employment for many people, forcing both men and women to accept 'bad' jobs, and making it imperative that both spouses in a family earn money in one way or another. Thus, like men and fathers, women and mothers are conceptualized and regulated primarily in terms of their relationship to the labour market. Now women's relationship to the (private) family is taken for granted and rendered as invisible as their relationship to employment used to be.

A major implication of recent welfare reforms is that single parents (mothers) have disappeared as a category of social assistance recipient. While there is continuing emphasis on mothers pursuing the putative fathers of their children for support under state legislation and policies, the formal rationale is couched in a different form of discourse. These mothers now have the role of the independent, self-sufficient, 'choosing' market citizen who is responsible for her bad choice of husband/father. Therefore, rather than looking to the state for support, they are required to take advantage of welfare-to-work programmes that will prepare them for paid employment and end their 'dependency' on the state. The importance of social reproduction in raising and caring for their children has vanished as a social good. State financial assistance is stringently means-tested, based on even narrower 'principles of less eligibility', contingent on moral behaviour (now conceptualized as industrious as well as asexual), and increasingly time-restricted and enforced, if need be through disqualification and/or criminalization. State financial assistance is no longer formally conceptualized as welfare or assistance; its provision is still temporary, but is now designed solely to move unemployed workers into the labour market.

The erasure of sole-support parents, first pencilled into Canadian welfare law only as mothers, has been completed. Their needs as mothers with responsibility for the care and upbringing of children have become as anachronistic as the very notion of social welfare itself. The challenge for those who remain committed to the principle of substantive equality and to the possibility of progressive social change is to continue to work to create social conditions and relations in which the poverty of single mothers and their children is neither inevitable nor denied. Until then, mothers need not apply.

Part II

Women's Agency and Activism in the Welfare State: Comparative and Historical Perspectives

3

Gender and the Rise of the Welfare State in Fin-de-Siècle New York City

The Case of Tenement Regulation

FELICE BATLAN*

I. INTRODUCTION

IN 1887, A New York City resident who identified herself only as a poor wash woman, wrote to the Mayor of New York City complaining of the odours emanating from the outhouse that served the dwellers of the tenement house in which she lived. She wrote that such odours were enough to 'kill' a person and that the resident women 'could not wash in safety'.[1] That a poor woman would write to the mayor of such mundane concerns might strike the modern reader as naïve. Yet letters such as these demonstrate both the everyday misery that tenement dwellers suffered as well as the growing understanding that the city was responsible for ensuring the welfare of its citizens, especially minimally adequate housing.

The question of the condition of New York City's tenement houses at the turn of the twentieth century was an issue that plagued a wide variety of state actors, reformers, and tenement dwellers. In bold relief it presented the question of what power the state possessed to regulate tenements, landlords, and the tenement population. This chapter explores how various historical actors, including reformers, courts, tenement

* Portions of this chapter have appeared in the *Southern California Interdisciplinary Law Journal* and *Law and Social Inquiry*. See F Batlan, 'Law and the Fabric of the Everyday: The Settlement Houses, Sociological Jurisprudence, and the Gendering of Urban Legal Culture' (2006) 15 *Southern California Interdisciplinary Law Journal* 235; F Batlan, 'A Reevaluation of the New York Court of Appeals: The Home, the Market, and Labor, 1885–1905' (2002) 27 *Law and Social Inquiry* 489.

[1] Letter from a Poor Wash Woman to Mayor Abram Hewitt (August 1887), Mayor's Papers, Abram Hewitt, Health Department, New York Municipal Archive (NYMA), Box 1344.

residents, and settlement house workers constructed the tenement problem and became proponents or opponents of state regulation. In the process it elucidates how discourses surrounding the tenement problem were deeply gendered.[2]

By focusing on tenement regulation, this chapter contributes to how we understand the interactions between welfare, regulation, law, gender and the state. Broadly it argues that welfare must be defined to include the state's efforts to regulate for the public good.[3] It also resituates the central role of the city in connection with the development of the welfare state. Indeed, by the turn of the twentieth century, New York City had already created what might be called a nascent regulatory welfare state. It was the municipality that most forcefully inserted itself into the daily life of city residents and it was the city that many residents called upon in times of need.

Such a nascent welfare state was also deeply gendered. So much so that by 1912, legal luminary Roscoe Pound labelled the vision of an activist municipality that provided services to its citizens and regulated capitalism as 'governmental maternalism'.[4] In doing so, Pound recognised the space of experimentation that the city provided and the feminine nature of a benevolent and caring state in which regulation played a crucial role.

The chapter begins with a discussion of late-nineteenth-century gender ideology and how gender mapped onto understandings of the public and the private, the home and the market. It argues that such concepts were crucial to determining what constitutionally could be regulated by the state. The chapter then explores how various reformers articulated the problem with tenements as being their lack of domestic privacy and incomplete separation from public space. This led to reformers and state actors seeking to regulate the tenement to create a private domesticity while simultaneously situating the tenement as part of the public and thus a constitutionally

[2] Many scholars who study gender and welfare focus on sites that specifically involve women, such as mothers' pensions and protective labour legislation for women. See, eg, KK Sklar, 'The Historical Foundations of Women's Power in the Creation of the American Welfare State, 1830–1930' in S Koven and S Michel (eds), *Mothers of a New World: Maternalist Politics and the Origins of Welfare States* (New York, Routledge, 1993); T Skocpol, *Protecting Soldiers and Mothers: The Political Origins of Social Policy in the United States* (Cambridge MA, Belknap Press of Harvard University Press, 1992); L Gordon (ed), *Women, the State, and Welfare* (Madison, University of Wisconsin Press, 1990); L Gordon, *Pitied But Not Entitled: Single Mothers and the History of Welfare, 1890–1935* (New York, The Free Press, 1994). Yet much regulation which appeared gender-neutral was in fact deeply gendered.

[3] Legal historian William Novak has demonstrated that a mass of state regulation existed in the United States before the Civil War. Novak, however, pays no attention to gender. See W Novak, *The People's Welfare: Law and Regulation in Nineteenth Century America* (Chapel Hill, NC, University of North Carolina Press, 1996). In addition, after the Civil War and the adoption of the Fourteenth Amendment, which made the US Constitution applicable to the states, state regulation became suspect as a potentially unconstitutional taking of property in violation of the Fourteenth Amendment.

[4] R Pound, 'The Administration of Justice in the Modern City' (1913) 26 *Harvard Law Review* 302, 312.

appropriate site for state regulation. Next, the chapter examines tenement dwellers', especially poor and working-class women's complaints about tenements and their understanding that as municipal citizens they had a right to decent housing. It continues by analyzing two court cases involving the constitutionality of tenement regulation. Finally, it explores the role of women settlement workers in the enforcement of tenement laws and how they became part of the growing regulatory welfare state.

II. THE IDEOLOGY OF GENDER: THE PUBLIC AND THE PRIVATE

In late-nineteenth-century debates regarding state regulation and the public good, gender functioned on multiple levels. Such gendered discourses could support or thwart regulation and it was also a way in which middle-class women were able to create a role for themselves within the developing welfare state. Likewise, in the conflicts that roared in late-nineteenth-century New York City regarding capitalism, citizenship, class, urban space and the role of the state, gender was a way through which rights and complaints were articulated, constructed and defined. Within these gendered claims and rhetoric, issues of the home and the market, the public and the private served as crucial dichotomies, which were themselves gendered.

In the market economy, which ebbed and flowed from the 1820s on, affecting different regions of the country unevenly, work became disconnected from the home. Wage labour was defined as work done outside of the home that was ideally performed by a male breadwinner. Eventually the market became the antithesis of the home, which represented a private metaphorical and literal space. The home, imagined as a women's sphere, was to be filled with theoretically non-commodified and unselfish relationships and provided an escape from the male, market-driven world of business suffused by self-interest and mendacity. Character traits such as self-sacrifice and virtue, symbolically embodied by the middle-class white woman, stood in opposition to the liberal conception of the market based on individual self-interest. Indeed, the very concept of the free male citizen whose wage labour provided for the family rested upon the ideal of a dependent wife and children who created the home as a refuge from the harsh realities of the marketplace.[5]

What precisely belonged within the imagined sphere of the home or the market, and even where to locate such boundaries, produced continual contestations and calls for new laws and state action. This relationship between state action, the public, and the private also drove what could be regulated while producing perplexing dilemmas and contradictions. Historical actors

[5] See AD Stanley, *From Bondage to Contract: Wage Labor, Marriage, and the Market in the Age of Slave Emancipation* (Cambridge, Cambridge University Press, 1998).

pondered whether regulation of the home was crucial in order to maintain it as a sphere divorced from the market. Could the market, which classical liberalism imagined to be outside of state regulation, be regulated to maintain the sanctity of the home? Did the unregulated market destroy the privacy of the home?

Furthermore, as scholars of women's history have long recognized, in the late nineteenth century middle-class women, the very bulwark of the private middle-class home, made extraordinary bids for public power, claiming that they would bring the virtue of home life and their expertise in domestic matters into the public sphere. In doing so, such women expanded the boundaries of the metaphorical home into public space.[6]

That the actual homes of neither the wealthy nor the poor could live up to such expectations and ideologies produced tremendous anxieties. Working-class and poor women not only worked in factories but engaged in paid homework. Within the tenement houses in New York City, families lived and worked producing goods that would be consumed by the middle class. Physically, the growing number of densely-packed tenements failed to live up to bourgeois conceptions of the privatised and sanitised middle-class home. Moreover, homes of the middle class could not be cordoned off from the physical environment of the city or the products produced in tenements that then entered middle-class homes. As a wide variety of reformers—men, women, working-class and elite—sought to examine, investigate and propound upon the importance of the sacrosanct and privatised home, the more public, the less private, intimate and sacred the home became. In fact, where the domestic physically, symbolically and metaphorically was located and its demarcation from the market plagued post-bellum nineteenth-century actors and the tenement functioned as a perfect symbol and actual location for such concerns.

III. LIMINALITY: HOME AND THE URBAN TENEMENT

Although the legal definition of a tenement, according to New York law, only meant that a building housed three or more families, virtually all New Yorkers understood that tenements were generally poorly constructed and vastly overcrowded apartment buildings in primarily immigrant neighbourhoods. Such apartments often lacked windows, ventilation and plumbing.

[6] On women's use of domesticity to expand their roles in public life, see, eg, Sklar (above n 2); P Baker, 'The Domestication of Politics: Women and American Political Society, 1780–1920' in Gordon (ed), *Women, the State, and Welfare* (above n 2); M Ryan, *Women in Public: Between Banners and Ballots, 1825–1880* (Baltimore MD, Johns Hopkins University Press, 1990).

In 1901, 83,000 tenements existed in New York City, which housed a population of nearly three million people.[7]

Tenements exercised an almost hypnotic effect over reformers of every ilk, as they were a visual reminder of New World poverty, the increasingly dense city, and the changing demographic of New York City's population. In microcosm, the tenements served to question the possibility of the Americanization of new immigrants and the physical and moral health of the city. In rhetoric that vastly overstated the problems of tenements, but that nonetheless reflected middle-class reformers fears, Jacob Riis wrote:

> In the tenements all the influences make for evil; because they are the hotbeds of the epidemics that carry death to rich and poor alike; the nurseries of pauperism and crime ... above all, they touch the family life with deadly moral contagion.[8]

The tenement, real and imagined, also represented a liminal site that stood on the precipice of the public and private. It was a space in which people lived their personal lives, yet one whose façade was exposed to the public. The dramas of family life played out within its interior spaces, then visibly spilled into hallways, courtyards, outhouses and streets. Simultaneously the tenement was deeply embedded in market relationships which involved landlords, sub-landlords, tenants, boarders and lodgers. Women, men and children lived and laboured within the tenements, manufacturing and producing cigars, clothing, artificial flowers, feathers and various food products including baked goods and shelled nuts which often were consumed in other people's homes.[9] These commodities easily crossed class lines, geographies, and the thresholds of homes, resulting in growing middle-class anxieties of contamination. In the tenements, women also laboured in the daily tasks of cleaning, cooking and providing for ubiquitous boarders and lodgers. Furthermore where a building was privately owned, the impact of the building overflowed its property lines, affecting neighbours and ultimately the city. Thus the tenement literally stood at the boundary of the public and private, challenging the concept and construction of both.[10]

[7] First Report of the Tenement House Department of the City of New York, vol 1 (1902–03).

[8] J Riis, *How the Other Half Lives* (1890) (Cambridge MA, Harvard University Press, 1970) 2–3.

[9] E Boris, '"A Man's Dwelling House Is His Castle": Tenement House Cigarmaking and the Judicial Imperative' in A Baron (ed), *Work Engendered: Towards a New History of American Labor* (Ithaca NY, Cornell University Press, 1991).

[10] Anne McClintock writes that the late-19th century middle class was preoccupied with the clear demarcation of boundaries between the private and public. This gave rise to an intense fetish for cleaning and a fetishistic preoccupation with liminal or boundary objects. A McClintock, *Imperial Leather: Race, Gender and Sexuality in the Colonial Contest* (New York, Routledge, 1995). For a discussion of the New York City apartment house as occupying a space between the public and the private, see EC Cromley, *Alone Together: A History of New York's Early Apartments* (Ithaca NY, Cornell University Press, 1990) 2.

The tenements' duality in blurring the public and private caused middle-class and elite reformers persistent angst. The tenement stood in sharp contrast to the idealized middle-class home with its sharp demarcation of public and private space and its clear boundary between the interior home and the street.[11] Again, Jacob Riis wrote of the tenements' absence of privacy, its halls that functioned as highways, and its failure to provide separate, decent and wholesome living space.[12] As one housing expert recommended to New York's 1894 Tenement House Committee, 'the tenement-house should not be like a portion of the street, but should be like a home; that the doors should be closed'. The Committee specifically found that the crowded condition of the tenements interfered 'with the separateness and sacredness of home life'.[13] A member of the New York City Board of Health testified to the US Senate that '[d]omestic privacy in these [tenement] houses was impossible'. This, he opined, caused bad 'moral effect'.[14] Late-nineteenth-century reformers importantly understood the appropriate home as deeply connected to the nation. As one reformer stated when arguing for state intervention in the area of tenements, '[d]omestic life creates a nation. The corollary is also true: Lack of domestic life unmakes a nation'.[15]

Even the most progressive social reformers engaged in such arguments. Florence Kelley wrote that the family was being destroyed by women and children forced to engage in paid homework. Not only did such homework produce unsanitary commodities that would find their way into the homes of the elite and middle class but they also produced extreme forms of domestic disorder—children uncared for, filthy homes, lazy men content to let their wives struggle, and family disintegration. Kelley continued that the protection of the home required the action of women for men had failed in their responsibility to guard the home. Arguments such as these, although employed for social improvement, served to reify the idea that the home, and women and children in it, needed to remain removed from the market and that only state regulation could adequately protect the home from the market.[16] Thus, appropriate domesticity mapped on to gender. A true home required a woman at its centre, who while engaging in unpaid housework would literally create the home.

[11] See G Wright, *Moralism and the Model Home: Domestic Architecture and Cultural Conflict in Chicago, 1873–1913* (Chicago IL, University of Chicago Press, 1980).

[12] Riis (above n 8) 119.

[13] Report of the Tenement House Committee (Albany NY, James B Lyon State Printer, 1895) 13, 444.

[14] US Education and Labor Committee, *Senate Report Upon Relations Between Capital and Labor* (1884) 650.

[15] ERL Gould, 'The Housing Problem in Great Cities' (1899) *Municipal Affairs* 109.

[16] F Kelley, 'The Invasion of Family Life by Industry' (1909) 34 *Annals of the Academy of Political Science* 90–96.

Resounding contradictions resided in such thinking. One of the great ironies of tenement reform was that in reformers' desires to demarcate the public and private and create what they understood to be the appropriately private home in the tenements, the tenements dwellers' home life became a matter of intense public scrutiny, public discourse and state action. Furthermore, as reformers continued to rally to the cry of domestic privacy, the increasingly public nature of urban life dramatically threatened understandings of private domesticity and private property. For example, the tenement dweller was mobile, unconfined to the 'tenement districts' and situated inside of the city itself. As one report stated, unclean tenement dwellers become 'traveling menaces to the health and comfort of the public'. The Tenement House Committee raised the question of whether the state could require the 'filthy' tenement dweller to bathe and change clothes. It wrote: 'Logically, it is as just to compel a man to refrain from permitting himself to become a nuisance to his neighbors ... as it is to compel him to refrain from permitting his building to become a public nuisance'.[17]

In part, it is this notion of the uncontained and the lack of clear boundaries between the domestic and the public, the poor and the middle class that so perplexed reformers and that resulted in the tenement serving as a fetish and symbol of late-nineteenth-century urban life. Yet it was also such concerns that propelled legislatures to pass increasingly strict tenement laws, and city agencies grew as they began to enforce such laws and regulations. In the process the tenement dweller received both the benefits of better housing and increasingly came under state surveillance.

IV. THE MUNICIPALITY, URBAN CITIZENSHIP, AND THE VOICES OF TENEMENT DWELLERS

By the early 1880s, as the tenement population grew fuelled by immigration from Eastern and Southern Europe, the New York City Department of Health understood one of its principal missions to be the policing of the conditions of tenement houses. It claimed that housing laws were crucial to ensure 'the highest development of the race, in body, mind and in moral character'.[18] As one Department official declared,

> it is the duty of the board of health to look after the habitations of those who are obliged to work with their hands; men whose incomes from their labors are limited ... [T]o make the houses which these people occupy as good in every respect as possible.

[17] Report of the Tenement House Committee (above n 13) 98.

[18] Letter from the Health Department to Mayor Thomas Gilroy (undated), Mayor's Papers, Thomas Gilroy, Health Department, NYMA, Box 1446, folder 83.

The official further stated that while the Board regularly inspected tenements on its own initiative, the houses of the 'well-to-do' received attention only when the Board received a complaint.[19]

Here, a number of points deserve emphasis. Although one can interpret the Board's actions as surveillance and control of the poor and working class, the Board understood its actions as protecting the tenement house dweller, who did not have adequate power to pressure landlords into making repairs. One Board official optimistically stated, 'they [the tenement population] receive [us] with great pleasure, and seem to regard the board of health as a friend who is determined to see that they are taken care of'. Further, the Board's activities clearly constituted state action and interference with market relationships, and it was recognised as such. As one US Senator articulated, the Department provided 'legal supervision' of 'the will of the [tenement] owner'.[20] Here, the Department provided protection to the tenement dweller, in part, by controlling the building owner. If contract represented the will of the parties, the landlord's will was now regulated. Thus the Health Department saw itself as a government agency that assisted the poor and working class in a deeply paternalistic matter and removed the landlord-tenant relationship from the pure realm of contract. As we will see, tenement dwellers had a very different understanding of the Department. Indeed residents used the Department and its powers to assert what they understood to be rights and entitlements—ones which over time actually would be enacted into law.

Although the Board of Health frequently boasted of its efficiency, by the mid-1880s, a host of reformers and city residents continually and publicly criticized it, creating an extraordinary space of public dialogue and legal debate. For instance, in 1887, the *Morning Journal* began to publicize the failure of the Department of Health to condemn numerous tenement buildings, which it claimed were 'unfit for human habitation'. The paper even created and published a 'black list' of the worst buildings in the city. After considerable wrangling, the Department eventually issued orders of repair against 58 houses.

Yet the Department, in correspondence with New York City's mayor, raised the vexing issue of what 'fit for human habitation meant'. As the President of the Board of Health wrote to the mayor, 'What would be unfit for a clean and well-conditioned citizen, is sought and enjoyed by those whose occupation would defile the best structure in New York'.[21] He further highlighted two of the principal questions that would haunt efforts to improve the tenement houses—What basic standard of living were tenement

[19] US Education and Labor Committee (above n 14) 642.
[20] *Ibid.*
[21] Letter from James Bayles to Mayor Abram Hewitt (26 August 1887), Mayor's Papers, Abram Hewitt, Health Department, NYMA, Box 1343.

dwellers entitled to? And was the condition of tenements the result of how tenants lived or how the structure was built? Furthermore where the Health Department equated national citizenship and appropriate domestic citizenship while at times blaming the inhabitants of tenements for their condition, tenement dwellers asserted their own claims to citizenship, and blamed landlords, the Health Department, and their neighbours.

The records of the Health Department and the Mayor's office are replete with the complaints of ordinary individuals disgusted by the condition of the buildings that they or their neighbours occupied.[22] Such complaints repeatedly demanded that the municipal government take action to ameliorate tenement conditions. As such, they represent one instance in the exercise of urban citizenship in which tenement dwellers demanded that the city government enforce what people understood to be their basic rights.[23] Gender played a role in such complaints. When reading late-nineteenth-century letters to various officials of the city, one is immediately struck that most of the writers are male. One major exception exists—the letters of women residents who complained of the intolerable condition of the buildings in which they lived. That women's letters are so prominent underscores women's responsibility for domestic space. More dramatically, it also indicates that poor and working-class women did not hesitate to make demands upon the municipal government and, at times, assert such claims in the language of citizenship.

For example, in 1894 Mrs M Reilly wrote to the Health Department complaining of her neighbour's lack of a sewage system. The cesspool that the landlord had dug caused fetid water to leak into her basement. She closed with the following words: 'The cellar is tenanted by a lot of poor Hebrews without light and air, and the stench is something terrible'.[24] Mrs Reilly called upon the city to exercise its power to force the neighbouring landlord to connect his building to the sewer system as required by law. But her complaint about the 'Hebrews' again elided the question of whether the problem was with the building or its occupants.

Another writer, who signed her letter 'A working girl', complained of overcrowding, filth and the lack of water in the building in which she dwelled.[25] A woman who identified herself only as a 'Poor wash woman'

[22] The Health Department received 23,455 complaints from citizens in 1892, and 22,046 in 1893. The Department found about 75% of these complaints valid. Report of the Tenement House Committee (above n 13) 485.

[23] Thomas Bender writes that in the 1890s intellectuals developed the concept of municipal citizenship and initiated a social politics grounded in the city. Through these citizens' letters, we can see the actual functioning of municipal citizenship. T Bender, 'Intellectuals, Cities, and Citizenship in the United States: The 1890s and 1990s' (1999) 3 *Citizenship Studies* 203.

[24] Letter from Mrs M Reilly to Mayor Thomas Gilroy (undated), Mayor's Papers, Thomas Gilroy, General Correspondence, NYMA, Box 1450, folder 121.

[25] Letter from A Working Girl to Mayor Abram Hewitt (1 July 1888), Mayor's Papers, Abram Hewitt, Health Department, NYMA, Box 1345.

wrote of the stench of a water closet, claiming, 'it is enough to kill you and we women can't wash in safety'.[26] In both of these letters, the women chose to identify themselves through their work, rather than any familial relationship, and implicitly claimed that as female workers they were entitled to live and work in clean dwellings with plumbing that functioned. Their self identification as working women served as a badge of citizenship, allowing them to make claims upon the city. In fact, they understood that the city could and should remedy such conditions.

Other letters were written anonymously by individuals or groups of tenants.[27] One letter from residents who identified themselves only as 'Six Sufferers' complained of three tenement houses from which 'the most terrible stench imaginable ... arises from the water closet'. The letter continued: 'It is constantly stopped up, which in this hot weather stagnates and the stench arising from the same ... is something which cannot be explained in words'. The 'Sufferers' claimed that such buildings violated the law requiring a sewer system connection, and demanded redress, asserting that the landlord 'would sooner let a poor human being perish then spend a few hundred dollars'.[28] These tenement dwellers clearly understood that the conditions in which they lived were deeply connected to the market.

Another writer to the mayor, who simply called himself 'a Tenant', complained of the lack of access to water which the law required. He wrote: 'the tenants on the top floors have to go in the yard for water and they spill it on the stairs and it freezes'. The condition of the yard and the toilets, he claimed, was filthy and he attributed his family's illness to the building's lack of water and cleanliness.[29] Unlike certain middle-class reformers and government officials, this writer had no doubt that his family's ill health was a result of the conditions of the building and its crucial lack of water, not the family's habits.

Numerous letter writers chose to identify themselves simply as citizens. In this language of citizenship, these writers expressed their understanding that they were members of a democracy, that municipal government was there to serve them, and that they had a right and entitlement to live in an habitable environment. For instance, a letter from a person who identified him or herself as 'A Citizen' contained the following: 'know [*sic*] water is to be had on floor till after 4 and sometimes 10 o'clock at night and the

[26] Letter from a Poor Wash Woman to Mayor Abram Hewitt (August 1887), Mayor's Papers, Abram Hewitt, Health Department, NYMA, Box 1344.

[27] The Health Department, in 1894, estimated that approximately 50% of the complaints that it received were from anonymous complainants. Report of the Tenement House Committee (above n 13) 484.

[28] Letter from Six Sufferers to Mayor Hugh Grant (undated), Mayor's Papers, Hugh Grant, Health Department, NYMA, Box 1393, folder 137.

[29] Letter from a Tenant to Mayor Hugh Grant (14 January 1889), Mayor's Papers, Hugh Grant, Health Department, NYMA, Box 1392, folder 131.

water closet is in a bad condition, also please half [*sic*] this sien to as soon as posibel'.[30] 'A Citizen of New York' complained of a house in 'terrible condition, filth, bad odor, toilets is broke and it is a regular cholera in the house'.[31]

This language of citizenship was not limited to men; rather it broadly encompassed men and women. In 1887, the Mayor received a short letter from a group of women complaining of pigeons and the dirt on the roof of their tenement building where they hung clothes to dry. Although the letter was anonymous, the women concluded that if the roof were cleaned it would 'oblige a great many citizens'.[32] A letter from a person who signed as 'One who is hoping for your good action in this matter', complained that the poor plumbing and stench in the building was making a number of children ill and stated that he expected that the mayor 'will give me my rights'.[33] These writers with their creative spelling understood themselves to be citizens of the metropolis, entitled to make demands on municipal government to enforce its own laws and to provide what they understood to be their basic rights. These letters did not plead, petition, or beseech but rather demanded enforcement of the laws as they understood them.

Perhaps even more surprising, the Health Department actually responded to these complaints. On a regular basis, the Department informed the mayor's office of the action that it had taken to remedy such complaints. Often the Department issued orders against the landlord to clean the premises, remedy structural defects, and supply adequate water.[34] In the event that such landlords failed to comply, the Health Department had the power to issue orders requiring that the premises be vacated.[35] Thus, tenants who complained about inadequate accommodation faced the prospect of losing their accommodations altogether. Furthermore, enforcement of the laws was most stringent when conditions in the tenements seemed to pose a threat to the health of the middle classes and elites outside the tenements.

As tenement residents sought to improve their living conditions, various elite and middle-class reformers launched their own campaigns. For example, the Working Women's Society, composed primarily of 'self supporting

30 Letter from A Citizen to Mayor Abram Hewitt (2 June 1888), Mayor's Papers, Abram Hewitt, Health Department, NYMA, Box 1345.

31 Letter from A Citizen of New York to Mayor Abram Hewitt (19 September 1888), Mayor's Papers, Abram Hewitt, Health Department, NYMA, Box 1345.

32 Letter from Anonymous to Mayor Abram Hewitt (25 July 1887), Mayor's Papers, Abram Hewitt, Health Department, NYMA, Box 1344.

33 Letter from One who is Hoping to Mayor Abram Hewitt (30 August 1887), Mayor's Papers, Abram Hewitt, Health Department, NYMA, Box 1343.

34 See, eg, letters from James C Bayles to Mayor Abram Hewitt (2 September 1887), (13 September 1887), (19 September 1887), (18 June 1888), (11 July 1888), (17 October 1888), Mayor's Papers, Abram Hewitt, Health Department, NYMA, Boxes 1343–1345.

35 New York Laws of 1882 (ch 410) s 659.

women', reported to the Board of Health numerous tenement violations.[36] They closely followed the Department's actions in connection with such complaints and continued writing to the Board, demanding results until their complaints were adequately addressed. In addition, they conducted an investigation of numerous tenements on Mulberry Street ultimately putting together a short report on their findings, which repeatedly mentioned the filthy condition of water closets and their proximity to tenement manufacturing establishments.[37] In emphasizing such physical proximity, the report suggested that the goods manufactured in such spaces possessed the possibility of carrying the foulness of the tenement water closet throughout the metropolis via the manufactured commodity. Again in 1893, the organization inspected two square miles of the tenement districts in search of violations of the tenement house laws and with the specific intent of testing the laws. It eventually filed 150 complaints with the Board of Health. The Board, however, stated that it could not bring legal action on the complaints, as the tenements had been built before passage of the 1887 tenement law.[38]

V. THE PUBLIC WELFARE AND PRIVATE PROPERTY: THE CONSTITUTIONALITY OF TENEMENT REGULATION IN THE COURTS

In many cases involving tenement dwellers' complaints and the outcry of reformers, the Department found its power significantly limited. In 1892, an intermediate New York appellate court ruled that a crucial 1887 law requiring the supply of water to each floor within a tenement house was unconstitutional.[39] Although involving only this one provision of the tenement laws, the Department believed that if challenged other provisions too might be struck down as unconstitutional. Tenement residents, the mayor,

[36] On the Working Women's Society, see EA Payne, *Reform, Labor and Feminism: Margaret Dreier Robins and the Women's Trade Union League* (Urbana IL, University of Illinois Press, 1988) 24, 28; J Waugh, *Unsentimental Reformer: The Life of Josephine Shaw Lowell* (Cambridge MA, Harvard University Press, 1997) 197–8; E Boris, *Home to Work: Motherhood and the Politics of Industrial Homework in the United States* (Cambridge, Cambridge University Press, 1994) 45, 85.

[37] Working Women's Society, Report of the Tenement House Committee of the Working Women's Society (New York, Freytag Printing Co, 1892).

[38] 'Special Correspondence from the Working Women's Society in New York', *The Woman's Tribune* (15 July 1893).

[39] Section 663 of the Consolidation Act as amended by ch 84 of the Laws of New York of 1887 provided in relevant part: 'Every such house erected after May 14, 1887 ... shall have Croton or other water furnished in sufficient quantity at one or more places on each floor, occupied or intended to be occupied by one or more families; and all tenement houses shall be furnished with a like supply of water by the owners thereof whenever they shall be directed to do so by the board of health'.

the Health Department, landlords, and a wide-variety of reformers understood the importance of the outcome of the case to municipal regulation.

On 20 March 1891, the Health Department served a summons on Trinity Church, New York's largest landlord, requiring it to renovate certain tenements by installing appliances to deliver water to each floor.[40] The water supply for families at two of Trinity's tenements consisted only of a fire hydrant in the yard.[41] To obtain water for cooking, house cleaning and bathing, tenants had to carry water into their apartments in buckets or tubs. Instead of making such renovations, Trinity challenged the constitutionality of the law.

In 1891 there was no New York precedent that directly addressed the constitutionality of tenement laws and a significant question existed as to whether such laws constituted a taking of property by the state in violation of the Fourteenth Amendment.[42] As the Comptroller of Trinity stated,

> I am satisfied that [the law] was an extreme exercise of the police power ... We determined that this decision had better be decided [by the courts], and we considered that it was more in the interest of the tenants, and a more sanitary rule not to have [the water] on all floors ... In many of the old houses the tenants are dirty and careless, and if there is water through the house they will throw all their slops in the sink.

The Comptroller further stated that for seven dollars a month, tenants could not expect landlords to provide all modern amenities.[43] Earlier cases in fact pointed to the New York courts' hostility to state regulation of the market and its broad interpretation of what constituted vested property rights.[44] Providing water to each floor in a tenement house required substantial and expensive renovations for houses that lacked adequate plumbing. The Tenement House Committee of 1894 found that landlords who did not provide water and failed to make repairs had a much higher profit margin than those who maintained their buildings in good condition.

On appeal, in a unanimous decision, the New York Court of Common Pleas found the statute unconstitutional. In hyperbolic rhetoric, the judges

[40] For a discussion of Trinity Church's property holdings, see JN Day, *Urban Castles: Tenement Housing and Landlord Activism in New York City, 1890–1943* (New York, Columbia University Press, 1999); E Blackmar, *Manhattan for Rent 1785–1850* (Ithaca NY, Cornell University Press, 1989).

[41] Trial Transcript, *Health Department of the City of New York v Trinity Church* (25 November 1891), Line 29, New York County Clerks Office, Old Case Division.

[42] The Massachusetts courts had found that a law requiring dwelling houses to have sewer connections and water closets was constitutional. See *Commonwealth v Roberts*, 155 Mass 281 (1891).

[43] Letter from the New York Churchmen (22 December 1894) in *Trinity Church Report as to Sanitary Condition of Tenements of the Church* (New York, Evening Post Job Printing House, 1895) 3, 5.

[44] In Jacobs, the New York Court of Appeals found unconstitutional a law that prohibited the making of cigars in tenement houses. *In Re Jacobs*, 98 NY 98 (1885).

wrote that the case concerned the gravest question of the 'essential securities of property', and that the statute constituted a taking of property for private use, since it was 'solely for the benefit of the tenants whom defendant is compelled ... to accommodate'.[45] The Court rejected the argument that the act was a legitimate exercise of the police power, finding it self-evident that there was no evidence that the lack of water on tenement floors affected the health of its occupants. The Court further stated: 'There is no necessity for legislative compulsion on a landlord to distribute water ... since, if tenants require it, self-interest and the rivalry of competition are sufficient to secure it'.[46] As a final flourish, the Court concluded with the following:

> The postulate upon which the legislation in question proceeds is the duty of government to exercise a paternal protectorate over the people; whereas the distinguishing characteristic of the American commonwealth is that it restricts the operation of government to the narrowest possible sphere; and reposes upon individual intelligence and effort for the development of a free and fruitful civilization. A conclusion contrary to the present decision would involve the essential principle of that species of socialism under the regime of which the individual disappears, and is absorbed by a collective being called the 'state'—a principle utterly repugnant to the spirit of our political system, and necessarily fatal to our form of liberty.[47]

The court's opinion adopted wholesale the rhetoric of laissez-faire economics. Such a rationale was particularly dangerous as it could be used to strike down most of New York's tenement house laws. The court reasoned that if tenants wanted indoor water, they would either bargain for it with their landlords or move to a residence with indoor water. The legislation, therefore, was invalid and ineffectual, because it interfered with the invisible hand of the market. The court also viewed the state's police power narrowly, and articulated the proper role of the state as abstaining from regulation which would interfere with an unfettered market. Here the welfare of society rested upon the individual's unregulated actions in the market. Further, government could not intrude to promote the welfare of the poor at the expense of the propertied.

The Board of Health appealed the intermediate court's decision to the New York Court of Appeals, New York's highest court. Trinity then had the misfortune of arguing the case to the New York Court of Appeals shortly after the Tenement House Committee of 1894 had finished its impressive investigation of the tenement house situation and presented its report to the New York legislature. Its findings included the assessment that over 32,800 tenement apartments were either dirty or very dirty, and 26,000 tenement

[45] *Health Department of the City of New York v Rector of Trinity Church*, 17 NYS 510, 513 (Ct Common Pleas, 1892).

[46] *Ibid*, 515.

[47] *Ibid*.

residents were 'unclean'.[48] The report claimed that the condition of immigrants' homes and their very bodies necessitated immediate state action.

Testimony given to the Tenement House Committee by some middle-class reformers such as Henry Rice of Hebrew Charities focused upon the dire need for water in the tenements while recognizing that such laws might interfere with vested property rights and constitutional concepts of liberty. Sanitary engineer Charles Wingate opined: '[W]ater should be provided inside the tenement-house, and hydrants in the yards abolished; it seems to me inhuman to oblige these people to carry up water to all the floors and carry the waste downstairs again'.[49] Wingate further saw the issue of water as specifically connected to making tenement dwellings private homes divorced from the street and public space.

Yet if water, in part, served to create a privatized home delineated from the public, how, as Trinity argued, could it be understood as benefiting the entire public rather than just the tenement dweller? As Trinity argued, '[w]here legislation destroys or impairs the property of the citizen or interferes with his rights, it is void, unless it is for the *public* good, not merely for individual ease and comfort, or the benefit of one class'.[50] Here, Trinity claimed that only the tenement dweller received any benefit.

Although gender-neutral on its face, the law, in actuality, not only benefited tenement dwellers as a whole but particularly affected women tenement dwellers. As some of the letters from women to the mayor and the Department of Health demonstrate, women required water to fulfill their domestic roles. Women were primarily responsible for carrying pails of water up dark and narrow stairs; they needed water to clean apartments, scrub floors, cook for families and boarders, and bathe children. Perhaps most difficult of all, women needed water and a clean space to wash clothing which required numerous trips up and down stairs. That water carrying was a woman's task was commonly recognized at the time. Although women tenement dwellers were seldom referred to in the 1894 Tenement House Committee Report, when discussing the carrying of water, the water carrier was often identified as a woman. For example, the Committee wrote: 'A woman going to the sink to fill her pail with water or to empty it in refuse water, is doubly likely to spill the contents'.[51]

As the case reached the Court of Appeals, two important questions emerged. Did regulation that required a positive expenditure of funds constitute an uncompensated taking of property by the state in violation of the Constitution? Secondly, could a regulation be used to benefit some

[48] Report of the Tenement House Committee (n 13) 101.
[49] *Ibid*, 444.
[50] Respondent's Brief, *Health Department of the City of New York v The Rector, Church Wardens of Trinity Church*, New York Court of Appeals Record, vol 13 (1895) 13.
[51] Report of the Tenement House Committee (above n 13) 93.

part of the population—in this case residents of tenements—at the expense of landlords or was the legislation constitutional because it benefited the entire urban public?

The Court ruled that legislation requiring a property owner to incur an expenditure was constitutional as long as the expenditure and the improvements required were reasonable. The Court further set forth its view of property, stating: 'There are sometimes necessary expenses which inevitably grow out of the use to which we may put our property, and which we must incur, whether voluntarily or else under the direction of the legislature'.[52] Thus, the Court found that in this case the expense required to furnish water was reasonable, given the legislature's determination of the importance of water to promote health. Yet, there was no evidence introduced at trial as to whether water delivered to tenement floors protected health. Rather, the Court based its decision upon its own construction of the relationship between the home, the market and public life. The court's understanding is worth repeating and analysing:

> [T]he free use of water, especially during the summer months, tends towards the healthful condition of the body ... The supply of water to the general public in a city has become not only a luxury, but an absolute necessity for the maintenance of the public health and safety ... The water is brought into the city so that it may be used in every house and building and, although we ... admit that no health law could practically be enforced which should provide that every individual inhabitant of the tenement houses should use water, yet we think it perfectly clear that facilities for the use of water will almost necessarily be followed by its actual use in larger quantities and more frequently than would the case be without such facilities, and to the great benefit of the health of the occupants of such houses. Those occupants require it even more than their more favored brethren living in airy, larger, more spacious and luxurious apartments. Their health is [a] matter of grave public concern ... That dirt, filth, nastiness in general, are great promoters of disease, that they breed pestilence and contagion, sickness and death, cannot be successfully denied. There is scarcely a dissent from the general belief on the part of all who have studied the disease that cholera is essentially a filth disease ... That opportunities, conveniences for the use of water in these tenement houses will unquestionably tend towards and be followed by more cleanly living on the part of their occupants of those houses.
>
> The tenement house in New York is a subject of very great thought and anxiety to the residents of that city. The numbers of people that live in such houses, their size, their ventilation, their cleanliness, their liability to fires, the exposure of their occupants to contagious diseases, and the consequent spread of contagion throughout the city and country, the tendencies to immorality and crime where there is a close packing of human beings of the lower order of intelligence and morals, all these are subjects which must arouse the attention of the legislator ... in order that

[52] *Ibid*, 42.

> such laws are enacted as shall directly tend to the improvement of health, safety and morals of those men and women that are found in such houses ... [W]here it is obvious that without the convenience of an appliance of the supply of water on the various floors of these tenement houses, there will be scarcely any but the most limited and scanty use of the water itself, which must be carried from the yards below, and when we must admit that the free use of water tends directly and immediately towards the sustaining of the health of the individual and the prevention of disease arising from filth either of the person or in the surrounding habitation, then we must conclude that it is more than a mere matter of convenience in the use of water which is involved in the decision of this case. The absence of the water tends directly towards the breeding of disease, and its presence is healthful and humanizing.[53]

The decision is remarkable on a number of levels. The Court of Appeals conceptualized the urban public as a unity and postulated that the health of the urban poor could not be separated from the welfare of the city as a whole. The Court understood that the poor immigrant body could not be segregated to protect the health of others. The poor were part of the city itself and the dense urban landscape created at certain and specific moments a sense of a holistic society.

In upholding the law, the Court removed water and domestic plumbing from the market. Water for domestic use, like the home as well as women's housework within the home, stood outside of the market. Water was to be untainted by commercial relationships, and its very purity could cleanse the poor and urban domestic space. The Court sought to de-commodify water such that water which flowed into the home was cleansed of the crassness and self-interest of the market. Yet in the Court's very attempt to exempt water from market exchange, it reified water as a commodity fetish. A commodity fetish is an object that substitutes for a social relation between people. As Anne McClintock writes about the role of soap in the late nineteenth century, soap was a spectacular commodity fetish even though it was promoted as the 'icon of nonfetishistic rationality'.[54] Like soap, water removed the dirt off the labourer, transformed the rich and the poor into brethren, and erased the capitalist relations that created the tenement house and class itself. The market-driven relationship between landlord and tenant was transformed into the relationship between tenement dweller and water.

The Court, like various reformers, also conflated understandings between the public and the private such that the intimate became public in order to produce the appropriately private domestic. Here the most personal acts of the tenement dweller—the washing of his or her body, the cleaning of the

[53] *The Health Department of the City of New York v The Rector, Church Wardens and Vestrymen of Trinity Church*, 145 NY 32, 33–7 (1895).

[54] McClintock (above n 10) 208.

rooms in which he or she lived became part of the court's public discourse and compelled state action. The condition of the tenement dweller's body and living space was defined as a matter of concern for the entire city. On one level, the home, the theoretical site of the private, became the crux of the public, necessitating government action and further distancing the idealised private home of the middle class and the immigrant abode of the tenement dweller. On another level, however, the tenement home of the urban poor now possessed the possibility of resembling the theoretically clean, privatised home of the middle class. In opening this path, the Court endowed water in the dwelling place with almost magical qualities and transformative possibilities. In the Court's words, it possessed not only the power to wash away filth but also the power to 'humanize'. Access to water, within the space of the home, now became a legal right as tenement dwellers themselves understood it to be, necessary to the welfare of the entire city.

The Court's decision upholding the law was profoundly important within New York, as it meant that the state had the ability to regulate tenements. Furthermore, although the New York Court of Appeals was understood to be an immensely conservative court that readily protected property and private interests, it articulated an understanding in which water and its ready accessibility were related to and crucial for the general welfare of the city. Indeed in the current world in which water is becoming privatized, resulting in the poor losing access to clean water, this opinion seems even the more remarkable.[55]

VI. THE GREAT TOILET DEBATE

The next great constitutional challenge to tenement regulation arose out of the regulation of tenement toilets. As *Trinity* focused upon the cleanliness of the immigrant body and dwelling place, the *Moeschen* case scrutinized the waste such bodies expelled and the process of its removal. In 1900, the Tenement House Commission was formed by the Governor of New York to once again study the tenement problem and to draft possible legislation.[56] In 1901, the Commission submitted its report and found that school sinks posed a serious danger to the occupants of tenements and their neighbours. School sinks were outhouses with toilets that did not flush. Rather the caretaker of a building would open a valve, which allowed water to rush into the bottom of the pipes, where matter collected, to flush it out.

[55] In recent years, municipal water is being increasingly privatized and water for home consumption redefined to be explicitly a commodity. It is only within the last 20 years that New York City began installing water meters. See, eg, M Specter, 'The Last Drop', *The New Yorker* (23 October 2006).

[56] See RW Deforest and L Veiller (eds), *The Tenement House Problem, Including the Report of the New York State Tenement House Commission of 1900* (1903).

In the early twentieth century, there were over 9,000 school sinks in tenements. As an earlier report stated,

> In many all cleaning process has been so long omitted that foecal matter has been found piled high above the seats. Tenants then turn to other portions of the privy houses and the result is a condition of indescribable filthiness, dangerous to the health and demoralizing to those brought in contact with it.[57]

As articulated, the question of the proper type of toilet was defined as both an issue of health and morals.

The Commission recommended that all school sinks in tenements be removed and replaced with water closets either in yards or indoors. In 1901, the legislature passed the Tenement House Act, which broke new ground in requiring that tenements have adequate windows, proper ventilation, fire escapes, square footage, and toilets.[58] The law mandated that all school sinks be removed, and that one water closet be supplied for every two families. The law applied only to tenement houses and allowed school sinks in non-domestic settings such as factories and schools to remain in place. Such exceptions point to the privileged place and emphasis on the domestic. The Tenement House Department asserted that the water-closet law 'was one of the most important steps ever taken in the sanitary progress of the city'.[59]

This new law reversed an 1870 statute requiring that privy vaults be replaced with what were then believed to be more sanitary school sinks. Thus the 1901 law represented a reversal of prior thinking by sanitary experts about school sinks. In fact, the renovations that the law required were so extensive that landlords of numerous tenements chose to tear their buildings down rather than attempt the renovations. Substantial evidence exists that while the law allowed water closets to be built outdoors, this option was all but impossible given New York City's weather conditions. The practical effect of the law therefore was to require indoor water closets.[60] In many tenement houses this necessitated converting valuable apartment space into bathrooms.

The condition of toilets was a constant source of consternation to reformers and tenement residents alike. For example, one letter to the mayor from a writer who identified him or herself as a 'Lover of Cleanliness and a Boarder', complained of the water closets for three buildings. This writer stated that six families and boarders lived in each of the buildings but

[57] Report of the Tenement House Committee (above n 13) 97.

[58] For a history of the 1901 Act, see R Lubove, *The Progressives and the Slums: Tenement House Reform in New York City, 1890–1917* (Pittsburgh, University of Pittsburgh Press, 1962).

[59] *Ibid*, 66.

[60] First Report of the Tenement House Department (above n 7) 69.

that only two water closets were 'in a properly clean condition'.[61] Another anonymous tenant dweller complained that,

> the house keeper clean[s] the closets about every three months and then the contents are put in the yard and left there for about (5) hours and then wash[ed] away all over the yard which r[a]ise[s] a very bad stench.[62]

Letter after letter complained of the foul condition of school sinks. Such letters once again demanded that the mayor and the Board of Health use its powers to remedy such conditions and they are poignant testaments to the misery associated with the most mundane moments of tenement life. Like the larger tenement question, where residents complained of filth and the lack of outhouse repairs, middle-class reformers located the lack of privacy as the source of the problem. Lillian Wald, founder of the Henry Street settlement, understood the lack of indoor toilets as an affront to decency and privacy. She wrote of walking across a courtyard on the Lower East Side, 'where open and unscreened closets were promiscuously used by men and women'.[63]

Stepping beyond the material and quotidian of stench, excrement, and neglectful landlords, the modern toilet also functioned on a symbolic level. As Anne McClintock recognizes, '[t]he Victorian bathroom [was] the inner most sanctuary of domestic hygiene and by extension the private temple of public regeneration'.[64] Lillian Wald, while searching for an apartment for herself and a companion on the Lower East Side, considered an indoor bathroom a necessity, writing: 'We set to work immediately to find quarters—no easy task, as we clung to the civilization of a bathroom, and according to legend ... there were only two bathrooms in tenement houses below Fourteenth Street'.[65] The Tenement House Department considered the school sink 'a relic of barbarism'.[66] Thus for reformers, the well-maintained and modern toilet carried with it the aura of proper civilization which necessitated that the bathroom be a deeply private and cleansed space.

Yet, in turn-of-the-century New York City the question was whether the toilets of the poor should be public or private and whether the privatized and indoor toilet would enhance or decrease the morality of the tenement dweller and the general welfare of the city. The legal battles that ensued over the legislation would be fought over such contested terrains.

[61] Letter from a Lover of Cleanliness to Mayor Thomas Gilroy (26 July 1893), Mayor's Papers, Thomas Gilroy, Health Department, NYMA, Box 1446, folder 88.

[62] Letter from an Anonymous Tenant Dweller to Mayor Hugh Grant (January 14, 1889), Mayor's Papers, Hugh Grant, Health Department, NYMA, Box 1392, folder 131.

[63] LD Wald, *The House on Henry Street* (New York, Dover Publications, Inc, 1915) 5–6.

[64] McClintock (above n 10) 214.

[65] Wald (above n 63) 9.

[66] First Report of the Tenement House Department (above n 7) 61.

In 1903, Katie Moeschen received a summons for failure to replace school sinks and install water closets in a tenement that she owned. Although it is unclear why Moeschen was chosen as a test case, it is clear that hers was financed by an association of real estate owners.[67] Perhaps Moeschen was chosen because her school sinks were relatively clean and she was a small landlord, holding only one building.[68] Perhaps she was chosen because she was a woman and her husband a plumber who testified to flushing out the school sinks personally every 24 hours. For whatever reason Moeschen was selected, the real estate owners association spared no expense, demonstrating the importance of this law to landlords.

Moeschen's lawyers presented the legal question as follows: 'Can the legislature require you to destroy that which it required you to create, unless it be established that the thing required to be destroyed is a nuisance *per se*'.[69] Furthermore, the defence repeatedly argued that the extensive and expensive renovations required by the law essentially destroyed any equity that landlords held in their buildings.[70] This, they argued, constituted a taking in violation of the Fourteenth Amendment to the US Constitution.

Although much of the trial testimony involved technical questions of sanitary engineering, issues of morality and gender also shaped the discourse and arguments. Attorneys for Moeschen had a woman occupant from each apartment submit an affidavit (obviously written by the attorneys since they were exact replicas of one another) stating that they would find an indoor toilet unsanitary. Such affidavits indicate that even the attorneys who argued the case understood that the household was within a woman's sphere, that such legislation especially affected women, and that women's opinions regarding household sanitation might be persuasive.

Experts for the defendant also argued that the private bathroom would allow young men and women a space for sexual encounters. Furthermore certain bathroom configurations created passage from one apartment to another, once again with ominous possibilities of sexual liaisons. Here middle-class conceptions of private domestic space were transformed into dangerous enclaves of working-class sexuality. In contrast to creating dangerous spaces of privacy, the defence argued that school sinks located in a communal yard with only semi-private petitions permitted residents to see

[67] R Deforest and L Veiller (eds), *The Tenement House Problem*, vol 1 (New York, McMillian Co, 1903) xvii.

[68] Unlike other tenement owners, Moeschen did not engage in the process of sub-leasing the building to a lessee who was responsible for managing the building and collecting rents. Because the lessee was paid from proceeds, sub-leasing created some of the worst tenement abuses. See Day (above n 41) 47–50.

[69] *Ibid.*

[70] *Ibid.*

the comings and goings of bathroom users, allowing them to police illicit activities.[71]

In the same way that school sinks preserved sexual purity, the defendant's lawyer also sought to demonstrate that they preserved domestic purity. Defence experts testified that odours would arise from indoor bathrooms, permeate kitchens, and pollute domestic space. They further sought to cast doubt on immigrant women's ability to appropriately clean toilets. In fact, the potential failure of such women's housekeeping skills was a relatively wide-spread concern even among reformers who worked for passage of the law. As one publication stated about the new tenement laws, 'the hard fought fight at Albany is but half a victory and the chance to really live is lost—lost because the tenement woman does not know how to make use of her opportunity'.[72] Here, the defence attempted to use these reformers' arguments, meant to justify the need for the training of immigrant women in domestic hygiene, against the reforms themselves. Thus for proponents and opponents of the law, immigrant women's imagined failures as housekeepers threatened to undermine (and in the defendant's case were fatal) to any benefit the law conferred.

Out of court, the attorney for the real estate owners association later argued that responsible landlords had built or purchased buildings in reliance on the old law in part to ensure that their widows and orphans would have a continuing stream of income which the new law would destroy. Far from endangering the sanctity of the home, he argued, the old law protected and provided support to the landlord's family.[73]

Where the defence focused on the unclean and immoral tenement dweller, the government attempted to make the connection between the tenement toilet and the larger health and welfare of the city, by focusing upon the tenement worker, and the role of the commodity in the stream of commerce. For example, one government witness (echoing earlier reports of the Working Women's Society) testified about filthy school sinks situated next to macaroni factories and bakeries. The witness stated: 'I have taken a great many pictures of sweat shops where girls worked within three feet and a half of the open doors of school sinks'.[74] Here, the contaminated commodity of the tenement, which would be consumed within other people's homes, carried with it the threat of contagion. Such contagion functioned on literal and metaphorical levels gesturing towards germs but also the moral contagion of an exploitative capitalism that brought women into factories to

[71] Trial Transcript, *Tenement House Department v Moeschen*, New York Court of Appeals Record 50 (1904) 32.

[72] *The Model Flat* (1903), np, Lillian Wald Papers, Columbia University, Reel 20.

[73] National Housing Association, 'The Tenant's Responsibility' vol II, (April 1912) 154.

[74] Trial Transcript, *Moeschen* (above n 71) 97.

produce commodities for home consumption thereby threatening the homes of the rich and poor alike.

On appeal, the Court of Appeals held that the statute clearly promoted the general health and was therefore a proper and constitutional exercise of the police power. The Court also stated that the financial burden placed upon an individual was irrelevant, given that 'it is not the hardship of the individual case that determines the question, but rather the general scope and effect of the legislation'.[75] Quite correctly, the defence attorney pointed out that the Court's opinion was 'absolute', 'far-reaching' and 'novel'.[76] Years later, the attorney remained perplexed regarding how a law could be constitutional that prohibited the existence of school sinks that earlier legislation had specifically required and that landlords had relied upon.[77] Yet, the Court specifically elevated the welfare of the public over any hardship caused to an individual's property interest. Here the undomesticated waste of the tenement dweller (by its very public-ness) threatened the health of the city and could therefore be regulated.

In *Trinity* and *Moeschen*, water, with its cleansing properties, and plumbing, which could instantly eliminate excrement, literally and figuratively had the ability to purify the home. By requiring the landlord to supply water and indoor toilet facilities, whether or not the tenement dweller bargained (paid) for it, the Court protected the domestic sphere from the commercial standards of the market place. The tenement dwelling moved a bit closer to becoming a 'home' which was pure, uncorrupted by the marketplace, sanitised by water, and a bit more private and cared for by an individual housekeeper. Yet in its very process of making such a ruling and its willingness to find the sanitary conditions of the tenement and the tenement dweller a matter of public concern—indeed a question of the welfare of the entire city—the Court also collapsed the distance between the private home, the public, and the state.

Further, the *Moeschen* case was significant for by implication it upheld the 1901 Tenement House Act, which radically imposed some of the strictest regulations of tenements in the country, including a prohibition on rooms without windows. Such legislation was one corner stone in creating a larger welfare state for a number of reasons. First, the rationale for such legislation was the clear understanding that tenement regulation was necessary for the general welfare of the tenement dweller, tenement districts, and the city as a whole. Secondly, such laws, as landlords frequently complained, functioned to indirectly redistribute wealth. Repairs and renovations on

[75] *The Tenement House Department of the City of New York v Moeschen*, 179 NY 325, 329 (1904).

[76] E Gould and A Bloch, 'The Tenants Responsibility by Emily Dinwiddie' (1912) 2 *Proceedings of the Academy of Political Science in the City of New York* 152, 158.

[77] *Ibid.*

tenements had to be paid for by landlords and such costs reduced landlords' profits while benefiting tenement residents.

The 1901 legislation also created the Tenement House Department, whose mission it was to enforce the new tenement house law. This was a significant move towards the creation of a bureaucratic regulatory welfare state—one in which specialized departments were charged with the enforcement of particular regulations and laws. The Department also broke ground as the first New York municipal department to hire women inspectors; nine in all. Unlike other areas of the developing regulatory state where women's jurisdiction was over other women, such as the case of women probation officers, no such separation occurred in the Tenement House Department. Rather the Department boasted that the women inspectors performed the exact same work as male inspectors.[78] The appointment of women inspectors served in part to recognize the significant role that elite and middle-class women were already playing in connection with tenement house reform. Further it was an appropriate role for women as it was connected to the home thus creating a site of what might be called 'public domesticity'.[79]

VII. MIDDLE-CLASS WOMEN, SETTLEMENT HOUSES, AND THE POLICING OF TENEMENT HOUSES

As will be seen, the role of elite and middle-class women in helping to construct welfare states during the late nineteenth and early twentieth centuries is quite remarkable given their lack of civil, political and legal rights. In the years between *Moeschen* and *Trinity*, as tenements became primary sites of public discourse about the city, state regulation, and home life, elite and middle-class women began to play an extraordinary role in connection with the enforcement of tenement house laws. In doing so, they essentially became quasi-state actors, who participated in the creation of a regulatory welfare state. One particularly important location of such women's influence and power were the settlement houses of New York City.[80]

[78] *Tenement House Department Annual Report* (1903).

[79] For a discussion of public domesticity see AG Richter, *Home on the Rails: Women, the Railroad, and the Rise of Public Domesticity* (Chapel Hill NC, University of North Carolina Press, 2005).

[80] Settlement houses were residences established by middle-class and elite women and men in poor urban immigrant neighbourhoods. Settlement workers often lived in the house for some period of time. The primary and secondary literature on settlement houses is vast. A small selection includes M Carson, *Settlement Folk: Social Thought and the American Settlement Movement, 1885–1930* (Chicago IL, University of Chicago Press, 1990); MK Simkhovitch, *The Settlement Primer* (Boston MA, National Federation of Settlements 1926); Wald (above n 63); AF Davis, *Spearheads for Reform: The Social Settlements and the Progressive Movement, 1890–1914* (New York, Oxford University Press, 1967).

Two of New York's most important settlement houses, College Settlement and Henry Street, were established by elite and middle-class women in the midst of immigrant tenement neighbourhoods. Settlement houses with their bourgeois furnishings and refined manners, in part, were meant to exhibit an appropriate domesticity in contrast to the imagined chaos of immigrant tenement life. Many settlement houses never tired of creating model tenement house apartments, demonstrating to immigrant women an appropriate interior and how the proper American wife created the sanitized American home.

To varying degrees, part of the settlement geist was an understanding that a proper domestic space would itself create American citizens. Yet settlement houses, which were open to all who lived in the neighbourhood, while also providing living space to often single middle-class women settlement workers, shared with tenements the porous boundaries between the public and private. Where settlement workers might hope to impress upon immigrant women the importance of an American household with American standards of cleanliness, housekeeping, food preparation, childrearing and privacy, in actuality they further blurred the distinction between the public and the private, domestic space and work space. Yet settlement workers ultimately became comfortable with an intense ambiguity as to where such lines could be drawn.

What is crucial to understand is that as the influence and activities of settlement houses grew, they became deeply connected to municipal government. Settlement houses often created model programmes such as those that provided free and pure milk, kindergarten classes, recreation, public baths, home nursing services and health care within the schools. It is no coincidence that so many of these programmes involved children, as women settlement workers were able to assert jurisdiction most easily over those issues understood to be within a women's sphere of concern.[81] Many of these programmes and initiatives eventually would be taken over by the municipal government.

A significant and early point of contact between the settlement houses and the city developed within the context of the policing and regulation of tenement houses. This makes sense, as the settlement houses were located in the heart of the tenement district. Furthermore as tenements implicated home life, women settlement workers could claim such issues as within their purview. The tenement house population used the settlements to report violations of tenement laws that settlement workers then would pass along to city agencies. In many instances, the settlement workers used their contacts to press government into rectifying violations where complaints of

[81] On this point see R Muncy, *Creating a Female Dominion in American Reform, 1890–1935* (New York, Oxford University Press, 1991).

poor immigrants otherwise would have been ignored. In other instances, settlements were able to report violations without using residents' names, thereby protecting them from a landlord's retribution. Municipal officials and reformers considered this system of anonymous reporting of tenement regulations so crucial that the Tenement House Department upon its creation adopted a similar system.

Years before the creation of the Tenement House Department, the all-female College settlement saw one of its most important functions as 'help[ing] towards the enforcement of the tenement house laws which make for better conditions of living'. In 1896, the settlement discussed how a neighbourhood father complained of conditions in the tenement where his family lived. The settlement explained:

> It proved to be a matter of great importance in tenement-house hygiene, and the proper authorities took prompt measures ... The heads of the various departments of City Government realize that through our many friends we are likely to know points of value, and they are quick to listen to our suggestions.[82]

Greenwich House settlement wrote: 'To protest on behalf of the neighborhood became a habit and the neighbors realized that the Settlement could be counted on to growl where it was dangerous or at least inexpedient for the private citizen to voice a protest'.[83] Thus, settlement houses provided a conduit through which women settlement workers claimed a voice in municipal administration while acting on behalf of their poor and working-class neighbours.

By actually living in the tenement districts, settlement workers could easily observe whether landlords were violating tenement house laws. For example, in 1905, Greenwich Settlement conducted an investigation of the standard of living in the surrounding area. While engaged in this house-to-house survey, they found numerous tenement house violations, which they reported to the Tenement House Department. Greenwich wrote that the Department quickly took legal action resulting in 'sanitary improvements'.[84] The settlement also created a system to record all reports that Greenwich made to the city, and the actions taken by officials in response. With such a system, Greenwich continually could pressure officials to respond to their complaints and concerns.

Simultaneously, however, Greenwich's interests in enforcing tenement laws conflicted, at times, with the interests of tenement residents in need of inexpensive housing. For instance, in 1906, Greenwich began lobbying the Tenement House Department to condemn and destroy numerous tenements

[82] *College Settlement Seventh Annual Report* (1896) 16–20.
[83] *Sixth Annual Report of Greenwich House* (1907) 5.
[84] See *Report of the Director of Greenwich House* (19 January 1905), *microformed on* The Greenwich House Records, Box 1, folder 18, Tamiment Library/Robert F Wagner Labor Archives (New York University).

that they believed to be unfit for human habitation.[85] Tenants, on the other hand, seldom wanted their homes destroyed but rather repaired. Here what Greenwich understood to be for the welfare of the community conflicted with the needs and interests of individual tenants.

At times, settlement workers were apologetic and sought to justify their role in reporting and enforcing laws to themselves and to others. Mary Simkhovitch, head of Greenwich House explained:

> While we [at Greenwich House] do not propose to involve any individual family or person in any difficulty, we do feel that any information that we may be able to give will help toward better legislation or a better enforcement of existing legislation in regard to some of those fundamental things that most deeply affect the life of our tenement-house population, it is not only desirable, but absolutely incumbent upon us.[86]

Somewhat contradictorily, she later wrote:

> We cannot give away our neighbors, we cannot get them into trouble, and yet we cannot be blind to the evils we see. But as a wise mother may overlook a wrong-doing from time to time in order to emphasize something more important when it comes up, so it is inhuman and unwise for a settlement to take over the office of law enforcement.[87]

Yet settlement houses often did just that. It is tempting to argue that Simkhovitch's statement imagined a more maternal state, engaged in caregiving, nurture and forgiveness, not power and punishment. Such sentiments, however, rarely prevented settlements from participating in the enforcement of municipal regulations. The concept of maternalism in which middle-class and elite women reformers saw themselves as mothers providing aid to the poor but also exercising authority over those who required uplift, included the power to punish. As settlements' connections and co-operation with the state grew, punishment could take the form of the exercise of state power.[88] Indeed settlement houses participated in creating and administering the developing municipal welfare state. Yet importantly this state was two headed—one side reflected the enhanced benefits and protection available through regulation. The other side was punitive and aimed at enforcement of such regulations.

Through the years, connections between city government and the settlements only strengthened. Greenwich, along with other settlement houses, provided lodging for women tenement house inspectors. Tenement inspectors, by

[85] *Ibid.*
[86] *First Annual Report of Greenwich House* (1903) 5.
[87] Simkhovitch (above n 80) 101.
[88] Linda Gordon writes: 'Maternalists imagined themselves in a motherly role toward the poor. Viewing the poor as in need of moral and spiritual as well as economic help, middle-class women sometimes imagined giving that help as a mother to a child, combining sympathy with authority'. Gordon, *Pitied But Not Entitled* (above n 2) 55.

living in the settlement houses and participating in their activities, became part of both the settlement community and the tenement districts.[89] With tenement house inspectors constantly available, settlements were able to exert strong influence over the Tenement House Department and resident tenement house inspectors constantly exerted their power over the neighbourhood. Indeed through the settlement houses' work, especially in regard to the enforcement of tenement house regulations, women settlement workers played a central role in building the nascent municipal regulatory welfare state.

VIII. CONCLUSION

By using the case of tenement laws in late-nineteenth-century New York City, this chapter has demonstrated how regulation was an important component in the creation of a municipal welfare state in the United States long before the New Deal. Furthermore, it has scrutinised the complex, gendered dimensions of even those laws that appear to be gender neutral. In the case of tenement regulation, the very concept of the idealized, private late-nineteenth-century home, like the woman who supposedly stood at its centre, was to be removed from the self-interested male world of the market. Tenement laws, which significantly affected the profits of landlords, indirectly redistributed income and challenged rigid concepts of private property, withstood constitutional challenges in the name of the public welfare, manifested in the desire to create an idealized private domestic space.

In contrast, tenement dwellers, especially women who lived in the tenements, understood that a minimum standard of housing was a right of municipal citizenship. At the same time, settlement workers, often women, played a central role in the enforcement of tenement regulations. Their day-to-day contact with tenement dwellers and their location in immigrant tenement districts, allowed them to function as the eyes of the state, placing neighbours and the urban environment under surveillance. Thus tenement laws at once had the power to create minimum standards of housing and provide tenants with various rights. The flip side is that the lives of the poor increasingly became a site of state action.

[89] See, eg, *Report of the Director of Greenwich House* (2 June 1905), microformed on Greenwich House Records, Tamiment, Reel 1.

4

'Mothers at Work'

The Welfare Rights Movement and Welfare Reform in the 1960s

PREMILLA NADASEN

I. INTRODUCTION

IN THE MID-1960s a powerful movement for welfare rights emerged in the United States.[1] Poor women on welfare came together in local, community-based organizations around the country and attempted to address violations of personal and civil rights, low benefit levels, and negative media portrayals of welfare recipients. In 1966, they formed the National Welfare Rights Organization, or NWRO. By 1969, at its peak, the organization had close to 30,000 members nationwide. It planned sit-ins, participated in militant public demonstrations, wrote pamphlets and position papers, and lobbied congress. Through their agitation, poor women on welfare engaged in the process of policy-making and influenced the direction of welfare reform. The history of the welfare rights movement illustrates that welfare is contested terrain on which competing notions of rights, justice, family and motherhood are played out.

The welfare rights movement entered the American political landscape in the wake of a racialized discourse about welfare. In the 1950s and 1960s, politicians, reformers, social scientists and journalists constructed a narrative of welfare, family, sex and reproduction that demonized black women

[1] For example see P Nadasen, *Welfare Warriors: The Welfare Rights Movement in the United States* (New York, Routledge, 2005). A Orleck, *Storming Caesar's Palace: How Black Mothers Fought Their Own War on Poverty* (Boston MA, Beacon Press, 2005). E Boris, 'When Work is Slavery' in G Mink (ed), *Whose Welfare* (Ithaca NY, Cornell University Press, 1999). R Williams, *The Politics of Public Housing: Black Women's Struggles Against Urban Inequality* (New York, Oxford University Press, 2004). F Kornbluh, *The Battle for Welfare Rights: Politics and Poverty in Modern America* (Philadelphia PA, University of Pennsylvania Press, 2007). G West, *The National Welfare Rights Movement: The Social Protest of Poor Women* (New York, Praeger, 1981).

on Aid to Families with Dependent Children (AFDC), a joint federal-state public assistance programme for single mothers. This narrative characterized recipients as promiscuous, lazy, unable to properly care for their children, and content to live off the government's largesse. Although based primarily on misconceptions and hyperbole, the narrative influenced the trajectory of the American welfare state. This article examines the development of this stereotype and how the welfare rights movement challenged the racialized and gendered constructions through its political mobilization. The ideological constructions of welfare functioned to marginalize and silence poor women on welfare, stigmatize the receipt of assistance, and discredit the welfare state, contributing to the ultimate demise of the welfare programme in 1996. The long-term whittling away of the welfare state is much more complex than ideology alone, and has to do with broad economic and political changes, the growing power of conservative forces, and the rise of neo-liberalism. But race and gender served as touchstones; as a lens through which welfare and many other political and economic transformations were viewed.[2] The image of what later came to be called the 'welfare queen' linked black poverty to assumptions of African American women's deviant gender and sexual practices.[3] Consequently welfare became a deeply contentious programme, laden with symbolism for people of different political persuasions. The stigmatization of welfare was also a foundation upon which the welfare rights movement built its political campaigns.

The welfare rights movement posited an alternative vision of welfare that advocated autonomy and independence for welfare recipients and in the process challenged normative constructions of family, gender and sexuality. The movement also nurtured poor black welfare recipients as political and legal actors by providing a platform for their involvement in policy making. They pushed for recipient representation in local welfare departments,

[2] See MK Brown, *Race, Money, and the American Welfare State* (Ithaca NY, Cornell University Press, 1999). E Reese, *Backlash Against Welfare Mothers Past and Present* (Berkeley, University of California Press, 2005). K Neubek and NA Cazenave, *Welfare Racism: Playing the Race Card Against America's Poor* (New York, Routledge, 2001). R Brewer, 'Race, Class, Gender and U.S. State Welfare Policy' in G Young and B Dickerson (eds), *Color, Class and Country: Experiences of Gender* (London, Zed Books, 1994) 115–27. R Lieberman, *Shifting the Color Line: Race and the American Welfare State* (Cambridge MA, Harvard University Press, 1998). H Sparks, 'Queens, Teens, and Model Mothers: Race, Gender, and the Discourse of Welfare Reform' in SF Schram, J Soss, and RC Fording (eds), *Race and the Politics of Welfare Reform* (Ann Arbor MI, University of Michigan Press, 2003) 171–95. Jill Quadagno in *The Color of Welfare* also discusses the connection between race and social policy, but she suggests that the civil rights movement was responsible for this association in the public mind because of its demand that War on Poverty programs be racially inclusive. In fact, AFDC became linked with African Americans much earlier—in the 1950s. J Quadagno, *The Color of Welfare: How Racism Undermined the War on Poverty* (New York, Oxford University Press, 1994).

[3] W Lubiano, 'Black Ladies, Welfare Queens, and State Minstrels: Ideological War by Narrative Means' in T Morrison (ed), *Race-ing Justice, Engendering Power: Essays on Anita Hill, Clarence Thomas, and the Construction of Social Reality* (New York, Pantheon Books, 1992) 323–63. A Hancock, *The Politics of Disgust: The Public Identity of the Welfare Queen* (New York, New York University Press, 2004).

at national conferences, and on policy advisory committees. They waged campaigns for a basic minimum standard of living for women on welfare and proposed a guaranteed annual income—an 'income floor'—below which no poor person would fall. They worked for economic security and political autonomy for poor mothers so they would have a choice about whether to stay home and care for their children or take paid employment outside the home, under what circumstances to have a child, and when they would enter or leave intimate relationships. Out of these campaigns, women in the welfare rights movement crafted a distinctive feminist politics that combined an analysis of race, class, gender and sexuality.[4]

II. WELFARE AND THE POLITICS OF RACE

The welfare rights movement emerged in conjunction with the civil rights movement and was a forerunner of the second wave of the women's movement, which gained traction in the late 1960s and early 1970s. Many of the earliest welfare rights activists got their political training and inspiration from the struggle for civil rights. Executive Director George Wiley, for example, had worked with the Congress of Racial Equality before his involvement with welfare rights. Catherine Jermany, a recipient active in California, was a member of the Southern Christian Leadership Conference. And Mildred Calvert, chair of the Northside Welfare Rights Organization in Milwaukee, was introduced to politics through local civil rights activity. In part because of its roots in the civil rights movement and in part because of the interconnectedness of race and welfare in the 1960s, the welfare rights movement was about 85 per cent African American, with some participation by Latina, white, and Native American women. So, although more white women than black women received welfare, the welfare rights movement was dominated and led by African American women, who made the racial politics of welfare central to their efforts to reform it.

NWRO comprised hundreds of local groups in nearly every state in the country. These groups sent representatives to an annual convention where recipients from different regions of the country could exchange ideas, show one another support, and begin to work together in a coordinated national effort. The convention elected a National Coordinating Committee with state representatives who met four times a year, and a nine-member Executive Committee that met nine times a year. Johnnie Tillmon was chosen as the first chairwoman and later became Executive Director. A mother of six, Tillmon headed a recipient group in Los Angeles, ANC Mothers' Anonymous, which was named after the state program in California, Aid

[4] See P Nadasen, 'Expanding the Boundaries of the Women's Movement: Black Feminism and the Struggle for Welfare Rights' (2002) 28 *Feminist Studies* 271–301.

to Needy Children (ANC). As a staunch advocate of feminism, interracial organizing and recipient control, Tillmon proved to be a formidable force in shaping the political culture of NWRO. In addition to the recipient leaders, a staff of mostly middle-class men, headed by George Wiley, an African American chemistry professor who resigned his academic position at Syracuse University to work full time in the anti-poverty movement, operated out of Washington DC. The staff was responsible for fundraising, hiring organizers and maintaining communication with the local chapters.

At its founding convention in 1966, NWRO adopted the motto: 'adequate income, dignity, justice and democracy', signifying its multiple goals of working to improve the administration of welfare, raising benefit levels, and creating a programme that fostered respect and dignity for recipients. The welfare rights movement used a variety of strategies to achieve these goals. They empowered recipients by educating them about the rules and regulations of welfare, arranged to have personal advocates for recipients in their meetings with caseworkers, and questioned caseworker decisions through a fair hearing process. They also waged a minimum standards campaign, holding mass demonstrations or sit-ins to force administrators to bring recipients up to a basic standard of living and ensure that recipients had all the items the welfare department deemed necessary, whether that was a bed for every child or a new winter coat every three years. NWRO protested at major department stores in an effort to have credit cards issued to recipients. It formulated a legal strategy with the help of legal aid lawyers to overturn the most abusive welfare regulations. Women in the welfare rights movement opposed mandatory work rules, sought to re-value their work as mothers, and campaigned to institute a guaranteed annual income. Through their campaigns, they challenged core features of AFDC that dehumanized and disrespected them.

From 1935, when welfare was first established during the New Deal as Title IV of the Social Security Act, until the 1960s, when the welfare rights movement emerged, AFDC underwent a dramatic transformation: from a non-controversial but still means-tested programme that served few needy African Americans to one that disproportionately aided African Americans and came to be viewed as largely black and corrupt. Aid to Dependent Children (ADC)—as AFDC was known prior to 1962—was a relatively minor programme in the 1930s and 1940s, made up primarily of widows, most of whom were white. It grew out of the mothers' pensions programmes of the Progressive Era, and was rooted in the male breadwinner/female homemaker model.[5] ADC was never a generous programme (many recipients needed to engage in paid work to make ends meet) and caseworkers

[5] L Gordon, *Pitied but Not Entitled: Single Mothers and the History of Welfare* (New York, The Free Press, 1994). A Kessler-Harris, *In Pursuit of Equity: Women, Men, and the Quest for Economic Citizenship in Twentieth-Century America* (New York, Oxford University Press,

went to great lengths to ensure that only the most deserving and morally pure recipients received assistance. Nevertheless, policy-makers and politicians agreed that poor women without husbands needed financial aid in order to fulfill their responsibilities as mothers. Considered a small but necessary programme in its earliest years, ADC was neither widely supported nor extensively criticized.

By the early 1960s, AFDC had come under intense scrutiny. First, some of the growing concern centered on the expansion of the welfare rolls—a fact repeated by journalists and conservative politicians countless times in this period. However, the number of families on welfare only grew from 652,000 in 1950 to 806,000 in 1960; hardly enough to warrant an outcry.[6] More importantly, critics pointed to an increasing number of African American women receiving benefits. The percentage of African Americans on the welfare rolls rose from 17 per cent in 1940 to 48 per cent in 1961. Reasons for this increase had to do, in part, with broader economic trends. Mechanization and other changes in agricultural production in the post-World War II South left many African Americans without work, fuelling migration to urban areas and the North. Between 1940 and 1960, more than three million African Americans made their way from the South to northern cities in search of employment. Although many found work in the service sector, de-industrialization in conjunction with widespread race and gender employment discrimination led to a disproportionately large number of unemployed or underemployed African Americans. In 1960, the official unemployment rate was 4.9 per cent for whites and 10.2 per cent for non-whites.[7] African Americans landing in the North and unable to find work may have turned to welfare departments for economic support as a last resort.

In addition, by the 1960s, most welfare recipients were not widows, but instead were never-married, divorced or deserted women. In 1937, widows made up 43 per cent of the ADC caseload; they fell to 7.7 per cent in 1961.[8] The Social Security Amendments of 1939 encouraged this trend by extending old age insurance coverage to widows and their children, in effect, removing 'deserving' women and children, whose husbands and fathers had died, from the ADC rolls and making them eligible for social security

2001). M Abramovitz, *Regulating the Lives of Women: Social Welfare Policy from the Colonial Times to the Present* (Boston MA, South End Press, 1989).

[6] US Bureau of the Census, *Statistical Abstracts of the United States* (Washington, DC, Government Printing Office, 1970): Table no 428, Public Assistance—Recipients and Payments by Program: 1950–1965.

[7] US Bureau of the Census, *Historical Statistics of the United States: Colonial Times to 1970* (Washington DC, Government Printing Office, 1975): Series D 87–101. 'Unemployment Rates for Selected Groups in the Labor Force: 1947–1970', p 135.

[8] US Advisory Council on Social Security, 1938 Final Report, pp 17–19 in R Bremner, *From the Depths The Discovery of Poverty in the U.S.* (New York, New York University Press, 1956) 535, cited in Abramovitz, *Regulating the Lives of Women* (above n 5) 321.

payments. Another factor is that the percentage of single mothers in all racial groups increased after World War II because of social and economic dislocations, as well as changing social mores. Between 1950 and 1960, out-of-marriage births increased by 31 per cent for white women and 20 per cent for non-whites.[9] But non-white women were disproportionately single mothers. In 1960 the official out-of-wedlock birth rate for whites was 23 out of 1000 births; for non-whites it was 216.[10] Obviously more women of colour had children out of wedlock. But there are additional reasons for the different rates of welfare receipt. Unmarried white women who became pregnant were well hidden from the public eye. They were sent off to birthing homes and their babies quietly put up for adoption. Unmarried black women had fewer institutional resources available. The lack of avenues for adoption, in addition to community values discouraging mothers from giving up their children, meant that single black mothers were much more likely to keep their children and raise them than white women.[11] This higher rate of black single motherhood, coupled with higher poverty rates, translated into a higher ADC rate for African American women.

As the composition of the welfare rolls changed in the 1950s and 1960s, the programme came under attack. These attacks were premised on a discourse falsely suggesting that most welfare recipients were black, sexually promiscuous, duplicitous, and undeserving of assistance. In their coverage of what was now referred to as the 'welfare problem' the press highlighted cultural pathologies and sexual immorality. In 1962, *US News and World Report* published an article about an investigator who reported that 93 per cent of ADC recipients in Washington DC were African American and that '[w]omen with several illegitimate children, by several different fathers, were often found living with men who were bringing home regular paychecks'.[12] Unlike a few years earlier when financial assistance was deemed necessary for single mothers to raise healthy and well-adjusted children, by the early 1960s welfare for single mothers was considered detrimental. It was believed to create a culture of poverty that was transmitted from one generation to the next. In 1963, *The Saturday Evening Post* commented: 'Today's welfare child, raised in hopelessness and dependency, becomes tomorrow's welfare adult, pauperized and helpless'.[13]

[9] R Grove and A Hetzel, *Vital Statistics Rates in the United States, 1940–1960* (Washington DC, US Department of Health, Education and Welfare, 1968) 185: Table 29, 'Ratios of Illegitimate Live Births by Color'.

[10] *Ibid*, 185.

[11] See R Solinger, *Wake up Little Susie: Single Pregnancy and Race Before Roe v. Wade* (New York, Routledge, 1994) and R Kunzel, 'White Neurosis, Black Pathology: Constructing Out-of-Wedlock Pregnancy in the Wartime and Post-War US' in J Meyerowitz (ed), *Not June Cleaver: Women and Gender in Postwar America* (Philadelphia PA, Temple University Press, 1994).

[12] 'Cheating on Relief: Investigation Shows This' *US News and World Report*, 16 July 1962.

[13] L Chevalier, 'The Welfare Mess', *Saturday Evening Post*, 11 May 1963.

This culture of poverty was located most specifically in African American migrants from the South. *US News and World Report* in 1965 attributed the rise in welfare rolls to the 'mass migrations of unskilled Negroes from the South' and their 'high rate of illegitimacy'. The increasing number of 'welfare babies' would 'breed more criminals, more mental defectives, more unemployables of almost every type'. The paper profiled the typical ADC recipient in Chicago: 'A poor Negro girl: ... She is insecure, uneducated, unsophisticated, frightened'.[14] One official in 1967 referred to children on AFDC as the 'children of illegitimate parents'.[15] Clearly the target in the welfare debate had become African American men and women, who were characterized as not wanting to work, unable to properly raise their children, and socially and culturally pathological. Thus, the press packaged and sold concern about ADC to the public through a racialized, gendered ideology. Promiscuity and laziness became synonymous with black women on welfare. No one definitively linked the increase in welfare rolls to the rise in out-of-marriage births rather than poverty rates, yet 'illegitimacy', in particular, was a catchword for evidence of the degeneracy of the black population and justified denying welfare to African American women.

The political discourses about the ostensibly dysfunctional nature of black culture and black women's sexual transgressions, prompted local welfare officials and legislators to investigate alleged welfare fraud and corruption, limit the size of the AFDC rolls, reduce monthly payments and put welfare recipients to work.[16] Caseworkers routinely checked up on women on welfare, sometimes conducting 'midnight raids'—impromptu home visits, often late at night—to ensure that a recipient was not involved in a relationship with a man. They applied stringent and humiliating eligibility criteria to prevent women from applying for assistance. This included probing questions about a recipient's past sexual experiences, or snooping inside her refrigerator to see the kind of food she was purchasing. Under constant scrutiny, recipients had to prove the soundness of their character, their destitution and, increasingly, their willingness but inability to work. Even when recipients qualified for assistance, their income was not always secure. Caseworkers could cut them off assistance without notice or explanation or reduce grants arbitrarily. Those getting monthly cheques found the amount hardly enough to provide the basic necessities for their children.[17]

Welfare rights activists responded to this racialized discourse by attempting to recast the image of welfare recipients. They wanted to draw attention

[14] 'The Mystery of Rising Relief Costs', *US News and World Report*, 8 March 1965.

[15] 'After 30 Years—Relief a Failure', *US News and World Report*, 17 July 1967.

[16] Y Zylan, 'The Divided Female State: Gender, Citizenship and US Social Policy Development, 1945–1990' (PhD Dissertation, New York University, 1994). J Patterson, *America's Struggle Against Poverty, 1900–1980* (Cambridge MA, Harvard University Press, 1981) 107–9. Reese, *Backlash Against Welfare Mothers* (above n 2).

[17] See W Bell, *Aid to Dependent Children* (New York, Columbia University Press, 1965).

to their work as mothers as a way to dispel myths that they were lazy and chose not to work. Concern for their children often spurred their involvement in the welfare rights struggle and many could not separate their status as mothers from their identity as activists.[18] They often referred to themselves as 'mothers' or 'mother-recipients', and sought to bring dignity and respect to their mothering work.[19] They challenged the artificial dichotomy between work and welfare by insisting that as mothers they did, in fact, work. In 1968 a Boston group said that 'motherhood—whether the mother is married or not—is a role which should be fully supported, as fully rewarded, as fully honored, as any other'.[20] One welfare recipient cleverly contrasted her situation with the reigning symbol of womanhood of the time when she asked: 'Jackie Kennedy gets a government check. Is anyone making her go to work?'[21] By attempting to re-fashion the popular portrayal of welfare recipients as worthy mothers engaged in meaningful and socially significant work, welfare rights activists sought to legitimize their receipt of public assistance. Placing value on their work as mothers challenged social norms that increasingly devalued the mothering work of poor women—especially women on welfare.

The welfare rights movement claimed welfare as a right, which meant financial assistance regardless of moral standing, personal behaviour or the capricious will of caseworkers. They argued that poverty was the only necessary qualification for receipt of welfare. Movement activists disseminated information about the rules and regulations of the welfare programme. Local groups gained access to departmental welfare manuals and, with the help of legal aid lawyers, wrote handbooks for members outlining their rights. Mothers for Adequate Welfare in Boston wrote 'Your Welfare Rights Manual', answering questions such as 'What do I get on AFDC?' 'What about Sheets and Furniture?' 'Can my Children go to College?' and 'How to Appeal a Decision by Your Caseworker'.[22] The Hinds County Welfare Rights Movement in Mississippi developed a handbook called 'Your Welfare Rights', counselling recipients: 'Welfare is not charity. If you are in need and meet the other eligibility criteria standards, you have a right to welfare help'.[23] Gaining knowledge about welfare regulations enabled

[18] For an excellent overview of the connection between mothering and activism, see A Jetter, A Orleck and D Taylor (eds), *The Politics of Motherhood: Activist Voices from Left to Right* (Hanover NH, University Press of New England, 1997).

[19] Massachusetts Welfare Information Center Newsletter, 7 April 1969, William Howard Whitaker Papers, Ohio Historical Society, Columbus, Ohio, box 2, folder 38.

[20] G Brumm, 'Mothers for Adequate Welfare—AFDC from the Underside' (1968) *Dialogues Boston* 11, Whitaker Papers, box 3, folder 3.

[21] 'Ohio Adequate Welfare News', 18 April 1968, Whitaker Papers, box 1.

[22] Brumm, 'Mothers for Adequate Welfare' (above n 20).

[23] Hinds County Welfare Rights Movement, *Your Welfare Rights*, Handbooks, July 1967 and March 1968. American Civil Liberties Union National Archives, Mudd Library, Princeton University, boxes 1134–6.

them to advocate for one another and to diminish the discretionary power of caseworkers. Their new-found knowledge brought a certain standardization and predictability to welfare policy.

Welfare recipients relied on an appeals process to question unfair caseworker decisions. They organized campaigns for fair hearings: formal non-judicial hearings before a State board of welfare to review a caseworker's decision. In these situations a recipient could bring an advocate or lawyer to the hearing with her. In New York City where the fair hearings were used most extensively, the Citywide Co-ordinating Committee of Welfare Rights Groups sponsored 3,000 fair hearing cases from August to October of 1967, a huge increase over the usual 50 cases a year.[24] Simultaneously with the fair hearing campaign, the welfare rights movement waged a legal struggle and won an important victory with the *Goldberg v Kelly* 1970 Supreme Court decision that guaranteed recipients the right to due process.[25] This ruling ensured recipients the right to a fair hearing before termination or reduction of their benefits. The appeals process shifted the balance of power between caseworker and client and gave recipients a bit more leverage in the face of a daunting welfare bureaucracy.

III. THE BLACK FAMILY AND THE POLITICS OF WELFARE

Another area of concern was the way in which AFDC supposedly damaged black families. A number of academic and policy studies attributed black poverty to deviant family practices. The most well-known study to connect welfare, poverty and race was *The Negro Family: A Case For National Action* by Daniel Patrick Moynihan, an official in the Department of Labor under President Lyndon Johnson. Published in 1965, the *Moynihan Report*, as it was more popularly known, explained black urban poverty by the rising number of female-headed households. Moynihan argued that '[a]t the heart of the deterioration of the fabric of Negro society is the deterioration of the Negro family. It is the fundamental source of the weakness of the Negro community'. He attributed the disproportionate number of black single-parent families—which he called a 'tangle of pathology'—to the 'matriarchal' black family structure.

Moynihan's thesis was not new. In fact, there was a long history of characterizations of the black family as matriarchal dating back to the work of black sociologist E Franklin Frazier in the 1930s. An anthropologist,

[24] No Author (Probably NWRO staff). Project in Lay Advocacy, 1967, George Wiley Papers, State Historical Society, Madison, Wisconsin; *New York Times*, 15 July 1968; AF Ginger (ed), *Civil Liberties Docket* (Oakland CA, Meiklejohn Civil Liberties Libraries, 1970) no 673, p 111.

[25] *Goldberg v Kelly*, 397 US 254 (1970).

Oscar Lewis, coined the phrase 'culture of poverty' in the 1950s to explain the persistence of poverty in poor communities of colour.[26] Collectively, these scholars focused attention on individual choices and cultural traits, while minimizing the significance of structural explanations for poverty.[27] They also posited the notion that the proliferation of two-parent, male-breadwinner families, rather than public assistance, was the solution to poverty. Although its argument was not original, the *Moynihan Report* nevertheless perceptibly affected welfare policy. With greater public concern about welfare and heightened attention to inner-city poverty because of urban uprisings in the mid-1960s, social policy and urban politics were at a critical juncture, making Moynihan's report invaluable to critics and reformers of welfare policy. Strengthening age-old arguments that poor single mothers should not receive government assistance because it contributed to family breakup, the *Report* linked race to welfare and single-parent families and made it difficult to talk about one without the others.[28]

Welfare rights activists defended their status as single mothers, disputed stereotypes that vilified them, and challenged the hetero-normative, two-parent family as the solution to the problem of poverty. They debunked the myth that single motherhood signified cultural deficiency and disagreed with the assumption that poor single mothers needed a male breadwinner. Welfare rights activists believed that women should have control over their sexuality and reproduction, and autonomy in choosing their partners. In their exaltation of motherhood, they did not advocate that women on welfare enter patriarchal relationships and accept a secondary position as mother and homemaker, but condemned the subordination of women in traditional family formations and suggested alternative models. Mothers for Adequate Welfare in Boston believed that marriage, with its 'fixed rules and obligations', was a 'means for domination more than a means for expressing love'.[29] As single mothers who were ostracized for not conforming to conventional norms, they were acutely aware of the social expectations to marry and establish traditional family relationships. Tillmon argued that if a woman was not married, people assumed she had 'failed as a woman because [she has] failed to attract and keep a man. There's something wrong with [her]'. The meager benefits and stigma attached

[26] Laura Briggs traces the emergence of the Puerto Rican 'welfare queen' in Oscar Lewis's *La Vida*. L Briggs, 'La Vida, Moynihan, and Other Libels: Social Science, Migration, and the Making of the Puerto Rican Welfare Queen' (2002) 14 *Centro: Journal of the Center for Puerto Rican Studies* 3–24.

[27] A O'Connor, *Poverty Knowledge: Social Science, Social Policy, and the Poor in Twentieth Century US History* (Princeton NJ, Princeton University Press, 2002).

[28] Spitzer makes a similar argument that race and welfare became inseparable in the mid-1960s. He ties this development, however, to the passage of the 1967 Social Security Amendments. SJ Spitzer, 'The Liberal Dilemma: Welfare And Race, 1960–1975' (PhD Dissertation, Columbia University, 2000).

[29] Quoted in Brumm, 'Mothers for Adequate Welfare' (above n 20).

to welfare served as an 'example' to let a woman know the consequences 'if she tries to go it alone without a man'.[30] These women examined how social pressures, the welfare system, and the institution of marriage inhibited autonomy by forcing women into unequal relations with men. Welfare recipients in Morgantown, West Virginia, wrote a handbook instructing others that 'an AFDC mother can have male visitors as often as she wants and go out on dates if she leaves her children in the care of a responsible person'. NWRO also brought a test case before the Supreme Court, *King v Smith*, that eventually outlawed substitute-father, or 'man-in-the-house' rules that cut a recipient off welfare if caseworkers found evidence that she had an intimate partner.[31] Through such strategies, welfare rights activists attempted to validate their status as single parents and assert their right to enter or reject the institution of marriage on their own terms.

This push for personal autonomy included reproductive rights. Welfare recipients wanted to choose for themselves whether or not and under what circumstances to have a child. Johnnie Tillmon wrote: 'Nobody realizes more than poor women that all women should have the right to control their own reproduction'.[32] Some manuals created by local welfare rights organizations educated recipients about birth control, but stressed that 'this is your choice'.[33] In addition to advocating access to birth control, women in the welfare rights movement opposed forced sterilization of women on welfare and made this part of their campaign for reproductive rights.[34] In 1971 the NWRO national convention included a panel on abortion, but, as Johnnie Tillmon explained,

> [w]e know how easily the lobby for birth control can be perverted into a weapon against poor women. The word is choice. Birth control is a right, not an obligation. A personal decision, not a condition of a welfare check.[35]

IV. WELFARE AND MANDATORY WORK

The growing political controversy around welfare led to momentum to put women on welfare to work. Welfare officials had, for many years, been aware that, even if unsanctioned, in practice poor women combined

[30] J Tillmon, 'Welfare is a Woman's Issue' (1972) 1 *Ms. Magazine* 111–16.
[31] *King v Smith*, 392 US 309 (1968).
[32] *Ibid*, 115.
[33] Chicago Welfare Rights Organization handbook, June 1968, Whitaker Papers, box 3; and 'Your Welfare Rights Manual' by Mothers for Adequate Welfare, undated, Whitaker Papers, box 3.
[34] For more on the history of African American women and sterilization abuse, see D Roberts, *Killing the Black Body: Race, Reproduction, and the Meaning of Liberty* (New York, Pantheon Books, 1997) and AM Smith, *Welfare Reform and Sexual Regulation* (Boston MA, Cambridge University Press, 2007).
[35] Tillmon, 'Welfare is a Woman's Issue' (above n 29) 115.

welfare receipt with paid employment.[36] The precursor of ADC, mothers' pensions programmes, rarely provided adequate assistance and poor mothers nearly always had to supplement their monthly benefits with paid work. In the 1950s, policy-makers and welfare professionals began to discuss employment as a way to address rising criticism of ADC.[37] Although their intent was to defend the programme, their willingness to experiment with work programmes was a slippery slope that lauded independence and dove-tailed with conservative attacks on assistance for poor mothers. And in the South, employment of welfare recipients during periods of labour shortage went hand in hand with the distribution of assistance when employment needs slackened. A field supervisor in a southern State in the late 1930s explicitly justified the exclusion of African Americans from the welfare rolls in this way:

> The number of Negro cases is few due to the unanimous feeling on the part of the staff and board that there are more work opportunities for Negro women and to their intense desire not to interfere with local labor conditions. The attitude that 'they have always gotten along', and that 'all they'll do is have more children' is definite ... [They see no] reason why the employable Negro mother should not continue her usually sketchy seasonal labor or indefinite domestic service rather than receive a public assistance grant.[38]

Despite this long-standing association between public assistance and employment, AFDC was, in theory, designed to reinforce women's domestic responsibilities and to support single mothers. As the racial composition of the welfare rolls changed, however, so did the intent of the programme. In the 1960s employment of welfare recipients became a permanent feature of federal welfare policy. In 1967 the Johnson administration mandated employment of women on AFDC with the Work Incentive Program (WIN). WIN required women with school-age children receiving AFDC to accept either job training or employment.[39] It also enabled them to keep a portion of their earnings without a reduction in welfare benefits. These increasingly restrictive ADC policies, which cut women off welfare if they refused or could not comply, made it harder for women, particularly black women, to receive assistance. Moreover, although few women were actually put

[36] J Goodwin, '"Employable Mothers" and "Suitable Work": A Re-Evaluation of Welfare and Wage Earning for Women in the Twentieth Century United States' (1995) 29 *Journal of Social History* 253–74.

[37] J Mittelstadt, *From Welfare to Workfare: The Unintended Consequences of Liberal Reform, 1945–1965* (Chapel Hill NC, University of North Carolina Press, 2005).

[38] MS Larabee, 'Unmarried Parenthood Under the Social Security Act', 1939 Proceedings of the National Conference of Social Work (New York, Columbia University Press, 1939) 449. Quoted in Bell, *Aid to Dependent Children* (above n 17) 34–5.

[39] For a discussion of the full range of government work programs and how they were targeted differently, see N Rose, *Workfare or Fair Work: Women, Welfare, and Government Work Programs* (New Brunswick NJ, Rutgers University Press, 1995).

to work, the WIN program redirected the focus of AFDC away from supporting mothers financially toward employment and independence.[40]

Members of the welfare rights movement unequivocally opposed the 1967 work rules, which gave them no choice about being full-time homemakers. They eloquently tied the welfare work requirements to the history of exploitation and slave labour. NWRO planned its first annual convention in Washington DC to coincide with the Congressional debates about the proposed work requirements for welfare recipients. At a public hearing, they argued that 'having a job is no guarantee against poverty' and called the Bill 'a betrayal of the poor, a declaration of war upon our families, and a fraud on the future of our nation'.[41] After the hearing, welfare rights activists adjourned to the Mall in downtown Washington for a 'Mothers' March', which drew 1000 people. At the rally, Margaret McCarty, welfare rights leader in Baltimore, invoked the historical oppression of African Americans as well as the racial pride of the period, when she said: 'lousy, dirty, conniving brutes' devised the Bill to 'take us back to slavery ... I'm black and I'm beautiful and they ain't going to take me back'.[42]

Welfare rights activists wanted to have a choice about working inside or outside the home. They supported the creation of child care centres to ease the problems of women who took paid employment. Johnnie Tillmon made day care 'one of the first priorities' of her welfare rights organization in California.[43] The NWRO office produced a guide for local welfare rights groups on how to organize a comprehensive community-controlled child care program, giving them advice on raising money, hiring staff and planning meals.[44] In 1972, the Clark County Welfare Rights Organization in Nevada successfully launched a day care programme with the help of local churches and a nutritionist employed by the Office of Economic Opportunity.[45] Although proponents of day care centres, women in the welfare rights movement, nevertheless criticized the dynamic created when poor women were hired to care for other women's children. Afraid of the way institutionalized child care could oppress underpaid women care workers, Tillmon warned that the fight for universal child care should ensure that it did not create 'a reservoir of cheap female labor' that 'institutionalized, partially self-employed Mammies'.[46] Thus, although day care centres

[40] For an extended discussion see Bell, *Aid to Dependent Children* (above n 17).

[41] *The Washington Daily News*, 20 September 1967.

[42] *Washington Post*, 29 August 1967. For a fuller discussion, see Williams, *The Politics of Public Housing* (above n 1).

[43] West, *The National Welfare Rights Movement* (above n 1) 253.

[44] NWRO, 'How to Organize a Comprehensive Community Controlled Child Care Program' NWRO pamphlet, Wiley Papers, box 16.

[45] J Evans, 'Quarterly Report to Campaign for Human Development', 1 February 1972, Wiley Papers, box 25.

[46] Tillmon, 'Welfare is a Woman's Issue' (above n 29) 115.

could potentially free some women from the constraints of child care, it could just as likely increase exploitation of other women.

The shifting discourse about welfare was a product of dominant perceptions of black women in the United States as paid workers rather than mothers. Since the emergence of racial slavery, labour force participation defined black women's social role. They reproduced for slave masters, and nannied white children, but most poor black mothers had little opportunity to nurture and care for their own children full time. Wage work for poor women and most black women often meant long hours, drudgery and meager rewards, not a fulfilling career. As late as 1950, 60 per cent of gainfully employed black women worked in private households or as cleaning women and 'help' in hotels, restaurants and offices.[47] For poor black women, paid employment was not necessarily a challenge to sexual inequality. On the contrary, requiring poor women to enter the world of paid work only reinforced the exploitation and oppression that many of them faced on a daily basis. The welfare rights movement's opposition to forced employment took into account black women's historical relationship to the labour market. Instead, they proposed adequate public support so that women would have the option of staying home. This, in itself, was a radical challenge to the socially-defined gender roles of poor black women, who had never been seen primarily as homemakers or mothers.

This historical association of black women and work underpinned the backlash against welfare. In 1972, during a Congressional debate of NWRO's proposal for a guaranteed annual income for all poor people, Senator Russell Long of Louisiana vocalized his opposition to the Bill by shouting out in the middle of the debate: 'I can't get anybody to iron my shirts!'[48] Fuelled by racial stereotypes, the new welfare regulations devalued the mothering work of black women and reinforced their status as workers, especially domestic workers who ought to be available to iron shirts. In the 1920s and 1930s, the architects of ADC constructed programmes to assist women as caretakers, but theirs was a racially-specific vision. They had in mind white single mothers. As black women increasingly applied for this entitlement around the country, single welfare mothers were portrayed as undeserving, licentious, welfare cheats.

Employment, motherhood, and the 'proper' social role for black women lay at the heart of the debate. Black women on welfare and middle-class women encountered vastly different expectations when it came to employment and motherhood. In the mid 1960s, most Americans opposed middle-class women, particularly women with children, entering the workforce.

[47] J Jones, *Labor of Love, Labor of Sorrow: Black Women, Work and the Family, From Slavery to the Present* (New York, Vintage Books, 1986) 257–8.

[48] J Welsh, 'Welfare Reform: Born Aug 8, 1969; died, Oct 4, 1972: A Sad Case Study of the American Political Process', *New York Times Magazine*, 7 January 1973.

A number of scholars have written about the persistence of the domestic ideal throughout the 1950s and 1960s. In her study of mothers and work in popular American magazines, Kathryn Keller argued that, throughout the 1950s, working mothers were considered maladjusted and their choice to work harmful to the child's development.[49] Although larger numbers of women entered the workforce in the 1960s, they did so despite public disfavour of working mothers.[50] For poor women the situation was different. A publication produced by the federal Department of Health Education and Welfare (HEW) revealed the disjuncture between what experts considered appropriate for middle-class white women versus women on welfare. HEW cited a report that children on AFDC had more behavioural problems when the mother stayed at home. Welfare children

> seem to have a higher incidence of serious disorders such as psychosis and appear to be more isolated, mistrustful, and anxious than the nonwelfare children ... The employment status of the welfare mothers also seems to affect impairment: children of working mothers have less impairment.[51]

The new welfare work rules in the 1960s, then, seemed to be more a result of the association of AFDC with poor African American women specifically rather than a transformation in the dominant gender roles and entrance of middle-class women into the workforce. The language used to characterize these two groups of women underscores the point. In the 1990s journalists and politicians routinely referred to middle-class women who didn't work outside the home as stay-at-home moms or 'soccer moms'—acknowledging their work and commitment to raising their children. They almost never applied these labels to women on AFDC, who were referred to as 'welfare mothers', highlighting their relationship to the state, rather than their relationship to their children. The public debate about women and paid work ironically chastised middle-class women for going to work and castigated poor women for not working.

V. A NEW VISION FOR WELFARE

Many of the welfare rights movement's goals converged in their demand for a guaranteed annual income. The movement lobbied for, and introduced into Congress, a proposal for a guaranteed minimum income for all poor people regardless of family status. In 1969, they set their base income

[49] K Keller, *Mothers and Work in Popular American Magazines* (Westport CT, Greenwood Press, 1994).

[50] B Linden-Ward and CH Green, *American Women in the 1960s: Changing the Future* (New York, Twayne Publishers, 1993) 92.

[51] *Welfare in Review* (1969), Quoted in DP Moynihan, *Politics of Guaranteed Income: The Nixon Administration and the Family Assistance Plan* (New York, Random House, 1973) 89–91.

at US$5500 for a family of four, an amount well above the poverty line and pegged to what they believed was a more accurate measure of living standards, the Bureau of Labor Statistics' 'low' budget for an urban family. NWRO envisioned their income floor working like a negative income tax—with a minimum income of US$5500, but, in order to maintain a work incentive, low-income families would get subsidies until their income reached just under US$10,000. Unlike the AFDC programme, the guaranteed income would disregard personal morality and homemaking skills and be based solely upon economic need.

This fight for a right to welfare and a guaranteed minimum income aided the welfare rights movement in its efforts to redefine the nature of welfare which, framed as a privilege rather than a right, had historically distinguished between worthy and unworthy recipients. Endorsing the concept of a guaranteed annual income served several purposes at once. It forced the state to recognize housework and child care as legitimate work, freed women from dependence on men, debunked the racial characterizations of black women as lazy by acknowledging the work they did as mothers, and gave women a viable option to degrading labour market conditions. In the 1960s advocates for some kind of 'income floor' spanned the political spectrum and included conservative economist Milton Friedman, radical groups such as the Black Panther Party, liberal Democrats in Congress, as well as Republican President Richard Nixon. While Friedman saw direct cash assistance as a way to reduce government bureaucracy, the Black Panther Party hoped it would be a means of economic redistribution. Congress discussed various proposals, including Nixon's Family Assistance Plan, which guaranteed families a basic minimum income of US$1600, and NWRO's plan for US$5500, which received endorsements from the AFL-CIO, the National Council of Churches, 21 members of the House of Representatives, as well as a special White House Conference on Food Nutrition and Health. In these Congressional debates NWRO's guaranteed income proposal became a standard by which other proposals were measured. By comparison, Nixon's plan looked measly and 'compromise' proposals attempted to find a middle ground between the two extremes. In the end, with the economic downturn in the early 1970s and the emergence of a more conservative political climate, none of these proposals was passed. Nevertheless, throughout the legislative process the welfare rights movement met frequently with Congressional representatives and members of the Nixon administration and participated in a political discourse about the needs of poor people and how best to serve their interests. They denounced aspects of the current welfare system that they found most intolerable and brought to the forefront of the debate issues of motherhood, children's rights and women's rights.

The welfare rights movement and its allies had a discernible impact on welfare policy in the 1960s. They eliminated some of the most egregious welfare regulations such as the residency requirement and the 'man-in-the-house' rules and established a legal precedent for their right to due process. They won thousands of dollars for recipients in special grants to bring them up to the basic minimum standard of living as defined by local welfare departments. They informed recipients of their legal and political rights and empowered them to claim these rights through collective action. By the early 1970s, welfare rights activists sat on presidential advisory committees, were consulted by the secretary of the Department of Health, Education and Welfare, and participated regularly in welfare conferences. Although in many cases their representation was token, it nevertheless signalled an important victory for poor black women who had historically been excluded from such deliberations. Although unable to achieve all of its goals, the welfare rights movement engaged in the political process, participated in the debate about black women's right to assistance, and contested the prevailing wisdom about welfare.

Through their organizing, women in the welfare rights movement articulated a black feminist politics that called for autonomy and choice for poor women. Their positions differed from other, more dominant strains of women's activism in this period. They centered poor women on welfare in the political discourse and integrated an analysis of gender, race, class, culture and sexuality. As such, they saw economic autonomy, financial support, and debunking the racialized, gendered stereotypes of AFDC recipients as fundamental to their feminist agenda. The movement gave voice to poor women who had been silenced and marginalized in the debate about welfare and made them active agents in social change and reform of public policy.

VI. CONCLUSION

Women in the welfare rights movement constructed a political platform that challenged the racist and sexist stereotypes associated with black single motherhood, which took shape in the 1950s and 1960s and informed both welfare policy and discussions of race. Black women's dependence on welfare, reformers and politicians argued, fostered criminal behaviour, discouraged work, encouraged promiscuity, and led ultimately to the next generation's dependence on welfare. Politicians and policy-makers employed the discourse of AFDC to discredit the social safety net as corrupt and to vilify poor African American women. Even though black women were not a majority of women on welfare, and most women on welfare never abused the system, politicians invoked racial stereotypes of welfare recipients in the 1960s to implement punitive policies and push for mandatory work. This transformed welfare from a programme that supported women in their work as mothers to one that encouraged or required women to enter the workforce, laying the foundation for its eventual dismantling in 1996.

In the 1960s, welfare recipients attempted to refashion the discourse that demonized them. The activism of the welfare rights movement opened up a political space that empowered one of the most marginalized sectors of American society. Welfare recipients became legal and political actors in the legislative process and in the public debate about welfare. They articulated economic demands that increasingly asserted a larger critique of gender roles, patriarchy and proscribed sexuality. For example, these activists sought to bring dignity to their work as mothers and defy a culture which for the most part devalued their mothering. They also challenged the belief that paid work was necessarily liberating and pointed to the exploitative labour market conditions under which most women, especially poor women of colour, worked. Rather than prescribing that women enter the work force or stay home with children, choose to marry or reject marriage, welfare activists demanded that women have the power to define their own lives. They fought for an increase in welfare benefits or a guaranteed annual income, which would enable them to make choices about parenthood, employment and sexuality. They believed that state economic assistance was not a form of dependency, but a source of liberation—liberation from patriarchal relationships and low-wage menial labour; and, if administered properly, liberation from control by the welfare bureaucracy. They came to see gender as central to the politics of welfare and increasingly identified as feminists. Black welfare activists formulated a distinctive and broadly-based analysis of women's liberation that spoke to the needs of many poor women.

Examining the evolution of welfare policy in conjunction with advocacy and agitation by welfare recipients, demonstrates how the politics of welfare was contested terrain in the 1960s. Welfare reformers, politicians, policy-makers, as well as welfare recipients battled about defining the terms of assistance for poor single mothers. Although they are not normally considered a part of the policy-making process, welfare recipients, especially organized recipients, participated in negotiating the terms of welfare. In their struggles welfare recipients targeted not just the mechanisms of welfare, but its ideological constructions as well. Consequently, this chapter highlights the importance of discourse and ideology and suggests that the struggle to roll back neo-liberal attacks or expand public assistance is, in part, about reframing the debate. The welfare rights movement's combined analysis of race, class, gender and sexuality can help us develop a broader notion of feminism to include the needs of poor women. Their particular brand of feminism calls for a public assistance programme that provides adequate economic assistance, challenges the normative two-parent family, and re-values care work. It is a model that may prove useful as we re-envision welfare in the twenty-first century.

Part III

The Precarious Citizenship and Legal Construction of Poor Women

5

Women in the Workforce in the Context of Neo-Liberalism

The Case of Israel

MIMI AJZENSTADT*

I. A SOCIETY OF DREAMERS

THE STORY OF Israeli society, spanning from the beginning of the twentieth century until today, is replete with utopian dreams and declarations of the freedom and autonomy of Jewish women. These ideas were already expressed in 'Altneuland', a utopian essay by Theodor Herzl (1860–1904), the founder of the Zionist movement, who called for the equality of women in the new Jewish society, claiming that 'it would have been blackest ingratitude on the part of men to relegate them [women] to the kitchen or the seraglio'.[1] Boris Shatz,[2] who played a central role in the establishment of the Bezalel Arts School, described his utopian vision of public buildings in Jerusalem. He envisioned that among the innovative establishments would be 'public dining rooms for all the people of Jerusalem. Women ceased working in their homes as cooks for their families ... Women were freed from the kitchen environment and its ritual, which perplex the brain'. The founders of the Kibbutz sought to ensure gender equality by establishing 'nursing' homes to attend to children's needs, which would liberate mothers to work together with male members of the communal societies.[3] The Jewish Women's Equal Rights Association of Palestine was established in 1919 to achieve 'one set of laws and one legal system for men and women'.[4] It envisioned a new society in which women

* The author would like to thank Mrs Hanita Kosher and Mrs Doirt Mesika for their research assistance.

[1] T Herzl, *Altneuland* ('Old Newland') (Haifa, Haifa Publishing [1902], 1960).

[2] B Shatz, *Jerusalem the Built up—A Daydream* (Jerusalem, 1918) (Hebrew).

[3] R Albiom-Dror, 'Women in the Zionist Utopia' (1992) 66 *Cathedra* 111 (Hebrew).

[4] S Azaryahu, '*The Union of Hebrew Women for Equal Rights in Eretz Israel': Chapters in the History of the Women's movement of Eretz Israel* (trans M Freedman) (Haifa, Women's Aid Fund [1948], 1977).

would enjoy the benefits of legal rights and of social and familial respect. The association demanded allocation of rights to women as an

> equal partner in the building of the State who would carry the burden of pioneering alongside the male and as human beings insisting on these elementary rights in our national organization ... [Women] wish to have equal rights with the males in political and civil life' (Central Zionist Archives J75–9, 1).

Half a century later, female members of the Israeli parliament (Knesset) called on the government to support policies to increase women's participation in the labour force and to 'enact social and just legislation' for women.[5] They claimed that both men and women should be seen as individuals eligible for equal rights as earners or house workers.[6]

Today, a century after the utopian dreams of Herzl and his successors, legal and economic autonomy remain elusive for many Israeli women. The public dining rooms celebrated by Shatz are now soup kitchens providing basic meals to the poor. Unfortunately, the number of women, including working women, visiting them continues to rise.[7] And, recently, the first Kibbutz, Degania, which symbolized the egalitarian ideology, was privatized, and services such as food preparation and care for family members were returned to the home.[8]

In the legal arena, Israel can be proud of a cluster of advanced labour laws securing women's rights as workers, and especially as mothers.[9] However, hotlines report a sharp rise in calls describing systemic abuse of these rights.[10] Finally, women workers do not yet enjoy economic independence or social recognition encouraging their participation in the workforce.[11] Rather, their entry into the workforce is considered to be a last resort among families struggling with a formidable financial situation.

Utopian dreams about women's independence and freedom emphasized the significance of women and mothers' participation in the labour market. The connection between women's autonomy and their employment is widely discussed by welfare state scholars addressing relations between

[5] Knesset minutes 21 June 1972, p 2959.

[6] See M Ajzenstadt and J Gal, 'Appearance Can be Deceptive: Gender in the Israeli Welfare State' (2001) 8 *Social Politics* 292.

[7] A Doron and J Gal, *Soup kitchens in Israel at the Beginning of the 21st Century* (Jerusalem, Paul Baerwald School of Social Work and Social Welfare, Hebrew University of Jerusalem, 2006) (Hebrew).

[8] S Fogiel-Bijaoui, 'Women in the Kibbutz: The "Mixed Blessing" of Neo-Liberalism' (2007) 13 *Nashim: A Journal of Jewish Women's Studies and Gender Issues* 102.

[9] F Raday, 'Women in the Labour Law' in RC Frances, C Shalev and M Liban-Koob (eds), *Women's Status in Israeli Law and society* (Jerusalem and Tel Aviv, Shoken, 1995) (Hebrew).

[10] T Tamir, *Women in Israel: Between Theory and Reality* (Ramat Gan, Women Lobby in Israel, 2007).

[11] N Lewin-Epstein and H Steir, *Division of Household Labour in Germany and Israel: Time Constraints, Resource Dependence and Gender Ideology* Discussion Paper No 1-2005 (Tel Aviv, The Pinhas Sapir Center for Development, Tel Aviv University, 2005).

women, family and the state.[12] Scholars claim that to understand these relations, their construction and legitimation, they must be contextualized in the wider social-political milieu as well as in the normative structure of the specific societies in which these relations are shaped and take place.[13] Drawing on those claims, this chapter examines the promised and actual state of mothers in the Israeli labour market during a decade of economic changes driven by neo-liberalism. The chapter begins with a theoretical discussion of the relation between mothers, work and the state. It then reviews these issues in the Israeli context, attempting to comprehend the influence of the neo-liberal ideology and its governance structure and policy as well as changes in the welfare state. It ends with a discussion on the gendered nature of the neo-liberal regime.

II. WOMEN, THE LABOUR FORCE AND THE STATE IN AN ERA OF NEO-LIBERALISM

Scholars of the welfare state have underscored the varying ideologies and policies of welfare regimes in relation to women's paid and unpaid work.[14] Broadly speaking, the various studies show that most Western welfare regimes that are tied to the capitalist social order of the nineteenth and twentieth centuries[15] adopted a 'breadwinner' model, characterized by a gender division of labour: men dedicated themselves to market work and women were occupied in unpaid care and domestic work.[16] This model led to men's control over the public spheres of work and politics and the relegation of women to the private sphere. It carried with it a notion of the dependency of the wife on the employed husband, leading to a limited independence, distinguishing between the family (private) and work (public) spheres.

The emergence of the post-industrial phase of capitalism in the United States[17] and in Europe[18] during the 1980s and the 1990s, and the emergence

[12] JS O'Connor, AS Orloff and S Shaver, *State, Markets, Families, Gender, Liberalism and Social Policy in Australia, Canada, Great Britain and the Unites States* (Cambridge, Cambridge University Press, 1999).

[13] See eg, I Ostner, 'Back to the Fifties: Gender and Welfare in Unified Germany' (1994) 1 *Social Politics* 32.

[14] L Brush, 'Changing the subject: Gender and Welfare Regime Studies' (2002) 9 *Social Politics* 161.

[15] N Fraser, 'After the Family Wage: Gender Equity and the Welfare State' (1994) 22 *Political Theory* 591.

[16] M Abramovitz, *Under Attack, Fighting Back: Women and Welfare in the United States* (New York, Monthly Review Press, 2000).

[17] M Abramovitz, 'Welfare Reform in the United States: Gender, Race and Class Matter' (2006) 26 *Critical Social Policy* 336; N Fraser, 'Clintonism, Welfare and the Antisocial Wage: The Emergence of a Neoliberal Political Imaginary' (1993) 6 *Rethinking Marxism* 9; N Fraser and L Gordon, 'A Genealogy of Dependency: Tracing a keyword of the U.S. Welfare State' (1994) 19 *Signs* 309.

[18] J Lewis, 'Gender and Welfare State Change' (2002) 4 *European Societies* 331; D Sainsbury, *Gender, Equality and Welfare States* (Cambridge, Cambridge University Press, 1996).

of late modernity[19] challenged this model and the accompanying assumptions about roles, status and the relation between women, work and the state. A new discourse, which defined society, the individual and employment, in terms of market metaphors and supported the marketization of the economic order, was accompanied by the decline of the welfare state and transformations in social norms and values associated with the traditional model of the nuclear, heterosexual family.[20] As a result of globalization, privatization, and limited job availability, fewer families could support themselves on one earner's wages alone.[21]

One apparent shift arising from these macro changes is the increased presence of women in the global labour market. Indeed, between 1975 and 1995, 65 per cent of advanced industrial countries and 51 per cent of developing countries experienced a sharp increase in women's labour force participation and a decrease in men's employment, leading to a change in the composition of the labour market globally.[22] Feminist scholars such as Kessler[23] and Orloff[24] anticipated that the increased female participation in the labour market might lead to greater equality for women because their independent income would enhance their position in the household and in society, and contribute to positive self-esteem and appreciation.[25] This increased household power, in turn, should lead to a more equitable division of domestic labour.[26] It would seem, therefore, that compared with the former position of dependency based on gender characteristics, paid work ought to facilitate more autonomy and independence, which together serve as important sources of a redefined empowered gender identity for women.[27]

The next section of the chapter examines these assumptions in light of the impact of neo-liberal governance on women's participation in the labour force in Israel.

[19] R Crompton, 'Employment, Flexible Working and the Family' (2002) 53 *British Journal of Sociology* 537.

[20] R Crompton, 'Gender Restructuring, Employment, and Caring' (2001) 8 *Social Politics* 266.

[21] Abramovitz, above n 17.

[22] G Standing, 'Global Feminization Through Flexible Labour' (1999) 17 *World Development* 1077.

[23] HA Kessler, *In Pursuit of Equity* (Oxford, Oxford University Press, 2001).

[24] A Orloff, 'Gender and the Social Rights of Citizenship. State Policies and Gender Relations in comparative research' (1993) 58 *American Sociological Review* 303.

[25] M Bittman, P England, L Sayer, N Folbre and G Matheson, 'When Does Gender Trump Money? Bargaining and Time in Household Work' (2003) 109 *American Journal of Sociology* 186.

[26] See discussion in H Steir and N Lewin-Epstein, 'Women's Part-Time Employment and Gender Inequality in the Family' (2000) 21 *Journal of Family Issues* 390.

[27] J Lewis, 'The Decline of the Male Breadwinner model: Implications for Work and Care' (2001) 8 *Social Politics* 152.

III. WOMEN IN THE LABOUR MARKET IN ISRAEL

Between 1948, with the birth of the State of Israel, and the early 1980s, the welfare state ideology dominated Israeli society. In 1985, Israel adopted a stabilization programme, which aimed to fight economic instability and to reduce the double-digit inflation rate.[28] Israeli society thus gradually moved from a collectivist, social and economic framework toward a more individualistic, materialistic, socio-economic regime, reducing state intervention and liberalizing the capital market.[29] During these years, the local market opened up to multinationals and imported goods, moving Israel toward a post-Fordist economy marked by a neo-liberal agenda, whose aim was to downsize the state and minimize its role in the market.[30] Privatization and globalization, accompanied by an ideology supporting reduced state responsibility for the welfare and the rights of individuals, governed policies in the labour market, as well as in areas of health, education and welfare. Support for the welfare state gradually lessened and health, education and welfare services were privatized.[31]

Neo-liberal perceptions came to dominate labour relations and the private sphere, collective rights were devalued and collective bargaining agreements were replaced by individual and special labour contracts. Until the 1980s, the Israel Federation of Labour, the Histadrut, had been a strong trade union, representing 80 per cent of Israeli workers.[32] It played a central role in collective bargaining over employers' wage payment and was highly involved in protecting workers' rights. During the 1980s, however, it lost its social and political strength and ability to protect public sector jobs and secure workers' rights.[33]

The pursuit of a neo-liberal agenda intensified in the first years of the twenty-first century, when Israel faced an economic recession due

[28] J Nitzan and S Bichler, *The Global Political Economy of Israel* (London and Sterling VA, Pluto Press, 2002); G Shafir and Y Peled, *Being Israeli: The Dynamics of Multiple Citizenship* (Cambridge, Cambridge University Press, 2002).

[29] A Razin and E Sadka, *The Economy of Modern Israel: Malaise and Promise* (Chicago, University of Chicago Press, 1993); M Shalev, 'Liberalization and the Transformation of the Political Economy' in G Shafir and Y Peled (eds), *The New Israel: Peacemaking and Liberalization* (Boulder CO, Westview, 2000).

[30] D Filc, 'The health business under neo-liberalism: The Israeli case' (2005) 25 *Critical Social Policy* 180.

[31] M Ajzenstadt and Z Rosenhek, 'Privatization and New Modes of State Intervention: The Long-Term Care program in Israel' (2000) 29 *Journal of Social Policy* 247; J Gal, 'The Commercialization of the Welfare State: Implications for Israel' (1994) 15 *Society and Welfare* 7 (Hebrew).

[32] F Raday, 'The Insider-Outsider Politics of Labour-Only Contracting' (1999) 13 *Comparative Labour Law and Policy Journal* 413.

[33] J Gal and N Achdut, 'A Safety Net Full of Holes: Changing Policy Towards Israel's Social Assistance Program' in A Uri, G John and J Katan (eds), *Formulating Social Policy in Israel* (Jerusalem, Taub Center for Social Policy Studies in Israel, 2007) (Hebrew).

to the renewal of the violent conflict with the Palestinians (the second Intifada), which led to a reduction in investments, in tourism and personal consumption. In addition, Israel was affected by the international economic slow-down. This led to the rise of unemployment to more than 10 per cent. The government's deficit ran at double the three per cent of the GDP inscribed in the budget. Benjamin Netanyahu, the then Finance Minster, who enjoyed strong support from Prime Minister Ariel Sharon, declared a recovery economic programme, which included cuts in taxes and the reduction of the government's involvement in the economy in order to free up resources for the business sector, as well as the increased privatization of state-owned companies.[34]

Other elements of the programme included massive lay-offs, especially in the public sector workforce, and wage reductions, cuts in the state budget and the curtailing of various benefit and transfer payments, especially child benefits, unemployment compensation and income support. In addition, during a short time span, the pensionable age for women was raised from 65 to 67 years and eligibility for the elderly allowance (which is not conditional on labour market participation) was raised for women from the age of 65 to 70. Finally, the state adopted stricter eligibility guidelines. In the case of income support programmes, for example, prior to 2002, single mothers were eligible for income support if their children were under the age of seven; however, since 2004 only mothers of children under two are eligible.[35]

These economic reforms led to an unstable workforce and the decline of real wages. Very few families could continue to make ends meet on a single earner's income. In 1998, for example, the difference between individual net income and average expenditures was 1,310 NIS (or approximately US$322). In 2004, this difference grew sharply to 1,487 NIS (or approximately US$371) (Surveys of Household Expenditure, Central Bureau of Statistics). Finally, Israel joined other countries in tying benefits to increased participation in the labour market. The main initiative was the adoption of welfare-to-work programmes.[36]

Similar to circumstances in other countries, this economic restructuring required Israeli women to look for work in order to increase households'

[34] A Doron, 'Thatcher: The Israeli Version' in R Rothental (ed), *The Roots: A New Discourse on Nation and Society* (Jerusalem, Keter, 2005) (Hebrew).

[35] N Ahdut, 'The Program for the Integration of Single Parents in the Labour Market: Resources and Obstructions for the Integration in the Employment Arena' (2007) 73 *Social Security* 69 (Hebrew).

[36] A Doron, '"From Social Relief to Work": A Threat on the Safety Net in the Israeli Social Security System' (2000) 58 *Social Security* 113 (Hebrew); J Katan, 'From Social Assistance to the Integration in the Workforce: An Easy Transformation or a Narrow Bridge' (2000) 58 *Social Security* 129 (Hebrew).

income and led to an increase in female labour force participation.[37] Indeed, women's participation in the labour market has grown steadily. In 1960, 27.3 per cent of the women in the civilian working-age population were employed, and in 2005, 50 per cent were in the labour market.[38] Although in the past, many women dropped out of the labour force after giving birth and returned only later in life, currently, many young mothers continue their labour market participation without interruption. In 2003, 53.7 per cent of women with children under the age of 14 participated in the labour market, and in 2005, that share increased to 54.9 per cent.[39]

A sharp increase in women's participation in the labour market is of course not new to Israeli society. During the 1970s, Israel witnessed a rapid economic growth, which led to an increase in consumption requiring an increase in workforce participation to overcome labour force shortage. Women were regarded by the government as potential workers who could respond to the needs of the expanding labour market.[40] The government of the time encouraged women to join the labour market and developed family policies and social protection to facilitate the integration of women into the labour force. Thus, a new infrastructure of day care centres was developed to care for children of working mothers.[41] In addition, working mothers were eligible to receive approximately 30 per cent of their day care fees.[42]

However, this ceased to be the case in the 1990s and the 2000s when neo-liberalism came to dominate Israeli politics. The government called upon the unemployed and especially women to 'get out and go to work'.[43] However, the government did not create family-friendly policies and affordable child care arrangements during regular working hours. Moreover, single mothers of young children who refuse employment in jobs that require their presence between 7.30–8.00 and 17.00 lose their eligibility for income support for two months.[44] The existing conditions in the labour market did not offer any assistance or protection to women who were left

[37] Clearly labour market participation rates in Israel are also affected by ethnic and religious affiliation (see eg, www.tamas.gov.il/NR/rdonlyres/0788A0C9-D2F6-4A96-9DD5-0F4563B782D6/0/nashimarviot.pdf; www.knesset.gov.il/mmm/data/docs/m02006.doc.) However, this subject is beyond the scope of this chapter.

[38] Manpower Survey, Central Bureau of Statistics (2005) at: www.cbs.gov.il/reader.

[39] *Ibid.*

[40] DN Izraeli, 'Culture, policy, and women in Dual-Earner Families in Israel' in SD Lewis, N Izraeli and H Hootsmans (eds), *Dual-Earner Families: International Perspectives* (London, Sage, 1992).

[41] Ajzenstadt and Gal, above n 6.

[42] H Bar and Y Markus, *Day-care: A Social Service for the Mother and Her Child: A Survey of Workers and Consumers* (Jerusalem, Institute for Applied Social Research, 1977) (Hebrew).

[43] See eg, Ministry of Finance, 'Discourse around Raising Women Pension Age to Women' (April 2008), at: www.mof.gov.il/hon/2001/pension/memos/plan2003_pres2.pdf.

[44] O Lotan, *Employment and Poverty Among Single Mothers* (Jerusalem, The Centre of Research and Information, The Knesset, 2007) (Hebrew).

almost alone to confront the free market forces, which created obstacles for their successful integration into the workforce.

A. Occupational Sex Segregation, Income Gaps and Part-Time Jobs

Women workers in Israel are concentrated in traditionally female, secondary sectors of employment. They are employed in personal, food and hospitality services, as well as nursing and teaching. The increase in women's labour force participation did not lessen the gender wage gap. In 2002, for example, the average hourly wage of a female worker was NIS 36.7 (or US$9.17), compared with NIS 45.3 (or US$11.30) for male workers.[45] In 2005 the average gross salary for female workers was 76.4 per cent of the average male salary in Israel.[46]

These gaps cannot be explained by gender differences in education. In 2005, 77.8 per cent of female workers had completed more than 16 years of studies compared to 76.8 per cent of working men.[47] Finally, the new economic structure hardly opened up new managerial options for women. In 2003, only 4.3 per cent of the Israeli female workforce was in managerial positions, compared with 9.2 per cent of males. By 2005, the participation rates in managerial positions for women had declined to 3.2 per cent compared to 7.9 per cent for men.[48]

Galin[49] found that 6% of women in the civilian labor force as compared with 19% of men were self employed or employers. Most of these women were concentrated in the traditional female occupations of day care, beauty parlours, coffee shops and restaurants, whose clients were mainly women.

Many women work in part-time jobs. Between 2000 and 2005, the percentage of women employed in part-time occupations in Israel increased from 34.7 per cent to 37.7 per cent.[50] Many other women worked in occupations defined as full-time positions but that consisted of reduced hours, leading to a reduced salary. Furthermore, part-time workers are not perceived as committed workers, and very few hold prime labour market positions.[51] This employment pattern reinforces their marginality in the

[45] Manpower Survey, Central Bureau of Statistics (2004), at: www.cbs.gov.il/reader.

[46] E Toledano, *Recipients of Maternity Leave Benefits: 2000–2005* (Jerusalem, National Security Institute, 2006) (Hebrew).

[47] R Halperin-Kaddari and I Karo, *Women and Family in Israel: Statistical Bi-Annual Report* (Ramat-Gan, Israel, Faculty of Law, Bar-Ilan University, 2007).

[48] Manpower Survey, above n 38.

[49] A Galin, 'The Impact of Flexible Work on Female Labour in Israel' in M Anat (ed), *Women, the Rising power: The Promotion of Women in the Workplace—Shattering the Glass Ceiling* (Tel-Aviv, Poalim, 1997) (Hebrew).

[50] Calculated from Manpower Survey, above n 38.

[51] Lewin-Epstein and Steir, above n 11.

labour market.[52] Women employed in part-time occupations usually work fewer hours (30.4 per week on average) than their male counterparts (41.7 hours on average).[53] Economic explanations for the high concentration of women in part-time jobs point to the preference of women to work in flexible jobs, which allow them to devote more time to rearing their children.[54] In Israel, most women claim that they would prefer to be occupied in full-time jobs; however, the lack of child care and strong social norms and ideology emphasizing the importance of child rearing prevented them from carrying out their wishes.[55]

B. Temporary Employment Agencies (TEAs)

Until the mid-1990s, the public service sector was the main employer of most women in Israel, as 60 per cent of the public sector workforce was female.[56] While most women were employed in low-paid clerical and service jobs in the public sector, they enjoyed job security and decent working conditions and their rights were protected. However, with the decline of unionized public sector jobs, many women turned to employment through temporary employment agencies (TEAs). Until the 1990s, TEAs supplied experts for specialized short-term projects. Since the 1990s, Israel has witnessed a proliferation of such agencies, the introduction of which was facilitated by the state. Raday[57] claims that 'the government was instrumental in establishing the legitimacy of this employment pattern by becoming a user of labour services acquired in this way'. Indeed, approximately one-third of the workers in government ministries are employed by sub-contractors, and 65 per cent of all workers employed through TEAs or sub-contractors are women.[58] On average, women are employed through TEAs for 26.2 months compared with 13.8 months for males. Women also seldom move to steadier work.[59] TEAs usually offer low-paid jobs which do not require professional skills and entail limited options for professional mobility. Workers in these jobs

[52] H Steir, 'Short-Term Employment Transitions of Women in the Israeli Labour Force' (1998) 51 *Industrial and Labour Relations Review* 269.

[53] 'Weekly Work-Hours per Employed Person and Per Employee, By Industry and Sex' from Manpower Survey, above n 38.

[54] P England, 'Gender Inequality in Labour Markets: The Role of Mothers and Segregation' (2005) 12 *Social Politics* 264.

[55] Halperin-Kaddari and Karo, above n 47; Galin, above n 49.

[56] Y Nakar, *Women in Israel 2001–2006* (The Knesset Information Services, 2006), at: www.miki.org.il/miki/files/1149584697390.doc.

[57] Raday, above n 32.

[58] R Warzberger, *Employment in Manpower Agencies* (Jerusalem, Knesset Centre of Research and Information, 2002) (Hebrew).

[59] M Tagar, *Working without Honor: Workers' Rights and Their Abuse*. A Report of the Association for Human Rights on the Occasion of International Human Rights Day 2006 (Hebrew), at: www.acri.org.il/hebrew-acri/engine/story.asp?id=1429.

are also too often exposed to unsafe working conditions and, as temporary workers, are denied basic benefits.[60]

Women employed through TEAs do not enjoy the benefits provided to women employed in the public service, such as paid medical leave if needed during pregnancy or for the purpose of fertility treatment, or paid leave for the care of a sick child. Their right to return to their jobs after giving birth is not secure, and they do not enjoy labour union protection,[61] which studies have shown is crucial for the protection and advancement of women and other disadvantaged workers.[62] Without union protection, women employed through TEAs do not enjoy the rights and benefits of union-negotiated wage contracts. In addition, according to the Women Lobby in Israel (2006), 19 per cent of women employed through TEAs were victims of sexual harassment compared with 13 per cent of independently employed women or women employed in public services.

In 1996, the Israeli parliament enacted the 1996 Employment by Labour-Only Contractors Law, which aimed to protect leased workers from exploitation (Proposal for Employment by Labour-Only Contractors Law). Section 13(a) of the Law equates the employment conditions of the leased worker with those in the workplace where he or she works. The Law provides that after three years of work, the workplace collective agreement will determine the leased worker's conditions. In 2000, the legislature introduced an advanced amendment, requiring TEAs to equalize temporary workers' conditions with those of in-house employees after only nine months of work (section 12(a)). However, in the 2003 budget, the amendment was postponed until 2007 and has not taken place to this day. This delay was achieved after campaigns were conducted by private entrepreneurs benefiting from the existing working arrangements. This legitimation and facilitation of working conditions stems from the principles of the new economy which favours reduction in expenditures, flexible work arrangements and higher mobility of workers, leading to the abusive work conditions of marginalized workers.

[60] N Dagan-Bozaglo, *The Right to Work: A Legal and Economic Perspective*. Adva Center 2007, at: www.adva.org\view.asp?lang=he&catID=452 (Hebrew).

[61] Warzberger, above n 58.

[62] See eg, Y Cohen, Y Haberfeld, G Mundlak and I Saporta, 'Unpacking Union Density: Union Membership and Coverage in the Transformation of the Israeli Industrial Relations System' (2003) 42 *Industrial Relations* 692; J Pontusson, FD Rueda and C Way, *The Role of Political Institutional Variables in the Making of Gendered Patterns of Wage Inequality: A Comparative Analysis of OECD Countries*. Institute for European Studies, San Giacomo Working Paper 99.4 (Ithaca NY, Cornell University, 1999).

D Weil, 'Individual Rights and Collective Agents: The Role of Old and New Workplace Institutions in the Regulation of Labour Markets' in RB Freeman, J Hersch and M Lawrence (eds), *Emerging Labour Market Institutions for the Twenty-First Century* (Chicago IL, University of Chicago Press, 2005).

C. Women and Mothers' Rights in the Labour Market

Soon after its establishment, Israel enacted the 1954 Employment of Women Law, which aimed to enable women, and especially mothers, to participate in the labour market. Over the years, the law was refined and extended, and together with other laws and regulations, it is now considered as being liberal and advanced, protecting women in the labour market.[63] Clause 6 of the Law provides for maternity leave for 14 weeks, and allows for leave during pregnancy and for pregnancy-related medical examinations. (Maternity payment for this period is regulated through the National Insurance Act). The Law further prohibits employers from demanding that women work during maternity leave. Clause 9a prohibits the dismissal of pregnant women or women undergoing fertilization treatment who have worked for at least six months with the same employer. An employer who wishes to dismiss a pregnant woman must obtain permission from the Minister for Industry, Trade and Employment. The minister is required to examine the request and grant permission only after being convinced that the request is not related in any way to the pregnancy or to the fertilization treatments. The law guarantees mothers the same position after returning from leave, and the 1998 amendment prohibits any cut-back in her wage. Clause 9d of the Law prohibits the employer from dismissing a woman living in shelters for battered women without permission. Mothers are entitled to be absent for up to an hour a day at the employer's expense for breast-feeding. According to section 7 of the 1963 Severance Pay Act, a mother who resigns within nine months after she gives birth to care for her child is entitled to a severance pay.

Other laws prohibit gender-based discrimination in the workplace. According to the 1996 Equal Pay Law, equal salary should be paid to employees of both sexes for comparable work. The 1988 Equal Employment Opportunities Law prohibits discrimination in the area of personnel recruitment, selection and promotion on the basis of attributions such as gender, sexual orientation, age, race, religion and nationality. The 1998 Harassment Prevention Act sets heavy punishments for incidents of sexual harassment in the labour market (section 3).

Although this set of advanced laws seems at first glance to protect female workers, an examination of the way in which they are enforced shows that rights of many women workers, and mothers in particular, are being abused and the impact of labour laws on their work condition is minimal. Fifty-three per cent of women who returned to their jobs after maternity leave were moved to another job by the employer.[64] Empirical data point to a

[63] Izraeli, above n 40.
[64] Tamir, above n 10.

steady rise in employers' requests to approve dismissal during pregnancy. The number of such requests increased by 33.1 per cent between 2000 and 2005, or from 907 to 1,208. Nearly one-half of these requests were approved.[65] An increase in the requests to discharge women undergoing fertilization treatment is also evident. In 2002, more than 50 per cent of these requests were approved.[66] To convince the Minister that the discharge is unrelated to pregnancy, employers cite a declining need of manpower in the workplace (in 2002, 26 per cent of the approved requests were granted for this reason), or that the worker did not comply with workplace rules, or the employer cites interpersonal problems preventing the worker from co-operating with colleagues, employers or customers (in 2002, 17 per cent of the approved requests were granted for this latter reason).

The women in these cases are allowed to present their case to the ministry during the process, and they may be represented by a lawyer. Few women take advantage of this provision, however, because most are unaware of their rights and have very limited resources to meet legal expenses.[67]

In addition, women and other members of marginalized groups usually do not apply to the courts owing to language and cultural barriers.[68] Left without legal assistance, many of the women (28 per cent in 2002) accede to some agreement with the employer, paving the way for their legal dismissal.[69]

This practice is under-reported, and therefore more alarming, given that employers often choose not to apply to the ministry and instead openly violate the law by dismissing pregnant women. When discharged, women could complain to the courts, but they hardly ever do.[70]

Until the 1990s, the Naamat organization, which was affiliated with the Histadrut and the Israeli Women Lobby, assisted women who filed complaints about abuse of their rights in various areas. In addition, the Ministry of Labour and Welfare established a service (SHEEL) providing similar help. During the past few years, there has been a proliferation of new non-governmental agencies and voluntary groups, such as 'My Sister', 'With You', and 'Yadid', as well as clinics adjunct to law schools and hotlines, all advising workers of their rights in the area of welfare and

[65] *Ibid.*

[66] R Halperin-Kaddari, *Women in Israel: A State of their Own* (Philadelphia PA, University of Philadelphia Press, 2004).

[67] See discussion on the scanty public civil legal aid available in Israel: M Ajzenstadt and B Ariel, *Civil Legal Aid in Israel* (Jerusalem, School of Social Work and Social Welfare, Hebrew University of Jerusalem, 2006).

[68] G Davidov, 'Enforcement Problems in "Informal" Labour Markets: A View From Israel' (2005) 27 *Comparative Labour Law and Policy Journal* 3.

[69] H Cohen, *Discharge of Pregnant Women. The Women Advocacy in Israel.* 2004 at: www.agenda.org.il/info/pages/sdulamatzeget.ppt (Hebrew).

[70] Nakar, above n 56.

work.[71] The various agencies report a steady increase of women workers complaining that their rights in the labour market are not secured. In addition to termination during pregnancy, women complain that employers refuse to employ pregnant women or mothers or offer them a different position, forcing them to lose their seniority when returning from maternity leave.[72]

Employers adopt a variety of techniques to bypass the laws. Thus, during pregnancy, employers reduce or limit women's work hours, reduce their shifts, change their work environment, move them to a smoking area, or try to force them to resign and thus save the employers the various payments they are required to make.[73] In addition, employers ask women to volunteer during their maternity leave as a condition of securing their job when they return from maternity leave.[74]

These violations are largely ignored by the Ministry of Industry, Trade, and Employment, responsible for labour law enforcement.[75] This weak labour law enforcement is probably not surprising. Sociologists of law have found that laws regulating employment relations are usually moderate and include broad and often ambiguous principles that allow organizations to flexibly interpret the law's meaning to their benefit.[76] The ambiguity leads to a 'process of definition during which organizations test and collectively construct the form and boundaries of compliance in a way that meets legal demands yet preserves managerial interests'.[77] In Israel, labour law violation takes place mainly among sub-contractors.[78] Most workers from these companies are from the lower strata of society and are desperate to hold on to their jobs, and thus are unlikely to take their employers to court since they fear unemployment.[79]

[71] See discussion on the 'NGOization' of civil society in H Herzog, 'Re/Visioning the Women's Movement in Israel' (2008) 12 *Citizenship Studies* 265.

[72] Tamir, above n 10; Tagar, above n 59.

[73] Cohen, above n 69.

[74] M Tabibian-Mizrachi, *Labour Laws: Do they Harm Women or Defend Them?* (Jerusalem, Knesset Centre for Research and Information, 2005) (Hebrew).

[75] G Davidov, *Enforcing Labour and Employment Laws: Lessons from Public-Sector Subcontracting in Israel*. Paper presented at the Law and Society Association Annual Meeting, Berlin 2007.

[76] HW Arthurs, 'Labour law Without the State' (1996) 46 *University of Toronto Law Journal* 1.

[77] LB Edelman, 'Legal Ambiguity and Symbolic Structures: Organizational Mediation of Civil Rights Law' (1992) 97 *American Journal of Sociology* 1531.

[78] Davidov, above n 68; R Hirschl, 'The "Constitutional Revolution" and the Emergence of a New Economic Order in Israel' (1997) 2 *Israel Studies* 136.

[79] K Bumiller, *The Civil Right Society* (Baltimore MD, Johns Hopkins University Press, 1987); W Felstiner, R Abel and S Sarat, 'The Emergence and Transformation of Disputes: Naming, Blaming, and Claiming' (1980) 15 *Law and Society Review* 631; R Shamir and M Shatry, 'Equality of Opportunities in the Labour Courts: Towards Sociology of the Legal Process' (1996) 6 *Labour Law Yearbook* 287 (Hebrew).

As mentioned above, during the past two decades, union power in Israel has weakened, leaving workers in various professions, and especially those employed by the private sector, unprotected. Collective bargaining and stable hierarchical structures of promotion have been replaced by individualized pay and a merit system, leaving workers belonging to marginalized groups less protected and with fewer tools for negotiating their pay and other work conditions.[80] Bamberger, Admit-Dvir and Harel,[81] who have studied the impact of protection in wage and promotion discrimination among scientists and professionals, concluded that women in unionized firms were less exposed to promotion discrimination and its negative earnings consequences. The limited access to justice and the marginalized social and economic position of many female workers create a 'fertile ground for employers wishing to cut costs by violating some labour and employment laws'.[82] As a result, low-income female workers remain unprotected, they are less likely to know their rights such as annual holidays, sick leave and others, and are systematically abused.[83]

D. Societal Attitudes toward Women Workers

Surveys conducted with several groups of citizens in Israel show that the increased participation of women in the labour market in Israel did not challenge the traditional perspective about the division of labour in society.[84] Most males and females strongly continue to support the belief that women have primary responsibility for family duties.[85] At the same time, Yishai[86] found that 71 per cent of employed women claimed that women should develop their own careers, even if this would cause discomfort in family life, and most women believed that women and men should share household responsibilities. However, in a survey conducted in 1996, 41 per cent of 400 women belonging to the civilian workforce in Israel claimed that they did not pursue a professional career because it would prevent their

[80] Y Elbashan, 'Access of Justice of Marginalized Groups in Israel' (2004) 3 *Allei-Mishapt* 497 (Hebrew).

[81] P Bamberger, M Admit-Dvir and G Harel, 'Gender-Based Wage and Promotion Discrimination in Israeli High-Technology Firms: Do Unions Make a Difference?' (1995) 38 *Academy of Management Resource Journal* 1744.

[82] Davidov, above n 68, 9.

[83] N Becker, N Abhasera and C Ziv, *Invisible Workers in the Public Service: A Report on Violation of Contractor's Workers Rights in Government Offices* (Jerusalem, Faculty of Law, Hebrew University of Jerusalem, 2006) (Hebrew).

[84] Halperin-Kaddari, above n 66.

[85] Lewin-Epstein and Steir, above n 11.

[86] Y Yishai, *Between Flag and the Banner: Women in Israeli Politics* (New York, Suny Press, 1997).

husbands from devoting the time required to advance in the labour market.[87] In addition, in the 2005 Social Survey, 19.3 per cent of married women said that they left their jobs to care for children, compared with only 6.3 per cent of males. In addition, more women than men reported that they shoulder most of the domestic duties, including caring for children or other family members.[88]

Women's financial contribution to their household is seen as a 'last resort' mechanism, enabling the family to survive, and not as an activity leading to equality or providing women the leverage to negotiate their share of household chores. Work is considered by most people, including women, as an extension of their domestic role and not as a way to improve their self-esteem or personal autonomy. Women workers continued to be defined by their family members, employers and themselves as supplementary wage earners.[89]

This traditional perspective reflects patriarchal ideas on women's role in the family. Its roots lie in the construction of motherhood in Israel as a family and national role. Motherhood is the means to increase the population, ensuring the continuation of the nation.[90] For most Israelis, the traditional family is a central keystone of the Jewish nation and the historical continuity with previous generations. The centrality of the traditional family to society is also a strong belief among the Arab population in Israel.[91] Against these entrenched ideas, women's labour market work is regarded as merely secondary. Moreover, the development of a career by a woman is stigmatized, and she is regarded as selfish and deviant.[92] Finally, Steir and Lewin-Epstein found that females working part-time suffer from a double disadvantage—in the labour market and in the family: 'their economic activity is devalued, they are not perceived as committed workers, and they are largely invisible in prime labour market positions'.[93] This practice preserves the gendered employment relations, and women's participation in the labour market goes socially and economically unrewarded.

[87] R Bar-Zuri, H Fisher and A Asher, *Women in the new world of work in Israel* (Tel-Aviv, The Israeli Institute for Economic and Social Research, 1997) (Hebrew).

[88] Halperin-Kaddari and Karo, above n 47.

[89] S Fogiel-Bijaoui, 'Families in Israel: Between Familism and post Modernism' in D Izraeli, A Friedman, H Dahan-Kalev, S Fogiel-Bijaoui, H Herzog, M Hassan and H Naveh (eds), *Sex, Gender Politics: Women in Israel* (Tel-Aviv, Kav Adom, 1999) (Hebrew).

[90] N Berkovitch, 'Motherhood as a National Mission: The Construction of Womanhood in the Legal Discourse in Israel' (1997) 20 *Women's Studies International Forum* 605; Izraeli, above n 40.

[91] Fogiel-Bijaoui, above n 89.

[92] M Ajzenstadt, 'Crime, Social Control and the Process of Social Classification: Juvenile Delinquency Justice Discourse in Israel, 1948–1970' (2002) 49 *Social Problems* 585; Izraeli, above n 40.

[93] Steir and Lewin-Epstein, above n 26, 22.

IV. THE GENDERED DIMENSIONS OF NEO-LIBERAL IDEOLOGY

This chapter sheds light on several issues concerning the gendered dimensions of neo-liberal ideology. First, because neo-liberalism is not simply an economic structure, but a philosophy encompassing individuals and society in market terms, rationalities and perceptions inherent in its logic should be explored to better understand its gendered features. Adopting a rational-economy philosophy, this perspective assumes a rational individual to be free to choose among various alternatives.[94] This 'rational economic man' makes cost-benefit analyses before choosing a specific activity in the workplace, aiming to maximize his or her utility to secure the highest possible wage.[95] The ethos of this ideology promotes individual responsibility and interprets failure as a sign and proof of an individual's weakness.[96] Economic dependency thus is explained as a choice preferred by certain individuals who choose unemployment or unprofitable occupations over productivity.[97] In this perspective, the growing availability of flexible jobs is considered as a rich source of opportunities to make strategic choices between an array of jobs and work possibilities.[98]

In this vein, the relegation of women to occupational segregation that results in low-paid and part-time work is considered an outcome of their calculated market decisions.[99] As was seen in this chapter, neo-liberal premises ignore social circumstances, such as childbearing and care-giver roles as well as practices of discrimination against women in the labour market, that prevent women from achieving the new challenges given them by society during this era of economic restructuring. Instead, women who occupy the lower ranks of the job market are blamed and stigmatized as lazy, unproductive and unable to achieve high status owing to their personalities and biological instincts.[100]

[94] See discussion in TC Patterson, 'The Turn to Agency: Neoliberalism, Individuality, and Subjectivity in Late-Twentieth-Century Anglophone Archaeology' (2005) 17 *Rethinking Marxism* 373.

[95] Crompton, above n 19; S Duncan and E Rosalind, 'Lone Mothers and Paid Work: Rational Economic Man or Gendered Moral Rationalities' (1997) 3 *Feminist Economics* 29; S Lash, 'Foreword: Individualization in a Non-Linear Mode' in U Beck and EB Gernsheim (eds), *Individualization: Institutionalized individualism and its Social and Political Consequences* (London, Sage, 2002).

[96] C Hay, 'The Normalizing Role of Rationalist Assumptions in the Institutional Embedding of Neoliberalism' (2004) 33 *Economy and Society* 500.

[97] Fraser and Gordon, above n 17.

[98] SP Vallace, 'Rethinking Post-Fordism: The Meaning of Workplace Flexibility' (1999) 17 *Sociological Theory* 68.

[99] See discussion in L McDowell, 'Love, Money, and Gender Divisions of Labour: Some Critical Reflections on Welfare-to-Work Policies in the UK' (2005) 5 *Journal of Economic Geography* 365.

[100] See discussion on the demonization of female victims and offenders in N Naffine, *Law and the Sexes: Explorations in Feminist Jurisprudence* (Sydney, Allen & Unwin, 1990); N Naffine, *Feminism and Criminology* (Malden MA, Polity Press, 1996); C Smart, *Women, Crime and Criminology* (London, Routledge & Kegan Paul, 1997); C Smart, 'Feminist

A central component of the neo-liberal individualistic agenda is its focus on individual rights and identities, which replace the conceptions emphasizing collective actions and responsibility that prevailed during most of the twentieth century.[101] This ideology promotes, among other things, the notion of individual responsibility for one's own career path without any reliance on communal arrangements, pre-earned and previously paved rights and promotion paths.[102]

A further premise of neo-liberalism is the cost-effective framework emphasizing the pursuit of efficiency, effectiveness and growth. Optimal productivity, this worldview suggests, should be achieved by shrinking government spending and reducing labour and other costs.[103] The disproportional employment of women in the private sectors in temporary, part-time and seasonal work (business models that maximize profits) advances the aim of gaining profits with limited financial investment. In this context, pregnant women and mothers of small children are considered unable to work sufficiently and even as hindering firms and organizations from economic progress. They thus have an adverse effect on the entire society. This further reinforces the image of women controlled by their bodies and their biological attributes, as they leave work for medical examinations or to breast-feed their babies, and is viewed as preventing them from becoming ideal devoted and productive workers in the global economy. The Israeli government forced women to join the workforce, framing this demand with the language of work choice and equality. However, in reality the social and economic circumstances did not provide this promised choice. It was not possible for working women to make 'real' or 'genuine' choices to 'work and care'.[104]

Secondly, women's incorporation into the labour force was not a means of promoting gender equality. Their labour is considered as a profit-generating activity and not as a mechanism enabling greater equality. Moreover, this trend did not change the traditional breadwinner model. Although it is true that almost half of the families in Israel have dual-income earning arrangements in which women contribute to the household economy,[105] further examination proves that the symbolic and ideological dimensions inherent in a model that assumes husbands are responsible for providing income for

Approaches to Criminology or Postmodern Women Meets Atavistic Man' in L Gelsthorpe and A Morris (eds), *Feminist Perspectives in Criminology* (Berkshire, Open University Press, 1990).

[101] See discussion in W Larner, 'Post-Welfare State Governance: Towards a Code of Social and Family Responsibility' (2000) 2 *Social Politics* 244.

[102] Crompton, above n 19.

[103] Abramovitz, above n 17.

[104] J Lewis and M Campbell, 'UK Work/Family Balance Policies and Gender Equality, 1997–2005' (2007) 1 *Social Politics* 4.

[105] H Steir and A Lewin, 'The Effect of Women's Employment on Poverty in Israel' (2002) 62 *Social Security* 28 (Hebrew).

the family has not disappeared or been replaced. Although women's roles in the family changed with increased female participation in the labour market, practical changes and discursive shifts in the meaning of the breadwinner model did not take place. Gender wage differentials occurring at all class levels reinforce the notion of women as supplementary wage earners dependent on primary male breadwinners. Women still bear the major responsibility for child rearing and other familial chores, as the division of labour in the household has not changed.

Attitudes toward women's employment are best explicated not by focusing on their participation rates, but by examining the gendered meanings attached to their work and income, which are further situated in the general societal attitudes toward women and their social role, which extends beyond the family structure. The ideology of domesticity, governed by cultural and structural factors, constructs women as secondary providers to their husbands' incomes. Instead of being liberated and in a position of acquiring power and autonomy through participation in the labour force, women once again are subordinate in both the workplace and in the home, a practice that has further contributed to their marginalization. Thus, the expansion of female employment was a condition insufficient for enhancing gender equality. Processes of globalization and privatization increased their confinement to poorly-paid, unstable occupations, left them unprotected in the unregulated market, and failed to provide them with negotiating power over their familial and personal status.

Thirdly, with women's increased involvement in the labour market, the boundaries between the private and the public sectors have become blurred. Women now have a more visible presence in the public arena via work. However, the confinement of women to the home has been replaced by an occupational segregation, allowing women only a limited representation in the workplace and mainly in selected occupations. The nature of their participation in the market can be seen as a spillover of family life into work, as it mirrors their gendered position in society in general and in the family in particular: women's jobs are often the extensions of their traditional roles of care-giver, and their work in both places is undervalued.[106]

The traditional gender ideology that supports the private-public dichotomy, ignoring women's unpaid contribution, now obfuscates women's significant and critical contribution to the household economy. Instead, their financial provision for the family is seen as a natural requirement and a means of assisting families to survive in the new economic regime. Women are required to negotiate between their familial work and economic production in the labour market, a demand that becomes more difficult in the context of the decline of welfare, health and education services amid

[106] Brush, above n 14.

the retreat of the welfare state. Women workers' dependency and their exposure to unregulated exploitation by those holding positions of power, reinforces gendered notions of weakness, victimhood and need.

Fourthly, the patriarchal nature of Israeli society, which requires women to simultaneously adhere to their familial role while contributing to the family wage, makes it difficult for women to develop careers and leads many women to become cheap, recycled labour, available to work under abusive work arrangements. The reconciliation of family and work responsibilities has not led to the redefinition of women's place in Israeli society.

Increased involvement of women in the workplace in Israel was not an outcome of comprehensive planning, leading to policies that enabled women to balance family and work. Such supportive policies as child care arrangements, tax benefits, and monetary remuneration for child care and housework could assist women's integration into the labour market, enabling them to reconcile work and family life. Moreover, the state did not institute measures to encourage women's labour force involvement. The new economic regime in Israel ignored gender equality, and women were unable to freely choose and shape the nature of both their paid and unpaid work.

The lack of these steps is not surprising, given the hegemony of domesticity in Israel, an ideal deeply rooted in the country's history and culture. This ideology continues to determine the meaning of women's employment inside and outside the family sphere. The traditional Israeli ideology, which centres on the notion of the nuclear family, secured the stability of the breadwinner model even at times of economic and social changes. In this case, these shifts succeeded in touching upon the external structure of gender relations but did not reach down to its ideological roots, which shaped the particular nature of women's position within the social structure of Israeli society during the neo-liberal regime.

In sum, neo-liberalism has brought both change and continuity in the practical and symbolic discourse relating to women's participation in the labour force. Women's unequal participation and the interpretation of their labour market work through neo-liberal principles reinforce motherhood and domesticity as strongholds of womanhood. As in other countries, the breadwinner model in Israel was externally modified but internally preserved; its traditional form may have disappeared, but its underlying assumptions were not altered,[107] and in some aspects they were even strengthened. Further research is needed to examine in detail the experience of women in lieu of the various global changes and their manifestations in various places in the world in an era of neo-liberalism.

[107] B Hobson, D Ann-Zolfe and K Hallden, 'Men and Women's Agency in Diverse and Changing Institutional Contexts' in J Lewis (ed), *Children, Changing Families and welfare States* (Cheltenham, Edward Elgar, 2006).

6

'Risky Women'

The Role of 'Risk' in the Construction of the Single Mother*

KAREN SWIFT

I. INTRODUCTION

THIS CHAPTER EXPLORES some effects of including the notion of risk in child protection law. Specifically, my focus is on Canadian legislation and on the policies, regulations and practices that support the legislation. I look particularly at the potential effects of legalized representations of risk on low-income mothers, usually single mothers, involved in child protection systems. In the conclusion, I make some observations about the construction of low-income single mothers in relation to risk. Two Canadian provinces, Ontario and British Columbia (BC), and their legislation and documents are used to illustrate the points.

The data analysis focuses on risk as ideology; that is, risk as a concept that serves to distort, gloss over and turn attention away from relations of class, race and gender that are structured into child welfare.[1] I examine how the treatment in child protection of risk as a real, identifiable and value neutral thing, supported in law, allows the construction of a 'risk class', composed mostly of low-income women, who can legitimately be intruded upon, scrutinized indefinitely and held to account for their daily activities. These intrusions can happen on the basis of what *might* happen in the future rather than on any actual harm to their children, with the result that more families become involved with child protection authorities for more reasons and often with more substantial consequences. I also point out

* Portions of this chapter appear in K Swift and M Callahan, *At Risk: Social Justice in Child Welfare and Other Human Services* (Toronto, University of Toronto Press, 2009). The Social Sciences and Humanities Research Council of Canada provided support for this research.

[1] K Swift, *Manufacturing 'Bad Mothers'* (Toronto, University of Toronto Press, 1995).

mechanisms that produce compliance by both workers and clients of the system. I argue for a more socially just approach to child welfare practice, one that considers all relevant factors necessary to produce healthy circumstances for children.

II. CONTEMPORARY DEBATES ABOUT 'RISK'

There is a substantial literature and much debate in academic and social policy circles about the nature, reality and meaning of risk. The idea of risk arises in societies that have a belief in science as an aid to controlling and changing the future. 'Science' in this context implies a belief that objective reality and truths about that reality can be identified through adherence to specific and standardized research methodologies—a belief of course challenged by critical theorists among others. The science of risk suggests that aspects of the future can be predicted through carefully controlled calculations of probabilities, based on selected aspects of the past. These predictions are viewed by many, including some scientists themselves, as being objective and value free: studies of past events are conducted, risks discovered and calculated, potential actions and victims are identified and mitigating activities recommended.

We now live in a context of increasing awareness of risk. The fallout from 9/11 has brought substantial public awareness of the idea of risk and considerable tolerance for extremely intrusive and inconvenient security measures. Even prior to 9/11, media 'amplification' of risk[2] brought attention to specific kinds of potential and often personal dangers. Accidents publicized in the media create pressure for new safety measures. Attacks on individuals, especially children, heighten fears and bring the attention of parents and others to safety measures believed to reduce the risk of such incidents happening again, even when it is far from clear that such security measures are actually effective. Nevertheless, the science of prediction has gained new traction in this period.

The science of risk builds on the actuarial techniques of the insurance industry. We are all familiar with the workings of insurance computations through which probabilities of harm for particular populations are predicted. Risk calculation builds on this approach, but in the social services moves beyond insurance thinking in its attempt to predict which people will be harmed and who will perpetrate that harm. In this kind of 'scientific' scenario, risks are viewed and treated as real. They are also treated as objective and value-free research findings.

[2] JX Kasperson and RE Kasperson, *The Social Contours of Risk* (London, James & James/ Earthscan, 2005).

An alternative view, taken especially by academics in the social sciences, poses risk as socially constructed.[3] These critics argue that the selection of factors and variables used to calculate risk reflect cultural and social norms.[4] From this perspective, the identification of 'risk' has the capacity to replicate and reproduce existing social relations and the norms of behaviour that apply to particular populations. By identifying departures from social norms through processes of assessing risk, blame for harms and problems can be attributed to particular people, even though nothing bad may yet have occurred. These scholars see risk as anything but neutral and certainly question the value of allocating substantial resources to the project of identifying departures from the status quo.

Through most of the twentieth century, the idea of social risk, albeit with a great many qualifications, was generally accepted as the basis of developing welfare programmes. Social welfare programmes created after World War II in Canada and elsewhere were based on a notion of the shared risks resulting from economic downturns and 'corrections'. This model assumed that anyone could be affected, that costs therefore should be shared and that blame need not be attributed to victims. In recent years, this model has lost favour in many Western countries and has been overtaken by a neo-liberal approach that individualizes risk.

Of course, the state and private sectors sometimes work together to 'spread the costs of risk and provide security'.[5] Heimer[6] has argued that both social and private insurers are becoming less willing to insure a broad range of risks, and that both kinds of insurers have the capacity to differentiate the worthy from the unworthy recipient. To be rejected by either a public or a private insurer, she points out, can substantially affect an individual's financial and social standing. Rejection implies that an individual is 'high risk' in some way that could be costly to the insurer. These identified risks can be used as eligibility criteria that lead to denial of other benefits and can even be used as criteria in hiring decisions.[7]

As neo-liberal ideas and policies gain ground, and as insurers become less willing to bear the costs of risk, individuals are increasingly expected to identify and take action against risks. Those who are identified as failing to calculate and act on their own personal risks are increasingly subjected

[3] D Lupton (ed), *Risk and Sociocultural Theory: New Directions and Perspectives* (Cambridge, Cambridge University Press, 1999).

[4] M Douglas and A Wildavsky, *Risk and Culture: An Essay in the Selection and Interpretation of Technological and Environmental Dangers* (Berkeley CA, University of California Press, 1982).

[5] R Ericson and A Doyle, *Uncertain Business: Risk Insurance and the Limits of Knowledge* (Toronto, University of Toronto Press, 2004) 4.

[6] C Heimer, 'Insuring More, Ensuring Less: The Costs and Benefits of Private Regulation Through Insurance' in T Baker and J Simon (eds), *Embracing Risk: The Changing Culture of Insurance and Responsibility* (Chicago IL, The University of Chicago Press, 2002).

[7] D Stone, 'At Risk in the Welfare State' (1989) 56 *Social Research* 591.

to formal risk assessments, legitimized by 'science' and carried out through the auspices of institutionalized human service organizations.[8] Critical theorists, meanwhile, continue to question whether people designated as 'risky' populations constitute a genuine threat to themselves or others or whether they are individuals who depart from norms and values preferred by society's elites.

III. RISK IN CHILD PROTECTION LAW

The assessment of risk has entered into many human service professions as an element of practice over the past several decades. Prison and parole services, mental health, domestic violence, youth justice and certainly child protection are fields that have introduced risk assessments into decision-making processes. Front-line staff members are asked to assess the risks that 'clients' pose to themselves and others through the use of instruments and tools devised for this purpose.

In child protection, risk has become a central feature of practice, supported in law and by complex practice requirements. In Canada, the concept of risk has played a significant role in the identification of families requiring intervention at least since the 1980s in Ontario, and shortly afterward in other provincial legislation. This new emphasis on risk in child welfare legislation occurred at a time when views of single mothers were beginning to change. Earlier in that decade single mothers in Canada were characterized in media in a rather positive way, and often seen as deserving of social programmes and assistance in doing their job of parenting.[9] However, as neo-liberal ideas and social policies gained traction, views of single mothers in general and low-income mothers in particular began to shift. They were more often characterized as needy, greedy and dependent.[10]

In the mid 1980s a protracted debate relating to changes in Ontario's child welfare legislation occurred, generally revolving around the question of whether 'risk of harm' or 'substantial risk of harm' to a child would be the legal criterion for intervention. One subtext of this debate was the question of whether social workers, mostly women, were too 'intrusive' in their work with clients, a claim feminists in particular viewed as a cover for

[8] Swift and Callahan (above n *).

[9] P Evans and K Swift, 'Single Mothers and the Press: Rising Tides, Moral Panic and Restructuring Discourses' in S Neysmith (ed), *Restructuring Caring Labour: Discourse, State Practice and Everyday Life* (Don Mills ON, Oxford University Press, 2000).

[10] E Power, 'The Unfreedom of Being Other: Canadian Lone Mothers' Experiences of Poverty and "Life on the Cheque"' (2005) 39 *Sociology* 643. See also M Abramovitz, 'Welfare Reform in the United States: Gender, Race, and Class Matter' (2006) 26 *Critical Social Policy* 336; M Little and L Marks, 'A Closer Look at the Neo-Liberal Petri Dish' (2006) 57 *Canadian Review of Social Policy* 16.

lowering programme costs by limiting the clientele. Eventually, the phrase 'substantial risk' was included in the law, with the result that cases to be dealt with by protection authorities were generally to be considered the more serious ones.

Numerous changes to Ontario's protection legislation, as well as that of other provinces, have occurred since the 1980s. Now, virtually every Canadian province includes risk in its definition of a child in need of protection as well as in other sections of child protection legislation, and the qualification that risk must be substantial in order for intervention to occur has disappeared in most jurisdictions. In Ontario, for instance, risk is used as a condition of finding a child in need of protection, now defined in legislation as a child who has been abused or is at risk of being abused.[11] Risk also appears in the 'Best Interests of the Child' provision of Ontario's Child and Family Services Act section 37(3): 'the risk that the child may suffer harm'. Likewise, in section 40(7)(b) and several similar provisions, risk justifies apprehension of a child without a warrant. The phrase 'there would be a substantial risk to the child's health or safety' provides direction to judges on the basis of risk. By virtue of section 72(1) and (2), even the public is required to make a report to protection authorities based on 'risk of harm to a child'. Other provinces also use the idea of risk in identifying a child needing protection. BC legislation[12] for instance uses the wording 'is likely' instead of 'risk' in similar provisions of protection legislation.

Notwithstanding ongoing epistemological and policy debates, the concept and meanings of risk itself have not been the subject of in-depth discussion by the professionals who assess parents for a variety of supposedly relevant risks related to child protection. Risk remains undefined in the legislation, although its meaning may derive from two related legal concepts. One is 'liability', referring to a condition for which a person is answerable and 'out of which arises a responsibility to perform in specific ways'. The other is 'foreseeability', from tort law, meaning that which should be anticipated as the consequence of particular actions or inactions.[13] This understanding is apparently assumed, for risk is treated in law as a matter of 'common knowledge', as a real thing, recognizable to professionals, parents and the public, which must be acted upon.

For institutional purposes, however, layers of instructions on how to recognize and manage risk have been developed over the years. These include regulations and official standards of practice that tie legislation to practice. Additionally, there are risk assessment tools, adopted and sometimes

[11] Child and Family Services Act (RSO 1990, c 11).
[12] Child, Family and Community Services Act (RSBC 1996 c 46).
[13] Program Development: Liability. Program Planning with Computer Applications 1, at: www.prm.nau.edu/prm275/liability.htm, accessed 22 January 2009; Your Dictionary.com: www.yourdictionary.com/foreseeability, accessed 22 January 2009.

required by provincial authorities, which spell out in list form the markers considered relevant for the identification of risks and their potential severity. These documents may also be tied to other institutional documents such as funding formulas, training plans and instructions on work practices. 'Risk' is essentially defined by this apparatus, and the work that is carried out by child protection workers supports, legitimizes and continually reinforces the ideas about risk contained in it. It is in this supporting apparatus that the mechanisms to construct particular women as legally and socially 'risky' are found.

In the following two sections, I examine the work of assessing and managing risk in the context of Canadian child welfare practice. Research for this chapter has been carried out on practices of risk assessment in child welfare in two provinces, BC and Ontario. The legislation and documents of these jurisdictions were examined, and a total of 46 interviews involving social workers, mothers assessed for risk and key informants were conducted in the years 2002 to 2006. Risk assessment tools used in other jurisdictions and by other professional workers were also examined. Some changes to risk instruments and their uses have been made since the data were collected. However, the dynamics of risk and its assessment remain firmly in place.

IV. ASSESSING RISK

It is estimated that in 2003, over 217,000 child protection investigations were carried out across Canada, most of them involving some kind of risk assessment. This represents a 78 per cent increase over the number of investigations done in 1998, a year when risk assessments were just beginning to be introduced across the country.[14] With the introduction of risk assessment came promises that 'children would be safer' as a result of its use: 'I have the privilege of presenting the BC Risk Assessment Model, a well-researched instrument designed to predict future harm to children' (Director of Child Consultation Services, BC).[15] This kind of public relations announcement would seem to imply that the scope of child protection was being extended to all children in the province. This of course is not the case. Elsewhere[16] I have argued that risk assessment processes in child protection are structured in such a way that low-income families

[14] N Trocmé, B Fallon, B MacLaurin, J Daciuk, C Felstiner and T Black, *Canadian Incidence Study of Reported Child Abuse and Neglect* (Ottawa, Minister of Public Works and Government Services Canada, 2005).

[15] Director, Child Consultation Services, *BC Risk Assessment Model* (Victoria BC, British Columbia Ministry for Children and Families, Child Protection Consultation Services, 1996) 3.

[16] K Swift and H Parada, 'Child Welfare Reform: Protecting Children or Policing the Poor?' (2004) 19 *Journal of Law and Social Policy* 1.

feel the most effects. The long history of child protection has been almost exclusively among the poor, those who do not have resources to solve the most immediate problems of child caring. Data from past and present Canadian studies confirm this argument. The National Council of Welfare[17] acknowledged the issue in one of the first national studies of child welfare: 'One fundamental characteristic of the child welfare system, however, has not changed appreciably over the years: its clients are still overwhelmingly drawn from the ranks of Canada's poor'.

The recent Canadian Incidence Study,[18] while it does not include data on income levels of families involved with child protection services, does confirm that the majority of families served are of low income. A large proportion (24 per cent) depends on social assistance, which is always below the poverty line in Canada. Many live in rental housing, and almost half (44 per cent) are single parents—mostly mothers. These of course are the groups that tend to have the lowest incomes in the country. Apparently, more parents in this group than ever before are being investigated for maltreatment of their children.

Simply being poor does not mean that a family will come under the scrutiny of child protection authorities, which is based on a reporting system. A child or family must be 'reported' by someone before any action will be taken to protect children. Most low-income families, poor or otherwise, are never reported, even though they share many characteristics of those who are reported. Many families who are reported will not end up becoming 'clients' of the system because they will be deemed 'ineligible'. On the other hand, children who are experiencing problems at home will not be served or protected if no report is made.

Protection staff, acting as 'screeners', take incoming calls and make decisions about whether and how to respond. They judge the seriousness of reports to some extent on the basis of who does the reporting. Reports by doctors and other medical personnel will almost invariably be viewed as serious. Reports by other professionals also will be seen as potential concerns, while reports by neighbours, relatives and members of the general public are more likely to be viewed as questionable, perhaps meriting a referral rather than an investigation. In general, professionals' concerns are more 'credible', and they are by far the most common callers, constituting more than three-quarters of all referrals.[19] Calls for help and resources from the mother herself are less likely to result in a case opening unless she is already well known to authorities.

[17] National Council of Welfare, *In the Best Interests of the Child* (Ottawa, December 1979) 2.

[18] Trocmé et al (above n 14).

[19] *Ibid.*

Workers who do this screening work look at the length of any past file, look at summaries of past case activity, which may or may not be accurate and certainly are not complete, and then seek the approval of the supervisor for their decision. Mothers who are screened out are constructed as 'coping'. Since there are no preventive child welfare services to speak of, clients who might potentially benefit from such services are screened out in the early stages of the investigation. Middle-class parents who are reported are more likely to resist involvement with child protection staff. People with some social power know they can refuse entry to investigators, hire lawyers to protect their interests, and purchase services that change the appearance or actuality of the situation. Poor people usually don't resist entry—they are recognized by workers as easier to coerce. As one worker remembered hearing, '[i]f you throw enough mud at them, something will stick'. Fathers are also more likely to resist becoming involved. They are less likely to be the custodial parent in any case, and more likely to elude or intimidate workers. This complaint process, similar in fact to police reporting, increases the likelihood that people who are 'socially acceptable to blame' will come under scrutiny, as Douglas and Wildavsky[20] point out. The individualizing of complaints further ensures that the protection of children will not be seen as a social risk requiring social resources to solve or mitigate.

Mothers, as the usual onsite parents, often feel they must co-operate. If they have any experience with child protection, they also know that resistance counts against them and can make their lives much harder. In the words of one worker interviewed, 'and if the client says: "Look, I have difficulty with what you're proposing", then that will be interpreted as a resistant client'. Once entry is gained, the level of intrusion required by the risk assessment process becomes intense. Some information about the family is generally acquired before they even know they are under investigation. Our study demonstrated considerable disparity between the two provincial study sites in the information given to parents about the risk assessment process. In Ontario, those under investigation were very frequently not told anything about the risk factors, scoring or the implications of scores. In BC, workers often shared the tool with parents and sometimes even negotiated scores with them.

Even when parents interviewed for our study were unaware of the assessment process, they quickly understood the importance of certain key items of information workers would be looking for. These include, for instance, any past history showing the parent was abused as a child. This item is based on the assumption that a 'cycle' of violence exists: abused children become abusive parents, an assertion with some validity but one also that

[20] Douglas and Wildavsky (above n 4).

can easily lead to false positives. Another key item on many risk assessment instruments deals with the level of compliance investigated parents demonstrate toward the worker and the process. This item appears based on an assumption that non-compliance equals guilt, but also indicates practicalities for the investigating worker: non-compliant parents make the work much harder. Other key items, drawn from literature in the field and practical experience, involve the existence of ongoing problems such as addictions, woman abuse, mental health diagnosis or disability; issues that parents may try very hard to hide in order to avoid the possibility that their children will be apprehended and placed in care.

Workers generally believe that risk assessment tools have been scientifically validated. Literature and statements put out by agencies suggest that this is the case. In fact, most tools introduced in 1998 or before had not been tested for validity or reliability. Since then more testing has been done on tools currently in use.[21] Even so, none have been widely accepted as beyond reasonable challenge in the scientific community, and some authors question whether they are indeed any more accurate than experienced clinical judgement.[22] Many risk assessment tools, including the one used in BC, Ontario and several other Canadian provinces, have been brought in from the United States and plugged into a screening and management process that is designed locally. Certainly the Canadian tools in use at the time of our study were not validated, although most workers we interviewed believed that they were. In fact, workers and managers often accepted risk assessment enthusiastically, based on the belief that the work was 'objective' and the more accurate conviction that workers' reports would be taken by the courts and other professionals as more credible than before.

Typically, as noted, tools focus heavily on past history of the family, especially the mother. One of our interviewees was stunned to read the contents of her file:

> I wasn't even born or whatever. It was ... I couldn't believe it when I seen that cause I looked at my file and said 'what the hell is this?' I said 'people are judging me from what happened years and years ago when I you know maybe I was just a newborn or whatever'.

At one level, assessments are highly individualized, focusing on past history of abuse, social location, available records—for instance police files—and

[21] C Baird and D Wagner, 'The Relative Validity of Actuarial and Consensus Based Risk Assessment Systems' (2000) 11/12 *Children and Youth Services Review* 839. See also J Rycus and RL Hughes, *Issues in Risk Assessment in Child Protective Services* (Columbus OH, American Resource Center for Child Welfare, 2003); A D'Andrade, A Benton and M Austin, *Risk and Safety Assessment in Child Welfare: Instrument Comparisons* (Berkeley CA, Center for Social Services Research, School of Social Welfare, University of California at Berkeley, 2005).

[22] D Baumann, J Law, J Sheets, G Reid and J Graham, 'Evaluating the Effectiveness of Actuarial Risk Assessment Models' (2005) 27 *Children and Youth Services Review* 465.

the identity of the reporter. At another, and more crucial level, assessments represent homogenizing processes that wash out both the social context and much of the personal context of the parent's life experience, including the circumstances in which they must do their parenting. Research[23] has shown that the mother's story is generally not viewed as an important feature of the investigation.

In our own study sites, which represent the most regimented form of risk assessment in Canadian practice, the parents' input is primarily in the form of answers to specific questions derived from the risk assessment tool, a tool that focuses on individual and family factors and that does not include social information of any kind. A mother's income level and source, her access to affordable housing, her proximity to health and other services are not considered as risk factors. The tools and information gathering processes select only some elements of information to be highlighted in the file. At the same time, however, the results of the assessment may very well be internalized by the mother, and viewed as part of her own or her family members' identities: 'I wasn't a very high risk. I was a low risk'. 'I'm not a risk anymore. Now it's my children that are speech delayed that is the risk'. In the beginning stages of assessment, workers concentrate on filling out the required forms and acquiring sufficient information to justify their scores to the supervisor and the system. Much of the assessment in fact can be made without the input of those under investigation. A story of risk is under construction, and the mother is a resource for information that must be quickly acquired. The worker is attuned (in the words of one of them) to 'mining for information', rather than understanding the totality of the situation. Selected pieces of the mother's life and experience are fitted into the tool and scored. The mother at this point has become a documentary 'bundle of factors'[24] with a score attached.

Workers carry out these tasks in an effort to meet the expectations of their supervisors for complete information on documents. Both worker and supervisor view the information in light of the potential for court involvement and possibly even an inquest in the event of a child's death later on. The worker may see the mother as someone she would like to get out of her own life, a case to be moved along. At the same time, she is a potential danger to the worker, someone whose actions could bring tragedy into the worker's own life if the future is not accurately predicted. Workers want to perform competently in the eyes of 'the system' and at the same time to accurately assess possible dangers. This tension for the worker, always present in child protection, has been intensified because of the widespread

[23] J Krane and L Davies, 'Mothering and Child Protection Practice: Rethinking Risk Assessment' (1999) 5 *Child and Family Social Work* 35.

[24] R Castel, 'The Foucault Effect' in G Burchell, C Gordon and P Miller (eds), *The Foucault Effect: Studies in Governmentality* (Chicago IL, University of Chicago Press, 1991).

belief that risk assessment, properly done, can accurately predict the future. If a child is hurt or dies, the worker's risk decisions can all be tracked and evaluated and she will be called to account. On the other hand, if the client is scored as a high risk, and no harm ensues, the worker likely will not be called to account for a false positive. Consequently, workers generally err on the side of higher scores:

> It's kind of a rounding up. If you think it's a '1', rate it '2'. You err on the side of caution, if you know what I mean.

> You're supposed to have one of these bullets [anchors] to decide the number. When in doubt, go up.

> I was trained to rate it higher in order to keep a case going. It's a safety thing to avoid missing a risk.

In this process, workers face an ongoing contradiction between their professional values of building relationships and offering needed assistance, and the requirements of agencies to identify risky parents. They also struggle to apply their tools consistently, as their instructions repeatedly suggest they should, and at the same time to see parents as individuals. Consistency generally wins out because of the comprehensiveness of the documentation required. Workers are supposed to complete the documents within prescribed time limits, to turn in documents with as few 'unknowns' ('9's in their computer language) as possible, since these are frowned upon, and to move the case along as the system requires. In this process details and complexity can be and often are lost. Procedures involved in working up a risk assessment construct parents investigated as a set of scores on selected risk factors. This record is inscribed in computerized information systems that are virtually permanent. If scores are high, the mother is constructed as a 'risky' parent, a person who is a danger to her children, possibly even as a potential killer.

V. MANAGING RISK

The focus on *individuals* as risky justifies the development of a risk reduction plan focused on the individual mother. Social risks such as poverty and poor housing availability are screened out and the need for social resources does not emerge from the assessment. Risk reduction primarily involves efforts on the mother's part to lower her risk scores on specific items with a view to getting the case closed. Often, both mother and worker share this goal, but it is of course the mothers who are now primarily responsible for achieving this outcome. During the risk assessment process, mothers are, in effect, objects—the objects of investigation. They may even be seen by workers as the 'bundle of factors' and scores produced by the assessment process. At the risk reduction stage, however, mothers must be reconstituted as active agents in the process. Without this transformation, in fact, the process would grind to a halt, as the worker has little to offer in the way of supports. To this end, 'contracts' spelling out mothers' responsibilities and goals are developed and signed. Refusal or resistance can lead to an even higher risk score.

One of the primary justifications for the identification of risk is that it creates a possibility for workers to focus on and target resources to the highest risk parents.[25] Certainly, decision makers responsible for child protection must have hoped that this approach had the potential to reduce the costs of services through more efficient deployment of resources. However, cost savings and efficiency have not been realized. As Figure 1 (below) illustrates, developing the risk assessment apparatus, training workers to use it and carrying out escalating numbers of complex investigations leading to an increased number of children in care has cost provincial governments a huge amount of money.

Further, Trocmé's Canadian study showed that only about three per cent of substantiated child protection cases involve actual physical harm to a child.[26] Presumably, this is the group which should receive the most substantial amount of resources. However, because of the 'rounding up' of risk scores, risk assessment processes identify a much higher percentage of parents as high risk, greatly increasing the 'target' population. It is also questionable whether resources have actually been targeted to their particular needs. Our study[27] showed that risk reduction plans involve almost

Figure 1: Ontario and British Columbia Nine-Year Comparison

	Total Expenditures	**Number of Children in Care**
Ontario 1998	$380,970,683	10,419
Ontario 2006	$1.221 billion	29,385
BC 1997–98	$424,022,000	8,524
BC 2006	$627,337,000	9,160

Sources:
Ontario Association of Children's Aid Societies (2006): www.oacas.org/newsroom/releases/october2007release.pdf.
Human Resources and Social Development Canada: Child and Family Services Statistical Report 1996–97 to 1998–99 (March 2001): www.hrsdc.gc.ca/en/cs/sp/sdc/socpol/publications/reports/2001-001347/page12.shtml.

[25] Rycus and Hughes (above n 21).
[26] Trocmé et al (above n 14).
[27] Swift and Callahan (above n *).

exactly the same activities and interventions that were on offer before the introduction of risk assessment. It further showed that the contracts mothers signed were remarkably similar to one another, bringing into question the reality of 'targeting'. In addition, high-risk ratings often lead to alternative care plans for children, and this is the most costly form of resource input in child protection work. The number of children taken into care, particularly in Ontario, escalated substantially after risk assessment was introduced, along with the provincial budget for child protection.

The number of children in care in BC also escalated following the introduction of risk assessment in the mid '90s, but began to decline by 2006 for several reasons.[28] These include an increase in the number of delegated Aboriginal agencies caring for children who do not appear in these statistics. Also, the Liberal government, elected in 2001, was committed to reducing the costs of welfare programmes. At this point, in response to rising numbers of children in care, the government instituted various measures aimed at keeping children out of care.

It is generally recognized now that even with the increased budgets for protection work, there is little left over for development or deployment of actual supports for families. Certainly, there is almost nothing for creative efforts to develop new supports or for preventive work. Even so, risk assessment continues to be justified by the idea that identification of risks specific to certain individuals will result in interventions tailored to their needs. But, as noted, much the same interventions that occurred prior to risk assessment continue to be used. Standard interventions include family support workers, public health involvement, monitoring by the family doctor, drug and alcohol assessment and treatment, parenting courses, anger management, mental health referrals, and shelters. We had no evaluations of their effectiveness prior to risk assessment, and have seen very few since. Flynn and Bouchard[29] do examine several intervention programmes routinely engaged by child welfare agencies. The authors conclude that only one study team published a paper producing a reliable evaluation of their programme design.[30] However, even the MacMillan study did not report levels of significance indicating that their intervention was successful with this client population. Flynn and Bouchard conclude

[28] LT Foster, 'Trends in Child Welfare: What Do the Data Show?' in LT Foster and B Wharf (eds), *People, Politics and Child Welfare in British Columbia* (Vancouver, University of British Columbia Press, 2007).

[29] RJ Flynn and D Bouchard, 'Randomized and Quasi-Experimental Evaluations of Program Impact in Child Welfare in Canada: A Review' (2005) 20 *The Canadian Journal of Program Evaluation* 65.

[30] H MacMillan, BH Thomas, E Jamieson, CA Walsh, MS Boyle and HS Shannon, 'Effectiveness of Home Visitations by Public-Health Nurses in Prevention of the Recurrence of Child Physical Abuse and Neglect: A Randomized Controlled Trial' (2005) 365 *The Lancet* 1786.

there is no convincing evidence available that these programmes provide effective interventions to parents who are assessed as high risks to their children.

It is telling that governments will pay for these types of programmes but will not give money to mothers directly. These programmes are nevertheless recommended because they remain all that the system has to offer. We know that some mothers repeat the required programmes many times, and some spend their whole week engaged in these required activities: 'But I did groups, all the groups ... Believe me, I have like dozens of certificates' (Mother). These mothers are constructed by their risk scores as people who need to be monitored on a regular basis, often by many professionals, a goal accomplished by participation in these programmes and activities. The theory is essentially a closed circle: we make children safer by monitoring their parents.[31] Does it work? To date, there is no evidence that these approaches do make children safer. We cannot even say that fewer deaths of children known to child protection authorities have resulted from the use of the risk assessment processes studied. Across Canada, over the past 30 years, an average of 35 children under 13 are listed as having been killed by their parents each year, a number that has remained stable since 1974, although peaking in 1997 at 52.[32] In individual provinces, including Ontario and BC, the verified numbers are too small for comparison, and record keeping is not necessarily reliable owing in part to complications in determining how children have actually died.

It can be helpful to look for direction in related areas of risk assessment. Risk assessments for mental health patients, as in child protection, have been designed to identify and target resources to those most likely to become violent, even though violent patients form a very small sub-section of the target population. As in child welfare, it is very difficult and probably impossible to design instruments that predict which people within this population will become violent. In the conclusions of a recent study, Munro and Rumgay[33] propose that homicides committed by mentally ill people could be more effectively reduced by 'improving the response to patients who start to relapse, regardless of their assessed potential for violence'. Their proposal flags the problem of the high cost of resources for risk assessment, which then reduces the potential for creating actual services.

[31] K Swift, 'The Case for Opposition' (2001) 47 *Canadian Review of Social Policy* 59.

[32] N Trocmé, J Lajoie, B Fallon and C Felstiner, *Injuries and Death of Children at the Hands of Their Parents* #57E (Toronto, Centre of Excellence for Child Welfare, 2007).

[33] E Munro and J Rumgay, 'Role of Risk Assessment in Reducing Homicides by People with Mental Illness' (2000) 176 *British Journal of Psychiatry* 118.

VI. SOME EFFECTS OF THE USE OF RISK TECHNOLOGIES

The widespread use of risk technologies in the practice of child protection and related human services has had profound impacts on the way relevant organizations structure themselves, how the actual work is done and, not least, the way professionals think about and relate to their clients. Here I explore three of these effects, focusing on those that are not necessarily obvious at first glance but which produce serious threats to equitable and ethical professional practice. These are: the ideological effects of risk practice, the enhancement of the legal apparatus of risk and unquestioning compliance with this system.

First, and perhaps most crucially, risk in the practice of child protection has introduced new kinds of ideological distortion into 'helping' practices. Risk assessment is generally presented to the public and to the human services professionals who will administer it with a promise of prediction and prevention. The surface reality of risk practice is that of a well-oiled machine: guiding documents are in place; individual parents are accountable for their own life projects and mistakes; professionals are accountable for their decisions; and necessary help is provided. However, this presentation hides and distorts an underlying reality, which is that risk can and usually does represent a convergence of many interests, not the least of which is to scrutinize and control low-income women.

The absence of social context from this apparently orderly picture, especially in an era of diminishing resources and supports, leaves individuals as the only visible targets for blame. Subjects of assessment appear to be floating free from the social relations of class, race and gender in which they are, in fact, embedded and which structure their lives and prospects in material and immediate ways. History appears as personal history. The historically-shaped conditions into which people are born and which they must daily accommodate simply vanish. Risk assessment is perhaps just one of the newest forms of ideology that serves to deflect attention from larger social issues and divisions. In the rush of completing the required work we may fail to ask, How is it that all these people being assessed, many of them minorities, many of them poor, most of them women, have become so 'risky'?

The positioning of risk assessment as scientific has the effect of presenting risk scores as incontrovertible 'truth'. Positivist science, with its focus on numbers, is legitimized, leaving critical science with no role to play. Dissent and even questioning become considerably more difficult in the face of what is accepted by most as scientific truth about an objective reality of risk. The presentation of risk as an objective 'thing' deflects attention from the actual material world of clients and creates the appearance of something bad lodged in actual people. Standardization and hierarchical work processes, posing as the solutions to problems of risk, conspire to contain dissent and discourage efforts to organize and challenge. Social workers, and no doubt other professionals, begin to lose contact with political movements[34] and even with the idea of advocacy and action. Support of 'high-risk' clients is a hard sell.

As we go about the onerous tasks prescribed in a risk regime, we may fail to ask whether recommended methods of risk reduction have proven to be effective. The legitimized 'science' is generally at the front end of the process, located in the tools for assessment. Evaluation of efforts for reducing risk in general receives very little attention. If, however, we don't know what is effective in reducing risk, what then is the rationale for assessing risk?

Risk in the practice of child protection creates a thick blanket of apparent meanings that covers over the reality that it primarily identifies and acts upon poor women. In fact, as Dean[35] has said, risk might be said to conflate class into risk. It is yet another way to classify troublesome and potentially expensive populations and to obfuscate what is going on, which in this case is substantial intrusion and surveillance of this group as well as the withholding of resources needed to do the job of parenting.

A second important effect of risk assessment as currently practised is an increasing emphasis on law in the practice of child protection. This new emphasis occurs in association with the shift from 'need' to 'risk' in social welfare generally and child protection in particular over the past several decades. By the 1990s in most Western welfare states 'dependency' had become a pejorative term that justified substantial reductions in state support of programmes and budgets. The job of many human service workers in this context has been to wean recipients away from supportive services provided by the state. By the end of the '90s, risk had been added to the lexicon of professionals working with 'troublesome' populations, and became thoroughly embedded in practice.

Risk assessment works to separate those who 'ought to be' independent from those deemed to be in need of monitoring. It creates gradations of 'risk classes' and justifies the application of 'appropriate' amounts of legally sanctioned surveillance to those groups. In child welfare, groups scored as less risky are engaged in risk reduction, which is aimed at a goal of 'independence'. Those scored as most risky are viewed as potential child killers. They are 'one step away from an inquest' (Worker), and are treated accordingly. In this circumstance, intensified legal action appears reasonable, even

[34] E Harlow, 'Why Don't Women Want to be Social Workers Anymore? New Managerialism, Postfeminism and the Shortage of Social Workers in Social Services Departments in England and Wales' (date) 7 *European Journal of Social Work* 167.

[35] M Dean, 'Risk Calculable and Incalculable' in D Lupton (ed), *Risk and Sociocultural Theory: New Directions and Perspectives* (Cambridge, Cambridge University Press, 1999).

though many of the actions taken occur on the basis of *what might happen*, and not what *has* happened.

At one level, risk may be just another way to construct the low-income single mum. She used to be needy, dependent and lazy. Now she is also 'risky'. At another more sinister level, risk assessment in child protection adds another group to the 'risk classes',[36] composed of people we are encouraged to fear, to blame, to control and to scrutinize. It is important to notice the role of law in constructing and maintaining a risk class. The presence of risk in child protection law, and the supporting apparatus that defines and constructs some people as risks to their own children, means that these identified women are not just subject to social labelling but also legal labelling. Their scores, their images, their records and reports remain in files in perpetuity. Their risk assessments are entered into court proceedings and become evidence in determining culpability. Meanwhile, mothers don't necessarily know of the existence of risk assessment and may have no idea that they have been scored. The placement of risk assessment information into this kind of legally-sanctioned context adds an extra and powerful layer to the construction of women, especially poor mothers, as threats to society. They join other high-risk groups ranging from mental patients to terrorists which society is encouraged to control; they are one of many groups now legally justifying reduced privacy and increased intrusion by authorities into personal life; they, along with others, act as powerful examples of the high cost of seeming to depart from social norms. The professionals whose work now involves identifying and managing such groups unwittingly spend large parts of their time helping to construct and legitimize such risk groups.

Given this increasing emphasis on legal processes, it is unsurprising that the size of legal departments and activity in child welfare have grown. As more investigations occur and more intrusive work with families is recommended, the work has become increasingly litigious. The apparatus of risk does seem to add weight to the recommendations made by child protection workers. The assessment tool is viewed by many allied professions, including lawyers, as an instrument capable of identifying the most risky cases; even as a sort of 'crystal ball' that forecasts potential disaster. In many circumstances, the risk ratings are quoted in court documents as a method for justifying the intervention recommended by the child welfare agency. At times, the legal department drives the focus and emphasis of the work in child welfare practice. One worker highlighted how he negotiated his way through the complexity of the system by aligning himself with the lawyers within his organization, whom he views as the organizational power

[36] P Rosanvallon, *The New Social Question: Rethinking the Welfare State* (Princeton NJ, Princeton University Press, 2000).

brokers: 'Child protection is a legal process ... and you end up in a more adversarial relationship (with clients) ... and so the power really rests with the legal department'.

Finally, whatever else risk practices have accomplished, they have instilled significant compliance into the system. Both workers and mothers try to shape how they are constructed by a system in which they are mutually involved, as there is much potential for both to be constructed as 'bad girls' who are non-compliant with system demands. Workers try to be seen as efficient and tough professionals who can't be fooled by the stories clients tell them. They try to 'move it along'. They work at being efficient gatherers of information. They make a goal of having no '9's and meeting the time requirements of the system. Mothers meanwhile try to 'prove' to workers that they are 'good enough' mothers who can do whatever is asked of them, even when they can't see the point. Language in legal supervision orders stresses compliance, risk reduction plans stress compliance, and mothers internalize the need to demonstrate compliance. Roast beef in the oven, cleaning the house, coaching the boyfriend, withholding information, keeping their lips buttoned, showing co-operation, attending classes, getting certificates form the centre-piece of their existence while under supervision, whether court ordered or not. Often, they do not know whether their case has been closed. This study revealed many examples of mothers who were unsure whether they remained under scrutiny. They looked out of their apartment windows at the approaching social worker to see if she was heading for them or someone else. But she might come another day...

VII. CONCLUSION: CAN RISK BE SOCIALLY JUST?

There is no evidence that new populations of dangerous parents have been uncovered through risk assessment methods. There is also no evidence that our risk assessment tools can predict what is going to happen to particular children in the future. The development of these tools more or less guarantees that what has been found will always be found. They are derived from past and current cases and their outcomes. Since past cases select low-income, often minority women for most attention, this is likely who will be found in the future as well. The tools are also geared to identify the same problems that have always plagued the clients of child welfare: developmental challenges and various kinds of health issues; addictions; and family dysfunction, especially violence, which is mentioned as a risk factor in over 50 per cent of cases.[37] The interventions prescribed also have not changed in any significant way. Mothers are still being told to go to parenting classes,

[37] Trocmé et al (above n 14).

anger management and budgeting courses. Large numbers of children are being apprehended. The front-end costs of risk assessment in fact have meant less money available for services. I am not trying to claim that no one is helped. Rather, I am suggesting that complicated tools and the magic of 'science' do not automatically lead to 'cures' or even to more helpful supports to this group of parents than before. And there is no reason to believe that children are safer than they were before, because the same resources and deficits are being applied to the same populations and problems.

With respect to child protection, it is important not to fall into the trap of seeing a challenge to risk assessment practices as a lack of concern for the safety of children. There are indeed parents who abuse and neglect. Current data, however, suggest this is a very tiny proportion of child protection cases, as shown in Trocmé's Canadian study.[38] This means that a great many cases are focused on something other than actual physical harm. It is common knowledge that many cases involve resource deprivation resulting from poverty. Problems of child care in these conditions are exacerbated by serious physical, mental and emotional problems of parents and/or children who for a myriad of reasons have not been able to get appropriate help and support. Some parents will never be able to do their parenting work adequately, and this must be recognized. Many, probably most, could provide better care of their children with adequate resources. This is the long-term problem of the child protection system: it has the capacity and mandate only to identify a narrow range of problems of child welfare among a narrow population.

Lewis et al[39] wrote some time ago of the inevitability that as time goes on 'only need defined as high-risk will receive service'. In other words, sanctioned definitions of risk rather than expressed need will act as the trigger for resource flow and the prioritizing of work activities.[40] In many risk assessment processes, the economic circumstances of the assessed individual are not part of the calculation of risk, even though economic issues are primary concerns for many service users. A social justice approach, in contrast, assumes need as the basis for resource eligibility.

Social justice is necessarily reflexive. As we have seen, risk technology has the capacity to produce a conceptual apparatus justifying considerable intrusion into lives and prospects and to justify the withholding of actual help. The ongoing critique of what we are asked to do and what we *actually* do is absolutely necessary to just practice in a socially-fluid context. Those

[38] *Ibid.*

[39] J Lewis, Bernstock and V Bovell, 'The Community Care Changes: Unresolved Tensions and Policy Issues in Implementation' (1995) 24 *Journal of Social Policy* 73.

[40] H Kemshall, N Parton, M Walsh and J Waterson, 'Concepts of Risk in Relation to Organizational Structure and Functioning within the Personal Social Services and Probation' (1997) 31 *Social Policy and Administration* 213.

professionals required to put risk into use must become more aware of the ongoing debates, meanings, agendas and implications of assessing for risk, including alternative and critical perspectives. Clearly professionals in many fields of practice have taken on technologies of risk without debate or real examination of their potential effects. Those helping professionals who are willing to develop informed perspectives of the meanings and implications of risk regimes and who are prepared to challenge orthodoxy when it is necessary have a much better chance to act ethically and in the interests of social justice.

Certainly, the abrogation of rights for some populations, rights that are assumed and accorded to others, often by law, constitutes social *in*justice. Chen[41] points out the importance of creating space for challenging the rationalizations that are used to defend unequal treatment for particular groups. Former US Secretary of Defence, Donald Rumsfeld, for instance, famously defended torture and other unlawful tactics at internment camps on the basis that they were dealing with 'terrorists'. Those people are different, he said, and so 'different rules apply'. I disagree that the rules ought to be changed or suspended for designated groups of 'different' people. Social justice means that the same basic rules protecting legal, social and civil rights do apply to all, including access to information about what is being done, why it is being done, and rights of appeal for decisions considered unjust.

How can feminists and others respond to the construction of women as 'risky' in a socially just way? First, we should question the risk mandates and practices of child protection itself. The apparatus of risk as currently deployed not only intensifies opposition between workers and mothers. It also creates a risk reduction model that separates mothers from each other. Each has her 'schedule' and list of tasks involving short-term programmes often located far from her home. Paradoxically, the content of these schedules looks remarkably the same for many. Yet each mother reports vertically to the system, and each follows a schedule articulated to programme availability. When programmes end, so do many of the constructive ties women might otherwise build with each other. A useful way to reconstruct the image of low-income single mothers in a positive direction would be to create the circumstances through which reducing risks would involve the building of community.

Secondly, we need to be asking some technical questions about these processes and practices. For instance, what role should 'risk' play in legislation? At the very least, legal and professional scholars should explore this aspect of legislation. Should an apparatus of risk that puts people under

[41] X Chen, 'Constituting "Dangerous Parents" Through the Spectre of Child Death: A Critique of Child Protection Restructuring in Ontario' in D Brock (ed), *Making Normal: Social Regulation in Canada* (Scarborough ON, Thomson Nelson, 2003).

intense scrutiny, sometimes without their knowledge, and supported by questionable scoring practices, be legally and professionally sanctioned?

Thirdly, we should be very concerned about the place of 'the social' in risk practices. At present, in much professional practice, risk and its management is an individual enterprise, with the idea of social risk all but disappearing from discourse as well as from everyday practice. If we are going to use risk assessment, why not look at the social conditions that create potential danger and 'risk' for particular groups and communities? The risk reduction efforts logically following from this calculation of risk would be more community based and more democratic than present practice allows.

Finally, and related to the previous point, we should be aware and concerned about the use of language in the construction of women. The present risk apparatus in child protection casts mothers as dangerous threats. Recasting low-income, single mothers as being 'at risk' rather than risky[42] opens up a completely different world of meanings related to the social and economic context. If risk assessment were applied not only to individual circumstances but to social and economic contexts of mothers, the idea of risk could be very useful, and the construction of these women and the professionals who work with them would take on a completely different complexion.

[42] C Brearley, *Risk and Social Work* (London, Routledge and Kegan Paul, 1982).

7

Intimate Intrusions

Welfare Regulation and Women's Personal Lives

JANET MOSHER

I. INTRODUCTION

WELFARE REFORMS OF the late twentieth century profoundly reconfigured the relationship of state and citizen. The principle of entitlement characteristic of the Keynesian welfare state that had rendered welfare a citizen's due was replaced by a narrow contractualism in which state benefits were made contingent upon participation in job readiness or other activities to foster 'self-sufficiency' and 'individual responsibility'. As 'flawed' or 'partial' citizens, those claiming state assistance were clearly marked as deficient, deviant and undeserving.[1] Consistent with this reconfiguration, the state's role has shifted away from beneficently meeting the needs of citizens, and further toward that of disciplining and reforming these flawed citizens. Of course, welfare systems have long played a role in disciplining the bodies of recipients, so I do not mean to suggest that this role is entirely new. Rather, while a familiar enough role, the techniques or tools have changed in important respects.[2]

[1] See J Mosher, 'Welfare Reform and the Re-making of the Model Citizen' in S Boyd, G Brodsky, S Day and M Young (eds), *Poverty: Rights, Governance & Citizenship* (Vancouver, University of British Columbia Press, 2007).

[2] See K Beckett and B Western, 'Governing social marginality: Welfare, incarceration, and the transformation of state policy' (2001) 3 *Punishment & Society* 43 on the rise of punitive social policy. As they have observed, reduced welfare expenditures are not indicative of state retreat but rather state reorganization toward a more exclusionary and punitive approach to the regulation of social marginality. Similarly Peck argues that 'rather than a straightforward diminution of state capacities, or indeed a reduction in the "size" of the national state, this "hollowing out" process typically entails a simultaneous roll-back *and roll-out* of state functions'; see J Peck, 'Neoliberalizing states: thin policies/hard outcomes' (2001) 25 *Progress in Human Geography* 445, 447. As I detail in the text, much of this 'rolling-out' function has focused upon fraud detection.

In these shifts single mothers in receipt of welfare have been dramatically repositioned. Early forms of mother's allowance were rationalized by a desire to keep (some) women out of the labour market, and in their proper place at home. While many single mothers did, in fact, participate in the labour market, the ideal of motherhood at least normatively, if not practically, placed women squarely in the home. Many feminists struggled over much of the twentieth century for a legitimate place for women in a male-dominated and -controlled labour market, while others highlighted the value of women's socially reproductive labour performed in the home. Attention to the value of the labour of social reproduction and a critique of the traditional patriarchal family underscored feminists' engagement with the welfare state, and in particular the call for enhanced welfare benefits so that women could live with dignity outside the confines of traditional patriarchal family structures.

While never fully realized in Ontario's welfare system, the legitimacy and value of the work of social reproduction was at least partially acknowledged. Prior to major reforms in the mid 1990s low-income single mothers were eligible for 'family benefits' pursuant to the Family Benefits Act. Grouped together with persons with disabilities, they constituted the deserving poor, enjoying slightly higher benefit rates, and free of the job search and other requirements of the able-bodied 'employable'. But the reforms of the mid 1990s redrew these boundaries of deservedness; single mothers were re-categorized as employable and subject to a new regime—revealingly called the Ontario Works Act[3]—that conditions benefits upon participation in work-related activities. A similar repositioning of single mothers has occurred throughout much of North America, where 'welfare-to-work' has become the organizing mantra.[4] Writing about the American context, Fitzgerald has argued that welfare reforms have 'fundamentally changed the status of women within U.S. capitalism'.[5]

While this shift has been important and profound, it has perhaps drawn our attention away from the ways in which welfare reforms have simultaneously re-tooled the welfare system to discipline and regulate women's intimate lives. As Kate Bezanson has suggested, welfare reforms have both de-familialization and re-familialization dimensions.[6] The repositioning of

[3] Ontario Works Act 1997 (SO 1997, c 25) Sch A [OWA].

[4] J Peck and N Theodore, 'Exporting workfare/importing welfare-to-work: exploring the politics of Third Way policy transfer' (2001) 20 *Political Geography* 427.

[5] J Fitzgerald, 'The Disciplinary Apparatus of Welfare Reform' (2004) *Monthly Review* 53, 53.

[6] K Bezanson, 'The Neo-liberal State and Social Reproduction: Gender and Household Insecurity in the Late 1990s' in K Bezanson and M Luxton (eds), *Social Reproduction: Feminist Political Economy Challenges Neo-Liberalism* (Montreal, McGill-Queen's University Press, 2006). There is a growing body of literature in the US examining the marriage promotion dimensions of American welfare reforms. See below n 18.

single mothers as workers and the turn to the market, rather than the state, to meet needs—de-familialization—has not replaced, but conjoined, in often uneasy ways, the regulation of women as mothers and wives and the shifting of responsibility to the private realm of family—re-familialization.

Drawing upon reforms in Ontario, I trace the various ways in which the intimate relational lives of women in receipt of social assistance are being regulated from both within and outside the welfare system. I attend to the cultural constructs, images, discourses and practices that operate as tools or technologies in the governance—both externally and self-imposed—of women's intimate lives.[7] I am particularly interested in the role of the welfare fraud regime in the regulation and disciplining of women's bodies. While some attention has been paid in the literature to the increasing convergence between the welfare system and criminal justice system and to the central place of criminal constructs—such as that of the welfare 'fraudster'—in the formation of modern welfare policies and practices, very little work has attended to the particular impact of these shifts on single women in receipt of social assistance.[8] Close attention to the intersections of the fraud regime and the concept of 'spouse' at play in Ontario's welfare system reveals that women's intimate relational lives are regarded as criminally suspect, and consequently subject to intense surveillance. While neither the state's interest in finding the men in the lives of single women nor the stigmatization of recipients as actual or potential fraudsters are new phenomena, profoundly important changes have occurred in how they are deployed as techniques of governance by the welfare system. The sweep and depth of surveillance, the ready acceptance of demeaning stereotypes and the pervasive characterization of non-criminal conduct as 'fraud' has created a dense, intractable web of control over women's relational lives. Forming an intimate relationship—something that is socially valued, particularly if heterosexual and leading to marriage—is profoundly fraught for single women on welfare, risking as they do being cut off benefits, forced into relationships of financial dependency, assessed with overpayment liabilities and charged criminally. Moreover, this form of discipline is deeply gendered, exercised upon the bodies of women but not men, and its character is patriarchal, often mirroring in precise detail the exercise of power and control by abusive men.

[7] C Watkins, 'It's Not Just About the Money: Governmentality and Resistance in Post-Reform Welfare Offices' (Ann Arbor MI, The National Poverty Center, 17 January 2006).

[8] See for example, Fitzgerald (above n 5); Beckett and Western (above n 2); J McCorkel, 'Criminally Dependent? Gender, Punishment, and the Rhetoric of Welfare Reform' (2004) 11 *Social Politics* 386; and K Gustafson, 'To Punish the Poor: Criminalizing Trends in the Welfare System' (Oakland CA, Women of Color Resource Center, Working Paper Series, No 3).

II. ONTARIO'S WELFARE SYSTEM

Welfare is a matter of provincial jurisdiction in Canada. That said, the federal government was a highly influential player in the unfolding of the Keynesian state welfare programs. Its influence came through its spending power, and more specifically through the development of cost-sharing agreements with the provinces negotiated pursuant to the Canada Assistance Plan (CAP).[9] Pursuant to these agreements, the federal government provided substantial funding for provincial welfare programs, provided that the provinces met certain conditions, including that benefit levels 'take into account the basic requirements of a person in need' and that no person be denied assistance 'because he [*sic*] refuses or has refused to take part in a work activity project'. The replacement of CAP in 1996 with a new block fund, the Canada Health and Social Transfer, that blended monies for health, education and welfare and attached no conditions, opened the door for provincial reforms.[10] The demise of CAP also signalled a new era of de-centralization, from the federal government to the provinces, and subsequently from the provinces to local municipalities.

Ontario lost no time in taking advantage of this opening to starkly alter its welfare program. Under the banner of a 'common sense revolution', a newly-elected Conservative government proceeded to quickly introduce major welfare reforms. Its new legislation, the Ontario Works Act,[11] and the Ontario Disability Support Program Act,[12] delineated two categories of recipients: those with statutorily recognized disabilities and all others. When introducing the legislation into the provincial parliament, the government identified three central goals lying at the heart of the reforms: making self-sufficiency the over-riding objective of social assistance (no longer a safety net for those cast off by the labour market, recipients were now assumed to be embraced and protected by that same market); fighting welfare fraud; and addressing the needs of those with disabilities (the only truly deserving beneficiaries). The Ontario Works Act, the focus of this discussion, expressly includes in its statement of purpose:

> The purpose of this Act is to establish a program that,
>
> (a) recognizes individual responsibility and promotes self reliance through employment;
> (b) provides temporary financial assistance to those most in need while they satisfy obligations to become and stay employed;
> (c) effectively serves people needing assistance; and
> (d) is accountable to the taxpayers of Ontario.[13]

[9] Canada Assistance Plan Act (RSC 1985, c C-1).
[10] Budget Implementation Act, 1995 (SC 1995, c 17) ss 31 and 32.
[11] OWA, above n 3.
[12] Ontario Disability Support Program Act (ODSP), 1997 (SO 1997, c 25) Sch B.
[13] OWA (above n 3) s 1.

The goals of self-sufficiency and individual responsibility are to be realized through a variety of legislative measures, but most significantly through mandatory participation in a variety of work-readiness activities, the details of which are contained in individual contracts called 'Participation Agreements'. As the then responsible Minister made explicit, '[p]eople have got to learn again to take responsibility for themselves and their families and not to leave it to everyone else to do'.[14] A moralizing discourse caricaturing those seeking benefits as lazy, dependent, and lacking a proper work ethic has been a central technique in the deployment of 'welfare-to-work' as the organizing logic of welfare provision.[15] A range of practices derived from this logic together weaves an intricate and tight web of intense scrutiny, surveillance and punishment for non-compliance. The effect has been to discipline not only welfare recipients as workers, but all those who are engaged in marginal, contingent work.[16] In this regard, '[w]elfare reform acts as the Panopticon of the poor, a disciplinary apparatus that places them under intense scrutiny and compels them to become docile workers'.[17]

The re-familialization dimensions of the legislation are less apparent on the face of the legislation; there is no explicit language of marriage promotion nor of family responsibility.[18] Yet a closer examination reveals several dimensions of the reforms that draw upon and shore up patriarchal familial relations, and that greatly expand the state's disciplinary apparatus over women's intimate lives. These include significant benefit cuts which have made it even more difficult to survive on existing benefit levels (a point to which I will return), a child support regime which predicates state benefits upon the demonstration of 'reasonable efforts' having been made to secure support from any man who might plausibly have a support obligation, and the concept of a 'spousal' relationship. It is to 'spouses' that I now turn.

[14] Ontario, Legislative Assembly, *Official Report of Debates (Hansard)* 36th Parl, 1st Sess, 28 September 1995.

[15] For a critique see Fitzgerald (above n 5) and M Fineman, 'Cracking the Foundational Myths: Independence, Autonomy, and Self-Sufficiency' (1999) 8 *American University Journal of Gender, Social Policy and the Law* 13.

[16] See Fitzgerald (above n 5) 58; Peck (above n 2); L Wacquant, 'The Penalization of Poverty and the Rise of Neo-Liberalism' (2001) 9 *European Journal on Criminal Policy and Research* 401; and J Mosher, 'The Construction of Welfare Fraud and the Wielding of the State's Iron Fist' in E Comack (ed), *Locating Law: Race, Class, Gender, Sexuality Connections* (Halifax NS, Fernwood Press, 2006).

[17] Fitzgerald (above n 5) 59.

[18] This is in contrast to American welfare legislation, the Personal Responsibility and Work Opportunity Reconciliation Act in particular; see G Mink, 'From Welfare to Wedlock: Marriage Promotion and Poor Mothers' Inequality' (2002) 11 *The Good Society* 68; AM Smith, 'The Sexual Regulation Dimension of Contemporary Welfare Law: A Fifty State Overview' (2002) 8 *Michigan Journal of Gender and Law* 121; JE Koons, 'Motherhood, Marriage, and Morality: The Pro-Marriage Moral Discourse of American Welfare Policy' (2004) 19 *Wisconsin Women's Law Journal* 1; CC Orr, 'Married to a Myth: How Welfare Reform Violates the Constitutional Rights of Poor Single Mothers' (2005) 34 *Capital University Law Review* 211; and JC Murphy, 'Legal Images of Fatherhood: Welfare Reform, Child Support Enforcement, and Fatherless Children' (2005) 81 *Notre Dame Law Review* 325.

A. Spouses

Women who seek financial support from the state in the form of welfare benefits have long been subject to intense moral scrutiny to determine whether they were (are) worthy or deserving of support.[19] While over time the categories of women eligible for state support expanded—from the widow, to the deserted wife, to the divorcee, and the unwed mother—various tests of moral worthiness continued to be at play. Women were required to demonstrate that they were 'fit and proper' or 'suitable persons', notions that turned largely on middle class expectations about how the home should be tended and children reared, and of course, on whether unmarried women engaged in sex. The 'suitable person' requirement was over time replaced by the concept of the 'single person'; a woman could apply in her own right for benefits provided that she lived as a 'single person'. While perhaps at first blush a more objective and less intrusive test than that of the 'suitable person', this was not the case in fact.[20] Rather, the inquiry focused upon whether a woman was involved in a 'marriage-like' relationship; an inquiry that once again subjected women to invasive scrutiny of their intimate relationships and to explicit moralizing. And the concept of 'marriage-like' (or cohabitation and consortium) was as malleable and ambiguous as that of the 'suitable person'. While limited attention was paid to the economic, social and familial aspects of the relationship, it appears that sexual factors were determinative in all but the most exceptional cases.[21] If found not to be living as a 'single person' but rather in a 'marriage-like' relationship, a woman was ineligible for benefits. As with her married counterparts, she was assumed to be dependent upon a male breadwinner. It mattered little that he had no legal obligation to support her, no means to support her, nor if the means, any inclination to support her; if the relationship was 'marriage-like' his support was simply imputed.[22]

In 1987, in response to a constitutional challenge, the Ontario government amended the welfare legislation, adopting a definition of 'spouse' that largely tracked provincial family law legislation. Significantly, this meant that a woman could co-habit with a man for a three-year period before they

[19] M Leighton, 'Handmaids' Tales: Family Benefits Assistance and the Single-Mother-Led Family' (1987) 45 *University of Toronto Faculty Law Review* 324; M Little, *'No Car, No Radio, No Liquor Permit': the Moral Regulation of Single Mothers in Ontario, 1920–1997* (Toronto, Oxford University Press, 1998).

[20] Leighton (above n 19).

[21] *Ibid*, 333.

[22] Although a few court decisions placed considerable weight on the provision of actual economic support, Leighton concludes from her review of the decisions of the Social Assistance Review Board that the decision-makers of that Board strongly resisted any attempt to give priority to economic obligation or actual support being provided, *ibid*, 333.

would be considered as spouses for welfare purposes, just as they would be for the purposes of the spousal support provisions of the Family Law Act. At the same time a provision was introduced to preclude the investigation or consideration of sexual factors in determining whether or not a person was a spouse. Not only did these changes to the legislation enable women to try out relationships without imposed financial dependence, they diminished the routine violations of women's privacy that had been a central feature of benefits to women since their inception. Additionally, the change to the definition of spouse impacted materially on the number of criminal fraud charges laid against women on welfare; for a three year period women could engage in intimate relationships with a reduced—not extinguished—fear of criminal sanction.[23]

This liberalized regime came to an abrupt halt in 1995 with the election of a Conservative government, and the unfolding of its 'common sense revolution.' The government acted quickly to amend the definition of spouse (other dramatic changes to the welfare system were to follow later), so that presumptively any two persons of the opposite sex who co-resided in the same residence were deemed to be spouses, and the onus was placed upon them to prove that they were not.[24] The provision introduced in 1987, precluding reliance upon sexual factors, remained in place, making it even more difficult to disprove the imputed status as spouses. The ambiguity of earlier days returned with a vengeance in a definition of spouse that turned upon whether one of two persons of the opposite sex who shared the same dwelling provided financial support to the other *or* there existed a 'mutual agreement or arrangement regarding their financial affairs' *and* the social, familiar and financial aspects of the relationship amounted to cohabitation'.[25] The new regulations were introduced on 1 October 1995 and by April 1996, 10,013 recipients had been declared ineligible directly due to the new definition. Of these 89 percent were women, 79 percent were sole support parents, and of the sole support parents rendered ineligible, 96 percent were single mothers.[26] Despite its gender neutral language, the

[23] It is telling to observe that in 1981–82, when the concept of 'living as a single person' was used to determine spousal status, 84% of welfare fraud charges were based upon an allegation of an undeclared spouse, resulting in 200 charges, 161 convictions, and jail in 42% of those cases. Two different background papers for a major review of social assistance undertaken in the late 1980s concluded that the definition of 'spouse' introduced in 1987 (tracking the Family Law Act) resulted in dramatic reductions to these high rates; see AM Gutierrez, *The Interaction of Criminal Law and the Income Maintenance System in Ontario*, a research report for the Social Assistance Review Committee, May 1987, 17 and 28; the Canadian Research Institute for Law and the Family (JE Wallace, ML McCall and JH Hornick), *A Literature Review of Welfare Fraud: Nature, Extent and Control*, a research report for the Social Assistance Review Committee, July 1987, 17.

[24] Family Benefits Act Reg 366, s 1(1)(d) as amended.

[25] *Ibid.*

[26] *Falkiner et al v Director, Income Maintenance Branch, Ministry of Community and Social Services & Attorney General of Ontario* (2002) 59 OR (3d) 481.

gendered impact of the new definition was abundantly obvious. And once again men were presumed to be breadwinners, responsible for both women and their children, when at law they had neither spousal nor in most cases, child support obligations.

The definition of 'spouse' introduced in 1995 was subject to a constitutional challenge in *Falkiner et al v Director, Income Maintenance Branch, Ministry of Community and Social Services and Attorney General of Ontario*.[27] The four applicants in the case each acknowledged that she co-resided with a man and that the social and familial aspects of their relationships amounted to co-habitation, but resisted the categorization of 'spouses' on the grounds that they were not financially inter-dependent. In fact, while each had a 'financial arrangement' with her respective intimate partner (indeed it is hard to imagine sharing a dwelling and not having some kind of financial arrangement) each maintained as much financial independence as possible.

The Ontario Court of Appeal found that the new definition of 'spouse' captured relationships which were not functionally spousal because they were characterized by neither economic inter-dependence nor actual support or support obligations. The Court concluded that '[t]he definition will thus capture relationships lacking in the permanence, the commitment, the legal obligation to support, the legal right to claim support, even the meaningful actual support that characterizes spousal or marriage-like relationships'.[28] The Court adopted the view expressed by the lower court that

> [i]t makes couples, or family units, out of individuals like the Respondents who have made no commitment to each other, with accompanying voluntary assumption of economic interdependence. There is all the difference in the world between a person, with her own money, sharing accommodation [note that if not spouses, his contributions toward the household will be taken into account in calculating the amount of her benefit cheque] in the hope that an inchoate relationship may flourish, versus a person whose financial support is largely in the hands of her co-habitant who has no legal obligation towards her or her children.[29]

Upholding lower court decisions, the Ontario Court of Appeal found the definition violated section 15 of the Charter, discriminating against the applicants on the basis of their sex, marital status and their receipt of social assistance.[30] In coming to this ruling, the Court found that the new definition disproportionately and adversely affected women, and perpetuated

[27] *Ibid.*
[28] *Ibid*, para 59.
[29] *Ibid*, para 60.
[30] *Ibid*, para 3 The government defended its new definition, arguing that rather than detracting from equality as the applicants alleged, it promoted equality as between 'common law' and married couples.

the historical disadvantage experienced by single mothers.[31] Again drawing from the lower court decision, the Court of Appeal observed that

> persons on social assistance are often stigmatized and feel themselves unworthy. The serious invasions of their privacy and the unwarranted assumption of their dependency upon a man occasioned by the Regulation can only reinforce this unfortunate aspect of their lives.[32]

Importantly as well, the court concludes that forcing women to become financially dependent upon men 'with whom they have at best a try-on relationship ... strikes at the core of human dignity'.[33]

The government sought to appeal the decision and was successful in its leave application to the Supreme Court of Canada, but just weeks before the appeal was to be argued, abandoned the appeal, ostensibly conceding the unconstitutionality of the definition and binding itself to the decision of the Court of Appeal. However, the definition of 'spouse' introduced subsequently largely tracks its 1995 predecessor, but grants a three month 'grace period;' that is, a three month period of cohabitation during which spousal status will not be imputed. And while the provision deeming those of the opposite sex who co-reside to be spouses and placing the onus upon them to prove the contrary was revoked in 2000, it seems that in practice a de facto presumption continues to operate.[34]

The definition of spouse for welfare purposes was also impacted by other litigation occurring in the context of challenges to the denial of benefits to same-sex couples. The Supreme Court of Canada's decision in *M v H*, which held that the definition of spouse under Ontario's Family Law Act that determined support obligations violated the equality rights of gays and lesbians, ultimately led to the reform of the definition of 'spouse' for welfare purposes.[35] Formerly governing relationships between 'two persons of the opposite sex', the welfare regime now governs relationships between 'any two persons' who co-reside. The current definition of spouse provides that,

> spouse, in relation to an applicant or recipient, means ...
>
> (d) a person who has been residing in the same dwelling place as the applicant or recipient for a period of at least three months, if,

[31] *Ibid*, para 96.
[32] *Ibid*, para 100.
[33] *Ibid*, para 101.
[34] That a de facto presumption continues to operate was confirmed by conversations with lawyers in Ontario's community legal clinics. The co-residency policy directive (#19) also affirms this; '[t]he Administrator requires evidence that satisfies him/her that the financial, social and familial aspects of the relationship do not amount to a spousal or same-sex partner relationship, in order for eligibility to continue'. Ontario, Ministry of Community and Social Services, *Ontario Works: Co-Residency Directive (Directive #19)* (Toronto, Ministry of Community and Social Services, September 2001).
[35] *H(D) v M(H)* [1999] 1 SCR 328.

(i) the extent of the social and familial aspects of the relationship between the two persons is consistent with cohabitation, and
(ii) the extent of the financial support provided by one person to the other or the degree of financial interdependence between the two persons is consistent with cohabitation.[36]

As with the pre-1987 regime, the ambiguity of the definition makes it difficult in many situations for women to know at just what point in the relationship they will be found to be 'co-residing' with a 'spouse' (two separate, but inter-related, inquiries). The relevant Ministerial policy directives point to a number of relevant sources of information to determine co-residency: driver's licence history; employment records; common phone numbers; and credit checks. Factors to be considered for 'spousal' determinations include an agreement about joint financial arrangements, contributions toward shared costs of necessities, shelter and services, money given or loaned, whether known by public authorities as a couple, arrangements for sharing household chores, groceries or meals, sharing childcare, caring for the other when ill, and receipt or acceptance of invitations as a couple. As the policy directive itself indicates, 'there is no correct number of questions that must be answered a certain way' to conclude either spousal status or co-residency; rather all factors must be weighed together. In practice, situations vary widely as to when persons are deemed to be spouses, and/or deemed to be co-residing.

In addition to the fear and uncertainty generated by this ambiguity, determinations of spousal status entail significant incursions into not only the private, intimate lives of women but their day-to-day social interactions. The spousal and residency questionnaires that must be completed probe into the minutia of daily life. One woman interviewed for the Woman Abuse and Welfare study,[37] who had left her abusive husband (but was still hopeful of reunification) and had moved into shared accommodation with a male roommate, said of the questionnaire,

> They were right in there, 'Well you must have had an affair and now you've moved in with your new boyfriend'. Just frustrating. I stayed there for the month and continued to look for another place; it was just too insane. I had a 5 page questionnaire about nit-picky kind of things like, 'Do you eat dinner together?

[36] O Reg 134/98 as amended. The definition of spouse also includes those who have declared themselves to be spouses, and those who have actual support obligations pursuant to family law legislation or a domestic contract.

[37] The Woman Abuse and Welfare Study entailed in-depth qualitative interviews with 64 women in Ontario who had been in receipt of welfare benefits for some period of time since 1995, when the major reforms began to be introduced and who had experienced abuse in an intimate relationship. See J Mosher et al, *Walking on Eggshells: Abused Women's Experiences of Ontario's Welfare System*, accessible at: www.oaith.ca/pdf/Walking_on_Eggshells.pdf. I have drawn from the original transcripts of that project in this article. Quotations in the text are all direct quotes from women interviewed for that project.

> Do you share a bank account? Do you share the same bathroom?' Stupid little things.

Another woman, whose aunt, when destitute, came to live with her temporarily recalled having to complete what was at the time the same-sex partner questionnaire; 'I found it very invasive and very insulting and I was really angry with them'.

Sandra Falkiner-Budgell, one of the applicants in the case of *Falkiner* has written of the questionnaire,

> I can't begin to tell you how humiliating and intrusive some of the questions were on this form. They asked what I called Reid's mother and what Reid called mine; they asked what my son called Reid, and if Reid ever bought him presents for his birthday; they asked if Reid ever babysat my son and whether he ever had any contact with my son's school; they asked who did the grocery shopping and who did the laundry; they asked anything and everything they could to help them 'determine if Reid was my spouse'.[38]

Invasions of privacy are not limited to what an applicant is required to personally disclose. Landlords, neighbours, teachers, and a host of others are asked to provide information and offer their opinions about the intimate lives of women. A routine form letter, in the particular instance mailed out to solicit information about a neighbour, explains,

> [w]e are conducting inquiries relating to an Ontario Works recipient and require information with respect to the above address. If you have any information regarding the tenants of the above address i.e.: number of occupants, sexes, names, employment, length of residence, or any other relevant information please do not hesitate to contact me. Your anonymity can be assured in responding to this inquiry.

In *Falkiner* evidence was proffered of one woman who was cut off benefits after a determination was made that she was co-residing with a spouse. Her evidence was that her imputed 'spouse' was in fact simply her landlord, and a close friend of her incarcerated boyfriend. The evidence which incriminated her was a series of statutory declarations from neighbours with whom the two had occasionally socialized. Apart from a change to the names of the alleged spouses, below is evidence taken directly from two of the statutory declarations,

> Jane and John are considered in my eyes as being a couple. They have come over for dinner or to play games in a manner that says they are living together ... they are always going to Jane's mother's house for dinner which to me shows that they are a couple. I have never seen anyone do this with their landlord before.

[38] Sandy Falkiner-Budgell, 'Busting Welfare: I Took the Tories' Spouse-in-the-House Law to Court and Won', accessed 20 April 2008, www.nowtoronto.com/issues/2002-06-06/news_story4.php.

> Jane and John are my neighbours. Jane was inteduced [sic] to me by John as his girlfriend. They had thanksgiving dinner with my family. They have come over to play card games as couple.[39]

Notice how what might be characterized as no more than gossip or speculative and subjective assertions of neighbours are accepted as proof of 'spousal' status. But note as well how the sharing of the minute detail of social existence fundamentally transforms social relations. When each and every social interaction has the potential be used as evidence of relational status—to potentially cut you off, throw you out and charge you criminally—the social relation is itself transformed into a moment of surveillance and all those who participate in the social fabric of one's life, be they neighbours, friends, teachers, shopkeepers or landlords, become potential informants.

Not uncommonly, persons are deemed to be spouses when they do not consider themselves 'spouses', when there exists no legal obligation of spousal or child support and where there is little, if any, financial interdependence. A traditional patriarchal family form is super-imposed upon relationships which are in fact, profoundly out-of-step with that model. The presence of a man signals economic wherewithal and contributions when in fact, many of the men who move in and out of the lives of women on welfare have little, if anything, to contribute financially. Long-term monogamous relationships are read onto fluid relationships with one or more partners, where change may be tied to economic need, to the ebb and flow in emotive relationships, or any number of other factors. And relationships are found where survival practices (using the address of a friend when you are without secure housing, jointly signing for credit to enable a friend, etc) are misread by those who have never experienced poverty, as proof of marriage-like relationships (because these are the only relationships wherein they can imagine these practices occurring).

The significance for a single woman is that if she is found to be co-residing with a spouse she will be cut off benefits, probably assessed with an over-payment (often substantial) and possibly charged with fraud. While in theory they may re-apply as a couple, this requires his agreement, that his financial assets be taken into account, and that he be prepared to comply with the welfare-to-work and countless other rules. Moreover, in all likelihood, he—as the imputed head of the household—will be the one to receive the welfare cheque. Women thus lose economic independence, and may be compelled into relationships of economic dependence upon men with no legal support obligations. For the applicants in *Falkiner*, each of whom had experienced abuse in past relationships and understood all too painfully how integral economic control is to the maintenance of abuse,

[39] Exhibits in *Falkiner* above n 26.

being compelled into relationships of economic dependence without an adequate 'trial' period of living together, was of paramount concern.

But the full impact of the current spousal regime can only be assessed and understood through an examination of its interplay with another construct, that of 'welfare fraud', and of the confluence of two areas of moral scrutiny; the promiscuous single woman living outside the normative borders of a proper patriarchal family and the equally deviant and destructive welfare 'fraudster.'

B. Fraud

Fighting welfare fraud has come to occupy a central place in welfare regimes, and has been successfully deployed to not only disentitle individual recipients accused of fraud, but more broadly to disentitle welfare recipients as a social group; to mark them as second-class citizens unworthy of respect and dignity.[40] In Ontario 'fighting fraud' (note the war metaphor) was, as noted earlier, one of three expressed goals of the reforms introduced in the mid-1990s. As a central tool of governance, fraud control has important discursive elements and material practices that are deployed by a wide array of actors in multiple sites.

State actors have played a central role in the construction of welfare fraud as a problem spiraling out of control. The use of terminology with explicit associations with criminality—fraudsters, theft, cheats, zero tolerance—and the misrepresentation of 'official' statistics regarding fraud, helped to manufacture the fraud problem.[41] And of course, the imagery of the welfare fraudster mapped neatly onto that of the lazy bum who preferred to stay home and do nothing, rather than work for a living, reinvigorating the historical association of poverty and criminality.

The fight against fraud in Ontario required and legitimized a new arsenal of weapons, which in turn, further solidified the claims regarding the severity of fraud and the depravity of recipients. Among the new weapons

[40] J Mosher and J Hermer, 'Welfare Fraud and the Constitution of Social Assistance as Crime', prepared for the Law Commission of Canada, at: osgoode.yorku.ca/osgmedia.nsf/0/271AE1B3D9D286D38525709A00521FBC/$FILE/Welfare%20Fraud%20Report.pdf, accessed January 3, 2009, and DE Chunn and SAM Gavigan, 'From Welfare Fraud to Welfare as Fraud: The Criminalization of Poverty' in G Balfour and E Comack (eds), *Criminalizing Women* (Halifax NS, Fernwood Publishing, 2006).

[41] In government reports 'fraud' was the term used to categorize all over-payments made to recipients irrespective of whether there was either the necessary criminal intent or in some instances the actus reus to establish the crime of fraud. The complexity, volume and counter-intuitive nature of the roughly 800 rules governing welfare receipt ensure not only that mistakes will be unavoidable but also pervasive. When these mistakes are characterized as fraud, fraud thus becomes a pervasive feature of the welfare system and recipients, actual or potential 'fraudsters'.

were those designed to detect and those intended to deter. Eligibility review officers were given new powers to investigate, and enjoy among other powers the right to question the person who is the subject of the investigation. The unfolding of the CVP (consolidated verification procedures) environment entailed a host of additional procedures and documentary requirements to prove one's eligibility on an on-going basis.[42] These procedures of proof and verification not only operate to disentitle those unable to comply but to signal the disingenuous, if not fraudulent, character of applicants. Information sharing agreements with other government departments enable vast amounts of informational exchange about recipients, and sweeping consents that must be signed by all members of the benefit unit further enlarge the amount of information gathered and stored. The introduction of a province-wide, toll-free snitch line, with active encouragement to report, enlisted new players (neighbours, teachers, landlords, etc) into the project of active surveillance. Some 6,527 calls were made to the snitch line in 2001–02; 9,348 in 2000–01. And in 2001–02, 38,452 fraud investigations were conducted (down roughly 14,000 from the prior year). No eligibility problems were found in 66.7 per cent of cases, 33.3 per cent (12,816) resulted in assistance being reduced or terminated, and only 393 convictions for actual criminal fraud resulted.[43] Despite the very low percentage of convictions in relation to the overall caseload (less than 0.1 per cent), very substantial numbers of recipients experience fraud investigations (and often benefits are cut off during the investigation), reductions and terminations.

Sanctions available under the Canadian Criminal Code for fraud (14 years for fraud over CAN$5000) were deemed inadequate, notwithstanding that those convicted of welfare fraud are already sentenced harshly compared with those convicted of other forms of fraud or other property crimes.[44] Ontario moved to create additional provincial sanctions—initially a three month ban on receipt of welfare benefits upon conviction for fraud (six for a subsequent offence) was introduced, but this was quickly followed by a revised regulation, increasing the severity of the sanction to a lifetime ban. While these bans on welfare receipt were rescinded in 2003 by a Liberal

[42] See A Mulzer, 'The Doorkeeper and the Grand Inquisitor: The Central Role of Verification Procedures in Means-Tested Welfare Programs' (2005) 36 *Columbia Human Rights Law Review* 663 who argues that verification procedures serve several functions. Mulzer observes that, '[s]tringent and invasive verification procedures stigmatize the receipt of benefits and express these concerns to claimants. At the same time, these procedures serve as a sign to the public that their concerns are well-founded … they serve to validate (and may even increase) the public's perception of welfare claimants as dishonest' (at 683).

[43] Ontario, Ministry of Community, Family and Children's Services, *Welfare Fraud Control Report 2001–02* (Toronto, Ministry of Community, Family and Children's Services, June 2003).

[44] Mosher and Hermer, above n 40; and DL Martin, 'Passing the Buck: Prosecution of Welfare Fraud; Preservation of Stereotypes' (2002) 12 *Windsor Journal of Access to Justice* 52.

government, a new policy directive was introduced to get tough on fraud, making mandatory a referral to police whenever there was reason to suspect intent to commit fraud.[45]

As the statistics noted above reveal, the policing of welfare 'fraud' rarely has much to do with actual criminal fraud or the protection of society from truly harmful behaviour. Rather the discourse of fraud and the new practices of surveillance and detection are deployed to demean, dehumanize and disentitle a entire social group. The now ready association drawn between welfare receipt, social disorder and crime effectively regulates not only the behaviour of those in receipt of welfare, but equally as important, the behaviour and attitudes of those who manage to live outside of welfare's strictures. For those in receipt of welfare, the threat of a fraud charge looms constantly in the air, generating fear, mistrust and anxiety.

To this point the portrayal of the operation of the welfare fraud regime I have offered suggests a sharper, more unified picture than in fact exists, belying the considerable variations in on-the-ground practices. *Ontario Works* is administered at the municipal level and significant differences exist in, for example, rates of fraud referrals to police. Notwithstanding the Ministry's Policy Directive that mandates a referral to police whenever there is reason to suspect the intention to commit fraud, some municipalities apply a dollar threshold, others consider a range of personal circumstances.[46] Moreover differences are often pronounced between the provincial and municipal levels of government, as was apparent in the strong opposition by many municipalities to the lifetime ban introduced by the province. Hence, whether a recipient risks an actual fraud charge varies considerably. But while less punitive responses can be seen in retrospect, they are impossibly difficult for recipients (or their advocates) to predict in advance.

C. Fraudulent Spouses

Actual criminal fraud requires a deceitful or dishonest act resulting in the deprivation of another. It requires that the accused have subjective knowledge not only of the prohibited act but that the act could have as a consequence the deprivation of another. Take an easy case where there is no factual contestation regarding spousal status nor co-residency. A couple is married and cohabiting; she has applied for *Ontario Works* benefits as a single person and has not disclosed that she is married, nor that she is cohabiting with her spouse. Her husband is employed and earning enough

[45] O Reg 456/03; Ontario, Ministry of Community and Social Services, *Ontario Works: Controlling Fraud Policy Directive (Directive #45)* (Toronto, Ministry of Community and Social Services, January 2004).

[46] Mosher and Hermer, above n 40.

income that they would not qualify as a couple were they to apply jointly. The prohibited act on these facts is the failure to disclose that she in cohabiting with her spouse; her behaviour may well be appropriately characterized as deceitful, and there seems little doubt that viewed objectively, it would be appropriately characterized as dishonest.

The reality, however, is that most cases are factually ambiguous. A single mother receiving *Ontario Works* benefits meets a man and they begin to date. Over the next several months he begins to spend a great deal of time at her home, and shares in many of the household tasks. They regularly go out socially together so many people in their neighbourhood and beyond will see them together. He moves some of his clothing into her apartment and he spends a few nights each week there. What she (or anyone for that matter) is unable to predict is at what point the welfare system would deem her to be co-residing with a spouse, and the three month grace period would begin to run.[47] Given this unpredictability, at what point does she engage in the prohibited act of deceiving *Ontario Works* about the 'true' nature of the relationship; that is, that she is co-residing with a spouse? As Wilkie has argued, it is highly problematic to 'label conduct criminal when not only is the categorization of that conduct highly subjective and discretionary but when … different legally-qualified tribunals come to opposing views on the same facts.'[48]

For recipients, what arises from these deep ambiguities is a diverse array of implied 'rules' regulating the permissible levels of intimacy. Women on welfare interviewed for the Woman Abuse and Welfare study expressed various conceptions of these rules:

> Once you are on welfare you are not allowed to, like, meet anyone else because if you are then they are supposed to be paying your bills and not welfare. So you sort of get that through reading between the lines.
>
> You know you get into trouble if somebody was there all the time. You have to keep them at arm's length, if you know what I mean?
>
> I believe I was allowed to have a man stay with me three nights a week, three nights a week, yeah … and he was only allowed so many pieces of clothing in my house and things like that.

Whether garnered through the sharing of information with other single mothers, direct edicts from their welfare workers or reading between

[47] As Gutierrez has observed, given that the determination of 'spouse' is a mixed question of law and fact, it is often exceedingly difficult to know when a woman on welfare would be considered a spouse for welfare purposes (above n 23, 39).

[48] M Wilkie, *Women Social Security Offenders: Experiences of the Criminal Justice System in Western Australia* (Nedlands WA, University of Western Australia Crime Research Centre, 1993) 44. Wilkie describes a case where the benefits tribunal had concluded on a balance of probabilities that there was not a spouse; while a criminal court on the same facts found that there was proof beyond a reasonable doubt there was a spouse.

the lines, the messaging to single women is that compliance with a set of implicit rules—that are difficult to discern with precision yet rule-like in their imposition from a governing authority and the punitive consequences that will flow from an imputed breach—is necessary to avoid trouble.

The Ontario Ministry responsible for welfare benefits (the Ministry of Community and Social Services), while acknowledging the complexity of the welfare system, suggests that concern about complexity is really beside the point. In its view, the rules may be complex, but what is asked of recipients is really quite simple—they are to report all changes in circumstances; it is the job of agents of the welfare system to apply the complex rules to determine whether and how the disclosed information impacts upon eligibility. In this crisp division of labour, recipients disclose all information and welfare workers make the complex determinations of eligibility.[49]

Reassuring though this approach may initially sound, it is in fact astonishingly punitive and disturbingly corrosive of women's autonomy. It is important to appreciate that a common view among welfare administrators is that the 'failure' to provide any piece of information that an administrator subsequently learns about and says in hindsight ought to have been reported constitutes criminal fraud. In other words, the obligation to disclose all changes in circumstances—the details of one's intimate, private life—is backed by the penal power of the state. So it is not only the failure to disclose a 'spouse' that may lead to an allegation of fraud, but also simply not sharing information that welfare wanted to know (irrespective of whether now knowing that information, the relationship would be deemed 'spousal').

In a strict legal sense the Ministry's position is wrong on two counts: the legislation itself does not require the reporting of all information, but rather changes in circumstances *relevant to eligibility*; and secondly, the mere omission of a piece of information does not, on its own, constitute criminal fraud.[50] But the regime within which single women on welfare struggle to

[49] Interview with Debbie Moretta, Director Ontario Disability Support Program, Ministry of Community and Social Services, 22 December 2004. Ms Moretta indicated that while the rules may be complex, what is asked of recipients is really quite simple; report changes in their circumstances. Similarly, in her affidavit in *Broomer v Ontario (AG)* (2004) 121 CRR (2d) 163, a constitutional challenge to the lifetime ban, Ms Moretta observes that 'the system is designed so that recipients make full disclosure of any changes in their circumstances to the program; individuals are not required to make any self-assessment of eligibility' (affidavit sworn 29 August 2003).

[50] The Rights and Responsibilities Form, for example, states: 'you are responsible for following the rules of the O.W. program, including honest reporting of all circumstances that *affect eligibility*' (emphasis added). Similarly, in the application form, the applicant acknowledges that 'I/we will notify the Administrator, the Director, or his/her representative as the case may be, of any change of *relevant circumstances* of any beneficiary of the allowance/assistance to be provided, including any change in circumstances pertaining to assets, income, living arrangements and my/our participation in Ontario Works activity as set out in the participation agreement' (emphasis added).

survive and comply (not always compatible endeavours) is structured less by the formal law than by the prevalent and invidious stereotyping of welfare recipients as fraudsters, and the mis-characterization of the retention of information about one's relationships as 'fraud.'

Imagine living within this regime that demands to know all changes in circumstances and that will characterize any perceived failure to do so as criminal misconduct? Does a woman have to report each time her boyfriend visits? Each time they go out together? Each time he cares for her children or buys a birthday gift for one of them? Each time they have sex? Each time he helps out around the house? Each time he buys groceries or pays a phone bill?

Within this regime the state assumes definitive control of how women's relationships will be characterized; it is the state that decides that she is a spouse, a girlfriend, a roommate or a caregiver. It is she who must live with the consequences. The state demands that women share the intimate details of their lives under threat not only of termination of the benefits that are crucial to survival but also of criminal charges. It is hard to imagine a more pervasive and intrusive system of control. The state, much like an abusive male partner, exploits economic dependence to exercise its power and control over women. It demands submission, compliance and obedience. And like possessive, abusive men, the state is acutely suspicious of women's sexual lives. Confident that there is another man, or men, that women are hiding in their homes, extensive measures of surveillance are justified to monitor, catch and punish women.

The inquisitiveness of front line workers, the policing powers of Eligibility Review Officers and the wide net of intrusive surveillance cast by measures like the snitch lines are all deployed to scrutinize the intimate lives of women in search of the 'other man.' Women's relationships with men—whether or not they are intimate—are regarded with acute interest, suspicion and often open hostility; they are, in fact, everybody's business. In this climate fear becomes a constant fixture in women's everyday lives. As mentioned above, the persistent surveillance by not only the state, but also neighbours, landlords, shopkeepers and others means that any interaction with a man might lead to an allegation of fraud.

The spousal and fraud regimes deployed by the state to control and discipline single women are also directly engaged by abusive men to extract their own forms of control and discipline over their intimate partners. Abusive men—whether current or past partners—frequently employ these tools of governance to their own ends. A man may report his past or current partner, claiming falsely that he (or another man) is living with her in order to have her cut off benefits and forced into dependence upon him. Or he may threaten to report her, hoping to increase her submission to his authority in exchange for his agreement—always tentative—not to report her. Or he may lend her a small amount of money or buy something for the household, only later to reveal his true intentions; to enhance his own power by now threatening to report her for having failed to disclose income.[51] As one woman, whose boyfriend had become increasingly abusive, described,

> I thought this relationship was my ticket off welfare ... 'great he's moving in ... I'm gonna' get off welfare' ... I thought he was going to take financial responsibility and I was gonna' be off welfare ... He lived off me, sponged off me. ... I couldn't tell them [welfare] what was going on [the abuse] because then they would cut [cancel] my cheque. I couldn't even tell them that this guy was sponging off me ... I mean you can't even get a guy outta' your house because now he has all the power in the world. Welfare fraud, welfare, that's what it's all about. They just gained the biggest stronghold they could ever gain and there'll by so many women that will be um, affected by that ... I just got into a relationship that I could no longer get out of because now someone could accuse me of fraud. Now I was bound because he, that just gave him the control ... See that's the whole problem with how it's set up now 'cause now women can't get out. Now they are definitely trapped. They are trapped ... they're going to basically life sentence you when you need some help.

This fear is not limited to instances where an abusive partner has uttered the threat or made the call; rather for many women it lingers constantly in the air. This fear makes it extraordinarily difficult to trust anyone, including the person with whom you may be forging a new relationship. As one woman explains, when a man in your life gives you money to help you out, he can also use it as a means of control by threatening to report you to welfare for fraud; he has the power to 'ruin you'.

> So it's hard for you to build a relationship properly because there's always that fear.... So you're in trouble if you do and you're in trouble if you don't [disclose the money]. One way you're in trouble with your relationship breaking down and you're in trouble with getting caught and losing the income. I need him. I needed a better vehicle to go the food bank half way through the month ... Your life is just, not your life when you're on social services. You have no life.

As noted, the fear of being reported relates not only to a potential finding of spousal status or the failure to report a change in circumstance but surrounds the small economic contributions that a boyfriend may make. Women often desperately need these small amounts of cash or the groceries or other household items that their boyfriends might purchase from time-to-time. While many know that this 'income' is to be reported, they

[51] The Woman Abuse & Welfare Research Project included a questionnaire sent to all area administrators of *Ontario Works*. 20 of 35 administrators responded affirmatively to the question, 'Are you aware of any cases where an abusive partner has reported to the welfare fraud hotline or elsewhere that his former partner is living with another man?' Of the 64 women interviewed, roughly 20% reported that their abusers had made, or threatened to make, a call to welfare to report them for fraud.

also know it is likely to be deducted dollar-for-dollar from their welfare cheques. It may also provide the traces of evidence of 'financial support' or interdependence, that while thin, may nevertheless be enough for welfare authorities to conclude they are spouses. Yet many also realize that not disclosing the 'income' may put them at risk of an allegation of fraud—not only from their welfare worker, but from those in their social networks, including their boyfriends. The women below capture the dilemma of deciding what information to share with welfare.

> They want to know everything ... but there are risks of telling them everything and of not.

> They want to know everything and that's where the fear comes in because they want to know everything and of course you're not gonna tell anything because you're afraid ... I mean every time you just tell them something, if you borrow money they may deduct it off of your cheque.

> I remember being told that you need to tell, you need to get all the facts. There's repercussions for that. A smart woman would not tell every intimate detail of her life because sometimes the man has got children of his own from a past relationship that he's supporting. And he's in your life. And he's dating you. He sleeps over occasionally or whatever. And he may contribute to the home. He may not be there 24/7 but he does because he cares for you and your children, he might bring something. Or he might give you some extra money. I don't think I need to tell social services that. To me that's prostituting myself.

> They told me if I had any boyfriend and he was living with me or gave me some money they needed me to report the income I receive, any money, any tip, any gift people gave me I have to report ... you need to report everything, even if you receive a dollar, or you find a dollar on the street you have to report it ... it doesn't make any sense!

Some of the women feared that providing any information at all about the relationship would result in termination. One woman explained that she would not disclose the abuse by her current boyfriend because she was confident that what would be heard and responded to is 'boyfriend' not 'abuse' and she would be investigated, potentially cut off and charged. Others explained:

> They tried several times to get information about him from me. But I would never say that I was in any type of relationship with him because then they would cut me off.

> Yeah just like my current boyfriend, he has his place and I have my place and we'd like to be family and everything. But I always tell him like, 'When I am working and you're working' because the way they are like any little slip and they have your life in their hands regardless of if you have kids or not. They wouldn't think twice about cutting you off and here you are, got rent pay and everything else. [She was particularly anxious because she had earlier been investigated when her housing worker came to her apartment and her boyfriend answered the door.]

Women in the Woman Abuse and Welfare study poignantly described other ways in which being on welfare made it extraordinarily difficult to build a new and healthy relationship. For many women, the men in their lives were not in a position to financially support them and their children. Women feared that if they provided information to their welfare workers about the evolving relationship they would be cut off and while for some the consequence would be forced economic dependence, others would opt, reluctantly, to end the relationship and preserve their welfare entitlements (as each of the Applicants in *Falkiner* said she would), and for others still, they were confident that the men in their lives would walk away, unable to assume the financial expectations imposed upon them. As one woman explained,

> I think that is such a serious issue. That is a major issue. Forming a relationship with a man is very difficult when you have social services. A good man that really cares about you, whether you're on social services or not, will always want to help you out. Nine times out of ten they do not have the income to take on your entire family. There's no concessions for that. So the bottom line is, if a man is coming into your life he should be able to take care of you and your children and you should be off welfare. Nine times out of ten they're not equipped, income wise, to take on that responsibility.

Another woman echoed this reality, imaging a man's reaction when he realizes that moving in together will shift all financial responsibilities onto his shoulders.

> [Imagine telling him] ... 'if you want me to move in right away, you'll have to pay everything' ... they're gonna be like, 'No'.

The expectation that men should (there is virtually no consideration of whether they *could*) assume financial responsibility for women and their children places women who want their relationships to continue in a difficult bind. While a man may not be able to contribute much, if anything, financially to the relationship, he may well bring other forms of crucial support—child care, adult company, or as the woman quote above explained, a means to get to the food bank. Tellingly the expectation that men should, and indeed do, provide economically carries through to the cases that are prosecuted as criminal fraud. There is frequently no inquiry at all of whether the men in women's lives are in fact providing for them financially, as the male breadwinner he is simply assumed to be providing, rather than 'sponging off' them.[52] Moreover, it is invariably only women who are charged with fraud for failing to disclose a spouse (the men who may benefit financially

[52] This is potentially relevant to the actus reus of the crime of fraud, which requires that there be deprivation of the state. In many circumstances, were they to re-apply as couple, they would in fact be entitled to receive higher benefits, so there is an argument that no deprivation has occurred.

are virtually never charged, although there is frequently little doubt but that they have been parties to any crime that may have occurred), and only women who carry the burden of over-payments (although there are civil remedies in the legislation that could be utilized to pursue men, these avenues to recovery are simply ignored).[53] And while there are few single fathers on welfare, there are plenty of single men on welfare, yet their intimate relationships are seemingly of little interest. There are very few reported welfare fraud cases based on spousal status that involve a male accused. Anecdotal evidence from community-based lawyers across the province indicates that the dense web of control regarding intimate relationships is profoundly gendered; men in receipt of welfare are investigated and charged with fraud, but rarely in relation to their intimate relationships or spousal status.

III. CONCLUSION

While welfare reforms of the late twentieth century discipline single women as workers, the above examination makes clear that the reforms simultaneously discipline their relational lives. The ambiguous character of the definition of 'spouse', the mischaracterization of the 'failure' to disclose either a 'change in circumstances' (read as anything and everything a state actor wants to know) or small amounts of financial and 'in-kind' assistance (groceries, meals, nappies, etc) as 'fraud', and the spinning of a pervasive discourse linking welfare receipt to crime, combine to render what might otherwise be considered the matter-of-fact details of daily social relationships as inculpatory evidence; as proof that women on welfare are not worthy, are not deserving, are in fact, the criminals we have suspected all along. The sweep of conduct potentially labeled as criminal is staggering, as is the intensity of the surveillance to which single women are subjected. Invasions of privacy are routinely carried out by not only agents of the state but also friends, neighbours, anyone and everyone.

Inevitably then, the regulatory power of 'spouses' and 'fraud' operates well beyond cases in which formal charges are laid; rather the looming threats of a possible fraud investigation (which as noted earlier, occur with significant frequency), of termination of benefits and of assessments of over-payments govern women's lives on a daily basis. Many do their best to comply; some avoid intimate relationships or sharing accommodation altogether to 'stay out of trouble' (often making it harder to get by),

[53] Pursuant to s 21(4) of the OWA, 'if a recipient had a dependent spouse when an overpayment was incurred, the administrator may give notice in writing to the spouse respecting the overpayment'. Once notice has been given the overpayment becomes enforceable as if it were an order of the Ontario Court (General Division).

while others attempt to discern what they can of the governing 'rules' and carefully structure their relationships to pattern those rules or to skillfully maneuver around them. But both compliance and resistance are extraordinarily difficult given the deep ambiguity of the concepts of 'spouse' and 'co-residency'; the 'rules' are literally, and perhaps intentionally, unknowable. This unknowability itself operates as a technique of control, expanding both the domains of surveillance for the concerned and watchful citizen and the array of social interactions where women must regulate their own conduct to avoid trouble.[54] In other words, the lack of clear referent points against which to model compliance or resistance results in the expansion, rather than the shrinkage, of the social spaces that are regulated. Unknowability also leaves women on tender hooks all the time; they never know just when the '*axe will fall*', nor whom they can trust.

Compliance is difficult not only because the rules are unknowable, but also because of the material realities of life on welfare. Benefit levels that are profoundly inadequate to meet even basic sustenance needs place many recipients in a position where they absolutely cannot refuse offers of small amounts of assistance from family, friends or intimates. Where disclosing this assistance will often result in dollar-for-dollar deductions from welfare benefits, recipients are placed in a horrendous moral double-bind. They cannot simultaneously comply with the demands of welfare to disclose all, and meet their own—and others'—expectations that they must provide adequately for their children.

The inadequacy of benefits, and the demeaning, dehumanizing and criminalizing processes of welfare receipt make women more desperate to get off welfare. For many, contrary to the hype of the welfare-to-work mantra, paid employment holds little promise, even if they were able to secure it. Finding a man becomes an explicit strategy to get off welfare (even if not out of poverty). Several women in the Women Abuse and Welfare study returned to, or were actively contemplating returning to, an abusive relationship, reasoning that life with their abusers was preferable to life on welfare. The message to 'get a man, any man, and keep him', although not explicitly spelled out in the legislation, is clearly being received by women. Diminished benefit levels, the definition of 'spouse', a hardening of stereotypes and explicit criminalization greatly reduce the options for women of living outside of patriarchal, nuclear families. As one woman in the Woman Abuse & Welfare project explained:

> They have pushed people into having to go into relationships ... they have pushed you into a situation where you have no choice but to live with somebody

[54] L Haney, 'Introduction: Gender, Welfare, and States of Punishment' (2004) 11 *Social Politics* 333 argues that ambiguity and contradiction render it difficult to know 'how to act or represent oneself' and play a significant role in 'keeping women in check'.

> in order to make the rent or to make the bills because of the cost of living has gone up and they are not prepared to give, you know, anymore than what is absolutely necessary. So, there is always going to be abuse with women because the government has put us into that kind of an environment.

And while women are pushed off welfare and into the arms (or fists) of men, the simultaneous valorization and glorification of marriage and family render marriage and traditional families a sought-after refuge for many. In other words, women are both pushed and pulled toward marriage and marital-like relationships.

Yet it is also clear that some women resist being pushed into patriarchal relationships of financial dependence; they are unwilling to enter private relations of dependence on the state's terms. For those low-income single women who continue to live outside the borders of the proper patriarchal family, the state practices its own form of patriarchal governance over their lives. Guardian of its patriarchal power, the state behaves as an abusive partner, harbouring deep suspicion that women may be courting other men. Constant surveillance, invasions of privacy, demeaning discourses and harsh punishments demonstrate the patriarch at work.

Irrespective of whether private patriarchal relations are re-constituted through welfare policies, all single women in receipt of welfare experience the curtailment of their ability to choose and determine the nature of their relationships. Their 'intimate associational liberty' is denied by the state.[55] As the Court of Appeal made so clear in *Falkiner*, women's dignity is thereby seriously compromised. All single mothers on welfare experience the fundamental erosion of their autonomy and the subjugation to the will of another. All single mothers on welfare are criminally suspect objects of surveillance. In sum, all single mothers on welfare are marked as deviant outsiders, undeserving of respect, support and dignity.

[55] This term comes from Mink, above n 18.

8

Retrenchment not Reform

Using Law and Policy to Restrict the Entitlement of Women with Disabilities to Social Assistance

JOAN M GILMOUR*

I. INTRODUCTION

WOMEN'S EXPERIENCES OF disability are constructed and regulated by systems of law and policy in many ways. In this chapter, I examine how this occurs in the context of establishing eligibility for social assistance, and contrast governments' discursive commitments with the reality of welfare law and policy. Government (cash funding) transfers are crucial to many who experience disability in Canada, a harsh economic reality that affects women more severely than men and makes them especially vulnerable, not only to program cutbacks, but also to uninformed judgements about eligibility and restrictive applications of the law. The current system, based on historical models of charity and distinctions between the deserving and undeserving poor, and a renewed emphasis on self-reliance and individual responsibility, is assessed against the measure of governments' own policy commitments to addressing broader determinants of health in order to improve population health, and to advancing the citizenship rights and inclusion of persons with disabilities. A striking feature of the cutbacks made to social spending and programs has been how little political cost governments incurred in doing so. The chapter highlights ways in which law facilitates the acceptance of these restricted and diminished norms and conditions. These changed (reduced) standards come to be accepted and internalized—becoming the new 'common sense'—with often profound effects for women's health and autonomy.

* This research was supported in part by the Social Sciences and Humanities Research Council of Canada. I am grateful for the research assistance of Kara Denny and Alexandra Raponi.

I begin with an introduction to two of the concepts that are central to this analysis: first, the influence of non-medical factors on population health, and secondly, disability. Next, I outline the social assistance system for people with disabilities in Ontario, focusing on how eligibility is determined, and how disability is conceptualized in the governing legislation. Finally, I analyze the role law plays in limiting possibilities in this system, and assess the prospects for reconfiguring legal norms to foster greater inclusion and citizenship rights for persons with disabilities.

II. DETERMINANTS OF HEALTH[1]

Keeping people healthy—doing what is needed to return individuals to health, maintain their health, prevent or slow the loss of health—is strongly associated with providing health care. 'Health' is equated with the absence of disease; health care, in turn, is most often thought of in terms of interventions available in acute care settings and provided by physicians. This has been as true in health policy as it has been in popular belief. We expect health care to be able to achieve all of those goals and more, and it is often essential in doing so. However, health status is influenced in important ways—indeed, often most significantly—by a range of factors in addition to the availability of appropriate health services. These are referred to as broader, or social, determinants of health. The process of identifying, understanding and determining how best to influence these factors in order to improve health is referred to as a population health approach.[2] That is the rubric that has been accepted for a considerable period of time by Health Canada (the federal Ministry of Health) and its provincial and territorial counterparts, as well as the Federal, Provincial and Territorial Advisory Committee on Population Health (FPTACPH) and a range of other government bodies.[3] In fact, the population health approach was endorsed by the

[1] This section draws from my co-authored article, J Gilmour and D Martin, 'Women's Poverty, Women's Health: The Role of Access to Justice' in P Van Esterik (ed), *Head, Heart and Hand: Partnerships for Women's Health in Canadian Environments*, vol I (Toronto, National Network on Environments and Women's Health, 2003).

[2] See generally M Hayes and J Dunn, *Population Health in Canada: A Systematic Review*, Canadian Policy Research Networks report #H-01 (Ottawa, Renouf Publishing, 1998) 7: 'Population health is the label used to describe the analysis of major social, physical, biological and behavioural influences upon overall levels of health status within and between identifiable population groups and subgroups'.

[3] See, eg, Canada. Standing Senate Committee on Social Affairs, Science and Technology, *The Health of Canadians: The Federal Role*, vol 4, Issues and Options (Ottawa, Government of Canada 2000) 123–4; Federal Provincial and Territorial Advisory Committee on Population Health (FPTACPH), *Toward a Healthy Future: Second Report on the Health of Canadians* (Ottawa, Health Canada, 1999). The Canadian Institute for Health Information established the Canadian Population Health Initiative in 1999 to expand public knowledge of population health (see generally: secure.cihi.ca/cihiweb/dispPage.jsp?cw_page=cphi_about_e), and one of

federal, provincial and territorial Ministers of Health in 1994, and has been identified by the Public Health Agency of Canada as a key concept and approach for policy development.[4]

The FPTACPH identifies the following as 'key influences' (determinants) of health: living and working conditions (socio-economic environment), physical environment, health services, early childhood development, social supports, personal health practices and coping skills, biology and genetic endowment, with more recent additions of gender, culture and membership in specific population groups.[5] It accepts the significance of absolute disparities among groups, but also recognizes that the scale of relative income inequities and social and economic differences within a society has been shown to be even more influential as a determinant of population health.[6] Consequently, one of the policy priorities it emphasizes to improve the health of the population is the importance of reducing income inequities.[7]

While proponents of a population health approach (let alone its critics) do not always agree about the factors that should be taken into consideration, nor about how they affect health status either singly or in combination, the population health framework does provide valuable insight into the roles played by conditions whose connection to health may not at first be apparent. Even more importantly for the purposes of this chapter, population health is the policy approach that has been widely accepted and promoted by various levels of government.[8] It is often the analytical framework explicitly adopted in government health policy documents.[9] Its 'penetration into policy discourse' has not, however, characterized the programs, legislation and regulations that have altered the landscape in

the 13 institutes that make up the Canadian Institutes of Health Research is the Institute of Population and Public Health (see generally: www.cihr-irsc.gc.ca/9466html).

[4] Canada. Public Health Agency of Canada, 'What is the Population Health Approach', at: www.phac-aspc.gc.ca/ph-sp/approach-approche/index.html.

[5] Gilmour and Martin (above n 1) 3; see also Public Health Agency of Canada, 'Key Elements of a Population Health Approach', at: www.phac-aspc.gc.ca/ph-sp/phdd/approach/approach.html#key_elements.

[6] FPTACPH, *Toward a Healthy Future*, above n 3, 184–5. See generally, R Wilkinson, *Unhealthy Societies: The Afflictions of Inequality* (London, Routledge, 1996); R Wilkinson, *The Impact of Inequality: How to Make Sick Societies Healthier* (New York, New Press, 2005). More recently, see: G Bloch, V Etches, C Gardner, R Pellizzari, M Rachlis, F Scott and I Tamari, 'Why poverty makes us sick' (2008) 75(5) *Ontario Medical Review* 32, on the links between poverty, illness and poor health.

[7] FPTACPH (above n 3). But see D Raphael, *Poverty and Policy in Canada: Implications for Health and Quality of Life* (Toronto, Canadian Scholars Press, 2007) 251–2 for criticism of the emphasis on relative inequality in a society as opposed to focusing on the absolute and profound concrete effects of material and social deprivation.

[8] M Hayes and J Dunn, *Population Health in Canada* (1998)—see especially: p 11, fig 1, 'Development of the Discourse'; see also: Public Health Agency of Canada, 'What is the Population Health Approach' (above n 4).

[9] See, eg, Statistics Canada, *How Healthy Are Canadians?* 2001 Annual Report (2001) 12(3) *Health Reports*, Statistics Canada Catalogue 82-003-XIE.

health, social services, housing, environmental protection and economic and labour market regulation. The contrasts between governments' policy rhetoric and the reality of reform—or more accurately, retrenchment—are striking.

In Canada, health care, income transfers to the disadvantaged and the construction and maintenance of a public infrastructure are some of the ways in which the state has supported and smoothed the processes of social reproduction. However, during the last several decades, the federal and provincial governments have significantly diminished their responsibilities in those areas, sharply reducing or eliminating many redistributive social programs and policies, and failing to adequately maintain those that remain.[10] Rather than responding to the clear connections between reduced access to social and economic resources for those least well off and significant negative effects on health status that have been identified not only in academic writing but in their own policy documents, the changes actually implemented for the most part have been consonant with a government agenda of restructuring and privatization of responsibility. Through these processes, governments have continued to reduce their economic role, cutting back on social spending and increasingly promoting private self-reliance.

Two examples from the mid-1990s illustrate this point: at the federal level, the demise of the Canada Assistance Plan (CAP); and at the provincial level, Ontario's decision to cut welfare benefits by more than 20 per cent shortly after the Conservative government came into power in the mid-1990s. From its inception in 1966, CAP put in place a system of federal/provincial cost-sharing for many provincial welfare programs, including social assistance.[11] As a condition of funding, provinces were required to meet certain conditions, including adherence to at least minimal national standards in order to qualify for federal transfers of funds. Although the flexibility allowed provinces in meeting those standards meant that individual challenges to the legality of decisions about social assistance payments were unlikely to succeed, the Supreme Court of Canada did recognize that an enforceable entitlement to benefits existed.[12] More significantly, however, the federal government had the power to take action in response

[10] J Gilmour, 'Creeping Privatization in Health Care: Implications for Women as the State Redraws Its Role' in B Cossman and J Fudge (eds), *Privatization, Law and the Challenge to Feminism* (Toronto, University of Toronto Press, 2002) 267; National Council of Welfare, 'Total Welfare Incomes and Poverty over Time' in *Welfare Incomes 2005*, at: www.ncwcnbes.net/documents/researchpublications/ResearchProjects/WelfareIncomes/2005Report_Summer2006/ReportENG.pdf; National Council of Welfare, 'Fact Sheet #1: *Welfare Incomes 2006*: Patterns and Trends', at: www.ncwcnbes.net/documents/researchpublications/ResearchProjects/WelfareIncomes/2006WebOnlylData/factsheet1ENG.pdf.

[11] Canada Assistance Plan, (RSC 1985, c C-1).

[12] *Finlay v Canada (Minister of Finance)* [1993] 1 SCR 1080, 1125–6.

to provincial breaches of those standards, whether or not these had been challenged by individuals.[13]

In 1995, the federal government repealed CAP and replaced the shared-cost funding of welfare programs with a new program, the Canada Health and Social Transfer (CHST), pursuant to which all federal contributions to provincial health, post-secondary education and social assistance/welfare programs were subsumed in one block transfer.[14] It also continued to reduce the amounts it transferred to support these programs, a pattern of unilateral decision-making the Supreme Court of Canada had previously accepted in a case unsuccessfully challenging federal alterations to the cost-sharing formula under CAP.[15] The CHST did not continue the national standards that had been part of CAP. CAP had required that assistance be provided to persons in need, that levels of assistance take into account the basic requirements of recipients in terms of food, shelter, clothing, fuel, utilities, household supplies and personal requirements; that welfare services continue to be provided and extended, that they not be tied to workfare; and that appeal procedures from decisions relating to assistance be made available, among other matters. The only one of the original conditions continued under the CHST was the prohibition on provincial residency requirements. In another significant shift, the federal transfer was no longer tied to maintaining a type or level of spending on social assistance, unlike the shared cost formula under CAP.

In the result, far from acting to reduce income inequities (a key determinant of health, targeted for government action in the FPTACPH Reports and accepted by the Public Health Agency of Canada[16]), on the legislative front the federal government eliminated its ability to enforce national standards in social assistance programs at a time when provincial governments were significantly cutting social services, even though transfer payments had become increasingly important as a major source of income for poor people.[17] In 2004, the CHST was subdivided once again, this time into a health component, the Canada Health Transfer, and the residue, the Canada

[13] G Brodsky and S Day, *Women and the Equality Deficit: The Impact of Restructuring Canada's Social Programs* (Ottawa, Status of Women Canada Policy Research Fund, 1998) 36, fn 73, note instances where provincial governments did have to change their programs to qualify for federal funding. As originally drafted, workfare schemes were not permitted.

[14] Budget Implementation Act, 1995 (SC 1995, c 17).

[15] *Reference: Re Canada Assistance Plan (BC)* [1991] 2 SCR 525.

[16] Public Health Agency of Canada, 'What determines health?', at: www.phac-aspc.gc.ca/ph-sp/determinants/determinants_e.html. Public Health Agency of Canada, 'Income Inequality as a Determinant of Health', at: www.phac-aspc.gc.ca/ph-sp/oi-ar/02_iincome.html.

[17] National Council of Welfare, 'Transfer payments to people living in poverty by family type, 2004' (Source: Statistics Canada Survey of Labour and Income Dynamics. Custom tabulation) in *Poverty Statistics 2004*, at: www.ncwcnbes.net/en/research/povertyprofile/webonly2004.html; D Ross, K Scott and P Smith, *Canadian Fact Book on Poverty 2000* (Ottawa, Canadian Council on Social Development, 2000) xxiii, 150.

Social Transfer. This realignment was not accompanied by a re-introduction of the conditions that had originally qualified provinces' entitlement to federal cash transfers for social assistance programs.

At the provincial level, after its election to power in Ontario in 1995, the Conservative government moved quickly to slash social assistance rates by 21.6 per cent.[18] Historically, social assistance benefits levels have been much lower than generally accepted poverty lines, leaving recipients living well below low-income cutoffs. As Corbett J noted in *Masse v Ontario (Ministry of Community and Social Services)* (a challenge to the government's action on the basis that it contravened recipients' constitutional rights under the Canadian Charter of Rights and Freedoms),[19] such a deep reduction in benefit levels would cause serious harm: 'There can be no doubt the effects of reduced income will be severe for all and devastating for some'.[20] The evidence before the court about the relentlessly debilitating effects of living in poverty was clear—poor health, inadequate housing, substandard nutrition, social marginalization, damaging effects on children, and many others.[21] It was also well known to the government.

Nonetheless, despite the court's recognition that the government's decision to cut benefits so substantially would cause extreme hardship, the application was unsuccessful. The court held that even though those affected were poor and suffered serious social, economic and political disadvantage and marginalization as a result, they were a disparate and heterogeneous group, and hence could not establish that they were members of a group whose equality rights were protected under section 15 of the Charter. More fundamentally, the court declined to inquire into what it termed 'policy/political' decisions in any substantive way, stating: 'The intractable economic, social and even philosophical problems presented by public welfare assistance programs are not the business of this Court'.[22] Its proper domain, the court asserted, was to determine whether the government *could* legally take this action, not whether it *should* do so. That, however, was precisely the question the applicants were posing, 'Was the

[18] The cuts were made to general welfare rates, not to benefits paid to people with disabilities. Ontario Disability Support Program rates have been increased somewhat in the intervening years, as have Ontario Works (general welfare) rates, but recipients of benefits are still far below the poverty line: National Council of Welfare, '*Welfare Incomes 2006*, Fact Sheet #3', p 6, at: www.ncwcnbes.net/documents/researchpublications/ResearchProjects/WelfareIncomes/2006WebOnlyData/factsheet3Eng.pdf; see also *infra* n 40 and accompanying text.

[19] The application asserted a breach of the right to liberty and security of the person under s 7, and of the right to equality under s 15 of the *Canadian Charter of Rights and Freedoms*, Part I of the Constitution Act, 1982, being Sch B to the Canada Act 1982 (UK), c. 11 (the Charter).

[20] *Masse v Ontario (Ministry of Community and Social Services)* (1996) 134 DLR 4th 20 (Ont Ct Gen Div), para 18 (Corbett J, dissenting in part), leave to appeal denied [1996] OJ No 1526 (Ont CA).

[21] *Ibid*, paras 37–42.

[22] *Ibid*, para 387 (O'Driscoll J).

government acting legally when it cut welfare payments, or did it breach constitutional rights?'. The court followed the approach articulated by the Supreme Court of Canada in the first Charter equality rights case it considered, *Andrews v Law Society of British Columbia*: 'Much economic and social policy making is simply beyond the institutional competence of courts; their role is to protect against incursions on fundamental values, not to second guess policy decisions'.[23]

Canadian courts have remained unwilling to recognize poverty as an analogous ground that triggers the equality rights and protection from discrimination guaranteed under section 15 of the Charter. Poor people are considered no more than a 'statistical aggregation' who are 'economically disadvantaged at the time for any reason'; an 'unstructured collective' not attracting Charter protection unless identifiable by some other recognized characteristic(s).[24] Nor have courts accepted that laws or administrative actions that impose great hardship on people who are poor breach their constitutionally protected rights to life, liberty and security of the person under section 7 of the Charter.[25]

Governments have acknowledged that ensuring people have adequate incomes and reducing income inequities are important initiatives to improve population health status. Yet the substantial reduction in social assistance payments in Ontario left those at the bottom, a disproportionate number of whom are women, worse off, and exacerbated the extent of income inequity. The situation has not improved since. The National Council of Welfare reports that between 2000 and 2006, five provinces, including Ontario, recorded their lowest level of welfare incomes for all household types it examined, including single people with disabilities.[26] Cutting welfare payments also has a ripple effect on other factors identified as important determinants of health: the ability to obtain adequate housing[27] and adequate nutrition, find employment, enable children to succeed

[23] *Andrews v Law Society of British Columbia* [1989] 1 SCR 143, 194.

[24] *R v Banks* (2007) 216 CCC 3d 19, 84 OR 3d 1 (Ont CA) paras 104–5, leave to appeal denied [2007] SCCA no 139. The Ontario Court of Appeal distinguished *Falkiner v Director, Income Maintenance Branch, Ministry of Community and Social Services & Attorney General of Ontario* (2002) 59 OR 3d 481, [2002] OJ no 1771 (CA) (discussed below nn 67–69 and accompanying text), as a case about impermissible differentiation in the social assistance regime on the basis of sex, marital status and 'receipt of social assistance', not a case about poverty. For a review of earlier decisions considering and sometimes accepting poverty as an analogous ground under s 15, see D Pothier, 'Equality as a Comparative Concept: Mirror, Mirror, on the Wall, What's the Fairest of Them All?' in S McIntyre and S Rodgers (eds), *Diminishing Returns: Inequality and the Canadian Charter of Rights and Freedoms* (Markham, LexisNexisButterworths, 2006) 135–50.

[25] *Gosselin v Quebec* (2002) 221 DLR (4th) 257 (SCC); *R v Banks*, above n 24.

[26] National Council of Welfare, 'Fact Sheet #1' (2006) (above n 10) 2.

[27] For similar conclusions from different sides of the political debate, see, eg M Trebilcock and R Daniels, *Rethinking the Welfare State: The Prospects for Government by Voucher* (New York, Routledge, 2005) 65, on the 'enormous health burden' of poor quality housing,

at school, and many others. Health policy-makers and the governments that employ them know this, as their own reports make clear. However, governments' actions repeatedly fail to address the links between poverty and ill health, despite their policy commitments.

The population health approach adopted by the FPTACPH set two general policy priorities:

> Improve the underlying and interrelated conditions in the environment [social, physical and economic] that enable all Canadians to be healthy; and
>
> Reduce inequities in the underlying conditions that put some Canadians at a disadvantage for attaining and maintaining optimal health.

It also noted that redistributive transfer payments and taxes have become increasingly significant in offsetting somewhat the growing income gap between Canadians with the lowest and highest incomes.[28] In light of that reality, government action drastically cutting social assistance payments seems aimed at achieving the opposite. Rather than reducing the persistent gap in health status between Canadians with high incomes and those with low incomes, it will make it worse.[29] Nor has government action been limited to cutbacks in welfare. It has also made establishing eligibility and access to benefits more difficult. These changes are felt particularly harshly by women, who already experience disproportionately high rates of poverty, head the largest percentage of lone parent households with limited economic resources, experience greater rates of disability, and take on the burden of becoming caregivers to those who are not, or are no longer cared for by the health and social services systems.[30]

and G Wekerle, 'The Shift to the Market: Gender and Housing Disadvantage' in PM Evans and GR Wekerle, *Women and the Canadian Welfare State: Challenges and Change* (Toronto, University of Toronto Press, 1997).

[28] The growing importance of transfer payments to those least well off in society is confirmed by other research as well—see, eg, National Council of Welfare (above n 17) and D Ross et al (above n 17).

[29] On the gap in health status, or 'health gap' between those who are well off and those who are not that persists in Canada despite universal health insurance, see FPTACPH (above n 3) 2, National Council of Welfare, 'Medicare: The Public Good and Private Practice' (Ottawa, Supply and Services, 1982); K Humphries and E von Doorslaer, 'Income-Related Health Inequality in Canada' (2000) 50 *Social Science and Medicine* 663. As Canadian social scientist D Raphael notes (above n 7) 205, 'The poverty and poor health relationship is one of the most robust associations known to the health and social sciences'.

[30] *Falkiner et al v Director, Income Maintenance Branch, Ministry of Community and Social Services & Attorney General of Ontario* (2002) 59 OR 3d 481, [2002] OJ no 1771 (CA); J Mosher and J Hermer, 'Welfare Fraud: The Constitution of Social Assistance as a Crime' (Ottawa, Law Commission of Canada, 2005); M Morris, J Robinson and J Simpson, *The Changing Nature of Home Care and Its Impact on Women's Vulnerability to Poverty* (Ottawa, Status of Women Canada, 1999); C Lochhead and K Scott, 'The Dynamics of Women's Poverty in Canada' (Ottawa, Status of Women Canada Policy Research Fund, 2000).

III. PEOPLE WITH DISABILITIES IN CANADA

More than 14 per cent of Canadians (4.4 million, or one out of seven) identified themselves as having a disability in 2006, an increase of over three quarters of a million people since 2001, when 12.4 per cent of the population (3.6 million people) reported a disability.[31] In addition, almost 3 million Canadians provide support to a family member or friend with a long-term health condition or disability. Disabilities vary in severity, duration, time of onset, and many other respects. Most are mild to moderate, but a substantial number are more severe. The majority of people with disabilities are women. Discrimination is a fact of life for people with disabilities, with associated social and economic exclusion. Adults with disabilities are less likely to be employed than their non-disabled counterparts.[32] When employed, on the whole they earn less than people without disabilities, and are disproportionately concentrated in precarious work.[33] Many are neither employed nor looking for work, in part because of concern about losing some or all of their current income or other support, such as drug benefit plans, should they become employed.[34] People with disabilities are significantly more likely to live in poverty than those without disabilities.[35] Government transfers and income support programs are crucial to many who experience disability, and have become increasingly important in sustaining low-income households in recent years, making up a substantial portion of household income in the lowest income quintile.[36]

[31] Statistics Canada, The Daily, 'Participation and Activity Limitation Survey', 3 December 2007, at: www.statcan.gc.ca/daily-quotidien/071203/dq071203a-eng.htm; Canada, *Advancing the Inclusion of Persons with Disabilities 2004* (Ottawa, Office for Disability Issues, Human Resources and Social Development Canada, 2004), ch 2, 8; Statistics Canada, 'A profile of disability in Canada in 2001', Statistics Canada Participation and Activity Limitation Survey (PALS) 2001, Catalogue no 89-577-XWE (3 December 2003), www.statcan.gc.ca.

[32] A Furrie, 'Profiling Canadians with Disabilities' in MA McColl and L Jongbloed (eds), *Disability and Social Policy in Canada*, 2nd edn (Toronto, Captus Press, 2006) 23.

[33] A Jackson, *Work and Labour in Canada: Critical Issues* (Toronto, Canadian Scholars Press, 2005); D Raphael (above n 7) 74–5; E Tompa, H Scott, S Trevithick and S Bhattacharyya, 'Precarious Employment and People with Disabilities' in L Vosko (ed), *Precarious Employment: Understanding Labour Market Insecurity in Canada* (Montreal, McGill-Queens University Press, 2006) 90–114; R Wilton, 'Working at the Margins: Disabled People and Precarious Employment' in D Pothier and R Devlin (eds), *Critical Disability Theory: Essays in Philosophy, Politics and Law* (Vancouver, University of British Columbia Press, 2006) 129–50.

[34] Canada, *Advancing Inclusion 2004* (above n 31) 32–3; see also MA McColl, 'Portraits of Disability in National Surveys' in McColl and Jongbloed, *Disability and Social Policy* (above n 31) 37.

[35] MA McColl, A James, W Boyce and S Shortt, 'Disability Policy Making: Evaluating the Evidence Base' in Pothier and Devlin, *Critical Disability Theory* (above n 33) 25; R Wilton, 'Working at the Margins' (above n 33).

[36] Ross et al, *Canadian Fact Book on Poverty 2000* (above n 17) xxiii; C Lochhead and K Scott (above n 29); National Council of Welfare, 'Average incomes of families living in poverty by primary source of income, 2004', at: www.ncwcnbes.net/documents/researchpublications/ResearchProjects/WelfareIncomes/2004Report_Spring2005/ReportENG.pdf.

By every indicator, women are more severely affected by the harsh economic realities frequently associated with disability than men, and consequently, are more likely to depend on government income support.[37] Among those who rely on Canada's various disability income support systems, women are less likely to be entitled to access income provided through insurance programs, either because these require prior labour force participation (such as the Canada Pension Plan), or target disabilities acquired through job-related accidents or illness (such as the Workplace Safety Insurance System). In addition, because they are more likely to have had low incomes, women with disabilities are less likely to benefit from the non-refundable tax credits provided for in the Income Tax Act, such as the disability tax credit and the medical expenses tax credit (primary mechanisms through which the costs associated with disability are recognized through the tax system). Because women are less likely to be able to meet the conditions for eligibility, the only disability support system open to them is often social assistance.

Social assistance levels have historically been far below low-income cutoffs (LICO), the proxy for poverty lines used by Statistics Canada.[38] In 2008, the maximum payment to a single person receiving benefits under the Ontario Disability Support Payments (ODSP) was CAN$999.00 per month, and the maximum for a lone parent with one child was CAN$1397 per month if the child was under 12 years, CAN $1456 if the child was between 13 and 17 years, and CAN$1583 if the child was 18 years or older.[39] The National Council of Welfare reported that in 2005, total welfare income for a single person with a disability in Ontario was 58 per cent of the poverty line (LICO), continuing a pattern of decline evident since 1994, when it was 71 per cent of the poverty line.[40] These two factors—the deep poverty in which many women with disabilities live, and their almost total reliance on government support—mean that they are particularly vulnerable to restrictions and cutbacks in government transfer programs.

The conditions for eligibility, the processes to establish and maintain entitlement, and the benefits provided under such programs are especially important to women. The relationship between poverty and resulting poor

[37] *Ibid* (Ross et al) 76; Canada. *Advancing the Inclusion of Persons with Disabilities 2006* (Ottawa, Human Resources and Social Development, 2006) 56, at: www.hrsdc.gc.ca/en/disability_issues/reports/fdr/2006/advancinginclusion.pdf.

[38] National Council of Welfare, 'Total Welfare Incomes and Poverty Over Time' in *Welfare Incomes 2005* (above n 10) 73–82, National Council of Welfare, Fact Sheet #1, '*Welfare Incomes 2006*: Patterns and Trends' (above n 10) 3.

[39] Payment under Ontario Works, ie general welfare, is a maximum of CAN$560 per month for a single person; a lone parent with 1 child can receive CAN$904 per month if the child is less than 13, CAN$921 if the child is between 13 and 17 years, and CAN$1072 if the child is 18 years or older.

[40] National Council of Welfare, *Welfare Incomes: 2005* (above n 10) 32, 74–5. For a single employable person—ie an individual in receipt of general welfare assistance rather than disability benefits—total welfare income was 34% of the poverty line, and for a single parent with one child receiving general welfare, it was 56% of the poverty line—*ibid.*

health is clear. Commenting on conditions of life on social assistance, a group of physicians concluded that '[l]iving on social assistance should be considered, with poverty, to be a major risk factor for ill health'.[41] Certainly, receipt of social assistance is strongly associated with significant health problems. Worse yet is an inability to establish or maintain entitlement to benefits—that can be devastating.[42]

IV. DEFINING DISABILITY

How disability is understood and treated reveals a great deal about how a society views its members who have disabilities, their place and potential in the world, and the scope, nature and basis of social responsibilities to them. It also constructs the experience of disability and the opportunities available to people with disabilities in important ways. It is beyond the scope of this chapter to do more than briefly sketch developments in thinking about disability, outline approaches among governments and policymakers, and touch on developments in disability scholarship. It is obvious, though, that different understandings of and theories about disability will have very different implications for the laws and policies that are developed.

Broadly speaking, disability has been conceptualized as arising either from individual pathology or (more recently) social pathology. The former is based on a biomedical approach, ie that 'disability is caused by a mental or physical condition that can be prevented or ameliorated through medical, biological, or genetic intervention ... mak[ing] the condition itself the focus of attention', or on a functional approach, which, although maintaining that the deficit stems from an individual condition or pathology, focuses on the impact the condition has on functional capacity.[43] In contrast, formulations of disability grounded in social pathology are explicitly political and

> start from a perspective that assumes that disability is not inherent to the individual. Rather, they assume that the disability is inherent to the social structure ... The pathology is that there is something wrong with the society that has to be fixed rather than something wrong with the individual that needs fixing.[44]

41 Bloch et al (above n 6) 34.

42 J Fraser, C Wilkey and J Frenschkowski, 'Denial by Design: The Ontario Disability Support Program' (Toronto, Income Security Advocacy Centre, 2003) 26, at: www.incomesecurity.org/paytherent/resources/pdf_R/ISAC.pdf.

43 M Rioux, 'On Second Thought: Constructing Knowledge, Law, Disability, and Inequality' in S Herr, L Gostin and H Koh (eds), *The Human Rights of Persons with Intellectual Disabilities: Different but Equal* (Oxford, Oxford University Press, 2003) 287; see also C Barnes and G Mercer, 'Disability, Work and Welfare: Challenging the Social Exclusion of Disabled People' (2005) 19 *Work Employment and Society* 527.

44 *Ibid* (Rioux). See generally M Oliver, 'Union of Physically Impaired Against Segregation [UPIAS] 1876' in M Oliver, *Understanding Disability: From Theory to Practice* (London, Macmillan, 1996).

Among those who conceptualize disability as a consequence of social pathology, Marcia Rioux identifies two variations, environmental and rights/outcome.[45] The former focuses on environmental arrangements (built, social, political, economic, etc), and on identifying and removing barriers to participation and inclusion. The latter is premised on the understanding that disability is a consequence of social organization, and the relationship of the individual to society at large. This approach concentrates on identifying and changing broad systemic factors that keep some groups from participating equally in society.

My own approach to disability builds on feminist and disability scholarship. As with many others, I begin from the social model of disability, which identifies disability as a political rather than a medical category, and locates what are often considered the causes of disability within society and social organizations. However, as some feminist and other critiques have noted, the social model can operate to erase or discount the embodied nature of people's experience of impairment, and for that reason, can be insufficient on its own.[46] This chapter, then, is an attempt to advance work I began and continue with others, that takes into account the politics of material, social and cultural disablement, as well as the material reality of embodied impairment.[47]

V. DISABILITY AND POLICY DEVELOPMENT

In reviewing developments in the perception and treatment of disability in social policy and scientific environments, Marcia Rioux observes that assumptions about disability

> are neither mutually exclusive nor temporally chronological. Some disciplines ... characteriz[e] disability as either solely a medical condition or personal deficit, while other have adopted either the framework of disability as a social and political condition or some hybrid of these two major schools of social thought. Consequently, policy and programming, both within the professional sphere

[45] Rioux (above n 43).

[46] S French, 'Disability, Impairment or Something in Between?' in J Swain, V Finkelstein, S French and M Oliver, *Disabling Barriers—Enabling Environments* (London, Sage, 1993); L Crow, 'Including All of Our Lives: Renewing the Social Model of Disability' in J Morris, *Encounters with Strangers: Feminism and Disability* (London, Women's Press, 1996); C Thomas, *Female Forms: Experiencing and Understanding Disability* (Buckingham, Open University Press, 1999); T Shakespeare, *Disability Rights and Wrongs* (London, Routledge, 2006); C Thomas, 'How is Disability Understood? An Examination of Sociological Approaches' (2004) 19 *Disability and Society* 225.

[47] C Frazee, J Gilmour and R Mykitiuk, 'Now You See Her, Now You Don't: How Law Shapes Disabled Women's Experience of Exposure, Surveillance, and Assessment in the Clinical Encounter' in Pothier and Devlin (eds) (above n 33).

> and coming from government, reflects attempts to accommodate these shifting understandings of disability as a status.[48]

Exemplifying this, when the federal government recently studied the many disparate definitions of disability in federal programs with a view to harmonizing them, it concluded that, because of the complex, multi-dimensional nature of disability,

> a single harmonized definition of disability may be impossible, given the many realities covered by the concept of disability. As well, a single definition may not capture the different policy objectives and needs of Canadians with disabilities [or, it may be added, the goals of government as program funder].[49]

Federal, provincial and territorial governments have, however, articulated a common statement of their policy goals in addressing disability issues, a view that strongly affirms the fundamental entitlement to equal citizenship of people with disabilities, and includes commitments to facilitate inclusion and participation as full citizens in all aspects of Canadian society, with provision of supports needed to achieve this goal.[50] However, just as with the gap between government rhetoric and the reality of its inaction on improving determinants of health for those least well off and reducing the extent of income inequality, the reality for people with disabilities often falls far short, and government action is much less supportive than its broad policy commitments would lead one to expect.

VI. SOCIAL ASSISTANCE: HOW ENTITLEMENT IS RESTRICTED

Income and employment supports are available under the Ontario Disability Support Program Act (ODSPA) to people with disabilities who meet the conditions specified in the legislation.[51] The statute sets out a mix of objectives that is marked by tension between benevolence and discipline. First, it states that the ODSPA is meant to provide for income and employment supports to 'eligible persons' with disabilities and 'effectively serv[e] persons with disabilities who need assistance' (ODSPA, section 1(a) and (c)). Secondly, however, this expansive understanding of state responsibilities

48 M Rioux (above n 43) 289.

49 Canada, *Defining Disability: A Complex Issue* (Ottawa, Office of Disability Issues, Human Resources Development Canada, 2003), at: dsp-psd.communication.gc.ca/Collection/RH37-4-3-2003E.pdf; Canada, *Advancing the Inclusion of Persons with Disabilities, 2004* (above n 31).

50 Canada, *In Unison: A Canadian Approach to Disability Issues* (Hull PQ, HRDC, 1998); Canada, *In Unison 2000: Persons with Disabilities in Canada* (Hull PQ, HRDC, 2000); MA McColl, 'Portraits of Disability in National Surveys' in McColl and Jongbloed (eds) (above n 32) 37.

51 Ontario Disability Support Program Act, Sch B to the Social Assistance Reform Act, 1997 (SO 1997, c 25).

is tempered by the statutory admonition that communities, families and individuals share responsibility with government, a justification for the state limiting and even contracting its role (ODSPA, section 1(b)). Thirdly, the statute emphasizes the need for cost control and discipline in its requirement that the program must be 'accountable to the taxpayers of Ontario' (ODSPA, section 1(d)). While one would expect this condition to be so basic an expectation of all government programs as to go without saying (as it generally does), the ODSPA is explicit in its call for fiscal responsibility, inferentially reinforcing fears of overtly generous benefit levels, fraud and recipients who are 'getting something for nothing'.

ODSPA requires that income support be provided to any Ontario resident over the age of 18 who meets the statutory definition of a person with a disability and is otherwise eligible for assistance.[52] The applicant bears the onus of establishing that she qualifies for assistance under the statute, and information must be provided on an ongoing basis. Social assistance is a complicated and difficult system, fleshed out with voluminous policy directives and forms that can often be accessed only with difficulty, if at all. Even judges have remarked on the complexity of the eligibility and reporting rules.[53] Yet penalties for breaking the rules are severe. Failure to comply with conditions of eligibility will result in refusal, cancellation or reduction in the income support payable (ODSPA, section 9). And although ODSP was introduced as an expansive new program formulated in response to what people with disabilities had requested, the enforcement provisions replicate those in the Ontario Works (general welfare) program.[54] It also tracks the same monitoring and surveillance systems used to detect breaches

[52] The initial precondition for eligibility is financial—the person and any dependents must have 'budgetary requirements' that exceed their income, and not have assets in excess of prescribed limits (ODSPA s 5). In addition, eligibility is contingent on both the person and his or her dependents providing information about personal identification, finances, and other information that may be prescribed, as well as having the information verified in the manner required (ODSPA s 5(d)). Applicants may have to meet other conditions as well.

[53] Relative to the predecessor legislation, see, eg: *R v Maldonaldo* [1998] OJ no 3209 (Ont ProvCt) para 41: 'The Regulations governing the question of entitlement are fiendishly difficult to understand' (on the recipient's failure to include monies received as a student loan in income); *Kerr v Metropolitan Toronto (Dept of Social Services)* [1998] OJ no 1890 (Ont Ct Gen Div), Archie Campbell J: 'a Kafkaesque Regulation so complex and ambiguous that it becomes a lawyer's nightmare', 'the sense or structure of the policy which might help a person on welfare to determine when he or she is breaking the law, is not apparent on the face of the Regulation' (on the degree of attachment to the workforce that would disqualify an applicant from consideration for receipt of social assistance benefits as an underage student).

[54] H Beatty, 'Ontario Disability Support Program: Policy and Implementation' (1999) 14 *Journal of Law and Social Policy* 1; J Mosher, P Evans, M Little, E Morrow and J Boulding, *Walking on Eggshells: Abused Women's Experiences of the Ontario Welfare System. Final Report of Research Findings from the Women and Abuse Welfare Research Project* (2004), at: www.oaith.ca/pdf/Walking_on_Eggshells.pdf.

and non-compliance. This includes the 'extensive and extremely punitive fraud control regime'.[55] Sanctions are identical as well.

How disability is defined has major consequences for people's entitlement to targeted benefit programs such as social assistance, because the definition underpins eligibility criteria. ODSPA defines a 'person with a disability' as someone with:

(1) a substantial physical or mental impairment that is continuous or recurrent and is expected to last a year or more, where
(2) the direct and cumulative impact of the impairment is to substantially restrict the person's ability to attend to one or more activities of daily living (specifically, personal care, and function in the community and workplace).[56]

The impairment, its likely duration and the restriction on the person's activities must all be verified by one of the types of health professionals prescribed by regulation.[57] This definition locates both the impairments and any limitations on the person's ability to attend to the activities of daily living squarely within the individual. In that, its adherence to a medical model of disability is clear—it is premised on the assumption that the person cannot participate because he or she is too impaired to do so. The statutory definition states that a person has a disability within the meaning of the Act if he or she has a substantial physical or mental impairment expected to last more than a year, and the *effect of the impairment* is to substantially restrict the person's ability to attend to personal care or function in the community or workplace. There is no recognition that barriers built into existing physical, economic and social structures and arrangements can be the cause of not only substantial limitations on the person's ability to participate but also complete exclusion from what are, as the statute recognizes, 'activities of daily living'.

Advocates active in representing claimants note that the ODSPA requirements to establish the presence of disability sufficiently 'substantial' to qualify for ODSP benefits exclude many people who would previously have qualified for benefits as 'permanently unemployable' under the predecessor Family Benefits Act.[58] These could be individuals who are substantially limited in one or more of the activities of daily living as the ODSPA definition requires, but not because of an impairment that is substantial in itself.

[55] J Mosher, 'Welfare Reform and the Re-making of the Model Citizen' in M Young, SB Boyd, G Brodsky and S Day (eds), *Poverty: Rights, Social Citizenship, and Legal Activism* (Vancouver, University of British Columbia Press, 2007) 124.

[56] Ontario Disability Support Program Act (above n 51) s 4.

[57] *Ibid*, s 4(1)(c); Ontario Disability Support Regulation, O Reg 222/98, s 46.

[58] I Morrison, 'Ontario Works: A Preliminary Assessment' (1998) 13 *Journal of Law and Social Policy* 1, 7; Beatty, 'Ontario Disability Support Program' (1999); Mosher et al (above n 54); Fraser et al (above n 42).

Rather, the restrictions may be the result of a combination of (less than 'substantial') impairments as well as age, work history, education and other conditions (some of which may themselves result from barriers the person faced because her impairments were used as a reason to exclude her from educational and employment opportunities).[59] Alternatively, the health care provider assessing an applicant may not consider that an impairment will substantially restrict the person's activities of daily living, or that it will be of sufficient duration—ODSPA requires that it be expected to last for a year or more.[60] Those caught in the status of 'nearly disabled' only qualify for Ontario Works (general) welfare, with its lower benefit levels and more onerous requirements, including employment expectations (workfare).

Since the social assistance system was revamped and Ontario Works and ODSPA introduced in 1998, courts have only infrequently considered administrative determinations of eligibility under ODSPA. However, even this small number of cases confirms concerns about how administrative determinations are made and the legislative criteria applied, particularly at the initial decision-making level. Under ODSPA, once financial eligibility is established, an administrative determination is made about eligibility, ie the existence of a qualifying disability. If found ineligible, the applicant may request an internal review, and if again found ineligible, she can appeal to the Social Benefits Tribunal (SBT), where there is an opportunity for a hearing (ODSPA, section 23). A further appeal lies to the Divisional Court on a question of law (ODSPA, section 31(1)). Throughout, the onus is on the applicant to establish that she is a 'person with a disability' as defined. Realistically, while appeals and reconsiderations are possible, the administrative determination is the beginning and the end of the road for many. For people who live in poverty and poor health with few resources, taking the matter further is often simply too difficult.[61] Thus, when bureaucrats interpret already narrowed eligibility criteria in a way that restricts these still further, they are likely to be the final arbiters of claims made.

[59] But see *Gray v Ontario (Director, Ontario Disability Support Program)* (2002) 212 DLR 4th 353 (Ont CA) para 13, asserting that the ODSPA definition of disability is more generous than its predecessor. The court noted (at para 27) that '[t]he assessment as to whether a person has a substantial physical or mental impairment must consider the various conditions individually and cumulatively. It is not necessary to break down the analysis to every part of the mind and body affected and find at least one disorder is substantial. Such artificiality would detract from the person centered and remedial purposes of the ODSPA. To analyze each physical or mental disorder separately and require that each separately result in a 'substantial restriction' would deprive 'cumulative' of any meaning in s. 4(1)(b) [of the statute]'.

[60] *Ontario v Matthews* [2000] OJ no 5305 (Ont Div Ct) para 16: the health care professional verifies the existence of the impairment, its likely duration, and the resulting restriction on activities; the tribunal determines whether those conditions are substantial; see also *Sandiford v Ontario (Director, Ontario Disability Support Program)* [2005] 195 OAC 143, 2005 CanLII 549 (Ont Div Ct) para 20.

[61] See generally Gilmour and Martin (above n 1).

Ontario (Director, Disability Support Program) v Gallier illustrates the administrative decision-making process.[62] The applicant (respondent on appeal) was a 59-year old woman with a sixth grade education who had worked in physically demanding factory jobs most of her life. After a number of serious falls over the course of several years left her with significant back pain, she obtained employment as a hotel sanitation worker. She was eventually laid off, but meanwhile, her condition had worsened. She had been absent from work for periods of up to six weeks because of back pain, and was only able to work about four hours a day. She applied to ODSP. Her physician had indicated in his report that 'The prognosis of her returning to gainful employment is not good'. She also suffered from pain in her knee and hip. The Social Benefits Tribunal overturned the initial administrative determination that she was not a person with a disability.

On appeal to the Divisional Court, the Director advanced a restrictive interpretation of the statutory definition. First, the Director argued that the Tribunal could not consider evidence of other impairments or treatment unless these were referenced in the medical forms submitted by the physician. The applicant had given evidence before the Tribunal about additional impairments (knee and hip pain) and her use of a brace to alleviate her back pain. The physician had not mentioned these on the forms. Secondly, the director challenged the Tribunal's finding that the applicant was substantially impaired in the workplace, as it did not take into account other employment possibilities of a more sedentary nature. The contrast between the abstract and limited inquiry the Director proposed to determine whether the impairment and restrictions on the applicant's activities were substantial, and her real life prospects is striking.

The Director's position was not accepted by the court. It held that the Tribunal could consider other evidence, including the applicant's own evidence about her condition. Nor need the health care provider verifying the applicant's condition provide 'minute detail'; the applicant can speak to additional conditions contributing to the limitations on her activities, as well as about other treatment, such as the brace. As for the restrictions on her activities, the Tribunal had concluded:[63]

> At her age and with her education and work history, her medical problems essentially preclude her being hired for or being able to maintain employment at any of the previous types of work, as well as making retraining for any other line of work impractical.

[62] *Ontario (Director, Disability Support Program) v Gallier* [2000] OJ no 4541 (Ont Div Ct).

[63] *Ibid*, para 11 (Sup Ct). See also *Sandiford v Ontario (Director, Ontario Disability Support Program)* (above n 60) (Social Benefits Tribunal (SBT) erred in deciding claimant did not have substantial impairment because there may be some job that she could do; this misapprehended the issue to be determined).

The court confirmed that it was appropriate for the Tribunal to apply the elements of the definition in the context of the applicant's own life. Where the Director favoured disregarding the applicant's circumstances in determining entitlement to income support, the court rejected this interpretation. As Lang, J observed, this is a remedial statute and as such, must be given 'such fair, large and liberal construction and interpretation as will best ensure the attainment of the object of the Act according to its intent, meaning and spirit'.[64] The court denied the Director's appeal.

A comprehensive review and assessment of social assistance jurisprudence is beyond the scope of this chapter. However, some of the decisions in which courts have affirmed and enforced the state's responsibility to provide social assistance and to read the statute as remedial in purpose rather than punitive are particularly significant when assessing the potential in legal remedies. In *Tranchemontagne v Ontario (Director, Disability Support Program)* the Supreme Court of Canada overturned decisions of the lower courts and the Social Benefits Tribunal that the SBT lacked jurisdiction to determine whether a provision in the ODSPA denying ODSP benefits to individuals who met the statutory definition of disability, but were disabled solely because of alcohol or substance abuse, contravened the Ontario Human Rights Code.[65] Provincial human rights legislation, which is accorded quasi-constitutional status in Canada, prohibits discrimination in the provision of services on the basis of, inter alia, disability. The Court held that, despite provisions limiting the tribunal's jurisdiction in its enabling statute, it was authorized to consider whether the ODSPA contravened human rights legislation. The majority was concerned that the protection against discrimination provided in human rights legislation should be accessible and available to members of the public, particularly those who are most vulnerable and marginalized. Diverting the applicants' claim to a tribunal specialized in human rights law after five years of challenges (the option favoured by the Ontario Court of Appeal) was not appropriate, given the policy underlying the legislation. When the matter was remitted to the SBT for reconsideration on this basis, the Tribunal concluded that the statutory provision breached the Ontario Human Rights Code, and declined to enforce a decision affirmed on appeal.[66]

Earlier, in *Falkiner v Ontario*, the Ontario Court of Appeal upheld a decision of the Divisional Court which had found the new version of the 'spouse in the house' rule adopted in Ontario in 1995 to be in breach of

[64] *Gallier* (above n 62) para 13. See also *Gray* (above n 59) paras 9–10, 16 (the legislation should be interpreted broadly and liberally in accordance with its purpose of providing support to persons with disabilities; any ambiguity in the Act should therefore be resolved in claimant's favour); *Sandiford* (above n 60) para 19.

[65] *Tranchemontagne v Ontario (Director, Disability Support* Program [2006] SCJ no 14.

[66] L Bisgould, 'Human Rights Cases Argued at Supreme Court' ARCH Alert (19 December 2005), at: www.cleonet.ca/instance.php?instance_id=1329; *Ontario (Director, Disability Support Program) v. Tranchemontagne* [2009] OJ no 1613 (DivCt).

the equality guarantee in section 15 of the Charter.[67] In a strongly worded decision, it affirmed that the applicants, who were single mothers receiving social assistance and living with men who were not the biological fathers of their children, but with whom they had various arrangements for sharing household expenses (although not ones they considered 'familial'), were not required to rely on these men for support, nor could their social assistance payments be reduced or eliminated simply because of the existence of such relationships. The court noted:[68]

> Beyond purely financial concerns, more fundamental dignity interests of the [applicants] have been affected. Being reclassified as a spouse forces the [applicants] and other single mothers in similar circumstances to give up either their financial independence or their relationship ... Forcing them to become financially dependent on men with whom they have, at best, try-on relationships strikes at the core of their human dignity.

Falkiner is notable not just because it affirms that the state is properly charged with primary responsibility for supporting women and their children when they need assistance, but also for acknowledging and giving weight to the effect on their dignity that being forced to give up their independence would have. The Supreme Court of Canada granted leave to appeal from this decision, but the Ontario government withdrew its appeal in September 2004.[69] That leaves the Court of Appeal's recognition in *Falkiner* that the three grounds of sex, marital status and receipt of public assistance can trigger application of the equality guarantees in section 15 of the Charter as the last word on the subject, at least in Ontario.

A review of the cases challenging determinations of ineligibility does indicate a solid rate of success on appeal, although of course, applicants do not always prevail before the courts, and certainly not in all cases before the Social Benefits Tribunal.[70] In particular, decision-makers at these levels evidence greater regard for ODSP applicants' legal rights and, in administrative law cases at least, for the reality of their lives as well.[71] The cases also make it clear that the strict legislative structure is not entirely responsible for the harsh reality of social assistance.[72] Myriad administrative and

[67] *Falkiner* (above n 24).

[68] *Ibid*, 512.

[69] See generally MJ Mossman, 'Choices and Commitments for Women: Challenging the Supreme Court of Canada in the Context of Social Assistance' (2005) 42 *Osgoode Hall Law Journal* 615. The notice of discontinuance was filed 1 September 2004—[2004] SCCB 130; see also O Reg 197/02.

[70] Fraser et al (above n 42) 25: In the 2000/2001 fiscal year, close to 50% of decided appeals of Disability Adjudication Unit decisions resulted in the original decision being overturned (citing Social Benefits Tribunal statistics, 2002).

[71] For a more detailed review and analysis, see Gilmour and Martin (above n 1).

[72] Nor is the line between statutory authority and statutory discretion always so clear—see L Pottie and L Sossin, 'Demystifying the Boundaries of Public Law: Policy, Discretion and

bureaucratic decisions interpreting and applying the law render it either more or less harsh. On the issue of eligibility for disability benefits, those decisions have tended to narrow the legislative provisions, screening applicants out, rather than using them to assist people broadly.[73]

A 2006 report by the Ombudsman of Ontario, 'Losing the Waiting Game: Investigation into Unreasonable Delay at the Ministry of Community and Social Services' Ontario Disability Support Program's Disability Adjudication Unit', highlights the prevalence of routine practices that ignore obvious failures in the operation of the system, are unnecessarily punitive, and transfer the cost of program failure to applicants.[74] The Report details the 'stifling' delays that have characterized the application process for ODSP benefits for years, the government's ineffective or non-existent responses, and the unjustifiable hurdles placed in the way of applicants and their families, even in cases that should have been a 'slam-dunk'.[75] It also highlights the needlessly restrictive approaches taken to applying the legislation and regulations. This is exemplified by the government's acknowledgement that although the cap it had imposed of four months' retroactive entitlement to benefits was unfair when delays were the result of its own inability to process applications in a timely manner, yet it did not take steps to eliminate this provision until prompted by the Ombudsman's investigation. Further, it had never used existing legislative provisions that would have allowed it to mitigate the effects of its own systemic delays on applicants.[76] Neither the applicants' vulnerability, nor the real hardships they endured as a result of the restrictive approach to applying the legislative regime, factored into the administrative determinations about the program's operations. Far from taking a large and liberal approach, as required with remedial statutes, administrative discretion was exercised to ration the benefits to which

Social Welfare' (2005) 38 *University of British Columbia Law Review* 147; Fraser et al (above n 42 and accompanying text).

[73] Gilmour and Martin (above n 1); Fraser et al (above n 42); D Herd and A Mitchell, 'Discouraged, Diverted and Disentitled: Ontario Works New Service Delivery Model' (Toronto, Community and Social Planning Council of Toronto, 2002), at: socialplanningtoronto.org/CSPC-T%20Reports/Discouraged.pdf; *Wareham and Adams v Her Majesty the Queen in Right of Ontario* [2008] OJ no 166 (Ont Sup Ct) (Crown was successful in having class action challenging administrative structures of the ODSP as improperly denying or delaying benefits to people with disabilities and claiming damages struck out as disclosing no cause of action).

[74] Ontario. Ombudsman of Ontario (A Marin) Final Report, 'Losing the Waiting Game: Investigation into Unreasonable Delay at the Ministry of Community and Social Services' Ontario Disability Support Program's Disability Adjudication Unit (May 2006), at: www.ombudsman.on.ca/media/3289/losing_the_waiting_game_20060531.pdf.

[75] *Ibid*, 8, paras 11, 21, 31.

[76] *Ibid*, 26, para 74, and 17, paras 46–7. Nor, as the Ombudsman pointed out, could the Ministry offer any justification for the four month time limit, or any evidence to suggest it was a reasonable length of time within which to expect applications to be processed—*ibid*, 25, para 71.

people were entitled. As the Ombudsman concluded, 'It is nothing short of shameful when the program is responsible for thousands of vulnerable individuals losing out on benefits'.[77] In response to the Ombudsman's Report, the government did make some changes to program operations, replacing the limit on retroactive support with a provision empowering the Director to determine the effective date of eligibility.[78] The Report, however, dealt with only one aspect of the Program; many examples of harsh interpretations and problematic administrative action and policies remain.

The record of positive results when matters are appealed is only somewhat encouraging. Success depends on deciding to appeal and on finding legal assistance to carry the appeal forward. Many people do not, or cannot.[79] In any event, appeals face formidable legal as well as practical hurdles, especially when the issue has been framed as a challenge to the social assistance system more broadly. In *Gosselin v Quebec*, a 2002 decision, the Supreme Court of Canada upheld provisions in Quebec's social assistance system that prescribed a lower level of social assistance benefits for people under 30 unless they participated in job training schemes.[80] It did so despite the provincial government's failure to provide sufficient places for all recipients under 30, consigning the applicant, Louise Gosselin, and others to very deep poverty. In a 5-4 decision, the Court held that neither the structure nor the deficient reality of the system the government had put in place contravened section 7 of the Charter, the right to life, liberty and security of the person. It also rejected the claim that equality rights under section 15 of the Charter had been breached, reasoning that the ameliorative purposes of imposing these incentives on young people receiving social assistance to participate in education and training was a sufficient answer, particularly as the 'reasonable person in the claimant's position' would not be demeaned nor her dignity assailed by a system meant to assist her in ending her reliance on social assistance.[81] More recently, in *R v Banks*, the Ontario Court of Appeal reiterated that despite its decision in *Falkiner*, poverty is not an analogous ground attracting the protection of the equality rights guaranteed by section 15 of the Charter.[82]

Despite some success in taking appeals to an administrative tribunal, and even more rarely, to the courts, the foregoing makes it evident that law and policy have been, and continue to be used to restrict women's entitlement

[77] *Ibid*, para 74.

[78] O Reg 231/06; *Wareham v Ontario (Minister of Community and Social Services)* (above n 73) para 13. Ombudsman Ontario, 'Case Update: Losing the Waiting Game', 2007–08 Annual Report, www.ombudsman.on.ca/en/what-we-do/selected-cases/losing-the-waiting-game-update.aspx.

[79] Fraser et al (above n 42); Gilmour and Martin (above n 1).

[80] *Gosselin v Quebec* (above n 25).

[81] See, eg Pothier (n 24).

[82] *R v Banks* (above n 24).

to social assistance, making their lives and those of their families more insecure, more difficult, and less healthy. As explained earlier, socio-economic factors, and in particular the degree of relative inequity in a society, significantly affect health status. Governments have recognized the iniquitous effects of great income inequality and (in their policy pronouncements at least) have committed to ameliorating the socio-economic situation of those worst off in society. Additionally, vis-à-vis people with disabilities, all levels of government in Canada have pledged to advance their inclusion and participation, based on the recognition that people with disabilities are entitled to full citizenship rights, as well as support to exercise those rights. As this chapter illustrates, however, in many instances the policies, programs and laws adopted have restricted entitlement to needed resources and intensified exclusion.

Despite this mixed and often discouraging record, can legal strategies be better deployed to challenge the status quo, and in particular the discriminatory barriers embedded in the structure and administration of the social assistance system, especially as they affect women with disabilities? Recent Charter scholarship is, on the whole, pessimistic about its transformative potential, and even its ability to protect existing systems, such as medicare, that are essential supports in the lives of those who are least well off (and many others as well). In commentary on trends and developments in Charter jurisprudence, a number of academic writers, practising lawyers and activists have analyzed trajectories in Charter interpretation since it first came into force.[83] The general thrust of their conclusions can be summed up in the title of a recent article by Mary Eberts on section 15 and remedies meant to advance systemic equality: '... You Can't Get There From Here'.[84] In other words, absent substantial changes in courts' interpretation of the Charter (especially sections 7 and 15, and the fraught question of whether and when the Charter imposes positive obligations on the state to act in order to meet its Charter obligations), these writers take a very guarded view of the potential in legal remedies to advance the cause of substantive equality, particularly those based on the Charter.

Other writers, looking to distance future legal challenges from disappointing Charter interpretation in the past, suggest that greater emphasis should be placed on human rights legislation rather than the Constitution. Although Charter and human rights cases have both borrowed substantially from each other during the combined lives of the two, these scholars are working to re-vitalize and emphasize the separate (and in their view,

[83] See, eg, S McIntyre and S Rodgers (above n 24); F Faraday, M Denike and MK Stephenson (eds), *Making Equality Rights Real: Securing Substantive Equality Under the Charter* (Toronto, Irwin Law, 2006).

[84] M Eberts, 'Section 15 Remedies for Systemic Inequality: You Can't Get There from Here' in McIntyre and Rodgers (above n 24).

different) goals, legislative frameworks, processes, applicability, scope, and remedies that distinguish human rights legislation from the Charter. They argue that, despite indications in some cases to the contrary, these distinctions are sufficiently significant to support arguments that human rights jurisprudence can and must develop differently, and not simply adopt (objectionable) Charter equality rights jurisprudence.[85]

Another approach suggested is to place less emphasis on courts and judicial interpretation of the law. This seems counter-intuitive, given the argument above that judicial and quasi-judicial decision-makers have often provided social assistance applicants' best hope of establishing entitlement to benefits, and that bureaucratic decision-making has tended to be even more harsh and onerous than the law required. However, proponents argue that the intent is not to abandon legal proceedings, but to focus more on improving other types of decision-making, including that of bureaucrats and policy-makers, in an effort to ensure equality rights and norms are taken into account from the beginning, by all the many different types of decision makers involved.[86] These authors emphasize the importance of inserting equality rights earlier and more broadly into institutional decision-making and power structures. As Pearl Eliades has pointed out, legal norms are often absent in policy-making, especially early in the process,[87] a deficiency that if remedied, would reduce the need to resort to the courts. Ensuring that policy-makers and administrators are aware of developments in legal norms, how these translate into practice, and the imperative of applying them, could multiply opportunities to affirm both equality rights and inclusion.

Still others urge continued attention to Charter equality rights analysis, and in particular, the importance of developing alternate approaches to the current judicial focus on defining the 'correct' comparator group in ways that hearken back to the 'similarly situated' analysis that the Supreme Court of Canada rejected in its first Charter equality rights case.[88] The Court's readiness to adopt an extremely narrow approach to identifying

[85] See, eg, L Reaume, 'Postcards from *O'Malley*: Reinvigorating Statutory Human Rights Jurisprudence in the Age of the *Charter*'; J Keene, 'The Supreme Court, the *Law* Decision, and Social Programs: The Substantive Equality Deficit'; A Wright, 'Formulaic Comparisons: Stopping the *Charter* at the Statutory Gate', all in Faraday et al (above n 83).

[86] See, eg, C Sheppard, 'Constitutional Equality and Shifting Conceptions of the Role of the State: Obstacles and Possibilities' in McIntyre and Rodgers (above n 24).

[87] P Eliades, 'Normative Approaches to Policy Development: Inscribing Charter Values in the Policy Process' in McIntyre and Rodgers (above n 24). Eliades explains *Falkiner* (above n 24), as an instance of policy-makers focusing on income and ignoring the impact of the negative change on welfare recipients—*ibid*, 244–5. I am not so sanguine about the reasons policy-makers and legislators chose this means of controlling women and their ability to decide about how they would live their lives and raise their families.

[88] D Gilbert and D Majury, 'Critical Comparisons: The Supreme Court of Canada Damns Section 15' (2006) 24 *Windsor Year Book of Access to Justice* 111.

the appropriate comparator is most glaringly evident in *Auton v British Columbia (Attorney-General)*.[89] The Court's comments are obiter, since it had already determined that the benefit sought was not one provided by law and hence, section 15 did not apply. However, its requirement of a precise parallel between the applicants and the comparator, enunciated for the first time at the final level of appeal in this case, without opportunity for response or new evidence from the claimant, is reminiscent of the old writ system, where failure to plead facts that would bring a case within the standard form and requirements of a writ precluded recovery by the plaintiff, even when the defendant had clearly acted wrongly.[90] The formalism of such an approach is likely to yield equally unsatisfactory results when applied to the question of identifying the correct comparator for purposes of analysis under section 15 of the Charter.

VII. CONCLUSION

I first began to work on the connections between women's health and women's poverty, the significance of broader determinants of health, and the possibilities in using legal remedies to challenge the debilitating and demeaning conditions that structure the lives of women with disabilities who depend on social assistance, in the wake of the Supreme Court of Canada's decision in *Eldridge v British Columbia*.[91] *Eldridge* was decided at a time when legal challenges seeking to establish that poverty was an analogous ground and hence triggered the equality guarantees in section 15 of the Charter, or that the worst of the legal assaults on people who were poor contravened their rights to life, liberty and security of the person under section 7, were being consistently rejected. Yet in *Eldridge*, which involved a challenge based on denial of access to health care, the Court affirmed that hospitals' and the public health insurance plan's refusal to fund sign language interpreters needed by applicants who were hearing impaired so that they could access the benefit of Canada's universally insured health care services, constituted government action and hence, had to comply with the Charter. The Court held that government's failure to fund interpreters breached the applicants' constitutional right to the equal benefit of the law without discrimination on the basis of disability, and could not stand. Given the almost iconic status of universal public health insurance ensuring access to medically necessary health services in Canada, and the Court's expansive understanding of what had to be covered, it

[89] *Auton v British Columbia (Attorney-General)* 2004 SCC 78, [2004] 3 SCR 657.
[90] G Fridman, *Introduction to the Canadian Law of Torts* (Markham, LexisNexis Butterworths, 2003) 4.
[91] *Eldridge v British Columbia* [1997] 3 SCR 624.

seemed that there could be potential to build on *Eldridge* to establish a more expansive right to health. In light of the devastating effects of broader determinants of health, especially economic insecurity and inequity, on the health status of those least well off, it seemed possible to use law to link the conditions needed to achieve and maintain health more explicitly to human rights.

Later decisions have increasingly diminished what can be expected of *Eldridge*. The Court has rejected claims seeking to expand public health insurance to include services for autistic children provided by health care providers when the latter are not already included under provincial public health insurance plans, despite evidence of efficacy.[92] Courts have also repeatedly confirmed that, when governments offer targeted benefit programs, they are free to determine their scope and beneficiaries, even if the scientific underpinnings for their decisions are lacking or outdated, and when it is clear that some people who clearly need assistance will fall between the cracks.[93] Meanwhile, the gulf between governments' rhetorical commitments to bettering the lives and health of those least well off in society and the reality of life under the policies and laws governments have implemented continues to grow.

While I am sceptical that courts will accept the invitation to develop radically divergent paths in their interpretations of the Charter and human rights legislation, this is certainly an avenue that should be explored. It may be that human rights tribunals can lead the way in developing more nuanced understandings of what constitutes discrimination; they certainly have done so in the past. Increasing the penetration of legal norms into initial policy-making and administrative determinations, and in particular increasing awareness of the linkages between health and human rights, is an important initiative. It must still be supplemented by the availability of legal remedies to enforce rights and carry forward challenges to administrative policies and determinations, including systemic issues. In that regard, scholarship and advocacy aimed not just at refining, but re-defining the judicial understanding of Charter equality rights are key. The impact of such work can be seen in a recent Supreme Court of Canada decision, *R v Kapp*, in which the Court acknowledged that its earlier decision, *Law v Canada (Minister of Employment and Immigration)*, had added to the burdens facing equality claimants, and allowed an unacceptable formalism to reappear in the form of 'artificial' comparator analysis focused

[92] *Auton* (above n 89): (public insurance coverage is generally limited to physicians and hospital services, with limited coverage for certain specific practitioners, such as physiotherapists).

[93] *Wynberg v Ontario* [2006] OJ no 2732 (CA); *Gosselin* (above n 25); *Granovsky v Canada* [2001] 1 SCR 703; *Flora v Ontario (Health Insurance Plan, General Manager)* [2007] OJ no 91 (Ont Div Ct), aff'd [2008] OJ no 2627 (CA).

on treating likes alike.[94] The Court specifically referred to the influence of critical academic commentary as it signaled its intention to draw back from these analyses.[95] Finally, it is essential to involve the communities of people with disabilities in structuring programs and supports so that they can achieve their (and society's) goals of inclusion, participation and equal citizenship. They are, after all, the people whom these benefit programs are meant to serve.

[94] *R v Kapp* 2008 SCC 41, paras 22–4; *Law v Canada (Minister of Employment and Immigration* [1999] 1 SCR 497.
[95] *Ibid*, para 22.

Part IV

Reconceptualizing State Forms and Socio-Legal Policy

9

Substantive Universality

Reconceptualizing Feminist Approaches to Social Provision and Child Care*

HESTER LESSARD

I. INTRODUCTION

WHAT DO WE mean by the term 'universal' with respect to the provision of benefits under publicly supported social programmes? This question floated quietly through my mind as I followed recent child care policy debates in Canada. My curiosity turned to bafflement during the campaign for the 2006 federal election, when, to great fanfare, the Conservative Party, as a key plank in its challenge to the incumbent Liberal government, announced its plan to implement a new universal child care benefit. As such, the benefit would be Canada's first new universal social programme in more than 40 years.[1] The Conservatives, in full-bore election mode, derided as empty the promises of the Liberals to expand the existing child care regime by increasing transfer payments to provincial and territorial governments earmarked for early learning and child care.[2]

* I would like to thank Dorothy Chunn, Shelley Gavigan, Mimi Ajzenstadt and Mimi Abramovitz for organizing the workshop at which this paper was first presented. I am grateful for the thorough and skilled research assistance provided to me by Jessica Derynck and Sharon Fox. As well I would like to thank a number of readers of the draft version who gave helpful feedback, namely Andrew Petter, Judy Fudge and Donald Galloway. Gillian Calder and Wanda Wiegers provided me with invaluable written comments. Katherine Teghtsoonian also provided inspiration and support by being a willing 'sounding board' and pointing me in the right direction in my searches through feminist child care policy literature. Finally I would like to thank Dorothy Chunn and Shelley Gavigan for their encouraging and meticulous editorial work.

[1] MJ Prince and K Teghtsoonian, 'The Harper Government's Universal Child Care Plan: Paradoxical or Purposeful Social Policy?' in GB Doern (ed), *How Ottawa Spends 2007–2008: The Harper Conservatives—Climate of Change* (Montréal, McGill-Queens University Press, 2007) 180. The authors explain that the last universal social programme initiated at the federal level was the 1964 Youth allowance programme: *ibid*, fn 1.

[2] *Ibid*, 183.

I undertake a closer look at the Conservative initiative, implemented shortly after their electoral success and dubbed the Universal Child Care Benefit (UCCB) in section III of this chapter. Briefly, the Conservative proposal reflects a typical pattern in the arena of family ordering, namely the articulation of conservative values to the neo-liberal priorities of privatization and marketization.[3] The tantalizing coupling of the language of universalism and 'social programme' was a mere ruse, covering over a programme aimed at universalizing a conservative conception of the family, subsidizing private market and familial 'choices', and further eroding the already meagre public infrastructure for accessible non-parental, centre-based child care.[4]

The Harper initiative was soon followed by the introduction of Bill C-303, the Early Learning and Child Care Act (ELCCA), by New Democratic MP Denise Savoie, around which a coalition of child care advocates quickly mobilized.[5] The proposed legislation, although it contains some compromises as well as large amounts of wishful thinking, aspires to put in place a regime that reflects the longstanding position of feminist activists and scholars in the child care field, namely a publicly-funded universal, accessible, high-quality regime of non-parental care.[6] As I write, my email inbox is ringing with incoming messages from listservs containing updates on the progress of the Bill and urging email and letter writing campaigns to key political actors.[7]

The use of the social democratic language of 'universal social programmes' by the Harper Conservatives to effectively capture the political and moral high ground while entrenching a socially conservative child care

[3] B Cossman, 'Family Feuds: Neo-Liberal and Neo-Conservative Visions of the Reprivatization Project' in B Cossman and J Fudge (eds), *Privatization, Law, and the Challenge of Feminism* (Toronto, University of Toronto Press, 2002) 169–217.

[4] Prince and Teghtsoonian, 'The Harper Government's Universal Child Care Plan' (above n 1) 181.

[5] Bill C-303, Early Learning and Child Care Act (ELCCA), 1st Session, 39th Parliament, 2006.

[6] The proposed ELCCA is structured as an exercise of the federal spending power. Under the legislation, provinces and territories are eligible for federal grants for an early learning and child care programme if the programme meets the legislative criteria, ie is 'of high quality, universal and accessible': *ibid*, s 5(1)(b). The legislation also requires delivery by non-profit providers, but licensed for-profit entities who provided services before the coming into force of the Act would continue to be able to do so: *ibid*, ss 5(1)(b) and 6.

[7] See, eg, www.buildchildcare.ca. The Bill was referred to the Standing Committee on Human Resources, Social Development and the Status of Persons with Disabilities after Second Reading. The Committee reported the Bill back to Parliament with amendments on 17 May 2007, at: www.cmte.parl.gc.ca/cmte/CommitteePublication.aspx?SourceId=206737. After the summer adjournment, the Bill was reintroduced and moved quickly through first and second readings. The presentation of and debate on the Committee Report took place on 20 and 21 November 2007. At the time of this writing, no third reading has taken place. See: www2.parl.gc.ca/HousePublications/Publication.aspx?Pub=Hansard&Doc=20&Language=E&Mode=1&Parl=39&Ses=2.

regime illuminates the difficulty with the language of universality. There are several lessons to be learned. The most obvious is that one has to be careful about what exactly is being 'universalized'. Another lesson is that there are many neo-liberalisms and, more to the point, many ways in which socially conservative norms and commitments can be harmoniously integrated into initiatives that also have the signature features—such as privatization and familialization—of neo-liberal ordering. As Shelley Gavigan points out, the merging of neo-liberal priorities with conservative values in the realms of family regulation and of much social programming that either directly or indirectly engages with familial relationships represents a continuity rather than a rupture in liberalism's relationship to patriarchal familial norms and practices.[8]

The ELCCA, Savoie's alternative legislative proposal, for the most part, rejects the patriarchal features of Harper's programme and returns the language of universality to its customary place, namely to a proposal that envisions a serious investment of public resources in a regime of non-parental centre-based care that has wide accessibility. To this extent, it captures the orthodox understanding of universality in terms of redistributive justice, or, more practically, in terms of a programme of social provision that provides meaningful material and institutional support accessible to all who come within a broadly defined social category, such as parents of children, regardless of need. However, in this chapter, I want to trouble the language of universality and its relation to feminist theorizing with respect to questions of social provision. My argument is that a feminist re-envisioning of social welfare must develop more nuanced understandings of universality, not simply to contend with the manipulative use of language by political opportunists but also to address in a substantive way the social and cultural complexity of gender and to engage more fully with the multiple dimensions of social injustice. In doing so, I am by no means rejecting the central importance of the redistributive character of universal social programmes nor their commitment to radical inclusion. Rather, I am arguing that the 'everyone' implied by the 'universal' in universality, must be examined more closely. Where the 'everyone' actually reinforces rather than redresses social inequalities it must, of course, be challenged. The trickier problem, however, is where the 'everyone' fails to deliver on its promise not because of a formal gap in coverage or a hidden 'claw-back' under another regime, but because of a failure to reflect significant historical, social and cultural differences

[8] SAM Gavigan, 'Something Borrowed, Something New, Something True: Patriarchal and "Privatized" Relations in Welfare and Family Law', manuscript on file with author, 4, 11. See also D Chunn and SAM Gavigan, 'From Mother's Allowance to Mothers Need not Apply: Canadian Welfare Law as Liberal and NeoLiberal Reforms' (2007) 45 *Osgoode Hall Law Journal* 733, 767–8.

and practices. My argument is that in this situation, the 'everyone' must be complicated rather than rejected.

I will start, in section II with a brief overview of the historical tension between universality and selectivity in social programmes, including the recent turn to the delivery of targeted benefits through tax regimes. In section III I rely on a short exploration of key Canadian government initiatives in the child care field in recent years to illustrate ways in which the turn to tax-based delivery of social benefits disrupts the universality/selectivity binary both at a conceptual level and as a benchmark against which to assess welfare state politics. The upshot, I argue, is that the strategic relevance of the universality/selectivity binary is much reduced. I will then discuss, in sections IV, V and VI, three additional, more fundamental reasons why a feminist re-envisioning of social provision must rethink or complicate the language of universality. Here I will draw on a range of feminist theoretical work, in particular that of Nancy Fraser, Ratna Kapur, and Wendy McKeen and Ann Porter. I will finish by examining the parallel between the conceptual and practical problems generated by the terminology of universality in social provision, and the conceptual and practical problems generated by the kindred language of equality in constitutional rights discourses. Feminist elucidation of the tension between formal and substantive equality, I argue, provides a useful guide for developing a feminist conception of universality that encompasses and addresses substantive differences in material conditions, social locations, needs and relationships.

II. THE UNIVERSALITY/SELECTIVITY BINARY

The universality/selectivity binary has provided a longstanding frame for categorizing approaches to social provision among liberal democratic regimes.[9] In theory, universal programmes are those conditioned only by citizenship or residence. In practice, such programmes are aimed at all who, in addition to meeting the citizenship or residence qualification, come within a broad classification such as an age or a family status category. However, the sub-categories inhere in the purposes of the universal programme and require no further application of eligibility criteria. Selective programmes are those which are accessible to individuals only on a case-by-case basis after they have met bureaucratically administered criteria, typically in relation to their economic means.[10] The universality/selectivity binary,

[9] One of the most heated debates over the relative merits of universal and selective approaches to social provisions occurred in Britain in the 1960s, and many of the themes of that debate continue to resurface today. See S Shaver, *Universality and Selectivity in Income Support* (London, Ashgate, 1997) 2–7.

[10] L Bryan, *Welfare and the State* (New York, St Martin's Press, 1992) 59–60.

however, does more than simply refer to programme design. In the debates of the past, the two modalities have reflected a much deeper normative and ideological divide. Universal programmes have been associated with social citizenship and thus with an emphasis on collective rather than individual responsibility for welfare, on entitlements as rights, and on liberal conceptions of a shared humanity.[11] The citizenship dimension, according to some proponents of universality, must provide not only equal benefits to all but also equal exposure to government administration and engagement in government institutions and services in order to reduce social distance by connecting everyone in a system of mutual giving and receiving.[12] The direct provision of universal services in kind—such as education, health care, or centre-based child care—achieves social integration in a tangible, publicly visible, community-enhancing, institutionally realized manner.[13]

Selective programmes, in contrast, have been linked to the presumption that welfare is primarily an individual and familial responsibility and that collective state responsibility is residual, reserved as a last resort for those who fail to provide for themselves and whose familial and private social networks have failed. Thus, at least at the level of theory, the universality/selectivity binary has reflected a starkly drawn divide between conceptions of the liberal community which tend, at one end, toward a social democratic vision of the political community, and, at the other end toward (classical) liberal and conservative variants of liberalism.[14]

This normative divide has been complicated by pragmatic arguments regarding efficiency and political support. Are selective programmes more efficient, as conservatives on the right insist, because they are targeted at the needy, or are they less efficient, as progressives on the left would have it, because they require large bureaucracies and surveillance?[15] Are universal programmes more viable politically because they benefit middle-class majorities who will not only sustain the programme but keep it running

[11] TH Marshall's articulation of social citizenship in terms of positive rights to a minimum level of material support provides the starting point for western, twentieth century conceptions of the welfare state. In Marshall's vision, such social rights, at least in the British context, have evolved over time from the civil and political dimensions of citizenship and are compatible with capitalist economies and some degree of economic inequality. See TH Marshall, 'Citizenship and Social Class' in TH Marshall (ed), *Sociology at the Crossroads and Other Essays* (London, Heinemann, 1963) 67–127.

[12] Richard Titmuss calls this the 'non-discriminatory objective' of welfare policy to distinguish it from the 'redistributive objective'. The non-discriminatory objective is crucial to 'social integration'. R Titmuss, 'The Role of Redistribution in Social Policy' in B Abel-Smith and K Titmuss (eds), *The Philosophy of Welfare* (London, Allen & Unwin, 1987) 211. See also J Barbalet, *Citizenship* (London, Open University Press, 1988) 50–51.

[13] Titmuss, 'Redistribution in Social Policy' (above n 12) 215, referring to Britain's National Health Service as the example.

[14] For a more in depth analysis of the universality/selectivity divide and the way in which it relates to a number of different welfare state typologies, see Shaver (above n 9) 7–20.

[15] Shaver (above n 9) 4.

at a relatively high standard of service?[16] Are the targeted beneficiaries of selective programmes inevitably stigmatized by criteria which single them out as needy, generating a political backlash against the programme and its clients?[17]

The implicit middle-class bias of universal social programmes has been particularly divisive, with some asserting that the middle class needs to be 'bribed' in order to support the poor.[18] The bribe has turned out to be considerable, calling into question the trade-off between electoral support and redistributive effectiveness. Social welfare scholarship in the 1980s clarified that universal programmes in areas of health, housing and education mostly benefit the middle classes.[19] In Canada, David Schneiderman has illuminated the ideological character of what he describes as middle-class support by examining the way in which universal as opposed to targeted social programmes are more likely to be defended by courts, in the name of constitutional equality rights, against erosion by neo-liberalising governments. Schneiderman argues that the jurisprudential pattern reflects a constitutional culture that is imbued with middle-class values, namely that privileges a conception of society organized around 'a gendered family structure with two income earners (female workers typically earning less or working part time) engaging in tax avoidance in order to maximize the family's discretionary income'.[20]

Dorothy Roberts, writing about income assistance programmes in the US context in which political backlash against the poor is entwined with racism, is sharply critical of the political viability argument in favour of universal programmes. She is sceptical that white Americans can be so easily

[16] Titmuss (above n 12) 216; Bryan, *Welfare and the State* (above n 10) 63.

[17] Titmuss (above n 12) 128–9, arguing that the American 'War on Poverty' of the 1960s failed because it created targeted services and benefits that stigmatised beneficiaries. See discussion below (nn 22–24) for a critique of the 'stigma' argument from an American critical race perspective. For a Canadian feminist analysis of targeting and the increased stigmatization of single mothers beginning with the restructuring of the postwar welfare state in the late 1980s, see J Brodie, 'Restructuring and the New Citizenship' in I Bakker (ed), *Rethinking Restructuring: Gender and Change in Canada* (Toronto, University of Toronto Press, 1996) 132, 137; and J Mosher, 'Welfare Reform and the Re-making of the Model Citizen' in M Young (ed), *Poverty: Rights, Social Citizenship, and Legal Activism* (Vancouver, University of British Columbia Press, 2007) 124–6, 132.

[18] D Schneiderman, 'Universality vs. Particularity: Litigating Middle Class Values under Section 15' in McIntyre and Rodgers (eds), *Diminishing Returns: Inequality and the Canadian Charter of Rights and Freedoms* (Markham, LexisNexis Butterworths, 2006) 371, citing C Offe, *Contradictions of the Welfare State* (Cambridge MA, MIT Press, 1992) 72.

[19] Bryan (above n 10) 124–31 surveys this scholarship. Bryan's main purpose is to broaden the frame within which we think about the welfare state by including consideration of economic welfare programmes, specifically occupational and fiscal welfare programmes. She also assesses social programmes which are identified more closely with the welfare state, such as housing, by including benefits delivered through the tax system, eg capital gains tax exemptions on sales of a primary residence.

[20] Schneiderman, 'Universality vs. Particularity' (above n 18) 368. Note that Schneiderman's analysis presumes a very broad conception of the 'middle class'.

persuaded to abandon the 'benefit' of having their own superiority and Black inferiority held in place by socio-economic disparities.[21] In addition, she argues that 'the universalist solution ... deliberately avoids an attempt to dismantle racist social structures as the price of appealing to whites' self interest'.[22] Although Roberts sees universal programmes as an improvement over the status quo, she warns that '[c]reating programs that maneuver around racism to make them more palatable to white Americans is likely to weaken their power to eradicate systemic oppression'.[23]

More recently this familiar debate has been complicated by the turn to new forms of programme delivery which, reinforced by the rise of neo-liberal conceptions of the 'consumer' or 'taxpayer citizen',[24] use the tax system to deliver a benefit that can be calibrated to income or the lack of it. While this turn has been particularly significant in Canada and New Zealand, other jurisdictions such as the United States have also embraced a greater reliance on tax-based delivery of social benefits.[25] The most common device for the delivery of a benefit through a tax regime is through tax expenditures, namely tax breaks such as credits, deductions or exemptions which are the equivalent of a public subsidy or spending provision.[26] The device also takes the more familiar (from a tax perspective) form of a revenue-raising measure which, viewed in its broader policy setting, is in fact a 'claw-back' of a benefit delivered through a companion programme. Finally, the programme can take the form of 'negative' income tax by means of which individuals receive 'top up' payments if their income falls below a certain level or if they have no income at all.

Benefits delivered through the tax system upset the universal/selectivity binary. They are sometimes described as 'universal' because they are, at the conceptual level, available to all, or at least to all who file tax returns or, in more limited programmes, all who earn enough to pay taxes; however, the adjustments through the tax system render the benefit more 'selective' in nature but without the public visibility, bureaucratic surveillance and stigmatisation for which selective benefits historically have been criticized. As

[21] D Roberts, 'Sources of Commitment to Social Justice' (1998) 4 *Roger Williams University Law Review* 175, 184.

[22] *Ibid*, 183.

[23] *Ibid.*

[24] J Brodie, 'Reforming Social Justice in Neoliberal Times' (2007) 1 *Studies in Social Justice* 93, 101 describes neo-liberal conceptions of citizens as consumers in relation to the transformation of social programmes into tax credits and deductions. J Shields and BM Evans, *Shrinking the State: Globalization and Public Administration 'Reform'* (Halifax, Fernwood Publishing, 1998) 80, use the term 'taxpayer citizen'.

[25] J Myles and P Pierson, 'Friedman's Revenge: The Reform of Liberal Welfare States in Canada and the United States' (1997) 25 *Politics and Society* 44, 47.

[26] N Brooks, 'Review of *Tax Expenditures* by Surrey and McDaniel' (1986) 34 *Canadian Tax Journal* 681, 681–5. Provides a brief synopsis of the development of tax expenditure theory.

well, the delivery of benefits through tax regimes appears to more effectively and efficiently target public resources at those who actually need them.

Myles and Pierson, writing in the mid 1990s, argued that, in Canada—where the turn to Negative Income Tax/Guaranteed Income (NIT/GI) regimes has been, in comparison to the United States, much more radical and comprehensive, including benefits targeted at non-working as well as working poor families—the impact has reversed, at least in the 'intermediate term', the favouring of middle- and high-income earners characteristic of universal and some selective programmes, and more effectively channelled the bulk of benefits to the poor.[27] Since then the trend to deliver benefits through NIT/GI regimes in Canada has, if anything, solidified. However, Canada is beginning to see steeper income inequalities.[28] Furthermore, critical voices, focusing on the way in which such regimes provide a wage subsidy for employers, have become more evident in the debate.[29] In addition, the NIT/GI model is a direct transfer in cash rather than kind which, in the case of support for child rearing, leaves social reproduction to individual (subsidized) choice in a mostly private market of (low-waged, gendered, racialized) providers. The missing elements are the institutional strategies and infrastructure which Roberts identifies as crucial to addressing systemic racial injustice and which, in the context of child care policy, many have identified as crucial to addressing the systemic gender inequalities rooted in relations of social reproduction.

Nevertheless, the turn to tax-based delivery of child care benefits, has produced alliances in Canada between conservatives and a broad spectrum of liberals, feminists, social democrats, child care advocates and anti-poverty advocates who support the promised reduction in income inequalities such programmes appear to deliver.[30] As well, the delivery of the benefit through

[27] Myles and Pierson, 'Friedman's Revenge' (above n 25) 445, 458.

[28] M Frenette, DA Green and G Picot, 'Rising Income Inequality in the 1990s: An Exploration of Three Data Sources' in DA Green and JR Kesselman (eds), *Dimensions of Inequality in Canada* (Vancouver, University of British Columbia Press, 2006) 95; A Yalnizyan, *The Rich and the Rest of Us: The Changing Face of Canada's Growing Gap* (Toronto, Canadian Centre for Policy Alternatives, 2007) 5 comparing income levels of Canadian families raising children today with families a generation ago.

[29] R Saunders, 'Making Work Pay' (Ottawa, CPRN, December 2005) at: www.cprn.org/fr/doc.cfm?doc=1350, cited in J Fudge, 'Beyond Vulnerable Workers: Towards a New Standard Employment Relationship' (2005) 12 *Canadian Labour and Employment Law Journal* 145, 169. Saunders argues that tax delivered supplements to the working poor must be accompanied by reforms raising the minimum wage in order to avoid the wage subsidy effect. *Ibid*. In the US, tax credits are restricted to the low end of the income scale in pursuit of a 'strategy of encouraging "flexibility" at the bottom of the labour market'. Myles and Pierson (above n 25) 445.

[30] Myles and Pierson (above n 25) 451; W McKeen, *Money in their Own Name: The Feminist Voice in Poverty Debate in Canada, 1970–1995* (Toronto, University of Toronto Press, 2004) 98–106; W Wiegers, 'Child-Centred Advocacy and the Invisibility of Women in Poverty Discourse and Social Policy' in Chunn, Boyd and Lessard (eds), *Reaction and Resistance: Feminism, Law and Social Change 1966–2000* (Vancouver, University of British Columbia Press, 2007) 246–7.

the tax system to individual families has been coupled with transfers made directly to provincial and territorial governments to enhance and expand publicly-funded early learning and child care programmes, thereby at least partially attempting to address the need for publicly-supported institutional strategies.

III. CANADIAN CHILD CARE POLICY

A brief look at current policy initiatives in the child care field in Canada illustrates some of these points. The starting place for understanding the Harper government's most recent intervention is the Canada Child Tax Benefit (CCTB), put in place in 1998 by the preceding Liberal government and retained in part by the Conservatives.[31] The CCTB consolidated an earlier move by Liberals to finally abolish in 1992 the family allowance, by then a taxed back allowance and thus no longer 'universal' in the traditional sense, and replace it with a combination of income-tested benefits and supplements. The CCTB continued this pattern. It comprises two components: a base benefit taking the form of a monthly, income-tested payment to families with children and an additional supplement targeted at low-income families, including families on social assistance. Both the targeted supplement and the basic benefit are paid monthly (in one combined payment for eligible families) by revenue rather than welfare authorities to the primary caregiver. The basic benefit is income tested and provided up to relatively high net family income levels (CAN$96,995 for a two-child family in the 2005–06 benefit year).[32]

The CCTB, as well as calibrating eligibility and benefit levels to reflect income, is subject to additional 'fine tuning', rendering it more selective than universal. For example, if a family claims a child care expense deduction under another part of the federal tax regime, then the benefit is reduced by 25 per cent of those deducted expenses.[33] As well, although the CCTB is not taxable, most provinces, with the approval of the federal government, claw back all or most of the Supplement either from their own child benefit or from social assistance benefits and reinvest those amounts in services aimed at low-income families.[34]

[31] This summary is drawn from C Young, *Women, Tax and Social Programs: The Gendered Impact of Funding Social Programs Through the Tax System* (Ottawa, Status of Women Canada, 2000) 19–40; Canada, *The National Child Benefit Progress Report: 2003*, ch 3; Canada, *The National Child Benefit Progress Report: 2005*, at: www.nationalchildbenefit.ca/ncb/Progress_Reports/2005/en/index.shtml.

[32] *The National Child Benefit Progress Report: 2005* (above n 31) ch 2.

[33] C Young, *Women, Tax and Social Programs* (above n 31) 33.

[34] While New Brunswick, Manitoba, Nova Scotia, and Newfoundland and Labrador make no adjustment, Prince Edward Island, Ontario, Yukon, Northwest Territories, British Columbia, Saskatchewan and Nunavut either offset social assistance benefits or offset a separate

Although the CCTB has many selective features, it is also possible to cast it as a quasi-universal benefit because of its location in the tax regime and its delivery by tax authorities up to fairly high levels of income.[35] Selective programmes are typically subject to strict eligibility criteria based on income, with the consequence that only a minority of persons or households are sufficiently impoverished to qualify as beneficiaries. The calibration of income to amount of benefit under the CCTB seems less rigorously residual in its application. The programme acts much more positively by taking steps to ensure that all Canadians have adequate income to care for their children. The targeted Supplement, from this perspective, when viewed in conjunction with the base benefit, can be seen as a way of more generously covering gaps at the low end of the income range. Thus, at the level of programme design, the CCTB can be viewed as a finely tuned programme that shields both itself and its key beneficiaries from stigmatization and political backlash by its quasi-universal character and its location in a tax rather than welfare regime.

However, although the federal benefit regime is an important source of support for some low-income families, its impacts are disastrously selective when looked at through a feminist anti-poverty lens. Wanda Wiegers points to a number of features responsible for this result: benefit levels do not address the depth of poverty; the provincial claw-backs erode in whole or in part monetary benefits for many families (disproportionately single mother families) on social assistance; and the programmes funded through the provincial claw-back are often contingent on employment. The latter feature fails to recognize the need for and importance of unpaid domestic labour.[36] As well, despite the touted accuracy of selective targeting through the tax system, reliance on the tax system and on the concept of family income means that many (often low-income) women do not receive the benefit because either they or their spouses did not file tax returns. Indeed, one study conducted before the current benefit regime was put

provincial child benefit. Canada, *The National Child Benefit Progress Report 2006*, ch 2, at: www.nationalchildbenefit.ca/ncb/Progress_Reports/2006/en/index.shtml. See also Wiegers, 'Child-Centred Advocacy' (above n 30) 243.

[35] Myles and Pierson argue that that programmes based on negative income and guaranteed income designs are different from traditional selective programmes because they reach persons at high levels of income thereby including 'electoral pluralities and, in some cases, even majorities.' For this reason they describe the turn to such programmes as 'a historically novel form of welfare state redistribution about which traditional welfare theory has little to say in regard to either origins or outcomes'. See above (above n 25) 444.

[36] Wiegers (above n 30) 243; Young (above n 31) 33–5 observes in addition that the CCTB is not fully indexed for inflation, and that the reduction of the benefit where a child care expense deduction is taken under other provisions in the tax regime compounds the unfairness stemming from the inadequacy of affordable child care and of the expense deduction itself.

in place, found that less than 40 per cent of those entitled to child care benefits actually receive them.[37]

Some of the inadequacies of the CCTB were partially addressed by its companion programme, the Early Childhood Development Initiative (ECDI), introduced by the Liberal government in 2000. The ECDI channelled resources to provincial and territorial governments for community institutions and infrastructure (pre-natal and infant screening programmes, family resource centres, pre-schools, child care and developmental programmes, and community supports).[38] However, Canadian government policy in the area of child development has generally relied on the work of human capital theorists concerned about economic efficiency rather than social justice.[39] Not surprisingly then, political justifications for the ECDI, although replete with references to children's well-being, made no mention of gender equality as an objective, invoking instead 'Canada's future social vitality and economic prosperity'.[40] Wanda Wiegers has summarized the impact of this policy orientation on women by observing that, in the end, many of the programmes supported by the ECDI seemed to 'minimize the levels of public responsibility and expenditure while potentially enlarging the individual responsibility of mothers'.[41] For example, resources were targeted at the poor, leading to investment in programmes aimed at screening for 'at risk' children, and thereby potentially subjecting parents to surveillance and stigma. As well, the social conservatism of the designers of the programmes funded through the ECDI was manifest in the manner in which many of the core programmes treated child care as a 'parenting deficit' to be addressed through parenting courses and child development programmes rather than as a social responsibility requiring significant public investment in child care institutions.[42]

The failure of the CCTB combined with the ECDI to live up to the promise of delivering greater benefits to those most in need has prompted some to call for a return to a universal, non-income-tested, approach to public support for families with children and others to call for an end to the provincial and territorial claw-backs which disproportionately disadvantage families who are in receipt of social assistance, who, in turn, are disproportionately lone mother families.[43] In addition, it has been pointed

[37] Young (above n 31) 31, citing G Cleveland and D Hyatt, 'Assessing Federal Child Care Policy: Does the Arrow Reach Its Target?' (1997) 18 *Policy Options* 20, 22.

[38] W Wiegers, *The Framing of Poverty as Child Poverty and its Implications for Women* (Ottawa, Status of Women Canada, 2002) 79.

[39] Wiegers (above n 30) 244–5.

[40] 'First Ministers Meeting Communiqué on Early Childhood Development', 11 September 2000, www.unionsociale.gc.ca/news/11090_e.html.

[41] *Ibid*, 244.

[42] *Ibid*, 244–5; Wiegers, *Framing of Poverty* (above n 38) 79.

[43] NAWL, *Bill C-80 and Related Measures: the National Association of Women and the Law, response to—the Department of National Health and Welfare's White Paper, the Child*

out that the amount of resources originally earmarked for the ECDI fell woefully short of what is required to 'even begin to provide comprehensive, high-quality, reliable and accessible child care'.[44]

Some of these concerns moved to the centre of public discourse during the campaign in the federal 2006 election. The incumbent Liberals, in response to their opponent's promise of a new universal child care benefit, announced they would more than double their commitment to early learning and child care to a total of CAN$10 billion with a projection of over one million more child care spaces by 2015.[45] In addition, the Liberals began to characterize child care as a 'public right'.[46] However, the ensuing electoral victory for a Conservative minority government not only foreclosed the expansion of the Liberal programme, it ultimately led to the cancellation of existing agreements made under the ECDI to transfer CAN$4.2 billion to the provinces for early learning and child care spaces and services. The Harper Conservative government also rolled the young child supplement—a component of the base benefit in the CCTB—into its own Universal Child Care Benefit (UCCB) and launched a Child Care Spaces Initiative.

The Child Care Spaces Initiative provided a quintessentially neo-liberal solution to the problem of lack of child care spaces. Like the UCCB, it was packaged in the neo-liberal language of choice.[47] The UCCB put money directly into the hands of parents to facilitate their child care choices; the Initiative turned to the private market in child care services to ensure sufficient child care spaces were available for those choices, promising 125,000 new spaces over five years. The Initiative's centre-piece is a tax credit for commercial and non-profit operators of child care programmes for capital assistance.[48] However, the tax credit did not yield the hoped for surge in new and expanded child care enterprises. An internal report prepared for the Minister of Human Resources a year after the implementation of the Initiative found that most companies and employers did not think the tax credit a sufficient inducement to get into the 'costly and complex' business

Benefit, a White paper on Canada's new integrated child tax benefit (Ottawa, NAWL, 1992) Six calls for a return to universality. Note that the NAWL paper describes a benefit such as the family allowance that is not calibrated to reflect income level but is, instead taxed back, as a 'universal benefit': *ibid*. National Council of Welfare, *Child Benefits: Kids are Still Hungry* (1998) 28 calls for an end to claw-backs.

[44] Wiegers (above n 38) 80.

[45] Prince and Teghtsoonian (above n 1) 6.

[46] *Ibid*.

[47] P Kershaw, '"Choice" Discourse in BC Child Care: Distancing Policy from Research' (2004) 37 *Canadian Journal of Political Science* 927, 929–31 surveys the literature analyzing choice discourse and its relation to neo-liberal child care policy.

[48] Canada, 'Aspire to A Stronger Safer Better Canada: The Budget Plan 2007' 124, 426–7, at: www.dsp-psd.pwgsc.g.ca/ explaining the promises made in the 2006 Budget.

of child care.[49] The lack of take-up by businesses was confirmed by a more recent study which found that although child care spaces had increased by 31 March 2007, it was the 'smallest increase in regulated child care in some years'.[50] Indeed, the only recent flurry of activity noted in the commercial child care sector has been the arrival of 123 Busy Beaver Learning Centres Ltd, a subsidiary of an Australian corporation, ABC Learning Centres Ltd, described as an example of 'big box daycare'.[51] Busy Beaver Ltd, attracted by the Harper tax credit, has been buying up commercial child care enterprises in Alberta and has shown interest in moving into the Ontario and British Columbia markets as well. Some fear has been expressed that, under international investment rules, extensive foreign investment in the private sector could make implementation of a public system of non-profit, publicly subsidized centre-based child care more difficult or costly.[52]

The Initiative has other flaws. In particular, some have observed that the lack of funding in the Initiative for operating costs will either depress wages and benefits for caregivers or result in high fees for parents.[53] As Prince and Teghtsoonian argue, both consequences have direct and negative impacts on women, who predominate in the child care sector of paid employment and who, as parents, are often the lower earner and thus come under pressure to forgo work where the costs of child care are high.[54]

To substitute for the lack of any extensive take up (other than Busy Beavers Ltd) for the tax credit offered by the Initiative, the Conservatives

[49] G Galloway, 'Few companies keen to provide child care', *The Globe and Mail* (Toronto edn), 27 October 2007, A4, quoting results of consultations obtained by *The Globe and Mail* under access to information legislation.

[50] *Child Care Space Statistics 2007* (Toronto, Childcare Resource and Research Unit, 10 April 2008) 1, at: www.childcarecanada.org.

[51] T McCharles, 'Opposition parties unite to fight big-box daycare', *The Toronto Star*, 1 November 2007, A1; T McCharles, 'Union report sounds alarm over foreign daycare chains', *The Toronto Star*, 2 April 2008, A17. See F Rush and C Downie, 'ABC Learning Centres: A Case Study of Australia's largest Child Care Corporation' (The Australia Institute, 2006) for an analysis of the quality of care provided at ABC's centres that is critical of both ABC as well as corporate delivery of child care: *ibid*, 37–8.

[52] McCharles, 'Big-box daycare'; McCharles, 'Union reports sound alarm'. See also L Monsebraaten, 'Activists urge freeze on daycare licences; Moratorium needed to keep multinational firm from buying out Ontario centers, advocates say', *The Toronto Star*, 3 March 2008, A6. The press coverage refers to a legal opinion prepared for the Canadian Union of Public Employees advising that international trade rules may render the introduction of a publicly subsidised system of non-profit child care centres costly in the face of extensive foreign investment in the child care sector. S Shrybman, 'Establishing a National System of Early Learning and Child Care in Light of Canada's Obligations Under NAFTA and the WTO', November 2004, on file with author.

[53] Canada, 'Aspire to a Stronger Safer Better Canada' Budget Plan 2007 (above n 48) 427. See also Code Blue for Child Care, 'What's Wrong With the Federal Child Care Spaces Initiative', at: www.childcareadvocacy.ca/resources/pdf/Whats_Wrong_with_Fed_CC_Spaces.pdf.

[54] Prince and Teghtsoonian (above n 1) 13–14.

promised and have carried through on an annual transfer payment of CAN$250 million to provincial and territorial governments.[55] However, the terms of the transfer have never been worked out. The transfer comes with no strings attached thus attracting the criticism that in fact there is no plan or accountability protocols in place, and that provinces are reducing support for programmes and promoting higher fees for parents.[56]

Finally, the Conservative government's Universal Child Care Benefit (UCCB) is a direct, flat-rate payment of CAN$1200 per year per child under six, made to all Canadians (citizens or non-citizens who are resident in Canada) regardless of income level. Thus the UCCB, unlike the CCTB, presents as a highly visible social programme that, at first glance, appears to be truly universal in the traditional sense, providing the exact same benefit to all who come within the designated group. The departure from selectivity is more apparent than real, as the UCCB is taxed back from the lower-income spouse (or from the parent in single-parent families), thus in fact bringing it more in line with the CCTB's selective, income-tested features.[57]

However, to understand the point that the universal/selective binary no longer provides a way to navigate welfare state politics, one must look at the substantive impacts of the UCCB. Although it has only been in place a short while, preliminary assessments point out that the UCCB delivers the most benefits for the breadwinner/caregiver nuclear family and the least benefits for the lone parent family.[58] This, of course, is not because of an oversight on the part of Conservative policy-makers; rather, it is because '*the central purpose of the UCCB* is to ... provide a symbolic endorsement of the decision by some parents—mostly mothers—to provide full time care for their children at home' (emphasis added).[59] What is universalized by the UCCB then, is the normative family of the post-war era—the gendered breadwinner/caregiver nuclear family—a familial ideal that is increasingly irrelevant for

[55] Canada, Budget Plan 2007 (above n 48) 124–5.

[56] Canada, Budget Plan 2007 (above n 48); Child Care Advocacy Association of Canada, 'Harper's Cut and Run Approach Hurting Families' 19 March 2007, at: www.action.web.ca/home/ccaac/alerts.shtml?x=98130&AA_EX_Session=ef518155bff531daa9df5be448269ef5. See also N Greenaway, 'Liberals, NDP jump on Ottawa day-care case; Families need a quality, affordable public system advocates insist', *The Ottawa Citizen (final edn)*, 1 November 2007, 5; M Sadava, 'Supply still falls far short of child-care demand; Province needs 14,000 more spaces in next three years', *The Edmonton Journal*, 15 April 2008, B5. The latter article cites concerns that 'extra transfers from the federal government have not gone into topping up the ... budget for child care'.

[57] Canada, Budget Plan 2007 (above n 48); Annex 5—Tax Measures: Notices of Supplementary Information and Ways and Means Motion at: www.budget.gc.ca/2007/bp/bpa5be.html.

[58] K Battle et al, 'More Than a Name Change: The Universal Child Care Benefit' (Ottawa, Caledon Institute of Social Policy, May 2006).

[59] Prince and Teghtsoonian (above n 1) 187.

all but financially advantaged families.[60] In addition, the UCCB deepens the divide between lower- and higher-income families not only by providing the least benefits to lone-parent families but also by eliminating the young child supplement of the CCTB. The supplement was available to families with lower and moderate incomes who could not access the generally greater savings provided by the child care expense deduction.[61] Indeed, the UCCB has been described as a 'windfall subsidy' for higher income families, coming as it often does as an addition to the relatively generous child care tax deduction, while the sum of CAN$1200, without more, does little to address the actual costs of child rearing.[62]

The ease with which the language of universality has been manipulated by the Harper government in Canada and the extensive resort to tax regimes to more finely tune the provision of ostensibly universal child care benefits points to either the strategic irrelevance of the language of universality or, at the very least, its potential to backfire. As noted earlier, feminist activism and scholarship with respect to child care has consistently advocated for a publicly-funded universal regime of non-parental centre-based child care. The demand for investment of public resources into centre-based care is rooted in an approach to child care that puts a premium on gender equality rather than child development, labour market priorities, or human capital development. The prioritizing of women's social equality directly challenges the socially conservative conception of the family that underpins both Liberal and Conservative child care initiatives in recent years.[63] On that basis alone, it might be important for feminists to eschew the language of universality and focus on exposing the continuity, at least with respect to the patriarchal theme, across the universality/selectivity divide as well as across the Liberal/Conservative divide.

Apart from these immediate and strategic concerns, I would argue, drawing on feminist theoretical work, that there are at least three additional reasons why the concept of universality in relation to social provision must be rethought or more carefully articulated. The first reason concerns the assumption in much liberal theory of what Nancy Fraser describes as a 'single, comprehensive public sphere'.[64] The assumption is belied by the

[60] Cossman (above n 2) 175.

[61] K Battle, *A Bigger and Better Child Benefit: A $5000 Canada Child Tax Benefit* (Ottawa, Caledon Institute of Social Policy, January 2008) 17–18.

[62] *Ibid*, 18.

[63] The Canadian trend in this regard may be part of a broader policy convergence and consensus about the appropriate allocation of responsibility between states, markets, and communities observed by Jane Jenson and Mariette Sineau in a study encompassing several European jurisidictions. See 'Citizenship in the Era of Welfare State Redesign' in J Jenson and M Sineau (eds), *Who Cares? Women's Work, Childcare and Welfare State Redesign* (Toronto, University of Toronto Press, 2001) 254–9.

[64] N Fraser, *Justice Interruptus: Critical Reflections on the 'Postsocialist' Condition* (New York, Routledge, 1997) 83.

variegated experience of citizenship across differently positioned social, cultural and economic groups as well as within those groups. In Canada, the assumption of a common political arena in which all can participate is most directly challenged by Aboriginal claims for self government. As well, it is both challenged and consolidated by Québec's resistance to interventions into the arena of social programmes at the federal level. Feminist theorizing regarding intersectionality and the essentialism underlying universalizing language in relation to identity and experience is useful here to delineate a more complex conception of (again borrowing from Fraser) 'multiple publics' or 'subaltern counter-publics'.[65] A second reason relates to what Ratna Kapur terms the transnational migrant subject.[66] The language of universality takes as an unproblematic given, a geographically bounded, liberal community the borders of which, in both past and present, often reflect and maintain a global pattern of exclusionary and oppressive practices. Fraser's recent revision of her critique of traditional liberal conceptions of the public sphere is also helpful on this point. In this regard, Fraser argues that both original conceptions of the public sphere as well as her own and other egalitarian critiques are captured and limited by the tacit assumption of a 'bounded political community with its own territorial state'.[67] A third reason concerns the need to integrate measures into any social provision programme that recognize and address the political nature of the relationship between provider and provided for. Welfare provision, as Wendy McKeen and Ann Porter argue, needs to be assessed from the perspective of how meaningfully programmes provide political space for the voice and agency of the groups that are the actual and potential beneficiaries of the programme. Again, Fraser's work on the 'representation' dimension of justice is of assistance in providing a theoretical foundation for a feminist approach to social provision that incorporates this attention to political engagement.[68] Despite these three concerns, however, universality's commitment to redistributive justice as well as its symbolic assertion of radical inclusivity remain important. In the conclusion, I point to the parallels between these dimensions of universality and analyses of formal and substantive equality. Feminist analyses advocating substantive conceptions of equality that address material and structural inequalities can be drawn upon to sketch out, in a preliminary way, a substantive conception of universality.

[65] *Ibid*, 83, 81.

[66] R Kapur, *Erotic Justice: Law and the New Politics of Postcolonialism* (London, Glasshouse Press, 2005) 137.

[67] N Fraser, 'Transnationalizing the Public Sphere: On the Legitimacy and Efficacy of Public Opinion in a post Westphalian World' in S Benhabib et al (eds), *Identities, Affiliations, and Allegiances* (Cambridge, Cambridge University Press, 2007) 46.

[68] N Fraser, 'Reframing Justice in a Globalizing World' (2005) 36 *New Left Review* 69, 75.

IV. UNIVERSALITY'S PUBLIC/PRIVATE SPLIT: GENDER, RACE, COLONIALISM AND CLASS

Feminists and other social movement activists and theorists have, in practice, refused to relinquish either the importance of recognizing multiple and overlapping dimensions of identity or the central role of material and structural inequality in sustaining patterns of exclusion and social injustice. In her argument for a more complex conception of justice, embracing and integrating redistribution, recognition and—in a recent revision of her original scheme—representation, Nancy Fraser identifies participatory parity as the 'normative core' of her vision of justice.[69] Participatory parity, on her terms, entails social relations that allow all adults to interact with each other 'on a par'. Such interrelations, she continues, are not possible without some measure of redistribution to guarantee the 'independence and "voice"' of individuals, nor without some measure of recognition. Fraser defines recognition in terms that emphasize social relations within a political community rather than cultural 'difference'. In short, recognition consists of 'institutionalized patterns of cultural value [that] express equal respect for all participants and ensure equal opportunity for achieving social esteem'.[70]

Participatory parity also presumes a set of political arrangements and practices, traditionally described as a 'public', that are radically inclusive, or, to put it differently, that are at least committed to the ideal of universality with respect to who counts as a political actor within the 'public'. In this latter respect, Fraser draws explicitly on Habermas's depiction of the liberal ideal of the public and his elaboration of this ideal in terms of a 'theater in modern societies in which political participation is enacted through the medium of talk'.[71] Fraser observes that Habermas's delineation of this discursive sphere, as distinct from both the state and the economy, is particularly useful for feminists because it counters the tendency to conflate the three spheres. She provides the example—particularly germane to child care debates—of the way in which feminist demands 'to de-privatize housework and child care are equated with their commodification'.[72] However, distinguishing herself from Habermas, Fraser illuminates not only the class but also the gendered and racialized dimensions of the original liberal ideal of the public. As she explains, the latter, exclusionary dimensions are implicit in the assumptions that persons can bracket their status and engage in

[69] N Fraser and A Honneth, *Redistribution or Recognition? A Political-Philosophical Exchange* (London, Verso, 2003) 36. Fraser reiterates the foundational role of participatory parity in relation to her revised three dimensional concept of justice in Fraser, 'Reframing Justice' (above n 68) 73.

[70] Fraser and Honneth, *Redistribution of Recognition* (above n 69).

[71] Fraser, *Justice Interruptus* (above n 64) 70.

[72] *Ibid.*

talk 'as if' they were social equals; that a multiplicity of competing publics signals the deterioration and fragmentation of democratic politics; that talk in the public sphere should be limited to the common good and any manifestation of private concerns or interests is negative; and that a clear divide between civil society and the state should be maintained.

On the basis of her critique of the liberal model, Fraser argues for a model that works against each of these assumptions. Thus her model rejects the bracketing of systemic inequalities in order to engage in 'talk' as an equal and, instead, insists that 'political democracy requires substantive social equality'.[73] Fraser also urges an ideal comprised of multiple publics instead of a single comprehensive public sphere. She observes that in societies which lack substantive social equality, subaltern counter-publics are required which permit the development of oppositional identities and discourses. As well, fully egalitarian societies require multiple publics in order to ensure the flourishing of 'diverse rhetorical and stylistic norms'.[74] Finally, Fraser rejects limits on discourse within the public sphere premised on a distinction between public goods and private interests, alluding to the ideological nature of the construction of both property relations and domestic or intimate relations as private.

It is Fraser's conception of multiple publics and her concomitant critique of the notion of a 'single comprehensive public sphere' that relates most directly to the analysis of universality in relation to social provision. Subaltern counter-publics provide a discursive space for the articulation of 'oppositional interpretations' of 'identities, interests, and needs'.[75] Using the example of the feminist subaltern counter-public, Fraser argues that within the discursive spaces of feminist bookstores, journals, festivals etc, women have been able to invent new terms to describe experiences of exclusion and to 'recast our needs and identities, thereby reducing, although not eliminating the extent of our disadvantage in official public spheres'.[76] However, Fraser makes it clear that such subaltern counter-publics are not simply correctives that offset the 'participatory privileges' of dominant groups, but also have crucial positive value as spaces within which identities are formed and enacted. Thus, in a culturally diverse egalitarian society, the insistence on a single comprehensive public sphere would be tantamount to an insistence on cultural homogeneity. As no discursive space is culturally neutral, homogeneity would 'effectively privilege the expressive norms of one cultural group over another, thereby making discursive assimilation a condition for participation in public debate'.[77]

[73] *Ibid*, 80.
[74] *Ibid*, 83.
[75] *Ibid*, 81.
[76] *Ibid*, 81–2.
[77] *Ibid*, 84.

Fraser's point can be concretely illustrated by the example of the interventions by indigenous voices in Canadian child care debates. Canadian indigenous scholars and activists have argued pointedly in relation to child care that proposals for a pan-Canadian programme are unlikely to be endorsed by their communities 'because of their historical experience with government assimilation policies' and because, from the perspective of such communities, 'child care is viewed as a vehicle for the transmission of culture and preservation of their languages'.[78] As one indigenous commentator, explaining the rejection of a universal child care programme, put it, '[t]he danger of universality and the fear of it on the part of many Aboriginal people is that our distinctiveness will be lost within it'.[79] The fear is rooted in the history of Canadian 'colonization of Aboriginal childhood' through 'the reserve, the residential school, the child protection system, young offender facilities, and jail'.[80]

Furthermore, the indigenous position makes it clear that indigenous child care, welfare and education practices, even within the traditionally 'private' sphere of family, are in fact themselves subaltern counter-publics, in short, are places where colonialism is resisted and subordinated cultural practices are sustained and reconceived.[81] The indigenous family, to the extent that it is the locus of 'identity and cultural realization',[82] is part of the indigenous counter-public,[83] much in the way that churches in African American communities at one time provided a cultural, social and political space for resistance to and critiques of racism embedded in US laws and policies.[84] A similar challenge to the designation, within liberal political discourse, of religious space as private is contained in Shauna Van Praagh's analysis of harm to children and the role of religious communities in which she argues that the self-conceptions of religious communities as 'parallel regulators of the family' should be recognized.[85] Both family and church in these examples

[78] M Greenwood and P Shawana, 'Aboriginal Perspectives on Child Care' in G Cleveland and M Krashinsky (eds), *Our Children's Future: Child Care Policy in Canada* (Toronto, University of Toronto Press, 2001) 234.

[79] R Budgell, 'The Needs of Aboriginal Children' in G Cleveland and M Krashinsky eds, *Our Children's Future: Child Care Policy in Canada* (Toronto, University of Toronto Press 2001) 348.

[80] A McGillivray, 'Therapies of Freedom: The Colonization of Aboriginal Childhood' in A McGillivray (ed), *Governing Childhood* (Aldershot, Dartmouth, 1997) 136.

[81] *Ibid.*

[82] Shawana and Greenwood, 'Aboriginal Perspectives in Child Care' (above n 78).

[83] K Anderson, *Recognition of Being: Reconstructing Native Womanhood* (Toronto, Sumach Press, 2000) 116–23, 205–12 for an elaboration of indigenous family relations as a place of strength and resistance for indigenous women.

[84] Fraser (above n 64) 75.

[85] S Van Praagh, 'The Youngest Members: Harm to Children and the Role of Religious Communities', in M Fineman and R Mykitiuk (eds), *The Public Nature of Private Violence: The Discovery of Domestic Abuse* (New York, Routledge, 1994) 152. Van Pragh's argument is directed at complicating our conception of the domestic sphere in relation to state intervention

function as public spheres in ways that, as Fraser notes with respect to churches, are 'unimaginable from the perspective of the liberal model of the bourgeois public sphere, with its Kantian secular-Enlightenment norms of publicity'.[86] The conception of family as a subaltern counter-public is a corollary of the feminist critique of the ideological construction of family as a private sphere in a manner that erases gendered patterns of intimate violence and of responsibility for care and other domestic work.

A different point emerges from Québec's interventions in Canadian child care policy debates. The constitutional position of Québec within the Canadian state as a separate province premised on Québec's historical, cultural and linguistic difference, has repeatedly posed challenges to efforts in Canada by feminists to mobilize broad-based support for pan-Canadian universal programmes, such as parental leave and child care, that are viewed as crucial to gender equality.[87] Québec's objection to national programmes is typically articulated in terms that view such programmes as simply another channel of Anglo-Canadian dominance, and that assert Québec's right—on constitutional, historical and cultural grounds—to self-government in areas of social policy. The jurisdictional argument is buttressed by the fact that, in the realm of social policy including that of support for families, Québec has generally been more generous than other Canadian jurisdictions.[88] Its record on child care provision is no exception.

However, Québec's insistence on its 'difference' has been pursued on terms that reflect the traditional project of the nation-state. In the child care arena, Québec instituted, in 1998, a provincial child care programme that provides, to all Québec residents, access to a high quality, affordable (currently seven dollars a day), publicly funded, non-parental centre-based child care, in short a 'universal' child care programme limited only by

in the family. However, it can also be seen as an argument for recognition of the quasi-public nature of religious community.

[86] Fraser (above n 64) 75. Iris Marion Young offers a similar argument in favour of a heterogenous public sphere that both relies on and is critical of Habermas. See IM Young, 'Impartiality and the Civic Public' in S Benhabib and D Cornell (eds), *Feminism as Critique* (Minneapolis MN, University of Minneapolis Press, 1987) 57–76. Young invokes the example of the 'linguistic and popular heterogeneity of the urban public' in 18th century Europe and America, a public she describes as 'wild, playful and sexy' where there was some mixing of sexes and classes. This 'wild public', she observes, did not survive the republican conception and institutionalization of a universalist state which 'reordered social life on a strict division of public and private'. *Ibid*, 64.

[87] G Calder, 'A Pregnant Pause: Federalism, Equality and the Maternity and Parental Leave Debate in Canada' (2006) 14 *Feminist Legal Studies* 99, 111–12, outlining the potential divide between feminists inside and outside of Québec over the nature of constitutional jurisdiction with respect to maternity and parental leave benefits delivered through an unemployment insurance regime.

[88] P Lefebvre, 'Quebec's Innovative Early Childhood Education and Care Policy and its Weaknesses' (March 2004) *Policy_Options* 53, at: www.irpp.org/po/archive/mar04/lefebvre.pdf.

Québec's territorial jurisdiction. While the Québec programme is enviable, preliminary assessments show that the programme, like other universal social programmes, has a clear middle-class bias. The 'one size fits all' approach means that 'parents working part-time or with non-standard hours and those with intermittent employment are excluded from the system'.[89] Not surprisingly then, several sets of data show that 'a very large majority of children in subsidized child-care services are from families in the upper income categories'.[90] In addition, 'socio-economically disadvantaged children are more likely to be cared for in poor quality services than are children from more affluent families'.[91] In other words, although Québec has consistently challenged Canada's assumption of a 'single comprehensive public sphere', it has deployed the very same assumption within its own territorial borders, reflecting what Fraser identifies as the original liberal ideal of the public as well as the homogenous nature of the 'imagined community' that underpins the nationalisms of Western liberal states more generally.[92] The functional reinforcement of systemic class and social divisions contradicts these dominant liberal narratives of inclusion and homogeneity. Nevertheless, Québec's clear identification of child care as a public responsibility and commitment to the ideal of universal access remains as the necessary, if not sufficient, condition of a more differentiated realization of that ideal, one that would more fully reflect the multiple subaltern publics within Québec society.

V. UNIVERSALITY'S 'SPATIAL LIMITS':[93] BORDERS, CITIZENSHIP AND FAMILY

A number of feminist activists and scholars have criticized the concept of universality in relation to social programmes by pointing out that the 'universal' has always evoked the deeply problematic figure of the citizen. Taking their cue from TH Marshall, universality advocates have typically sought to enhance the fundamental nature of certain entitlements by linking them to a theory of social citizenship. The concept of citizenship, however, comes laden with inherently exclusionary notions of membership in political community. While limits inherent in the nature of the benefit

[89] *Ibid*, 56.

[90] *Ibid*. Childcare Resource and Research Unit, *Trends and Analyses 2007: Early Childhood Education and Care in Canada 2006* (Toronto, 10 April 2008) 7, at: www.childcarecanada.org/pubs/other/TandA/Trends_Analysis07.pdf.

[91] P Lefebvre, 'Quebec's Innovative Early Childhood Education' (above n 88).

[92] Fraser, 'Transnationalizing the Public Sphere' (above n 67) 46.

[93] D Ferreira Da Silva, 'Toward a Critique of the Socio-Logos of Justice: the Analytics of Raciality and the Production of Universality' (2001) 7 *Social Identities* 421, quoted in Kapur (above n 66) 140.

may be unavoidable, limits that map over broader systemic patterns of marginalization and exclusion directly contradict and undermine the promise of inclusion associated with universality. For example, Canada's historical roots in white settler society, entailing both the colonization of indigenous peoples and the pursuit of explicitly racialized immigration policies, produced a national identity and set of citizenship practices that 'imagined' Canada as white.[94]

In Canada today, the overwhelming majority of immigrants are from Asia, Africa, the Middle East, and South and Central America, causing a demographic shift that challenges the imagined community of Anglo-European settlers underpinning the immigration laws and policies of the past.[95] The 'keep Canada white' immigration policies have been replaced today by more formal, neutral criteria as well as designations indicating levels of citizenship, such as citizen, permanent resident, refugee and visitor, and 'classes' of migrants, such as business- and family-class applicants, students, seasonal agricultural workers, live-in care-givers, tourists and guest workers. However, these more neutral categories often map over gendered, raced and colonial patterns of advantage and disadvantage. Thus even a robust conception of the welfare state and of social citizenship, when transposed onto the specific historical, material and social relations that underpin the development of the Canadian nation and its territorial jurisdiction, risks consolidating a fundamentally racialized and gendered global order.[96]

Ratna Kapur, borrowing from Denise Ferreira Da Silva, calls the contradictory character of universalist claims 'the other side of universality', arguing that 'assumptions about universality, neutrality and objectivity on which legal concepts are based' are 'products of the ruptures produced in and through colonial encounters'.[97] She points to the co-existence of European struggles for freedom and equality with European colonial endeavours and practices such as empire and slavery.[98] The current 'exclusion of the other from the project of universality', Kapur posits, is most visible at the borders of the nations that comprise 'the West', in particular in the legal construction of the transnational migrant subject, under both international and domestic laws.[99] However, examples abound of internal 'bordering' processes that reinforce broader gendered and racialized social relations.

[94] S Thobani, 'Nationalizing Canadians: Bordering Immigrant Women in the Twentieth Century' (2000) 12(2) *Canadian Journal of Women and the Law* 279.

[95] E Carasco et al, *Immigration and Refugee Law: Cases, Materials and Commentary* (Toronto, Emond Montgomery, 2007) 27.

[96] Thobani (above n 94) 290.

[97] R Kapur (above n 66) 139–40, citing Da Silva (above n 93) 422.

[98] *Ibid*, 137.

[99] *Ibid*, 139, 141.

For example, many universal programmes resort to concepts of residency rather than, or as an alternative to citizenship to more fully include persons who are functionally, if not formally, members of the political community. However, residency as a legal classification comes with its own gradations and levels. Some jurisdictions—the United States, Britain and other parts of Europe—have taken steps to pare back access to social provision by restricting it to citizens as of right and to those who have become naturalized or attained permanent status.[100] In Canada, similar differentiations can be found in Ontario's social assistance regime. Provisions in Ontario social assistance regulations from 1994 to 2001, automatically deducted CAN$100 from social assistance payments made to persons who had come to Canada as sponsored or family-class members under the immigration regime. Because most sponsored immigrants are women (and most female immigrants come to Canada by this route) such provisions have a gendered as well as racialized impact.[101] As a part of this trend, Ontario has also limited access to health care through a restrictive redefinition of residence and the imposition of waiting periods for eligibility, provisions that were unsuccessfully challenged under the Charter.[102] Audrey Macklin observes that 'the combined effect of immigration law and Ontario provincial social welfare legislation explicitly denies sponsored immigrants (many of whom are women) equal citizenship long after and despite the acquisition of legal citizenship'.[103]

The sponsorship undertaking set out in the Immigration and Refugee Protection Act[104] (IRPA) is central to the production of a gendered and racialized bordering process in Canada. The provisions allow Canadians and permanent residents to sponsor family members who seek permanent resident status without going through the regular admission process. According to its current terms, the sponsorship undertaking commits the sponsor to repay any social assistance that the sponsored applicant may collect in the first 10 years after landing.[105] As noted above, the sponsorship option is how most women immigrate to Canada. As such, it corrects what would otherwise be an immigration process that overwhelmingly favours men. However, while it might introduce more numerical equality in the gender composition of immigrant groups, the arrangement often enforces a

[100] TA Aleinikoff and D Klusmeyer, *Citizenship Policies for an Age of Migration* (Washington DC, Carnegie Endowment for Peace, 2002) 65–8.

[101] A Macklin, 'Public Entrance/Private Member' in B Cossman and J Fudge (eds), *Privatization, Law, and the Challenge of Feminism* (Toronto, University of Toronto Press, 2002) 241.

[102] *Ibid*, 245.

[103] *Ibid*, 245–6.

[104] Immigration and Refugee Protection Act (SC 2001, c 27).

[105] Immigration and Refugee Protection Regulations (SOR/2002-227) s 132(1)(b)(ii)(A). Social assistance recipients who are sponsored immigrants can also be subject to provincial rules that reduce their benefits on the basis that they are sponsored. Macklin (above n 101) 244–5, giving the example of Ontario.

relationship of dependency between (male) sponsors and (female) family-class migrants, rendering some women 'especially vulnerable to financial, physical, and sexual abuse from men who choose to exploit this imbalance of power'.[106] Thus, while imagining a more numerically balanced community with respect to gender for Canada, the sponsorship provisions also entrench substantively unequal, gendered power relations within that community.

Audrey Macklin emphasizes that the sponsorship undertaking is by no means a neo-liberal initiative but rather is firmly rooted in the consolidation of a Keynesian inspired notion of the Canadian welfare state in the post-war period. As she puts it, 'the more responsibility governments undertook to ensure the welfare of those over whom they exercised their authority, the greater the perceived need to narrowly circumscribe the social and geographical boundaries of eligibility for those benefits and perquisites'.[107] The dependency relations enforced by the sponsorship undertaking also fit comfortably with the assumption, central to the post-war welfare state in Canada (and often re-inscribed by neo-liberal reforms heavily inflected by socially conservative values) that women's economic security is best addressed through attachment to a male breadwinner.[108]

The terms of sponsorship set out in federal legislation also stipulate that persons in receipt of social assistance for a 'reason other than disability' cannot themselves act as sponsors.[109] Persons that seek to become sponsors are often immigrants themselves, attempting to assist family members to join them in Canada. In recent litigation challenging the social assistance bar on the basis of its inconsistency with constitutional equality rights, the Federal Court upheld the legislation, explaining that the restriction was an acceptable device for ensuring that the state reaps the economic benefits of immigration.[110]

The impacts on children of this 'bordering' process reveal the ease with which the privileges of full, formally recognized citizenship can be severely compromised in the name of ridding the nation of undesirable elements. Child citizens in jurisdictions such as Canada, the United States, Britain and other European countries, generally have difficulty asserting even the most basic entitlement of citizenship, namely the right of 'non-deportability' or to reside indefinitely in one's country of citizenship, in situations where

[106] Macklin (above n 101) 242.

[107] *Ibid*, 241–8. See also J Brodie (above n 24) 98, who notes that in the post-war period, 'social citizenship discourses were interwoven with an emerging narrative of pan-Canadian nationalism'.

[108] H Lessard, 'Charter Gridlock: Equality Formalism and Marriage Fundamentalism' in McIntyre and Rodgers (eds), *Diminishing Returns: Inequality and the Canadian Charter of Rights and Freedoms* (Markham, LexisNexis Butterworths, 2006) 313–14, discussing pension regulation.

[109] IRPA (above n 104) s 133(1).

[110] *Guzman v Canada*, 2006 FC 1134, 1135.

their parents lack full citizenship status.[111] As well the increasingly restricted access for non-citizens to social benefits often has discriminatory impacts on the citizen children who 'live within the same, typically constrained, family budget'.[112]

While Kapur posits the figure of the transnational migrant subject in order to expose the gendered and racialized character of conceptions of citizenship that are tightly bound to the territorial state, the interplay between social welfare and immigration regimes foregrounds the transnational migrant family. Jacqueline Bhabha observes:

> The assumption of a unitary family, all of whose members share the same nationality, live in the same country, travel together or following the male breadwinner, have the same short- or long-term interests, and have easy access to each other, is outmoded. It is disrupted by new patterns of mobility: wage earners, visitors, students, entrepreneurs who embark on transnational migration leaving family members behind; calamities of war, upheaval, persecution that destroy, separate, or disperse families; children born in host countries to parents with different nationalities and immigration statuses; settled immigrant situations disrupted by visa expiry, criminal conviction, family breakup, economic vulnerability.[113]

Rather than opening up legal and social spaces for transnational families, income assistance, immigration, family and child welfare regimes are more likely to subject such families to harsh discipline on the basis of the suspect or uncertain citizenship status of their members. The Canadian jurisprudence regarding sponsorship of adopted children who are members of the adoptive parent's extended family provides an example. The focus of much of the jurisprudence is on whether the adoption is 'genuine' or is instead, a 'sham', based on the desire to expand the educational and economic opportunities of the sponsored adopted child.[114] The normative family in these cases is constructed as emphatically nuclear, while attempts to remold cultural variants, such as extended familial networks of obligation, to fit into the dominant model are viewed sceptically as 'adoptions of convenience' and thus attempts to 'cheat' or break the rules.[115]

[111] J Bhabha, 'The Mere Fortuity of Birth? Are Children Citizens?' (2004) 15 *Differences: A Journal of Feminist Cultural Studies* 91, 94. For a Canadian example, see *Langner v Canada* (1995), 184 NR 230 (FCA).

[112] Aleinikoff and Klusmeyer (above n 100) 70. The authors observe that three-quarters of all children in immigrant families in the United States are US citizens.

[113] Bhabha, 'The Mere Fortuity of Birth' (above n 111) 96.

[114] See, eg, *Kwan v Canada* (2001) 17 Imm LR (3d) 167 (FCTD) in which the Court refused to overturn the decisions below rejecting the applicant's bid to adopt the daughter of his wife's cousin on the grounds that the parent child relationship between the child and the adoptive parents was not 'genuine': at 170–71 and 201.

[115] National Anti-Racism Council of Canada, *Racial Discrimination: The Status of Compliance by the Canadian Government with the International Convention on the Elimination of all Forms of Racial Discrimination* (2002) 36–8, at: www. narcc.ca/index.html. A cross-Canada survey conducted in 1998 found that only 3.6 per cent of child care centres

How would a child care programme that was inclusive of the transnational migrant and her family differ from one centred on families that more closely resemble the unitary, geographically stable nuclear family? Eligibility criteria and the substantive content of programmes are key mechanisms for 'bordering' child care and other benefit programmes. A glance at the current array of federal child care benefits in Canada, whether described as selective or universal, shows that some steps have been taken to recognize an array of different interests and social locations. By making child care benefits such as the UCCB available to 'residents' regardless of citizenship status, more families are included in the programme. In addition, the Canadian government acknowledges the need to channel resources into language programmes at child care centres aimed at recently immigrated children who lack fluency in either of the official languages, although programming in this regard is meagre.[116] The increased diversity of children, especially in large urban centres, also signals a need for programming that reflects and supports cultural and linguistic difference.[117] The shift of resources overall under the current Conservative government toward an individualized, market-based approach no doubt puts constraints on these efforts. Nevertheless, in our lexicon of social provision of child care there are institutional and practice elements already in place which reflect the contextual variety of needs at the community level and a fluid, less formal conception of political membership.

A more thoroughly inclusive approach would not only enlarge the dedication of resources to these commitments but also challenge the hiving off of immigration law, in particular deportation and sponsorship provisions, as well as social assistance, child welfare, employment and health care regimes, from child care regimes. The racialized and gendered 'bordering' practices that occur under these other regulatory systems not 'only directly shape access to "universal" programmes but also differentially shape child care needs and priorities'.[118] Ultimately, however, the 'softening' of borders

offered English or French second language training while '40.1% of centres had at least one child whose first language was neither English nor French'. G Doherty et al, *You Bet I Care! A Canada Wide Study on: Wages, Working Conditions, and Practices in Child Care Centres* (Guelph, Centre for Families, Work and Well Being, University of Guelph, 2000) 121.

[116] OECD Directorate for Education, *Organization of Early Childhood Education and Care Policy: Canada: Country Note* (2004) 22, at: www.hrsdc.gc.ca/en/cs/sp/sdc/socpol/publications/reports/2004-002619/page00.shtml.

[117] M Friendly, *Canadian Early Learning and Child Care and the Convention on the Rights of the Child* (Toronto, Child Care Resource and Research Unit, University of Toronto, 2006) 5, notes that '50% of kindergarteners in some classes in Toronto, Vancouver, and Montreal were born outside Canada or are from recently immigrated families'.

[118] GE Galabuzzi, *Canada's Economic Apartheid: The Social Exclusion of Racialized Groups in the New Century* (Toronto, Canadian Scholar's Press, 2006) 188 discusses generally the way in which high levels of residential segregation experienced by racialized groups and immigrants impedes access to 'civil services like education, health care, and recreational services'.

challenges at a fundamental level, not only our assumptions about who is entitled to public goods and protection, but also about who is entitled to a political voice in their design and allocation and what is required to make that voice meaningful.[119] In the next and concluding section, I further explore this question and its relation to debates about universality. In particular, I examine the argument that while universal programmes represent a crucial commitment to redistributive justice, they need to be realized through institutional practices and structures aimed not only at recognition of difference but also at creating political space for representation with respect to the substantive nature and content of the programme itself.

In sum, the interplay between immigration and social welfare regimes makes it clear that different levels of membership within liberal societies such as Canada have, indeed are expected to have, material and social consequences and to differentially shape individual relations to the state and to state benefits in more than simply formal ways. While I do not mean to suggest that any spatial limits on public responsibility for social provision or any requirements of 'territorial belonging'[120] are unacceptable, I do want to argue that when those limits or requirements continue to reproduce material, gendered, racial and other cross-global as well as internal patterns of inequality under the rubric of 'universality', we need to probe more deeply the conceptual and ideological dimensions of the language of universality as well as the institutional arrangements for social provision that are too easily equated with universality.

VI. CONCLUSION: FORMAL OR SUBSTANTIVE UNIVERSALITY AND THE PROBLEM OF POLITICAL AGENCY

The project of reconceptualizing universality in a way that preserves its commitment to redistributive justice and radical inclusion while at the same time opening up rather than shutting down space for difference, has a parallel in the feminist project of reconceptualizing equality. Formal equality, like universality, signals radical, infinitely expandable inclusion, a commitment to everyone's shared humanity. As such it is fundamentally liberating at the level of principle but fundamentally exclusionary at the level of application. By emphasizing our shared humanity, formal equality constructs us as interchangeable persons, rendering irrelevant to the equality calculus,

[119] See J Mostov, 'Soft Borders and Transnational Citizens' in Benhabib et al (eds), *Identities, Affiliations, and Allegiances* (Cambridge, Cambridge University Press, 2007) for the implications of the 'softening' of borders in Europe for the allocation of public goods and the recognition of interdependencies and multiple, overlapping attachments.

[120] Bhabha (above n 111) 93 uses this term to describe the normative core of the legal conception of citizenship.

the material conditions, practices, structures, attributes and attitudes that entrench socially experienced inequalities.

Universalism in the realm of social and economic benefits seems to move beyond the 'formal' in formal equality by giving material content and support to the core commitment to every person's humanity, prompting one theorist to argue that universal social rights are an oxymoron—that social rights by definition respond to socio-economic difference through redistributive measures calibrated to redress difference.[121] In other words, social rights and entitlements—as some of the critics of universality from the progressive side of the political spectrum argue—are properly selective. Selectivity in this approach, however, has been disentangled from its association with a residual conception of the state's role in relation to social well-being. The latter conception, while tolerating minimal amounts of material support in the form of publicly-funded social benefits, is deeply and philosophically opposed to redistribution. Rather, selectivity is being used here almost tongue in cheek, to signify the necessity in any seriously redistributive initiative to develop nuanced responses to the particularities and diversity of human needs.

Universality in social provision, conversely, is associated with a robust commitment to redistribution. Nevertheless, as explained in the two previous sections of this chapter, despite the redistributive character of universal social programmes and their rhetorical commitment to 'all', the presumption of sameness underlying universalism often contradicts and undermines its radically inclusive promise. Sheila Shaver calls this the tension 'between the status content of citizenship and the substantive content of social rights'.[122] In short, the presumption of sameness underpinning formal citizenship status obscures, erases and ignores the social, economic and cultural differences that both legitimize and maintain exclusion on the one hand, and that sustain and texture community, social relations and identities on the other. The transnational subject and her family bring into focus the link between these internal stratifications and differences and global patterns of inequality. The experience of social provision by transnational migrants and their families is often simply one dimension of their formal and functional exclusion from the deliberative processes—such as voting, political candidacy, participation in mainstream civil society institutions—of the official public sphere of the polities within which they reside, work and parent.[123]

Feminist theories of substantive equality provide a potentially rich source for rethinking universality without rejecting it altogether. Such theories challenge the sameness principle and reject rigidly comparative approaches.

[121] Barbelet, *Citizenship* (above n 12) 67–72.

[122] Shaver, *Universality and Selectivity in Income Support* (above n 9) 12.

[123] Aleinikoff and Klusmeyer, *Citizenship Policies for an Age of Migration* (above n 100) 43–60.

The latter measure equality in relation to unstated norms which implicitly privilege dominant perspectives and needs. Substantive equality theories, in contrast, aspire to give material content to equality claims, often described as social equality or equality of outcomes or results.[124] Thus the 'substantive' in feminist substantive equality theories, has come to signify at least two important features: a redistributive element and an attention to historically and socially-mediated differences.

A substantive conception of universality might similarly carefully distinguish between the powerful liberal principle of a shared humanity underpinning both formal equality and universality, and the inherent and intractable complexity of social and political relations, especially in deeply stratified societies and in the context of populations and issues that can no longer be contained within the Westphalian frame of the nation state. In short, we need to develop a conception of substantive universality that retains the commitment to redistribution associated with universal social provision while at the same time foregrounding difference across social, cultural and economic locations. The way that conceptions of substantive equality directly engage with the inherent and ever-shifting complexity of social and political relations provides a model here. Indeed, shorn of the institutional, material, and ideological constraints that inevitably constrain any conception of equality in the legal rights arena, a more explicitly substantive conception of universality in relation to social provision might open up greater political space for the institutional variety and normative pluralism required of any truly 'substantive' approach.

However, the language of 'difference' and 'context', like the language of universality, is itself detachable from the specific context of political relations and therefore can easily be manipulated. Thus a concept of universality would, reflecting Fraser's recently updated conception of justice, require attention to a third dimension. The hidden and not so hidden 'bordering' processes that underpin many universal and selective approaches to social provision point to what Fraser identifies as the injustice of misrepresentation, in particular, the 'misframing' of the political community which occurs when 'the community's boundaries are drawn in such a way as to wrongly exclude some people from the chance to participate *at all* in its authorized contests over justice'.[125] As she puts it, '[c]onstituting both members and non-members in a single stroke, this [frame-setting] decision effectively excludes the latter from the universe of those entitled to consideration within the community in matters of distribution, recognition, and ordinary-political representation'.[126]

[124] NC Sheppard, 'Equality, Ideology and Oppression: Women and the *Canadian Charter of Rights and Freedoms*' (1986) 28 *Dalhousie Law Journal* 195, 218.

[125] Fraser (above n 68) 76.

[126] *Ibid*, 77.

Fraser's argument, however, is driven by her concern about the largely formal exclusions that occur as a result of the increasing gradations of membership in Western liberal democracies, aimed at maintaining the borders on which state territorial jurisdiction is founded. Wendy McKeen and Ann Porter raise similar concerns with respect to the political agency of persons who, although they may be full members of society in formal legal terms, face institutional and structural barriers to full participation in society. In reflecting on the feminist literature about the nature and development of the welfare state, particularly in light of recent neo-liberal shifts, they argue that it is insufficient to analyze welfare state developments simply in terms of the relations between states, markets and families. Rather they urge that feminists working in this area need first, to develop a lens that measures the ability 'to create the networks of support that can provide a sense of community and reduce the isolation' that so often accompanies social reproductive work.[127] Secondly, they argue that we need not only material resources and opportunities to care and care for, but also 'to have a political voice that helps shape the policies that govern us'.[128] Both of these elements point to a focus on political agency that the authors argue must be more centrally located within the models and frameworks used to assess welfare state developments. Thus, in terms of recent changes to federal child care policy, not only is the increased poverty flowing from restructuring important to highlight, but also the reduction of potential political spaces and networks facilitated by community-based public providers of goods in kind rather than in cash.[129] Social provision 'in cash' rather than in kind, as in the example of the delivery of child care benefits through tax regimes, shuts down or 'privatizes' those potentially political spaces and erases the political nature of the provider/provided for relationship underpinning benefit programmes.[130] While the dismantled Liberal plan to transfer resources into government hands for the expansion of early learning and childhood development programmes may have simply expanded the apparatus of surveillance aimed at children at risk and deficient parents, it at least took the first step of marking out a public institutional space at the community level. Such public spaces and nodes of social connection are potentially political spaces and nodes of political connection and coalition for marginal actors and voices. From these concrete places, one can at least imagine the

[127] W McKeen and A Porter, 'Politics and Transformation' in L Vosko and W Clements (eds), *Changing Canada: Political Economy as Transformation* (Montreal, McGill-Queen's University Press, 2003) 113.

[128] *Ibid*.

[129] *Ibid*, 119–22.

[130] The issue of delivery of benefits 'in cash' or in kind raises complex issues for social justice, feminist, and anti-poverty advocates. For a more extended discussion than I am able to provide here, see M Young, 'A Guaranteed Annual Income and Canadian Women' 23 May 2007, draft chapter on file with author.

transformative politics that McKeen and Porter urge and the 'authorized contests over justice' which Fraser envisions. Within the space of the community child care centre, one can at least take the first steps to challenge and contest the substantive content and scope of child care provision.[131]

There is no quick and easy path to the democratization of what Fraser calls frame-setting in a globalizing context. Indeed her rejection of the formal apparatus of citizenship concepts tied to exclusionary conceptions of the nation state and its territorial jurisdiction begs the question of how one navigates a wider, open-ended, more institutionally variegated, and less bordered and territorially constrained vision of democratic politics. Fraser herself argues that a starting point would be to supplement the Westphalian state-territorial principle for the demarcation of community with the 'all-affected principle' that looks not for 'geographical proximity' but for 'co-imbrication in a common structural or institutional framework' as the basis for determining who has standing as a subject of justice and politics.[132] Julie Mostov emphasizes 'a common present and a potentially common future' rather than 'long shared histories or deep cultural ties' as the ground for the politics of 'public goods'.[133] John Borrows, writing from an indigenous perspective, sees territory playing a transforming rather than restrictive role in giving content to a conception of citizenship that embraces indigenous relationships with land without denying the 'hybridity, displacement, and positive potential of our widening circles'.[134] All of these approaches offer glimpses of a different kind of politics of social provision than that provided by either the Keynesian-Westphalian frame or the increasingly dominant neo-liberal frame which accords a more flexible, global conception of citizenship only to capital. However, the starting point for such a politics should be a substantive conception of universality in social provision that would bring together the three elements—redistribution, recognition and representation—identified by Fraser as key dimensions of justice. The latter representational element, however, not only makes sharply visible and open to contest the framing of the community that stands behind and gives content and shape to any 'universal' social programme, but also requires more attention to the institutional and spatial elements that underpin such political engagement.

[131] See, eg, S Prentice, 'The Case of Community-Governed Child Care Services' and P Milton, 'Education and Child Care: confronting new realities' both in G Cleveland and M Krashinsky (eds), *Our Children's Future: Child Care Policy in Canada* (Toronto, University of Toronto Press, 2001).

[132] Fraser (above n 68) 82. See also C Maier, '"Being There": Place, Territory, and Identity' in Benhabib et al (eds), *Identities, Affiliations, and Allegiances* (Cambridge, Cambridge University Press, 2007) 67–84, who explores how difficult it is to disentangle community identities from space, place, and territory.

[133] Mostov (above n 119) 141.

[134] J Borrows, *Recovering Canada: The Resurgence of Indigenous Law* (Toronto, University of Toronto Press, 2002) 145.

10

*Women's Work and a Guaranteed Income**

MARGOT YOUNG

I. INTRODUCTION

THE IDEA OF a guaranteed income has been a topic of some currency for a number of decades within the Canadian feminist community. In 1970 the Royal Commission on the Status of Women recommended payment of a guaranteed annual income by the federal government to the head of all one-parent families as one way to address women's persistent poverty.[1] More recently, a number of feminist academics and activists have issued clear calls for implementation of a 'guaranteed adequate income'. In 2004, a group of scholars and activists released the *Pictou Statement*, a short manifesto stating, among other things: 'Women demand an indexed guaranteed living income for all individual residents set at a level to enable comfortable living'.[2] In 2006, the Victoria, British Columbia-based Women's Livable Income Working Group published a study funded by Status of Women Canada entitled *Women's Economic Justice Report on Guaranteed Livable Income.*[3] This report, a compendium of testimony in wide-ranging favour of a guaranteed income, speaks strongly and passionately for a guaranteed livable income.

* An earlier version of this chapter is forthcoming in M Cohen and J Pulkingham (eds), *Public Policy for Women: The State, Income Security and Labour Market Issues* (Toronto, University of Toronto Press, 2009). Thanks are due to Dorothy Chunn and Shelley Gavigan for their thoughtful oversight of this chapter. Funding for the research on this chapter was gratefully received from the Social Science and Humanities Research Council of Canada, Community University Research Alliance programme in connection with the Economic Security Project.

[1] Royal Commission on the Status of Women in Canada, *Report* (Ottawa, Information Canada, 1970) 325.

[2] L Lakeman, A Miles and L Christiansen-Ruffman, 'Pictou Statement: Feminist Statement on Guaranteed Living Income' (2004) 23 *Canadian Woman Studies Journal* 204.

[3] Women's Livable Income Working Group, *Women's Economic Justice Project: An Examination of How Women Would Benefit From a Guaranteed Livable Income* (Victoria, Victoria Status of Women Action Group, 2006).

But the feminist community is not of one mind on the call for a guaranteed income. Opposition to this idea also has strong heritage in Canadian feminist thought, particularly in response to the concrete guaranteed income proposals that have issued from more mainstream or right-of-centre organizations over the last 30 years or so. Feminist commentaries on the Macdonald and Forget commissions'[4] proposals for variants of a guaranteed annual income, for instance, were critical of the family orientation of proposed guaranteed annual income plans and of the balance of benefits these plans would bring about. In 1987, in a representative article entitled: 'A Good Idea Goes Bad: Guaranteed Income or Guaranteed Poverty?', Marjorie Cohen castigated the range of guaranteed income proposals in circulation at that time as dangerous sell-outs—intentionally or naively—to business and market forces.[5] Today, feminist politics on the issue remains split: many see a guaranteed income as essential to addressing women's poverty while others raise suspicions about why, given current ascendant neo-liberal politics, there is a resurgence in calls—nationally and internationally—for a guaranteed income.

This discussion between feminists needs to become an important part of the overall debate. Feminist appreciation of the specific income security needs of women, and of particular groups of women, has much to add to consideration of guaranteed income proposals. Feminist analyses of marriage, of employment, and of citizenship, for example, lend valuable and considerable insight into the dynamics and issues relevant to income security reform.[6]

The discussion that follows has several distinct parts. It begins, in section II, with a brief reminder of the disproportionate poverty Canadian women experience and of some of the critical features of women's reliance on current provincial social assistance (welfare) systems. That section is followed in section III by an overview of the idea of a guaranteed income, at least as this chapter uses that notion in the analysis that follows. The lengthiest section, section IV sets out the advantages and disadvantages of guaranteed income proposals in relation to women, with a specific focus on the issue of work and its place in welfare reform politics from a feminist perspective. Finally, section V provides an assessment of some aspects of the practical viability of a guaranteed income, and concludes with articulation of a particular understanding of guaranteed income proposals that, while sure not

[4] Royal Commission on the Economic Union and Development Prospects for Canada (Macdonald Commission), *Report*, 3 vols (Ottawa, Minister of Supply and Services Canada, 1985); Commission of Inquiry on Unemployment Insurance, *Report* (Ottawa, Minister of Supply and Services Canada, 1986).

[5] M Cohen, 'A Good Idea Goes Bad: Guaranteed Income or Guaranteed Poverty?' (1987) 21 *This Magazine* 19.

[6] C Pateman, 'Democratizing Citizenship: Some Advantages of a Basic Income' (2004) 32 *Politics and Society* 89.

to please the strongest advocates, nonetheless lays claim to what I believe is most progressive and powerful about the notion of a guaranteed income.

II. WOMEN'S POVERTY IN CANADA

Like the United States, Canada 'discovered' post-war poverty in the late 1960s. Today, despite being one of the richest nations in the world, Canada remains a country with a poverty rate that is unacceptably high, particularly for certain groups of people.[7] We are also a nation increasingly characterized by deep income and wealth inequality.[8] The concentration of incomes and wealth at the very top of the distributional curve is growing dramatically. In 2007, the richest 10 per cent made 82 times more than the poorest 10 per cent. In 1976, those at the top made 32 times more.[9] Our society is thus increasingly composed of two groups: distributional winners and losers. Those at the bottom are disproportionately immigrant families, lone mothers, younger households, unemployed and work-poor households.[10] These individuals and their families face very real struggles to make ends meet.[11]

The economic and political restructuring that is responsible for this growth in income and wealth inequality, and that marked neo-liberalism's arrival on the Canadian scene, has not been gender-neutral in impact. Women have disproportionately experienced increased and more severe poverty (particularly in female-headed households), seen their consumption curtailed and workloads increased as a result of loss of household income, been most directly affected by cuts to social services spending, and seen reductions in quality and conditions of paid employment options in both the private and public sectors.[12] The simple and clear outcome is that progress towards gender equality has been significantly stalled.

[7] The National Council of Welfare recently wrote that 'Canada has a poverty problem' National Council of Welfare, 'Solving Poverty: Four Cornerstones of a Workable National Strategy for Canada' (2007) 126 *National Council of Welfare Reports* iii.

[8] A Yalnizyan, *The Rich and the Rest of Us: The Changing Face of Canada's Growing Gap* (Toronto, Canadian Centre for Policy Alternatives, 2007); Canadian Centre for Policy Alternatives, *Growing Gap, Growing Concern: Canadian Attitudes Towards Income Inequality* (Toronto, Canadian Centre for Policy Alternatives, 2006); M Lee, *New Perspectives on Income Inequality in B.C.* (Vancouver, Canadian Centre for Policy Alternatives (BC Office), 2004).

[9] T Hennessy, 'Foreword' in Hennessy, *Why Inequality Matters, In 1000 Words or Less* (Toronto, Canadian Centre for Policy Alternatives, 2007).

[10] G Esping-Anderson, 'Households, Families and Children' (Paper presented to the RC 19 Annual Conference 'Old and New Social Inequalities: What Challenges for the Welfare States?', delivered at the International Sociological Association (ISA) Oviedo, Spain, 7–9 September 2001) unpublished, on file with author.

[11] Hennessy, *Why Inequality Matters* (above n 10) 5.

[12] J Brodie, *Politics on the Margins: Restructuring and the Canadian Women's Movement* (Halifax NS, Fernwood Publishing, 1995).

Nowhere is this more evident than in low-income or poverty statistics. In 2003, 53 per cent of low-income Canadians were female.[13] Unattached women, Aboriginal women, immigrant women, women with disabilities, senior women and women of colour are also disproportionately poor, both when compared to other Canadian women, and to their male counterparts.[14] For example, in 2003, 36 per cent of Aboriginal women, 23 per cent of immigrant women, 29 per cent of women of colour, and 26 per cent of women with disabilities lived in poverty.[15] As well, 19 per cent of senior women were poor.[16] In 2003, 38 per cent of Canadian families headed by sole-parent mothers had incomes that fell below Statistics Canada's after-tax 'Low Income Cut-offs', compared to 13 per cent of families headed by sole-parent fathers and just seven per cent of non-elderly two-parent families with children.[17] Many of these groups intersect: for instance, Aboriginal and African-Canadian women are more likely to be lone parents.

The situation in Canada has attracted international criticism. In January 2003, the Committee on the Elimination of Discrimination against Women conducted its fifth periodic review of Canada under the United Nations Convention on the Elimination of All Forms of Discrimination against Women.[18] In its concluding comments, the Committee expressed astonishment about 'the high percentage of women living in poverty'.[19] A similar statement was made in 2006 by the United Nations Committee on Economic, Social and Cultural Rights.[20]

Consistent with other chapters in this Part, this chapter's consideration of a guaranteed income pays particular attention to women with the highest rate of low-income status: lone mothers. While certainly not a new phenomenon, lone-mother-led families are an increasingly common and unexceptional family form. In 2001, there were 1,311,190 lone-parent families in Canada (15.6 per cent of all families), of which 81.3 per cent

[13] Statistics Canada, *Women in Canada 2005: A Gender-based Statistical Report* (Ottawa, 2005).

[14] *Ibid.*

[15] *Ibid.*

[16] *Ibid.*

[17] The figure of 38% represents the numbers across Canada. It is higher, however, in some regions. Notably, in 2004 British Columbia had a rate of poverty for lone-mother-led families of 49%, a considerably higher figure: J Pulkingham, 'Bucking the National Trend: Poverty among Lone Mothers' (2006) 9(3) *Canadian Centre for Policy Alternatives BC Commentary* 5.

[18] Convention on the Elimination of All Forms of Discrimination against Women (CEDAW) (adopted 18 December 1979, entered into force 3 September 1981) 1249 UNTS 13.

[19] UN Committee on the Elimination of Discrimination against Women, *Report of the Committee on the Elimination of Discrimination against Women*, 28th Session (13–31 January 2003) and 29th Session (30 June–18 July 2003) UN Doc A/58/38 (Supplement no 38) para 257.

[20] UN Committee on Economic Social and Cultural Rights, *Consideration of Reports Submitted by States Parties under Articles 16 and 17 of the Covenant*, 36th Session (1–19 May 2006), UN Doc E/C. 12/CAN/CO/4, E/C 12/CAN/CO/5 para 15.

were lone-mother-led households.[21] Divorce, or relationship breakdown, is the main reason for the incidence of lone-mother families.[22] While these numbers reflect a series of evolving norms in Canadian society, they also represent a hard-fought victory for women to be able to choose their sexual and life partners, and to choose whether or not they will raise their children in a conjugal relationship with another parent. A woman's ability to parent outside a traditional family form is a necessary freedom in any society that lays claim to basic respect for women's equality.

Yet, families headed by lone mothers have by far the lowest income of all family types: their income is 38 per cent of the average income for non-elderly two-spouse families with children and less than 60 per cent of the average income of lone-parent families headed by men.[23] Between 2001 and 2003, the average income of lone-mother families dropped, while the average income of other family types rose.[24]

There are good reasons for using the needs and circumstances of lone mothers as a context for thinking about guaranteed income. First, this group implicates key foci of gender analysis—family formation, division of labour, assumptions of dependency and independence—that are critical to policy discussions.[25] Secondly, lone mothers really are among the poorest of the poor in Canada, so solutions to poverty must take their needs into account. Thirdly, renewed calls for what is being called a guaranteed livable income are coming from feminist grassroots organizations for which lone-mother-led families are paradigmatic of those in need of the benefit.[26] And, fourthly, the circumstances of these women and their families, because these families disproportionately must rely on social assistance schemes, illustrate the problems with the current income support system, not the least of which is a benefit level that is grossly and cruelly inadequate.

A. Lone Mothers and the Current Welfare System

Welfare typically is formally conceived of as a programme of last resort—a safety-net for those individuals whose basic needs are not met by individual or family personal wealth, earned income from the paid labour force or some other government programme. In practice, of course, this far understates

[21] Canadian Council on Social Development, *CCSD's Stats and Facts: Families: A Profile of Canadian Families*, at: www.ccsd.ca/factsheets/family/index.htm.

[22] National Council of Welfare, *Poverty Profile, 2001* (Ottawa, Minister of Public Works and Government Services Canada, 2004).

[23] Statistics Canada, *Women in Canada 2005* (above n 14).

[24] *Ibid.*

[25] W McKeen, *Money in Their Own Name: The Feminist Voice in Poverty Debate in Canada 1970–1995* (Toronto, University of Toronto Press, 2004).

[26] Women's Livable Income Group, *Women's Economic Justice* (above n 4).

the central role welfare has come to play. In 2003, point-in-time numbers showed that 1.7 million children, women and men (5.5 per cent of the population) were on social assistance in Canada.[27]

Welfare programmes, which are provincially based, are plagued by inadequate benefit provision, unfair and unduly difficult access to benefits, stigma and illegitimacy, punitive and coercive treatment of applicants and recipients, and unnecessary complexity and lack of transparency.[28] Details of provincial welfare plans as they pertain to lone-mother families show that two phenomena are particularly striking. First, benefits levels are set so as to insure that lone-mother families reliant on welfare remain the poorest among the poor. For example, in British Columbia (BC), the monthly income on provincial welfare for a Vancouver family with one adult and two children over five is CAN$1623.82 as of April 2007. This figure reflects all available income, including the base welfare rate of CAN$1036, tax credits and benefits, and the National Child Benefit. This (even recently raised) rate amounts to just 74 per cent of the 2005 Statistics Canada's after-tax Low Income Cut-Off for this same family.[29] Indeed, the Dietitians of Canada have regularly noted that welfare rates in BC fail to provide an income adequate for core nutritional needs.[30]

Secondly, the rules that structure these families' eligibility for income support and related benefits are, in most provinces, strikingly inconsistent with basic values asserted elsewhere in our political and social system. Rhetoric, both governmental and private, abounds about the central social importance and sanctity of the family, of children, and of meaningful employment. Yet, social assistance programmes, as they relate to lone-mother families, stand in sharp contradiction to these professed values. Welfare programmes ensure that children of these families face malnutrition, inadequate child

[27] K Battle, M Mendelson and S Torjman, *Towards a New Architecture for Canada's Adult Benefits* (Ottawa, Caledon Institute of Social Policy, 2006).

[28] *Ibid.*

[29] Canada has no official poverty line. Statistics Canada's 'low-income cut-offs' are one of the most widely used measures of low income. These figures, generated by Statistics Canada, vary by household size and area of residence population. Statistics Canada defines a low-income household as one that spends a disproportionate amount on basic necessities—food, shelter and clothing. Low-income cut-offs are generated using either pre- or post-tax income.

[30] Dietitians of Canada, *Cost of Eating in British Columbia: Annual Report 2006* (Vancouver, 2006). Anecdotal reports also reveal that many women on income assistance are forced, by the inadequacy of that assistance, into violent and degrading situations. Reports out of both Ontario and British Columbia tell us that the economic insecurity characteristic of welfare receipt forces women to stay within or go back into abusive relationships. Simply put, poverty ensures that women remain or become vulnerable to violence in their intimate relationships. Further, some women on welfare reveal in a recent BC study that they have been force to trade sex for money in order to feed themselves and their families (J Mosher et al, *Walking on Eggshells: Abused Women's Experiences of Ontario's Welfare System* (Ontario, Women and Abuse Welfare Research Project, 2004); S Klein and J Pulkingham, *Living on Welfare in BC: Experiences of Longer-Term 'Expected to Work' Recipients* (Vancouver, Canadian Centre for Policy Alternatives BC and 'Raise the Rates', 2008) 11.

care and substandard housing. And the mothers, forced to take available work as soon as their youngest child turns, for example, three years (in British Columbia) or even one year (in Alberta), have limited opportunities for combining meaningful employment or training with their care responsibilities.

The best one can say about current welfare provision is that it is geared for short-term alleviation of the worst effects of poverty for these women. It is true that the existing welfare state, to the extent that it gives some women some economic independence from patriarchal relations within the family, has emancipatory effects.[31] But, welfare provisions remain shaped by the goal of 're-inserting' women into those institutions—the market and the nuclear family—that are most ill-suited for these women and their families' current needs and circumstances.[32]

A number of recent reports examining Canada's income security system from a range of perspectives all agree that the system is a failed one. No one defends the current mix and character of programmes. But the problems are cast widely and the solutions all over the political map.[33] It is not surprising that alternative and novel forms of collective economic provision for the most vulnerable among us are tremendously appealing and that the task of re-imagining our income security system has such take up. Current policy proposals promise to cut through the dilemmas of welfare—and, leading the pack—if volume of argument is any guide—is the raft of proposals for a guaranteed income.

III. A GENERAL MODEL OF A GUARANTEED INCOME

This paper uses the term 'guaranteed income' for the policy proposal under study. Commentators name their guaranteed income proposals variously—'guaranteed annual income', 'negative income tax', 'citizen's income', 'basic income', 'social wage' and 'social dividend'—but what matters are the details of any one proposal, not simply its formal terminology. The idea of some form of guaranteed income, funded by the state, paid to individuals or households on a regular basis, has adherents across the political spectrum. What one commentator proposes under the rubric of a guaranteed income can have very different ideological roots and practical outcomes

[31] F Fox Piven, 'Ideology and the State: Women, Power and the Welfare State' in L Gordon (ed), *Women, the State and Welfare* (Madison WN, University of Wisconsin Press, 1990).

[32] A McKay, *The Future of Social Security Policy: Women, Work and a Citizens' Basic Income* (London, Routledge, 2005) 87.

[33] A report from the Caledon Institute of Social Policy, for instance, calls for 'a new "architecture" of social policy for the twenty-first century': Battle et al (above n 28) 1. And, the National Council of Welfare notes that 'income irregularity is increasing and for most Canadians income security is decreasing. Our many programs have become a tattered patchwork': *Solving Poverty* (above n 8) 1.

than another commentator's version. Thus the details of any proposal are critical. And, the debate among advocates of guaranteed income is fierce over the specifics of income level, programme delivery, programme implementation, and so on.

This chapter relies on a simple, but strong version of a guaranteed income: the provision of an adequate floor income provided on a continuing and regular basis, regardless of work involvement, to all members of society. The benefit would be financed through general state revenue funds, delivered by the national government directly to all resident in Canada.[34] Not coincidentally, this is the version of guaranteed income most like the reform currently advocated by a number of grassroots Canadian women's groups.[35]

The key distinguishing characteristics of this model of guaranteed income (and indeed of most models) are universality and unconditionality. As a universally granted benefit, the income would be equally available to every individual adult member of society. Such a benefit is contrasted with targeted or means-tested benefits which selectively deliver benefits to a more narrowly defined sub-group on the basis of some characteristic, say, income level. The only distinguishing trait of those in receipt of a universal guaranteed income would be age (adulthood), although the benefit could be extended (probably at a lower level) to children.

Payment of a guaranteed income could be made either to households or to individuals, or to both at different levels. An analysis sensitive to the gender politics of households, and to the regulatory and disciplinary impact of state designation of household status, urges payment to individuals, regardless of individual living arrangements. (Of course, choice of the individual, not the household, as the benefit unit leaves unaddressed concerns about the economies of scale achieved by larger households composed of several benefit recipients.)

As an unconditional grant, the benefit payment is made regardless of the kind of administrative or behavioural conditions currently in vogue in Canadian welfare regimes. Such concerns as how the money is spent, how a recipient's time is spent, the co-habitation patterns of recipients, recipient reporting, programme attendance, or availability for supervisory visits, and so on are all irrelevant to continued receipt of the full benefit.

The impact of these two features of a guaranteed income—its universality and its unconditionality—is to make a core level of financial capacity a basic entitlement of membership in Canadian society. Thus a guaranteed income can be understood as a right of citizenship, as central to economic or social citizenship as the right to vote is to political citizenship.

[34] Most advocates argue that a guaranteed income should not be taxed, although a variety of different tax schemes are proposed for income earned on top of the guaranteed income. I leave these delivery details for another time.

[35] Lakeman et al, 'Pictou Statement' (above n 3); Women's Livable Income (above n 4).

Of course, much hinges on what is encompassed by the notion of adequacy. The question inevitably involves consideration of various poverty lines and ideally calculation by some reasonable and humane method of a minimum livable income. The range of proposed income levels—when commentators get sufficiently concrete enough to specify benefit levels (and most do not)—is significant. For example, the Macdonald Commission recommended in its 1986 Report an income of roughly one-third of the poverty line.[36] Senator Hugh Segal, a member of the Canadian Conservative Party and a current advocate of a variant of guaranteed income, recently advocated a level of CAN$3,000 over the Statistics Canada's Low-Income Cut-Offs.[37] This chapter proceeds with a more general formula: that of a guaranteed income paid at a level sufficient to satisfy basic needs and to allow a degree of meaningful social inclusion. Thus, my model for discussion of a guaranteed income is more generous than many actually proposed.

The following sections of this chapter undertake an overview of some of the attractions and disadvantages of a guaranteed income from a perspective that is sensitive to feminist concerns around paid and unpaid work, the gendered division of care-giving, and the split between public and private spheres of responsibility more generally. The purpose, then, is to map out broadly those arguments most referenced in the feminist debate over guaranteed income policy. The overview does not, for example, engage fully in arguments about impact on the labour market or economic incentive structures. But it does focus on the issues that emerge perennially around discussions of women, care-giving, and work.

IV. A FEMINIST APPRAISAL

A. Why Feminists Might Like a Guaranteed Income

The attraction of a guaranteed income is immediately obvious. A guaranteed income, set at an adequate level, offers to significantly reduce poverty. It promises more equal sharing of society's resources by redistributing resources to those least well-off.[38] Receipt of a regular, unconditional income would go far in addressing the current material and social deprivation of low-income Canadians and low-income Canadian families. The result, all other things remaining equal, could be a fairer and more equitable society, a political community that delivered substantively on a promise of social citizenship.

[36] Macdonald Commission (above n 5).

[37] Comments made by Senator Hugh Segal, World Congress on Basic Income (Dublin, 20–21 June 2008).

[38] R Theobald, *Free Men and Free Markets* (New York, Anchor Books, 1965).

More specific benefits follow from a guaranteed income's features of universality and conditionality. As a universal payment, a guaranteed income renders irrelevant a significant number of problems faced by targeted or means-tested programmes. Universal benefits reduce the stigma of receipt and, some argue, promote social cohesion by minimizing social stratification generated by selective benefit receipt and dependence. Universal programmes are typically cheaper to administer, more efficient, less intrusive, and, arguably, encourage broad middle-class support for the benefit.[39]

A guaranteed income also has a potential advantage of great importance to low-income women. The benefit, if payable to the individual, holds out a promise of freeing some women from a great deal of the worst and most coercive aspects of their intimate economic relations with men. Women and mothers, in particular, are potentially cast as independent economic agents, at least in the terms specific to benefits eligibility and delivery. Adoption of a guaranteed income could then communicate a particular positive set of ideas about women's economic citizenship and about social organization generally.[40] On a practical level, as a universal benefit, and if set at an adequate level, a guaranteed income would protect women somewhat from economic coercion to stay with abusive partners[41] and from 'survival sex', that is, involvement in the sex trade as a means to generate an income. It would also enable women to feed, clothe and house themselves and their families more adequately and reliably.

As an unconditional grant, the most signal feature of a guaranteed income is that it breaks the long-standing link between income and employment, making an individual's economic wellbeing independent of involvement in the paid labour force. Refusal to work or to look for work would no longer constitute a problem for benefit eligibility, nor would a guaranteed income policy worry about 'welfare to work' strategies. The existing income security policy of using welfare programmes to encourage work at almost any cost would have to be abandoned.

A guaranteed income is thus attractive for women, but especially for lone mothers, because of women's vulnerable status in labour markets. Women are more likely than are men to work part-time (less than 30 hours a week): seven out of ten part-time employees are women.[42] Specifically, lone mothers are more likely to experience both exclusion from and marginalization within the labour force. Women who must leave the labour force to care for children or other family members are at greater risk of

[39] S Lerner et al, *Basic Income: Economic Security for all Canadians* (Toronto, Between the Lines, 1999).

[40] Brodie, *Politics on the Margins* (above n 13).

[41] Mosher et al, *Walking on Eggshells* (above n 31).

[42] C Lindsay and M Almey, 'Paid and Unpaid Work' in *Women in Canada: A Gender-based Statistical Report*, 5th edn (Ottawa, Statistics Canada, 2006) 102, 109.

non-standard employment. Some lone mothers are separated long enough from the paid labour force that they exist for the long term in poverty, primarily dependent on welfare for income. Others are involved within the paid labour force but work in casual, low-level jobs. Such employment carries the risk of low wages, unemployment, under employment, few pension, health or other benefits, often no union membership and protection, and a limited career path. Some forms of non-standard employment (such as in domestic and farm work) also fall outside the protections of labour standards legislation, with the result that these workers are denied overtime protections, minimum wage guarantees, maternity and paternity leave and vacations. Linking these individuals' income security to labour market participation does little to address their poverty. For these workers, the workplace promises more injustice than justice.[43]

The discourse of 'choice' and of enabling women's choice is dominant in the guaranteed income advocates' argument. Proponents argue that a guaranteed income would permit an individual to structure her work activity in ways most responsive to the changing circumstances of her life-cycle; to make 'real choices with reference to economic and non-economic activities'.[44] It is certainly true that Canadian women disproportionately attribute involvement in part-time work to the need to do child care or carry out other personal or family responsibilities. In 2004, 18 per cent of all women in the paid labour force gave these reasons for working part-time, as opposed to two per cent of the men working part-time.[45] Women between the ages of 25 and 44 were even more likely (34 per cent) to be employed part-time because of personal or family responsibilities.[46] Income support programmes that incorporate conditionality based on specific patterns of labour force involvement or availability mismatch the life circumstances of women (and mothers, in particular) and thus virtually guarantee many women's vulnerability to poverty.[47] Pateman, a leading feminist advocate of a 'basic income', argues that male-pattern employment dictates the central terms of our income security system.[48]

So, it is argued, a guaranteed income (or a basic income)—because of its unconditional decoupling of income security and paid employment—holds the promise of enhanced freedom. One can choose not to work at all, or not to work under exploitative, poorly paid conditions. By contrast, the current provision of an income floor (welfare) in Canada is marked by the contingency of benefits on labour market availability. The 'welfare to work'

[43] B Ackerman and A Alstott, 'Why Stakeholding?' (2004) 32 *Politics and Society* 41, 60.
[44] McKay, *Future of Social Security* (above n 33).
[45] Lindsay and Almey, *Women in Canada* (above n 43) 102 and 109.
[46] *Ibid*, 102–3.
[47] McKay (above n 33).
[48] Pateman, 'Democratizing Citizenship' (above n 6).

mantra resounds and the boundaries have been punitively cast between those considered 'employable' and those legitimately excused from generating their own income in the paid labour force.[49] Women with unpaid caregiving responsibilities are caught and punished by distinctions based on a norm of paid employment involvement. Thus a guaranteed income represents for its feminist advocates a significant liberation from a model of self sufficiency through paid employment that is understood to be oppressive to women.

Equally powerful for feminist proponents is the fact that the unconditionality of a guaranteed income eliminates the regulatory 'curiosity' of the state into the conditions and terms of welfare recipients' lives—such as their living arrangements. The maze of conditions, of rules, to which a provincial welfare recipient is typically subject have been described by Mosher as both unknowable and impossible,[50] and thus overwhelmingly intrusive and disciplining. The rules—resting on the framing of welfare recipients by the state and dominant political discourses as lazy, work-avoidant, morally suspect and dependent—result in 'an intricate and tight web of intense scrutiny, surveillance and punishment for non-compliance'[51] that typically, Mosher later adds, is, in most provinces, profoundly gendered and disproportionately targeted at women recipients.[52] Removal of the regulatory and disciplinary gaze of the welfare state from women's lives is a considerable benefit of an unconditional form of income security. Income support is, in this way, 'de-sexed'. The gendered history of income support for women is bypassed by the recipient homogenization that a guaranteed income, because of the benefit's unconditionality, accomplishes. It matters only that the recipient meets the conditions of the universality of the grant—other details particular to any one recipient before and during benefit receipt are irrelevant to the state as income guarantor.

Different theorists have different ways of generalising these benefits of a guaranteed income. Pateman stands out by framing a guaranteed income as not merely the instantiation of economic liberty and opportunity but as also a grant of self-government or autonomy.[53] A guaranteed income becomes a 'badge of [political] citizenship',[54] its economic benefits the means to effective self-government and public civic involvement and self-realization.

[49] J Mosher, 'Welfare Reform and the Re-making of the Model Citizen' in M Young et al (eds), *Poverty: Rights, Governance & Citizenship* (Vancouver, University of British Columbia Press, 2007).

[50] J Mosher, 'Intimate Intrusions: Welfare Law and Women's Personal Lives', ch 7 in this volume.

[51] *Ibid.*

[52] *Ibid.*

[53] Pateman (above n 7).

[54] R Lister, *Women's Economic Dependency and Social Security*, EOC Research Discussion Series No 2 (Manchester, Equal Opportunities Commission, 1992) 453.

Unlike the current political rubric where the male work pattern grants entitlement to citizen status, and other social contributions—notably care work—are unacknowledged, unvalued, and thus irrelevant to citizenship, a guaranteed income shifts the terrain.[55] Adequacy of benefit income allows a 'modest but decent' standard of living but also permits the degree of self-direction, self-governance and public participation that freedom requires and citizenship ought to grant. Thus, Pateman writes that a guaranteed income could 'end the mutual reinforcement of the institutions of marriage, employment and citizenship'.[56]

A guaranteed income removes the necessity to judge if an individual's poverty is her own fault or the product of systemic factors and, therefore, could remove the policy relevance of the distinction between deserving and undeserving. A guaranteed income could set in force a new order of social citizenship—a different set of assumptions about what the individual can demand from the collective. Lone mothers, in particular, might no longer be cast as a problem for the state—as undeserving, employable but unemployed, and as dependent in the worst sense of that notion.[57]

Other proponents promote a guaranteed income as the best path to the kind of economic flexibility the market now demands, given globalization and rapid technological change. This flexibility would allow a wider range of paid work—such as part-time and temporary jobs, contract work and so on. This is work women already disproportionately do. It would also recognize and value those human activities that extend beyond paid work and are an integral part of a cohesive and rich society, such as care-giving and provisioning.[58] Again, this is work that women already disproportionately do. This argument is elaborated in the next sub-section as part of the response advocates of a guaranteed income give to concerns about labour market impact.

To summarize, this list of positive arguments about a guaranteed income is potent: an end to poverty; recognition of women's citizenship; valuing of women's caring responsibilities; facilitation of a broader, more socially

[55] Pateman (above n 7).

[56] *Ibid*, 90. Pateman moves beyond the more traditional notions of individual opportunity and liberty some male commentators claim as the outcome of guaranteed income programmes. Pateman understands freedom more substantively as self-government and autonomy, an expanded sense of freedom due largely to the enhanced sensitivity of her analysis to the different relations and forms of power that circulate in women's lives. So 'government' in marriage, in the workplace, are critically important to Pateman, in addition to more traditional understandings of political government. A guaranteed income is, for Pateman, an element of 'democratic social transformation': it allows women to recapture power and self-direction in a broader range of both intimate and public spheres. A guaranteed income could, Pateman argues, support citizens' general civil and political participation by opening up opportunities for citizens to expand political capacities and skills.

[57] N Fraser and L Gordon, 'A Genealogy of Dependency: Tracing a Key Word of the U.S. Welfare State' (1994) 19 *Signs* 309; Brodie (above n 13).

[58] Lerner et al, *Basic Income* (above n 40).

responsive range of human activities; a significant reduction in the punitive and disciplinary intervention of the state in women's lives; and empowerment of women to escape domestic violence. No wonder many feminist groups, faced with a society deeply, and increasingly, marked by gendered economic injustice, call for a guaranteed income.

B. Some (Significant) Cautions About a Guaranteed Income

The simplicity and appeal of an idea that proposes guaranteed, regular and unconditional cash infusions for low-income families makes critique of such an idea necessarily complicated—both theoretically and politically. Nonetheless, there are a number of outstanding concerns with the notion of a guaranteed income. First, there are straight-up concerns about the merits of the idea. Secondly, there are concerns about the pragmatic dangers of implementation. I will deal with the concerns about the merits in this subsection and leave the pragmatic concerns to the conclusion.

A number of concerns about the substance and merits of guaranteed income proposals, just like arguments in favour of a guaranteed income, focus on the characteristics of universality and unconditionality. Traditional concerns so structured are not notably feminist, but these concerns nonetheless provide important structure to the existing debate within the feminist community.

The strongest of the traditional concerns argues that, most simply, paying a benefit to everyone, independent of labour market involvement, raises the issues of, first, prohibitive costs and, secondly, negative work incentives.[59] These two common critiques are straightforward, in that they are easy to understand and anticipate, and challenging to meet. The cost issue depends much upon benefit levels, tax-back rates (not always a feature of guaranteed income proposals), and savings that result from the abatement of poverty and the rationalization, simplification and possible elimination of other social welfare delivery systems and programmes. Some of these savings are straightforward to calculate, many are not. But, in any case, it is fair to say that a fully adequate guaranteed income will likely mean radical redistribution of resources and priorities. The second concern—negative work incentives—warrants a lengthier discussion.

The traditional issue of work disincentives is widely explored in the literature and the critique gains cogency from the image of the lazy, able-bodied lout, more than eager to take the benefit and spend it surfing, skiing or simply lying around. Bound with this critique is the moral principle of reciprocity—that one ought not to receive something for nothing—in

[59] McKay (above n 33).

addition to more pragmatic concerns about the impact on the economy and economic growth of large numbers of individuals opting out of paid work.

In response to this concern, Van Parijs, perhaps the best known international proponent of guaranteed income, has argued that a guaranteed income will actually enhance labour market involvement.[60] To elaborate on a point made earlier, a guaranteed income, functioning as an employment subsidy to the potential worker, increases worker options in job selection and even job creation,[61] can abolish or reduce the unemployment trap by making work always mean a positive income differential, and, finally, encourages job-sharing by better allowing sabbaticals from work or part-time work.[62] The argument is that a guaranteed income, rather than discouraging active labour market participation, could help to establish a labour market more responsive to technological and work pattern changes. The result, it is argued, is income security policy that promotes both social justice and economic efficiency.[63]

The critique of this defence of a guaranteed income is that it assumes that formal labour market involvement is always something to encourage. The defence ignores other positions with regard to economic and non-economic activities and presents a limited approach to the issue of social policy reform. Indeed, the focus on paid work, and on avoiding paid work through reliance on a guaranteed income, is, Pateman argues, a particularly andocentric concern.[64] Thus, critiques of traditional social programmes and some of the standard defences of guaranteed income policy have, although from different perspectives, an obsession with paid work. Arguments about rational economic behaviour that structure the debate apply best to men, whose lives are much more culturally accountable in the terms of 'the traditional work-and-pay relationship'.[65] The 'life experiences of women are largely ignored'.[66] Reform of social security policy that better fits the pattern of women's, and of mothers', lives necessarily must depart from this norm.

The answer, McKay (a feminist proponent of guaranteed income) argues, is recognition of the positive contribution of non-work activities.[67] Not all human interactions and activities can be explained through appeal to

[60] P Van Parijs, 'Basic Income and the Two Dilemmas of the Welfare State' (1998) 67 *The Political Quarterly* 63.

[61] For instance, guaranteed income recipients could start up their own business ventures and thus create employment for themselves where none existed before. This is because of their independence from needing to find paid work.

[62] *Ibid.*

[63] McKay (above n 33).

[64] Pateman (above n 7).

[65] McKay (above n 33) 113.

[66] *Ibid*, 114.

[67] *Ibid.*

market-based economic structures.[68] Notably, much of the care-giving work and family sustenance work women traditionally do fall outside a model of productive work. And, freed from the inevitability of justifying income maintenance measures in terms of the workings of the market economy, new conceptions of the desired outline and workings of income maintenance policy can be imagined.[69] But this more gynocentric perspective will not satisfy traditional concerns about the efficient operation of the paid labour market in the face of universal and unconditional adequate income support.[70]

So, the debate over impact on work incentives is a detailed one, with an interesting feminist perspective on labour market impact and on what kind of activities a guaranteed income will allow to be recognized and affirmed, including activities that lie outside a traditional market analysis. But the fact remains that a benefit programme that does not, in some manner, rest upon assumptions about traditional productive labour to earn benefits, is controversial. Regardless of qualifications of the work incentive issue that proceed from guaranteed income proponents like Van Parijs, a guaranteed income sits in clear tension with the principle of reciprocity, traditionally understood.

And, in contrast to Van Parijs's argument about improved labour market flexibility as a good thing, others point to the risk that a guaranteed income will result in even worsened exploitative conditions. From this angle, the guaranteed income is simply a way to compensate for what is perceived to be the 'inability of a large section of the workforce to be absorbed by the economy at an adequate wage'.[71] An unconditional guaranteed income would thus constitute a floor beneath labour market earnings, enabling employers to offer a less-than-living wage. Some advocates argue this is good, enabling 'continued participation of low earners in paid work'.[72] From another perspective, however, a guaranteed income starts to look too much like a subsidy to employers and an incentive to lower wages. From this latter perspective, a guaranteed income simply institutionalizes low wages and results in the socialization of business costs.[73]

Advocates of a guaranteed income argue, in turn, that the assurance of a guaranteed income would enable workers to refuse sub-subsistence wages, ensuring employers had incentive to make employment more attractive.[74] For low-wage, unattractive work, this may mean, some advocates argue,

[68] *Ibid.*

[69] *Ibid.*

[70] *Ibid.*

[71] RJ Van der Veen, 'Real Freedom versus Reciprocity: Competing Views on the Justice of Unconditional Basic Income' (1998) 46 *Political Studies* 140.

[72] *Ibid.*

[73] Lerner et al (above n 40) 32.

[74] G Standing, 'Seeking Equality of Security in the Era of Globalisation' reprinted in Lerner et al, *Basic Income: Economic Security for all Canadians* (Toronto, Between the Lines, 1999) 101–6.

that workers will be able to leverage better work conditions (or better pay) since a guaranteed income functions as a hedge against 'desperation bidding' by workers with no other economic options.

Whatever the case is about work incentives—whether unconditional income is good or bad for paid work involvement—and leaving aside the albeit important debate about the effect on wage levels of a guaranteed income, what gets ignored in this debate is that women who have children stand in a more complicated relation to paid employment than is acknowledged by the assertion that separating income security from work is liberating. Here the feminist discussion of a guaranteed income adds substantially to the debate. And it moves the argument away from preoccupation with work incentives to broader questions of choice, public versus private provision, and citizenship.

To begin, the character of women's labour force involvement is a critical feature of this debate. The twentieth century saw a transformation of women's relationship to paid employment. Mid-century only 10 per cent of married women were in the paid labour force.[75] Now, in the twenty-first century, 'paid employment increasingly dominates many women's adult lives'.[76] This increased participation of women in the paid work force has been termed 'one of the most significant social trends in Canada in the past quarter century'.[77] While women are less likely than men to be employed, the majority of women, even those with young children, are part of the paid labour force.[78] Indeed, the growth in the employment rate of all women with children has been especially sharp: 73 per cent of women with children under 16 years were employed in 2004, as contrasted with 39 per cent in 1976. For women with children under three years, the increase is even more dramatic, to 65 per cent in 2004 from 28 per cent in 1976. And, most employed women with children have full-time jobs. In 2004, close to three out of four employed women with at least one child under 16 years at home were employed full time. Female lone parents are less likely that mothers in two-parent families to be in the paid labour force but, nonetheless, in 2004 68 per cent of these mothers with children younger than 16 years were employed, although, only 46 per cent of lone mothers with children under three years were employed in that same year. The result is that even most lone-mother-led families, despite this family type's disproportionate reliance on social assistance schemes, derive the majority of their income, not from the social assistance system, but from paid work.[79] Women, even those who

[75] A Duffy et al, *Few Choices: Women, Work and Family* (Ontario, Garamond Press, 1989) 10.

[76] *Ibid.*

[77] Lindsay and Almey (above n 43) 102–3.

[78] *Ibid*, 118.

[79] Statistics Canada (above n 14).

lone-parent, are importantly already a feature of the paid labour force. Any analysis of women's economic status and of their income security needs and preferences must take this into account.

Simply removing the obligation of paid employment is not necessarily an ideal solution for the economic and social justice issues that affect mothers. Indeed, some studies of mothers in Europe show that the majority of women would, in fact, choose some mix of their care-giving work and employment—quality employment—in the labour market.[80] Some women will want to stay out of the labour market completely during their child-rearing years; others will want to be in full-time paid employment. Many women may want some resolution that allows both continuing care-giving work and significant involvement in paid work.

A guaranteed income will not resolve this issue of paid and unpaid work, of the mix of care-giving and paid labour many women face, either by choice or necessity. It will not transform the existing paid labour market into one that is more compatible with being a primary care-giver of children. Most importantly, as Pateman points out, the availability of a guaranteed income may simply reinforce traditional assumptions that, ideally, women who can afford to do so should stay home to look after their children. The irony is that prevailing dominant norms about who does child care work may mean that any 'choice' a guaranteed income seems to grant women will merely obfuscate the continuing force of gender and familial ideologies. It may make such ideological 'truths' all the more certain when women, because of an unconditional guaranteed income, are encouraged to leave the paid labour force to do unpaid care labour. A guaranteed income may provide women with a much needed economic 'leg up', while at the same time restricting the range of choices about how to balance unpaid care-giving work and paid work that are socially assertable. If a woman has to work in the paid labour force to support her family economically, she may be judged less harshly for making that 'choice'. If she does not need to earn an income, because of a guaranteed income, she may experience real pressure to 'stay at home', even if that is not her inclination. Women remain without full liberty to balance being a parent and worker as they wish, and, as Pateman asserts, men will continue to free-ride on the care-giving work of women.[81]

To summarize, a guaranteed income does nothing to increase the relative value of women's unpaid domestic work and to change the traditional gendered division of labour within the domestic economy.[82] Rather, it risks further institutionalization of women's location within the family, with a

[80] Esping-Anderson, 'Households, Families and Children' (above n 11).

[81] Pateman (above n 7).

[82] A Orloff, 'Comment on Ann Withorn: Is One Man's Ceiling Another Women's Floor?' (unpublished paper presented at Basic Income Guarantees: A new welfare strategy? at the University of Wisconsin-Madison, US 6–8 April 1990), as cited in McKay (above n 33).

consequent failure to liberate women from the very social assumptions and hierarchy that construct the domestic characterization and devaluation of women's work.[83] A guaranteed income may mean an increase in leisure and self-development opportunities for some, but it is unlikely that those individuals will be mothers.

The irony, then, is that in working to ensure women's economic independence, an emphasis on women's economic security as mothers also reinforces separation of women from the public realm. Of course, as Pateman notes, it is true that enhanced economic security could enable a more public citizenship for women by allowing a greater degree of social inclusion.[84] But in a society where an important 'public' arena is the paid workplace, women's choice to be present in this public sphere must be facilitated, acknowledged and supported by public policy. For many women, as for many men, the workplace is a critical and central site of personal identity, development, and social interaction. Many women want to engage in paid work and spend many years in training to do so in a fulfilling and engaging context. A good workplace connects its inhabitants to the larger public and facilitates the public and collective citizenship that theorists like Pateman so value. Of course, the paid labour force is also a site of significant oppression, exploitation, and suppression of self-development and expression for many workers. This is an issue any programme of economic and social justice must face. However, it is not the case that the answer to the current economic and social injustices women face lies in an imagined world populated by the liberated surfer, the paid male worker, and the economically secure 'at-home' mother.

Moreover, a guaranteed income alone does little to improve the conditions of paid employment for women. We know women want to, need to and, indeed, in large numbers, do work outside the home. Yet, the character of that work, the kind of work that women hold relative to the work men do, has not changed enough over the 30 years that has seen women's presence in the labour force rocket. Many commentators have written about the issue of 'precarious' work (job stability and quality) and women. For example, women are still more likely than men to hold part-time employment. In 2004, over 20 per cent of women aged 25 to 54 worked part time, compared with under five per cent of men in this group.[85] Women are also slightly more likely than men to have temporary employment. In 2004, 14 per cent of employed women, compared with 12 per cent of employed men, had temporary employment. Women typically have lower incomes than men; lone-mother-led families have by far the

[83] McKay (above n 33).
[84] See n 57 above.
[85] Lindsay and Almey (above n 43) 109.

lowest incomes of all family types.[86] The gender wage gap shows stolid persistence,[87] so a feminist income security reform policy must be far more complicated that are many guaranteed income proposals.

Simply put, the call should not be for freedom from paid employment but for freedom from coercion to do paid work and to do bad paid work, and for freedom from coercion to withdraw from paid work. It should be for the freedom to engage in activities that do not traditionally code as 'work', like provisioning and other 'non-productive' yet critical activities.[88] But, from a feminist perspective, it must also involve advocacy of freedom from the assumption that the caring work of society is properly only, or even primarily, women's work. That is, to recall a traditional feminist touchstone, reform must include the freedom from the assumption that care work is women's work or, at least, certainly not men's work. Only this complete package of 'freedoms' promises radical and adequately gender-sensitive progressive social reform for women who are mothers.[89] We must recognize the importance of care work to our society but not fix women within this role. This is no novel observation but it bears repeating in this context.

The lesson of feminist analysis of the state is also worth repeating. As Brodie argues, women are not simply acted upon by the state, do not merely react to state actions as a group of social actors standing outside any one state manifestation, but come to understand their material situations, their social options, gender relationships, and their distinct identities and interests through state action and policy.[90] Individual choice—particularly along such a critical and central ideological fault-line as care-giving responsibilities—is appropriately recognized as inevitably socially configured and constrained. What comes to be regarded as natural, as normal, as incontestable is strongly influenced by the forms of institutions embedded in society by the state. Of course, these understandings, interests, or options are anything but natural or inevitable—they are historically-specific, political, and partial. Different state forms 'weave different meanings into our everyday lives' and these meanings are normalized by law and policy, not merely imposed through state programmes and institutions.[91] Individuals tell their own stories and choose their own paths using narratives and forms that exist as part of larger social contexts and economies. Social welfare reform thus must be self-conscious about what it is institutionalizing, normalizing, and reinforcing.

[86] C Lindsay and M Almey, 'Income and Earnings' in *Women in Canada: A Gender-based Statistical Report*, 5th edn (Ottawa, Statistics Canada, 2006) 133, 134.

[87] British Columbia Government Employees Union, *Labour Data* (May 2008), at: www.bcgeu.bc.ca/reports_and_briefs.

[88] McKay (above n 33).

[89] McKeen, *Money in Their Own Name* (above n 26).

[90] Brodie (above n 13).

[91] Brodie (above n 13) 27.

Calls for a guaranteed income also ignore key feminist critique of the oppressive function the public/private split has in another way. Guaranteed income proposals typically over-emphasize the importance of private action, inadvertently, at least, ignoring the roles that public responsibility, public provision, and public ordering of community institutions can ideally play in securing individual and community welfare. For example, many advocates of a guaranteed income point to the possibilities for involvement in volunteer community work that a guaranteed income allows.[92] Yet, community infrastructure surely is critical enough to warrant concerted, and state financed, support. It is great to have community centres with an active volunteer corps, but surely it is even better to have community centres with adequate, trained, and (well) paid staff.

A programme for women's economic security, or, more specifically, for mothers' economic security, that emphasizes only the provision of a guaranteed income thus risks reinforcing the classical liberal divide between the public, the market and the private family. This 'sociopolitical map'[93] of classical liberalism, and now extended in neo-liberalism, assumes it is sensible to understand a realm of private concern subject to individual or market sovereignty—such as the family or the market, now even social services—presumptively out of reach of state or public reordering or interference. Feminist theorists have long disputed the notion that this divide is natural and a-historical, their critiques revealing that any line drawn reflects particular political manipulations that work to deny the role public interests play in shaping and enforcing private relations. Indeed, the line between the public and the private shifts constantly, the two spheres both determine and define each other, and the divide, far from being natural or inevitable, implements one selective and historically-located set of political and economic interests over others.

The specific economic redistribution a guaranteed income accomplishes does recast the boundaries between the state (or the public) and the distributional outcome of the market (or the private) somewhat. It widens the realm of the public by engaging the state in redistributing base income more broadly and more fairly. However, emphasis on a guaranteed income alone as the centre-piece of social welfare provision leaves intact and separate from collective purview much of the workings of the market—both the market's provision of services and its treatment of workers. We know how crucial this public/private partition is to the perpetuation of unequal and oppressive class, gender and racialized relations. Thus, a reform programme that does little else than put some money into everyone's pockets is unlikely to be the front-piece of an adequate redistribution of social

[92] See, eg, Women's Livable Income (above n 4).

[93] M Walzer, 'Liberalism and the Art of Separation' (1984) 12 *Political Theory* 315.

and economic resources. Indeed, if a guaranteed income is also used as an excuse or reason to cancel other forms of social spending and social programming—as some right-wing advocates of the plan envision—the overall distributive effect of a guaranteed income implementation may be regressive and less just.

Some traditional advocates of a guaranteed income unduly 'biographize'[94] (or individualize) the social and economic fates of guaranteed income recipients. The individual is imagined to be financially empowered to supposedly now determine the conditions of her life on her own terms—to continue to labour under the myth that she alone can 'write' her own story, this time with adequate income in tow. Thus, the remedy to poverty is individualized and fiscalized; structural remedies are not necessarily envisioned or encompassed within income security reform. But a guaranteed income, alone, cannot redress or alter structural problems responsible for poverty, for disempowerment and its (gendered) distribution in Canadian society.

Moreover, guaranteed income proposals cast citizenship primarily in terms of the citizen as consumer, empowered by that citizenship to purchase social welfare needs in the market. This is consistent with what one commentator calls 'elite neo-liberalism', focusing on the 'individual liberties of a mass consumerist society'[95] and fits with an understanding that sees the economy as generated and expanded through consumptive spending. Thus, progressive and often well-intended proposals for welfare reform of this sort can reinforce what Bourdieu terms 'the undivided reign of the market and the consumer, the commercial substitute for the citizen'.[96] The 'public good' of social welfare becomes a 'private good'[97] and the market is understood as the source of individual wellbeing. Public expectations about what ought to be collectively provided change accordingly, and community is corroded.[98] Yet, not all necessary social welfare goods can be provided adequately by the private market alone, or even at all. Many require collective, public provision—like medical care, forms of insurance, education and so on. No matter how adequate a guaranteed income is, there will still be services and goods that individuals will need—and that any just society would not see them go without—that an equal income spent in the private market could not guarantee.

There is another irony, then, to guaranteed income proposals. For many proponents a guaranteed income, by de-linking income and participation in the labour market, fosters a kind of anti-consumerism or an abstinence

[94] I owe this expression to comments from Janine Brodie.

[95] D Long, 'Liberalism, Imperialism, and Empire' (2006) 78 *Studies in Political Economy* 201.

[96] P Bourdieu, *Acts of Resistance: Against the Tyranny of the Market* (New York, New Press, 1998) 25.

[97] *Ibid.*

[98] Brodie (above n 13).

from accumulation of material goods by de-throning the work ethic that is ideologically and historically central to capitalism and to capital accumulation. A guaranteed income, by ducking the capitalist imperative to labour and earn, frustrates the idea that freedom is fostered by more and more consumption.[99] However, by understanding economic injustice as resolvable simply by cash payments to the citizen, a guaranteed income also, as discussed above, reduces the citizen to merely market consumer and participant.

Typical guaranteed income proposals also inadequately challenge the purely formal (rather than substantive) equality aspirations of dominant neo-liberal political discourse. The idea that economic and social needs can be best met by a universally established guaranteed income that delivers (roughly) the same amount to everyone ignores that some individuals and groups of individuals have significantly different and more extensive needs and ought therefore to have greater and different entitlements from the collective universal benefit.[100] For example, a universal and fixed grant of health care access would over-insure some and under-insure others. A mother with a diabetic child has different and more extensive income and programme needs. Indeed, all universal programmes suffer the false equality of formal equality alone.[101] Reform to the welfare state must recognize that key areas of human welfare require more than equal allotments of cash. Some guaranteed income proposals take this into account but not enough do.

So, two general points distinct to a feminist perspective on a guaranteed income stand out. First, social welfare reform must be sensitive to the complex nature of women's relationship to paid work. Simply discounting the need for women who are parents to have some meaningful involvement in the paid labour market may misstate what is desired by many women. Secondly, some calls for a guaranteed income lend support—albeit unknowingly or unintentionally—to many assumptions of social and economic ordering that are suspect: the gendered division of labour; an under-emphasis on public citizenship and substantive equality; and a shrinking of public service provision. While one must be careful to recognize that there is much that is liberating for women—particularly the most oppressed—in aspirations of liberal economic individualism and the formal equality that underpins it, one also must be cautious in engaging such an alignment uncritically. The (neo-) liberal goods of economic liberty and formal equality resound strongly for women—but they are loaded freight and also function to justify much of modern economic and social relations that are deeply oppressive and unequal for women.

[99] Pateman (above n 7).

[100] Some guaranteed income proponents do argue for benefit rates that take account of such features as family size, disability and age. However, all important differences cannot adequately be factored into a universal programme.

[101] My thanks to Hester Lessard for this insight.

V. CONCLUSION

Left undiscussed so far is the issue of political saleability and feasibility—the pragmatic considerations of bringing about an actual guaranteed income programme in Canada. In turning to these issues, it should be noted at the outset that the political resonances with neo-liberalism and traditional gendered notions of labour described above are greatly troubling. Particularly worrying are the inevitable compromises involved in achieving social policy proposals in an age of Canadian neo-liberalism and what this might mean for a guaranteed income in practice. The ideological resonance of a guaranteed income with plans for the dismantling and recasting of the welfare state already in progress should make us uneasy. This results in a number of specific issues of pragmatic concern.

Because it will be difficult to sell the idea of a guaranteed income that grants an adequate income, for the reasons of cost and reciprocity discussed above, the adequacy of the benefit is likely to be subject to political compromise. This risks what Ackerman and Alstott characterize as the 'chump change' problem—that benefits under any guaranteed income that is politically feasible will be miniscule and trivial.[102] In the guise of providing all that is liberating about a guaranteed income, the neo-liberal state will provide an income that is far from adequate, using the legitimacy of the progressive argument, while ensuring continued impoverished conditions for many Canadians. The problem of poverty will be touted as fixed; the reality will be that the poor—particularly lone-mother-led families—will be less and less visible or credible as objects of political concern and attention.

Some progressive proponents of a guaranteed income see a strategy of gradual implementation—an initial very small guaranteed income that over time grows as the public gets used to the idea—as answer to the issue of political saleability. But these theorists often ignore the risk that conjoined with such a version of guaranteed income could very well be the continued or even enhanced dismantling of existing social welfare programmes. That is, the right will support the left's advocacy of a guaranteed income because a guaranteed income will serve as a means of getting rid of our messy welfare state. Other publicly-provided income security benefits will be folded into the guaranteed income and other publicly provided benefits and services—like childcare, and so on—will have no political viability. The public goods of the Keynesian welfare state will become the private goods distributed through the neo-liberal market. And, the outcome would be the worst of both worlds: an inadequate guaranteed income enabling the reduction or continued non-provision of all other aspects of the social welfare state. Instead of gradually acclimatizing the public to the idea of an

[102] Ackerman and Alstott, 'Why Stakeholding?' (above n 44) 52.

adequate guaranteed income and a fuller welfare state, the implementation of an inadequate guaranteed income will normalize minimal and residual state presence in economic security provision.

Another variant of staged, partial implement involves compromise of the notion of universality. Guaranteed incomes could be granted to different select groups of individuals in need. Such a programme of guaranteed income would not be universal to all adults, say, but would be unconditionally guaranteed to those members of some designated sub-group of the population. Canada's current Old Age Security plan is an example of such a more selective but unconditional income security programme. The Child Tax Benefit, introduced in 1984, was at one time touted as seed for an eventual form of guaranteed income for families with children. And some form of guaranteed income for persons with disabilities circulates in and out of various current policy discussions. Of course, not surprisingly, those welfare recipients deemed most 'undeserving'—single, employable adults without children—do not feature largely in proposals for more limited versions of a guaranteed income. The danger is that the rhetoric and justifications for a guaranteed income could be used to reinforce, rather than dismantle, the punitive and damaging stereotypes already in play in existing welfare programmes about who deserves public support and who does not. And the needs of only some of the poor will appear to merit attention.

Nonetheless, there is much that is engaging and empowering about the idea of guaranteeing every Canadian a decent and fair share of economic resources. The insistence on substantive equality and economic citizenship that underpins the aspirations of progressive guaranteed income proponents must be part of any income security reform. But there are three other essential elements to income security reform as well—elements particularly essential to the economic health of lone-mother families.

First, we need to think separately about continued and enhanced collective provision of essential goods—goods and services that everyone should be able to access. These are things such as education, health care, child care, social housing and so on. These goods are best provided universally by government. Without the base of a well-developed welfare state, people will remain in need, despite guaranteed income grants. So, '[a] fully developed welfare state may deserve priority over Basic Income because it accomplishes what Basic Income does not; it guarantees that certain specific human needs will be met'.[103] It is increasingly true that some proponents of a guaranteed income couch their advocacy of the policy in terms of it being a piece of, not the whole of, the social welfare offerings of a state. But these comments figure more in oral than

[103] BR Bergmann, 'A Swedish-Style Welfare State or Basic Income: Which should have Priority?' (2004) 32 *Politics and Society* 117.

written advocacy of guaranteed income and so a strong caveat of this sort is needed, particularly as the more mainstream proponents of a guaranteed income can neglect this point.

Secondly, labour market policy is critical, especially for those most vulnerable in the paid labour market such as lone mothers. It is critical that the discussion of income security for women be accompanied by a discussion of the conditions of work women face today. Given the positive value a good job can have in women's lives, it is important that the issues of precarious work and workplace justice be part of any programme of income security advocacy.

For example, we must ensure that it is not contradictory to be both a primary care-giver for children and a paid worker. This will require such things as a higher and decent minimum wage, better care-giving leave for days when children and other family members are sick, timetable flexibility and other family-friendly workplace practices, such as decent maternity and parental leave support and so on. Labour market policy must be an important focus of women's calls for social welfare reform. Parenting and wage work should both be possible, without 'suffering from the second-class work citizenship of part-time workers in a world run by full-time workers'.[104]

Thirdly, from a feminist perspective on women's economic security, all roads lead to universally available, affordable, accessible and quality public daycare. Child care is so central to women's equality that it deserves specific mention. With good employment policies and universal, affordable, available, quality child care, significant numbers of lone mothers will leave their poverty behind. Sweden, for example, has a poverty rate of five per cent for its lone mothers—a number Esping-Andersen attributes to not only a more substantive welfare system but also, importantly, to sound employment policies and daycare availability.[105]

Finally, as the other three points illustrate, it is unlikely that any one single social programme can provide fully the range of services and income support our society ought to guarantee. Thus, a guaranteed income alone cannot satisfy the full scope of collective and public responsibility a just society bears for the welfare of its population. Proponents of a guaranteed income should be cautious about too singular a focus in their welfare reform urgings.

But, a guaranteed income surely captures powerfully at least part of what a just and fair society will guarantee to everyone: an adequate degree of unconditional economic independence and empowerment, more simply put, a decent level of personal income. In this way, then, a guaranteed

[104] Orloff, 'Comment on Ann Withorn' (above n 83) 4–5, cited in McKay (above n 33) 109.

[105] Esping-Anderson (above n 10).

income can be understood less as a concrete policy proposal and more as a political aspiration. The question of a guaranteed income is critically taken up—if only to set out a metric of minimal expectations for a just income security system. Virginia Woolf emphasized the importance of 'a room of one's own' to women's intellectual participation in society.[106] The feminist ideal of a guaranteed income endorses and expands Woolf's 'opinion',[107] recognizing the importance—even if not the sole importance—of 'money of one's own' to women's social, economic and political emancipation.

[106] V Woolf, *A Room of One's Own* (New York, Harcourt, Brace & World, Inc, 1929).
[107] *Ibid*, 4.

Index